FOUNDATIONS
OF THE CONCILIAR THEORY

STUDIES IN THE HISTORY

OF

CHRISTIAN THOUGHT

EDITED BY

HEIKO A. OBERMAN, Tucson, Arizona

IN COOPERATION WITH

HENRY CHADWICK, Cambridge
JAROSLAV PELIKAN, New Haven, Connecticut
BRIAN TIERNEY, Ithaca, New York
ARJO VANDERJAGT, Groningen

VOLUME LXXXI

BRIAN TIERNEY

FOUNDATIONS
OF THE CONCILIAR THEORY

FOUNDATIONS
OF THE CONCILIAR THEORY

THE CONTRIBUTION OF THE MEDIEVAL CANONISTS
FROM GRATIAN TO THE GREAT SCHISM

BY

BRIAN TIERNEY

ENLARGED NEW EDITION

BRILL
LEIDEN · NEW YORK · KÖLN
1998

The first edition of this work was published by Cambridge University Press (1995).

This book is printed on acid-free paper.

Library of Congress Cataloging-in-Publication Data

Library of Congress Cataloging in Publication Data is also available.

Die Deutsche Bibliothek - CIP-Einheitsaufnahme

Tierney, Brian:
Foundations of the conciliar theory : the contribution of the medieval canonists from Gratian to the great Schism / by Brian Tierney. – new enl. ed. – Leiden ; New York ; Köln : Brill, 1998
  (Studies in the history of Christian thought ; Vol. 81)
  ISBN 90–04–10924–2

ISSN   0081-8607
ISBN   90 04 10924 2

PRINTED IN THE NETHERLANDS

PATRI MATRIQUE

CONTENTS

Introduction to this Edition ix
Acknowledgment xxx
Preface xxxi
List of Abbreviations xxxiii
Introductory: The Conciliar Theory and the Canonists 1

PART ONE

DECRETIST THEORIES OF CHURCH GOVERNMENT
(1140–1220)

Chapter One   Pope and Church 21
  1. *Tu es Petrus* 23
  2. *Romana Ecclesia* 32

Chapter Two   Pope and General Council 43

Chapter Three   Pope and Cardinals 62

PART TWO

ASPECTS OF THIRTEENTH-CENTURY ECCLESIOLOGY

Chapter One   Changing Views on Church Government .. 81
  1. Papal Monarchy 81
  2. Decretalist Corporation Concepts 89

Chapter Two   The Structure of a Medieval Ecclesiastical
Corporation 98
  1. Head and Members 100
  2. The Prelate as Proctor 108
  3. Episcopal Vacancies 117

Chapter Three   The Whole Church as a Corporation 121
  1. *Corpus Mysticum* 121
  2. *Plenitudo Potestatis* 129
  3. Hostiensis and the Roman Church 136

PART THREE

CONCILIAR IDEAS IN THE FOURTEENTH CENTURY

Chapter One   John of Paris 143

Chapter Two   Conflicting Criticisms of Papal Monarchy 162

Chapter Three   The Attitude of the Academic Canonists 180

Chapter Four   Franciscus Zabarella 199

Conclusion 215

Appendices
   Appendix One   Huguccio's Gloss on the Words *nisi
      deprehendatur a fide devius* 227
   Appendix Two   Passages of Joannes Teutonicus on the
      Authority of Pope, Church and Council 229
   Appendix Three   Notes on Canonists and Anonymous
      Works Mentioned in the Text 233

List of Works Cited 241

Index of Names and Places 249

Index of Subjects 253

INTRODUCTION TO THIS EDITION

Habent sua fata libelli. This book had an odd fate. It was published simply as a medieval monograph without any allusion to contemporary ecclesiastical affairs; then, a few years later, it emerged as a frequently cited text in a vigorous debate among Catholic scholars about the right ordering of the Church in the modern world.

The idea of investigating the views of medieval canonists on the authority of General Councils was suggested to me in 1948 by Walter Ullmann. It seemed an interesting research topic for a young medievalist, a little recondite perhaps, but pleasantly remote from any modern strife or dissensions. At that time, in the days of Pope Pius XII, the institutional structure of the Catholic Church seemed immutable, fixed for all time. The governance of the Church by a highly centralized papal monarchy was seen as divinely ordained; the decrees of the First Vatican Council made any other arrangement almost unthinkable. It was also widely assumed that the definitions of papal sovereignty and infallibility promulgated in 1870 had excluded the need for any future General Councils. In these circumstances fifteenth-century Conciliarism seemed a dead-end of history, of interest only to a few medieval specialists.

The situation was transformed in January 1959 when Pope John XXII announced his intention of summoning a new Vatican Council. As one might expect, the Pope's announcement stimulated a spate of new writing about the history of General Councils and their role in the life of the Church; it is not so obvious, though, why so much of the new work should have focused on the Council of Constance and the conciliar doctrines that animated its decrees. The reason for this renewed interest was that many Church leaders hoped to see a more collegial style of government emerge from the deliberations of the new Council, and the decrees of Constance represented the last significant attempt to establish such a system for the Catholic Church. In these circumstances, the argument presented in my book seemed appealing to some of the reform-minded scholars who contributed to the discussions leading up to the Council. They were especially interested in the suggestion that the ideas of the medieval Conciliarists were not some kind of heretical aberration, not 'something accidental and external, thrust upon the Church from outside', but rather 'a logical culmination of ideas that were embedded in the law and doctrine of the Church itself'.[1] Two theologians in particular who were to be influential at the Council, Yves Congar and Hans Küng, made use of my work in their own writings and discerned in it significant implications for modern ecclesiology. I do not suppose that any of the Council Fathers actually read *Foundations of the Conciliar Theory*, but possibly, through the mediation of Congar and Küng, the book influenced the thinking of some of them. Cardinal König of Vienna, for instance, mentioned the argument of *Foundations* in an address given at Freiburg in 1964, after the second session of the Council. He suggested that the objective of Vatican Council II should be to achieve a synthesis between the teachings of the First Vatican Council and the Council of Constance.[2]

The interest in fifteenth-century Conciliarism evoked by the events of the 1960s did not die away once the Council was over, and the material presented in my book came to be assimilated into a burgeoning new literature on various aspects of conciliar thought. A recent work by Ansgar Frenken, describing modern research on the Council of Constance, provided a bibliography of over 1500 items, most of them written since 1960.[3] There is also a substantial new literature on the Council of Basle. Some studies have provided overviews of the whole conciliar epoch. Outstanding among them is Alberigo's *Chiesa conciliare*.[4] Other works have dealt in detail with particular Councils (Brandmüller, Franzen and Müller, Krämer, Helmrath).[5] Several major studies have explored particular themes that were of central importance to the Conciliarists, e.g. papal depositions (Zimmermann),[6]

---

[1] *Foundations of the Conciliar theory*, p. 12 (in the present edition).

[2] F. König, 'Die Konzilsidee von Konstanz bis Vatikanum II', in *Konzil der Einheit. 550-Jahrfeier des Konzils zu Konstanz.*

[3] A. Frenken, 'Die Erforschung des Konstanzer Konzils (1414–1418) in den letzten 100 Jahren', *Annuarium historiae conciliorum* 25 (1993), 1–509.

[4] G. Alberigo, *Chiesa conciliare: Identità e significato del conciliarismo* (Brescia, 1981). The works cited in the following notes represent only a sampling of the very extensive modern literature.

[5] W. Brandmüller, *Das Konzil von Pavia-Siena*, 2 vols. (Münster 1968–74); *idem, Das Konzil von Konstanz* (1414–1418), 1 (Paderborn, 1991); A. Franzen and W. Müller, eds., *Das Konzil von Konstanz. Beiträge zu seiner Geschichte und Theologie* (Freiburg, 1964); W. Krämer, *Konsens und Rezeption. Verfassungsprinzipien der Kirche im Basler Konziliarismus* (Münster, 1980); J. Helmrath, *Das Basler Konzil 1431–1449. Forschungstand und Probleme* (Cologne, 1987).

[6] H. Zimmermann, *Papstabsetzungen im Mittelalter* (Graz, 1968).

appeals from Pope to Council (Becker),[7] Church reform (Stump, Pascoe).[8] Other works have considered the lives and thought of individual Conciliarists (Oakley, Posthumus Meyjes, Sigmund, Watanabe).[9] To review all this work would require a book-length study like that of Frenken. Here I want only to respond to some criticisms and comments evoked by *Foundations*, and then to explain briefly some of the ways in which my own thinking about Conciliarism developed after the writing of the book.

Criticisms and Responses

For me, the most precious appraisal of my book came from Yves Congar. When *Foundations* was reprinted in 1968 he wrote, 'S'il est un livre qui a profondément renouvelé l'histoire des doctrines ecclésiologiques sous l'aspect de théories constitutionelles, c'est bien celui de B. Tierney....'[10] At the other extreme a few less sympathetic critics suggested that the book had little new to offer since earlier writers—the ones mentioned in my Introduction—had already suggested a canonistic origin for conciliar thought.[11] I would certainly want to acknowledge my debt to preceding scholars, especially to my own mentor, Walter Ullmann. But, as Francis Oakley has recently pointed out, although several authors had mentioned the canonists as a source for conciliar theories, none had actually carried through an investigation of the relevant texts.[12] So my book, which presented a substantial body of new canonistic material and situated this material for the first time in a coherent argument flowing from the twelfth-century Decretists to the mature Conciliarism of Zabarella, did have

---

[7] H.-J. Becker, *Die Appellation vom Papst an ein Allgemeines Konzil* (Cologne, 1988).

[8] P. H. Stump, *The Reforms of the Council of Constance* (1414–1418) (Leiden, 1994); L. B. Pascoe, *Jean Gerson: Principles of Church Reform* (Leiden, 1973).

[9] F. Oakley, *The Political Thought of Pierre d'Ailly* (New Haven, 1964); G. H. M. Posthumus Meyjes, *Jean Gerson, zijn Kerkpolitiek en Ecclesiologie* ('s-Gravenhage, 1963); P. E. Sigmund, *Nicholas of Cusa and Medieval Political Thought* (Cambridge, Mass., 1963); M. Watanabe, *The Political Ideas of Nicholas of Cusa* (Geneva, 1963).

[10] *Revue des sciences philosophiques et théologiques* 54 (1970), p. 105.

[11] See e.g. the rather grudging remarks of R. Bäumer, 'Die Erforschung des Konziliarismus', in R. Bäumer, ed., *Die Entwicklung des Konziliarismus* (Darmstadt, 1976), pp. 3–56.

[12] F. Oakley, '*Verius est licet difficilius*. Tierney's *Foundations of the Conciliar Theory* After Forty Years', in G. Christianson and T. M. Izbicki, eds., *Nicholas of Cusa on Christ and the Church. Essays in Memory of McCuskey Brooks* (Leiden, 1996), pp. 15–34.

a certain freshness and originality for many readers. Nearly all the authors who wrote on medieval Conciliarism during the controversies of the 1960s—Jedin, De Vooght, Fink, Congar, Küng, Gill—referred to *Foundations* as a significant reinterpretation of conciliar origins.

Occasionally a criticism of *Foundations* seems based on a misunderstanding. J. H. Sieben, for instance, in one of his far-ranging studies on the idea of a General Council, presented a series of Decretist texts asserting that such a Council had to be convoked and presided over by the Pope. He further noted that those who derive conciliar thought from canonistic sources argue entirely from certain exceptional situations envisaged by the canonists, and that we ought rather to emphasize the normal relationship between Pope and Council in their writings. As to that, he continued, nothing could be more clear. The Council could not exist without the Pope but certainly the Pope could exist without a Council; so it followed that the Council was of its nature subordinated to the Pope.[13] Constantine Fasolt saw these words as 'an outright assault on the central element of Tierney's thesis'.[14] I do not know whether Sieben intended such an outright assault. Earlier in his book he wrote that conciliar thought is intelligible only when considered against the background of earlier canonistic writing and referred to my own work as 'pathbreaking'. In any case the points he makes do not invalidate anything I wrote. Of course the canonists taught that, in normal circumstances, the Pope should summon and preside over a General Council. But so did all the mainstream Conciliarists at Constance.[15] (The point is discussed in more detail below.) This did not mean, however, either for the

---

[13] H. J. Sieben, *Die Konzilsidee des lateinischen Mittelalters* (847–1375) (Paderborn, 1984), p. 255.

[14] C. Fasolt, *Council and Hierarchy. The Political Thought of William Durant the Younger* (Cambridge, 1991), p. 19. It is not easy to understand Fasolt's underlying attitude to conciliar thought. In his *Introduction* he referred to Durant as one who 'played a major role in the history of the conciliar theory' (p. 10). In his *Conclusion* he wrote that 'there can be no history of the conciliar theory . . . because no such thing as the conciliar theory ever existed . . .' (p. 318). Fasolt was perhaps making in a muddled fashion the point I noted in *Foundations* (p. 3). 'In strict accuracy, no doubt, one should speak of a collection of conciliar proposals rather than of "the Conciliar Theory"; and yet there was sufficient unity of thought among the various writers to render the latter expression significant and useful'.

[15] Here, for instance, are some remarks of Zabarella. 'Et dicitur generale (concilium) quia a papa emanavit generalem potestatem habente' (*Commentaria ad* X.3.37.4). 'Nota quod in generali concilio papa disponit concilio approbante' (*Commentaria ad* X.5.33.23).

canonists or the Conciliarists, that Councils were simply subordinate to Popes. Sieben indeed went on to quote here some of the Decretist texts asserting that the pope was bound by the decrees of preceding General Councils in matters touching the faith and the general state of the Church.

As to the argument that the relevant canonistic discussions dealt only with exceptional situations, there are two points to be made. The structure of corporation law developed by the Decretalists, an essential component of later conciliar thought, was intended to regulate the life of the Church in normal circumstances, not only in emergencies. And, insofar as the conciliar program was a response to an emergency situation—as was certainly the case at the Council of Constance—we should not too readily assume that this fact diminishes its enduring significance or the significance of the canonistic texts that had envisaged such an emergency. Often the true character of a person or an institution is most clearly revealed in a time of crisis. A man might betray his trust in some extreme emergency. An institution might reject its own best traditions for the sake of mere survival. But the Conciliarists of Constance were not driven to such an expedient. They knew that Christ had promised to be with his Church through all the ages. They were convinced that the Church could not lack the power to maintain itself in being, whatever vicissitudes might befall its leaders. And, in their time of crisis, they found that they could reach back into the tradition of the Church itself—especially the constitutional law of the Church—to overcome the dire emergency that they faced.

For many readers the principal value of *Foundations* was that it rendered untenable the view, still widely accepted at the time I wrote, holding that the real origin of conciliar thought is to be found in the 'heretical' works of William of Ockham and Marsilius of Padua.[16] Some critics, however, pointed out that certain of the Conciliarists did in fact know the works of Ockham and Marsilius, and made use of them in their own writings. This observation is true. But it does not provide a decisive answer to the question of origins. We need to

---

[16] This was emphasized by Michael Seidlmayer in a long and generous review of *Foundations*—the more generous since at the time I wrote I was unaware of Seidlmayer's own important work. See *Zeitschrift der Savigny-Stiftung für Rechtsgeschichte. Kan. Abt.* 74 (1957), pp. 374–87 at 387. 'Die "ockhamistische Konzilstheorie" hat auf Grund des Buches von Tierney endgültig den Platz zu räumen'.

ask further where Ockham and Marsilius derived their ideas from and what elements of their thought were important for the later Conciliarists. At the time when I was completing *Foundations* I also wrote a separate study dealing with Ockham's use of canonistic sources and his influence on conciliar thought. There I wrote: 'The personal idiosyncrasies of Ockham were largely ignored; the Conciliarists preferred to build their systems around doctrines that Ockham himself had borrowed from earlier writers and especially from earlier canonistic writers'. And so, I argued, 'The somewhat paradoxical conclusion emerges that Ockham was most influential precisely when he was least original'.[17]

One might make a similar point about Marsilius. The Paduan did not rely overtly on canonistic texts as Ockham did—he depended more on Aristotelian philosophy and on his own interpretation of scripture and Church Fathers—but the whole argument of the *Defensor pacis* was based on an underlying juridical conception of the church and the state as corporate entities, which functioned according to the normal rule of corporation law specifying that the consent of a whole community could be expressed by its greater part, taking into account 'the quantity and the quality of the persons'.[18] Paul Sigmund established a direct influence of Marsilius on Dietrich of Niem and Nicholas of Cues by quoting passages from their works that were closely dependent (though without acknowledgment) on similar passages in the *Defensor pacis*.[19] But, again, it is important to know what particular doctrines of Marsilius were used by the later writers. In fact, in the texts quoted by Sigmund, Nicholas used Marsilius to prove that legitimate government must be based on consent and that consent could be expressed by the weightier part of a community; and Dietrich quoted the *Defensor pacis* to prove that a criminal or heretical pope could be deposed, and that the pope did not possess both 'swords' of spiritual and temporal power. Presumably both authors copied their arguments from Marsilius because they had his work

---

[17] 'Ockham, the Conciliar Theory, and the Canonists', *Journal of the History of Ideas* 15 (1954), pp. 40–70 at pp. 68–70.

[18] *Defensor pacis*, 1.12.3. Marsilius used the term *valentior pars* to express this idea. The standard canonistic formula was *maior et sanior pars*. I discussed Marsilius and canonistic corporation theory in an early article, 'A Conciliar Theory of the Thirteenth Century', *Catholic Historical Review* 36 (1951), pp. 415–40.

[19] P. E. Sigmund, 'The Influence of Marsilius of Padua on XVth-Century Conciliarism', *Journal of the History of Ideas* 23 (1962), pp. 392–402.

conveniently at hand, but the points they were making could equally well have been sustained from orthodox sources, and indeed from canonistic sources. The point is that even Marsilius could not be heretical all the time; that would have called for too much originality. Along with his own idiosyncratic opinions he also presented teachings that were commonly found in other, more respectable medieval writers on law and political philosophy. And the Conciliarists did not borrow from Marsilius the most distinctive and really unorthodox elements of his thought—e.g. his view that the Papacy was not divinely established or that the Church received no coercive jurisdiction from its Founder.

Theology and Canon Law

A common comment on my work, not usually presented as a hostile criticism, pointed out that there was an important theological element in conciliar thought that I had not discussed, and that many of the outstanding Conciliarists of the fifteenth century were indeed theologians. Joachim Stieber, for instance, wrote that, 'Tierney's persuasive argument . . . should *not* lead to the mistaken conclusion that the appeal to canon law literature was more important than the recourse to the New Testament. . . . In the end, the advocates of the supreme authority of general councils in the church tended to be theologians rather than canonists'.[20] I was conscious of this fact when I wrote *Foundations* and, with the hopeful wariness of a young scholar seeking to ward off an anticipated criticism, I carefully noted that the book did not pretend to be 'a complete history of conciliar thought down to the time of the Great Schism'.[21] Such a history would have to include the work of some eminent orthodox theologians and not only the 'heretical' Ockham; but the same issues arise as with Ockham. For a full understanding of the development of conciliar thought, we need to consider the influence of canonistic sources on the theologians themselves even, or especially, when they were having recourse to New Testament texts.

---

[20] J. W. Stieber, *Pope Eugenius IV, the Council of Basel and the Secular and Ecclesiastical Authorities in the Empire* (Leiden, 1978), p. 390. For a similar remark by Antony Black see his *Council and Commune* (London, 1979), p. 5.

[21] *Foundations*, p. xxxi.

The body of earlier theological argumentation that most influenced the Conciliarists grew out of the secular-mendicant disputes of the mid-thirteenth century. Some of the Franciscan and Dominican masters argued that local bishops could have no right to resist the papal privileges conferred on the friars because the bishops' own jurisdiction was derived wholly from the supreme pontiff. This position was maintained by such great theologians as Bonaventure and, more cautiously, by Aquinas. Their adversaries, the defenders of the bishops and secular clergy, acknowledged that Christ did indeed establish Peter as head of the Church, but they held that Christ also conferred jurisdiction directly on the other apostles. They then went on to argue that the bishops, as successors of the apostles, received their authority directly from Christ, not as a grant from the Pope. Such ideas later formed an important strand of thought in fifteenth-century conciliar theories, especially in the work of Gerson.

The point that particularly concerns us is that, although the defenders of episcopalism were theologians, engaged in theological discourse about some crucial texts of the New Testament, they also relied extensively on canonistic sources in interpreting those texts. This is especially evident in the writings of William of St Amour, the doughty defender of the bishops in the early stages of the controversy. In his *De periculis*, for instance, William quoted *Dist.* 21 c. 2 of the *Decretum*.

> In the New Testament, after Christ the sacerdotal order began from Peter.... The other apostles indeed received honor and power with him in equal fellowship and they wanted him to be their leader ... when they died bishops succeeded in their places.... Also seventy-two disciples were chosen of whom priests are the image.[22]

This text became a cornerstone of the episcopalist case. It is actually from pseudo-Isidore but genuine patristic doctrine lies behind it. The teaching that the twelve apostles prefigured the order of bishops and the seventy-two disciples the order of priests comes from Bede, and the assertion that the other apostles received equal honor and power with Peter goes back to Cyril. But, although both texts are ancient, it was the concatenation of the two passages as presented in the *Decretum* that was especially important for the episcopalist case. Among

---

[22] William of St Amour, *De periculis novissimorum temporum* in *Opera omnia* (Constance, 1632), pp. 17–72 at p. 24.

various other Decretist texts, William of St Amour also cited *Dist.*
99 c. 5 where Gregory the Great rejected the title of universal bishop
and C. 25 q. 1 c. 6 which asserted that, although the Roman pontiff
could make new laws, he could not destroy what had been established 'by the Lord and the apostles and the holy Fathers'. Recalling
another common Decretist phrase William wrote that if the Pope
did seek to undercut the authority of the bishops he would 'perturb
the whole state of the church'. William interwove texts from scripture and the ordinary gloss to the Bible into his arguments and these
texts were emphasized by later episcopalists; but a substructure of
argument derived from canonist sources was always present. This is
especially evident in the memorandum drawn up on behalf of the
French bishops in 1289. It consists mainly of a patchwork of references to the *Decretum* and *Decretals*.[23]

It happened that the old mendicant-secular dispute broke out again
at Paris in the years just before the Council of Constance. Writing
on behalf of the theology faculty, Gerson vigorously defended the
rights of inferior prelates—their rights to preach, to hear confessions,
to receive tithes.[24] Then, a few years later, he assimilated this material
into his conciliar treatise, *De potestate ecclesiastica*.[25] The authority of
General Councils would be as nothing, he wrote, if the Pope were to
usurp for himself all the rights of lesser prelates in the Church. Gerson
based his argument here on texts of scripture and the Church Fathers.
It seems a good example of a distinctively theological approach to
the problems of Conciliarism; but to understand Gerson's position
fully we also need to be aware of the earlier tradition that he relied
on, and of the elements of canonistic teaching that were incorporated
into it.[26]

---

[23] K. Schleyer, *Anfänge des Gallikanismus im 13. Jahrhundert* (Berlin, 1937), pp. 156–
200.

[24] P. Glorieux, ed., *Jean Gerson. Oeuvres complètes*, X (Paris, 1973), p. 33.

[25] *Oeuvres*, VI (Paris, 1965), p. 242.

[26] One could trace a similar interplay between theology and canon law in the
conciliarists' conception of a mixed constitution for the church. Aristotle's idea of a
mixed constitution entered medieval thought in the theology of Aquinas (*Summa
theologiae*, 1.2ae. 105.1). But the Thomist doctrine became associated with a canonistic
teaching concerning the authority of the College of Cardinals derived from Hostiensis.
Eventually, in the work of D'Ailly and Gerson, the cardinals figured as the 'aristo-
cratic' element in the constitution of the church. The assimilation of the canonist
doctrine produced a theory very different from that of Aquinas—not to mention
Aristotle. On this theme see my *Religion, Law, and the Growth of Constitutional Thought,
1150–1650* (Cambridge, 1982).

While several readers of *Foundations* pointed out correctly that theologians contributed significantly to the development of conciliar thought, a few asserted—more emphatically than I had done myself—that late medieval Conciliarism was indeed derived from canonistic sources; but then they found in this fact a reason for rejecting the central doctrines of the Conciliarists. Joseph Gill, for instance, pointed out that the decree *Haec sancta* of the Council of Constance, which defined the authority of a General Council in relation to the Pope, was really addressing a theological issue. But, he continued, a merely canonistic tradition could not provide an adequate foundation for a theology of the Church. The great theologians themselves, people like Bonaventure and Aquinas, were strong supporters of papal absolutism, Gill noted.[27] (This is true, but one might add that, as regards the specific issue involved in the dispute of the thirteenth century, the 'great' theologians were wrong and their adversaries were right according to modern ideas, at least concerning the status of bishops.) In a similar fashion Heinz Hürten wrote that, although the doctrine of the conciliar theologians was 'prepared for and grounded in the canonistic writings of the Middle Ages', still this did not ensure the dogmatic validity of their teachings. Eventually, he suggested, the papal position was victorious because it was more in accord with the Church's traditional faith.[28] Hürten also quoted Hans Barion who, a little earlier, had insisted that we should not confuse the *opinio communis* of the canonists with the faith-consciousness of the Church. The Conciliarism of the fifteenth century, Barion wrote, was only 'an outmoded private opinion surviving in a false flowering'.[29] Gill likewise commented that, 'The mistake was to try to graft theology onto a canonistic stock. . . . The graft did not take. The fruit was still canonistic, not theological, and sound in proportion to the firmness of its roots'.[30] That is to say, for Gill the conciliar 'fruit' was unsound.

This approach may reflect an inadequate appreciation of the canonists' achievement. The twelfth-century Decretists were not just legal technicians interpreting casuistically an established code of law.

---

[27] J. Gill, 'The Canonists and the Council of Constance', *Orientalia Christiana periodica* 32 (1966), pp. 528–35.

[28] H. Hürten, 'Zur Ekklesiologie der Konzilien von Konstanz und Basel', *Theologische Revue* 59 (1963), pp. 361–72.

[29] H. Barion, Review of L. Buisson, *Potestas und Caritas. Die päpstliche gewalt im Spätmittelalter*, in *Zeitschrift der Savigny-Stiftung für Rechtsgeschichte. Kan. Abt.* 45 (1960), p. 515.

[30] *Art. cit.* p. 534.

Their great source book, Gratian's *Decretum*, presented an array of texts that reflected the experience of the Church in the world for a thousand years. The canonists who grappled with this material and sought to shape out of it a unified structure of law were engaged in a great intellectual enterprise, a task that attracted some of the foremost intellects of the age. It seems simplistic to suppose that the generation of great jurists who first gave a universal law to the Catholic Church had no adequate understanding of the nature and structure of the Church itself, and to dismiss their views as 'outmoded private opinion'. Perhaps it is the private opinions of their modern critics that should be viewed with a certain caution.

The coexistence in modern scholarship of the two lines of argument I have mentioned, one asserting that there was a theological basis for the conciliar vision of the church and the other insisting that the Conciliarists relied on an inadequate canonistic tradition, suggests a need for some further reflection on the relationship between theology and canon law in the growth of conciliar thought. In fact it is very difficult to disentangle two separate strands of argument. When they wrote on the topics discussed in *Foundations*, the canonists were discussing ecclesiology, which is nowadays regarded as a branch of theology. In the twelfth century this field of study was regarded as a proper province of canonists rather than theologians. But the Decretists were arguing from what we should consider theological source material that had been assimilated into the *Decretum*— not only the texts of Church Fathers like Augustine and Jerome, and the decrees of early Church Councils but also the key texts of the New Testament referring to the authority of Peter and the apostles. When major theologians turned to the study of ecclesiology in the thirteenth century they drew on the earlier canonistic material. A little later we can find canonists making use of theological sources. Guido de Baysio for instance used Thomas Aquinas and Alexander of Hales to explicate Gratian's doctrine of natural law in his *Rosarium*, a voluminous commentary on the *Decretum*. In *Foundations* I discussed the Conciliarism of John of Paris, treating him as a theologian who incorporated canonistic ideas into his teaching on church government. Ockham's work displays the same characteristic. And a similar pattern can be found in the writings of the papalists of the fourteenth century. Alvarus Pelagius was a canonist who used theological sources; Augustinus Triumphus was a theologian who made use of canonistic texts. The same pattern persists in the fifteenth-century

Conciliarists. D'Ailly, a theologian, cited the texts of the *Decretum* very frequently in his conciliar writings. Nicholas Cusanus was a canonist by training but we now remember him more as a great theologian and philosopher. Johannes de Turrecremata, an eminent theologian, wrote a commentary on the whole of the *Decretum* to show how his papalist views could be expounded in terms of jurisprudence. Panormitanus, a Conciliarist and perhaps the greatest canonist of the age, relied extensively on Aquinas in his unfinished commentary on the *Decretum*.[31]

Of course the disciplines of canon law and theology did remain distinct, with separate faculties in the medieval universities. Some themes of theology had nothing to do with canon law and some aspects of canon law, like court procedure, had nothing to do with theology. But writers on ecclesiology, on the nature and structure of the church, typically found it necessary to call on both traditions of thought. A complete history of medieval conciliar thought would need to consider in detail this interplay of canonistic and theological traditions from the twelfth century onward. I think that such a history would continue to show that canonistic doctrines provided an essential core around which the various conciliar theories clustered. But it remains true that a comprehensive account of the growth of conciliar thought would have to deal with more sources than those that are discussed in *Foundations*. I once set out to write such an account— we still need one—but, in working on the medieval source material, especially the writings of Ockham, I became more interested in another aspect of medieval ecclesiology and the book, I finally wrote dealt with a different theme.[32]

Paths of Research

Since it is now more than forty years since *Foundations of the Conciliar Theory* was first published, some readers may be interested in the further pathways of research that the book opened up.

---

[31] The interplay of theology and canon law in medieval ecclesiology is discussed more fully in my paper, 'Canon Law and Church Institutions in the Late Middle Ages', *Proceedings of the Seventh International Congress of Medieval Canon Law*, ed. P. Linehan (Vatican City, 1988), pp. 49–69. On Panormitanus's use of Aquinas see A. Black, 'Panormitanus on the *Decretum*', *Traditio* 26 (1970), 440–44.

[32] This was the work on papal infallibility discussed below.

One path led to a study on the history of papal infallibility. I was intrigued by the fact that, in the controversies of 1870, both sides assumed that the doctrine of infallibility was taught in the writings of the medieval canonists. The only difference was that opponents of the new definition considered the canonists' teaching to be a regrettable innovation based on 'forgeries and fictions' (in the words of Döllinger), while the defenders of infallibility saw the canonists as simply witnessing to the ancient faith of the Church. But in my reading of the canonists I had not encountered any doctrine of papal infallibility at all. There were many assertions of papal sovereignty but they were associated with a widespread concern that an individual pope might become a heretic and mislead the church by teaching false doctrine. This led me to ask how the doctrine of papal infallibility did in fact grow into existence. My conclusion was that the doctrine first emerged in the controversies over Franciscan poverty in the late thirteenth and early fourteenth centuries.[33]

Another line of argument that I pursued in later work concerned a broader theme, the role of the canonists and Conciliarists in the whole history of Western constitutional thought. Long before my book was written, John Neville Figgis had maintained that the ideas of the Conciliarists exercised a continuing influence on secular political theory in the early modern era.[34] But I argued in *Foundations* that the central doctrines of the Conciliarists had already been suggested in earlier canonistic writings. There seemed, then, to be a possibility of presenting a coherent history of the growth of Western constitutional thought from twelfth-century jurisprudence to the fully developed constitutional theories of the seventeenth century. I tried to address this theme in a little work of synthesis published in 1982.[35]

Still another line of research was suggested by the multiple definitions of the term *ius naturale* that one encounters in the early glosses on the *Decretum*. Sometimes the words were taken to refer to a 'force' or 'power' or 'faculty' inhering in human persons—something more akin to our idea of a subjective natural right than to the old concept

---

[33] See my *Origins of Papal Infallibility, 1150–1350. A Study on the Concepts of Infallibility. Sovereignty and Tradition in the Middle Ages* (Second Impression with a Postscript) (Leiden, 1988). The Postscript discusses various criticisms of the book.

[34] Figgis's original insight has been amply confirmed in the more recent work of Francis Oakley. The relevant articles of Oakley are collected in his book, *Natural Law, Conciliarism and Consent in the Late Middle Ages* (London, 1984).

[35] *Religion, Law, and the Growth of Constitutional Thought, 1150–1650* (Cambridge, 1982).

of natural law. Starting out from this observation, I tried to trace out a history of natural rights theories from the twelfth century to the seventeenth—from Gratian to Grotius. In the course of this work I discussed *inter alia* the relationship between Gerson's conciliar theory and his teaching on natural rights.[36]

Although the argument presented in *Foundations of the Conciliar Theory* could lead on to these different paths of research, its principal relevance of course was for the understanding of fifteenth-century Conciliarism itself. However, my book was indeed limited to foundations. It stopped short of considering the attempt to implement a conciliar program at the Council of Constance. But the legislation of Constance, especially the crucial decree *Haec sancta*, became a major focus of debate in the years of Vatican Council II and I discussed this theme in a group of later articles.[37] I would like finally to explain here how this later work was related to the argument presented in *Foundations* and to the concerns of modern writers on problems of contemporary ecclesiology.

Haec sancta declared that everyone of whatsoever state or dignity, 'even if it be the papal', was bound to obey the statutes of the Council of Constance, and also those of any other General Council, in matters touching the faith, the schism, and the general reform of the Church in head and members. Subsequently the decree *Frequens* provided that General Councils should meet at regular intervals in the future to carry through the general reform mentioned in *Haec sancta*.[38]

The language of *Haec sancta* evoked the most varied judgments in the debates of the 1960s. Some commentators—Gill, Hürten, Pichler—held that the decree was simply invalid. Jedin and Brandmüller argued that *Haec sancta* was a valid decree but that it applied and was intended to apply only to the immediate circumstances of the existing schism. De Vooght and Küng, emphasizing the reference to 'any

---

[36] *The Idea of Natural Rights. Studies on Natural Rights, Natural Law and Church Law, 1150–1625* (Atlanta, 1997).

[37] 'Hermeneutics and History. The Problem of *Haec Sancta*', in *Essays in Medieval History Presented to Bertie Wilkinson*, ed. T. A. Sandquist and M. R. Powicke (Toronto, 1969), pp. 354–70; '"Divided Sovereignty" at Constance. A Problem of Medieval and Early Modern Political Theory', *Annuarium historiae conciliorum* 7 (1975), pp. 238–56; '"Only the Truth Has Authority": The Problem of "Reception" in the Decretists and in Johannes de Turrecremata', in *Law, Church and Society. Essays in Honor of Stephan Kuttner*, ed. K. Pennington and R. Somerville (Philadelphia, 1977), pp. 69–96.

[38] *Conciliorum oecumenicorum decreta*, ed. G. Alberigo et al., 3rd ed. (Bologna, 1973), pp. 409–10, 438–39.

other General Council', treated *Haec sancta* as a dogmatic decree possessing permanent validity, but they assumed that it would come into play only in future emergencies like that of the Great Schism. Francis Oakley held that the decree was a valid dogmatic pronouncement intended to regulate the normal life of the church and that, as such, it was in direct conflict with the decree *Pastor aeternus* of Vatican Council I. Oakley concluded that 'the claim to attach infallibility to *particular* conciliar or papal pronouncements must simply be dropped.'[39]

My own contributions to this discussion—influenced by my earlier work on the canonists—suggested that *Haec sancta* was intended as a permanently binding statement of positive constitutional law but not as a dogmatic definition of faith. I also argued that *Haec sancta* was intended to regulate the normal life of the Church and not to apply only in emergency situations. But my further point was that the decree can properly be interpreted in a moderate sense. It should not be understood as making the Popes mere subordinate agents of future General Councils. *Haec sancta* was enacted in an atmosphere of crisis. A form of words had to be found that everyone could accept. Understandably, therefore, the text finally adopted contained ambiguities and compromises,[40] and this was especially true, I suggested, as regards the key words referring to future General Councils.

There can be no understanding of *Haec sancta* unless we start out from an awareness that the Conciliarists assembled at Constance were, in a sense, all papalists. They did not seek to abolish the Papacy and establish some form of republican government for the Church; on the contrary the central purpose of the assembly was to reunite the Church under a generally recognized Pope. The Fathers of Constance claimed supreme authority for themselves at a time when there were three would-be pontiffs, all of doubtful legitimacy.[41] (John XXII's

---

[39] F. Oakley, *Council Over Pope? Towards a Provisional Ecclesiology* (New York, 1969). Oakley also provides an overview of the other opinions mentioned above. For further discussions of them see my article 'The Problem of *Haec sancta*', and especially, H. Schneider, *Der Konziliarismus als Problem der neureren katholischen Theologie* (Berlin, 1976). It seems to me that, without insisting specifically on the dogmatic validity of *Haec sancta*, one might question on other historical grounds the assertion of *Pastor aeternus* that the doctrine of infallibility formed part of 'a tradition received from the beginning of the Christian faith.' The issue is discussed in my *Origins of Papal Infallibility*.

[40] Various ambiguities in the text of *Haec sancta* were discussed by T. Morrissey, 'The Decree "Haec Sancta" and Cardinal Zabarella', *Annuarium historiae conciliorum* 10 (1978), pp. 145–76.

[41] The point was emphasized by Brandmüller, *Konzil von Konstanz*, 249.

legitimacy was called into question when he threatened to prolong the schism by fleeing from the Council.) Looking to the future, the Council Fathers also declared that future Popes were to be bound by the statutes of other lawfully assembled General Councils in the three defined areas. But, in normal times, once the schism was ended, the statutes of General Councils would be statutes of Pope and Council members legislating together, not decrees of members acting against the head. According to a strict interpretation of *Haec Sancta*, it was statutes of this kind that would be binding on future popes. *Haec sancta* did not declare that the members of a Council should prevail against a certainly legitimate Pope as has been commonly assumed. Some members of the Council no doubt favored that opinion, but they did not succeed in enacting it into law.

This way of understanding *Haec Sancta* can be supported by considering both the traditions of thought explored in *Foundations* and the actual proceedings at the Council of Constance. Among the Decretists, there was a generally accepted view that a pope was bound by the statutes of General Councils in matters touching the faith and the general state of the Church; but the relevant texts typically referred to preceding Councils supported by the authority of earlier Popes. They did not assert that the members of a Council were greater than its head. The *Glossa Ordinaria* to the *Decretum* maintained the contrary position—that, in case of dispute, the judgment of the Pope should prevail.[42] Very rarely a Decretist author did argue that, in matters of faith, the members of a Council possessed a greater authority than the Pope, but always in contexts where they were considering the judgment of a pope for heresy.[43] Explaining this view, Alanus wrote 'Perhaps it is so . . . because there is a doubt whether he is Pope.'[44] I doubt if any Decretist would have insisted that the members of a Council should prevail against a certainly legitimate and orthodox Pope in the conduct of church affairs. On the other hand, they commonly held that Pope-and-Council together possessed a greater authority than the Pope alone when the faith was concerned or 'the general state of the church'. This common opinion of the

---

[42] Gloss *ad* C. 24 q. 1 c. 6. See *Foundations*, p. 49.

[43] Many more Decretist texts, supplementing those in *Foundations*, were printed in my article 'Pope and Council: Some New Decretist Texts', *Medieval Studies* 19 (1957), pp. 197–218.

[44] *Art. cit.* p. 218.

Decretists was crisply expressed in a phrase of an English canonist, later repeated by John of Paris, 'A Pope with a Council is greater than a Pope without a Council'.[45]

In another area of canonistic thought, the corporation theory of Hostiensis that Zabarella explicitly relied on, we find again that major affairs touching the well-being of the whole group were to be decided by head and members acting together, not by the head without consent of the members nor the members acting in opposition to the head. Among the churchmen assembled at Constance there were many canonists and prelates who were advised by canonists. Such people knew perfectly well that a definition of the Pope's obligation to obey the statutes of General Councils did not necessarily imply that the members of a Council, separated from the head, could impose their will on a legitimate pope. Of course *Haec sancta* did not favor the opposing view either—that the judgment of the Pope should prevail in a dispute. The issue was not resolved. The wording of the decree was ambiguous and, I think, deliberately so. When, later on, an irreconcilable dispute arose between the Pope and the members of a conciliar assembly at the Council of Basle, the Conciliarist, Panormitanus, and the papal supporter, Turrecremata, both presented a mediating position that had already been suggested in the twelfth century by Huguccio. In case of such a dispute, they suggested, the church should follow the opinion that was most in accord with reason and scripture.[46] Neither author supposed that the issue had been settled once and for all by *Haec sancta.*

If we turn back now to the debates at Constance we find that, *after* the enactment of *Haec sancta*, speakers of various shades of opinion continued to maintain that, when a legitimate Pope existed, supreme authority in the Church inhered in a General Council that included the Pope as its head—not in the Pope alone or in the members of the Council alone. During the debate on tyrannicide in

---

[45] Caius College, Cambridge, MS. 676, Gloss *ad* C. 24 q. 1 c. 1 cited by J. A. Watt, 'The Early Medieval Canonists and the Formation of Conciliar Theory', *Irish Theological Quarterly* 24 (1957), pp. 13–31 at p. 28. For John of Paris see F. Bleienstein, *Johannes Quidort von Paris: Über königliche und papstliche Gewalt* (Stuttgart, 1969), p. 185, '. . . papa cum concilio maior est papa solo. . . .'

[46] On this see especially H. Schüssler, 'Sacred Doctrine and the Authority of Scripture in Canonistic Thought on the Eve of the Reformation', in G. F. Lytle, ed., *Reform and Authority in the Medieval and Reformation Church* (Washington, D.C., 1981), pp. 55–68. The issue is further discussed in my '"Only the Truth Has Authority"' (above, n. 42).

the Summer of 1415—after *Haec sancta*—one of the cardinals referred any question of faith involved in the dispute to 'the Roman pontiff in a future General Council'.[47] In September Leonard Statius, the master-general of the Dominicans, urged that language about the power of the Council and the Pope should be understood as referring to a union of Pope and Council not to a division between them. Later the Dominican argued that, in a General Council, the exercise of supreme power belonged wholly to a Pope who was 'legitimately presiding and residing' in the Council and not to the Council itself.[48] This was certainly not the opinion most commonly accepted at Constance. But the point is that it could not have been argued before the Council at all if *Haec sancta* had already decreed that the members should prevail against the head.

Leonard Statius was an exceptionally propapal spokesman but more conciliar-minded prelates also maintained that, in normal circumstances, a General Council must include the Pope as its head. Both D'Ailly and Gerson asserted that a General Council was greater than a Pope precisely because the Pope was a necessary and intrinsic part of the Council. And, they argued, 'every whole is greater than its part'. D'Ailly observed that the Pope was the head of a General Council and then added, 'If plenitude of power is in the supreme pontiff, the same or a greater plenitude of power will be in any body *of which he is head*' (emphasis added).[49] Gerson upheld the usual view that the whole church assembled in a General Council was greater than the Pope with a similar argument. He maintained that 'plenitude of papal ecclesiastical power' existed as an integral part of a whole and therefore was not greater than the power of the whole Church. Gerson, however, acknowledged that the papal power was greater than 'the rest'; but, he continued, 'the rest' could not constitute a General Council since such a Council must necessarily include the papal authority.[50]

---

[47] Mansi, XXVIII, col. 799.

[48] H. Finke, *Acta Concilii Constanciensis*, II (Münster, 1923), pp. 418, 705.

[49] H. von der Hardt, *Magnum oecumenicum Constantiense concilium*, VI (Frankfurt, 1700), col. 53. D'Ailly went on to quote the gloss of Johannes Teutonicus to *Dist.* 93 c. 24 asserting that the statutes of a Council were preferred to those of a Pope in case of conflict (see *Foundations*, p. 252).

[50] *Oeuvres*, VI, p. 233, ". . . plenitudo ecclesiasticae potestatis papalis superior et major est ad reliquas. Sed jam illud quod reliquum est nullo pacto potest constituere generale concilium . . . generale concilium in sua ratione formali includit de necessitate papalem auctoritatem sive papa sit sive non sit'. A little earlier (p. 222) Gerson

D'Ailly and Gerson and all the Conciliarists at Constance held that, if a Pope became a 'heretic or overt tyrant' (as d'Ailly put it) or if he refused to summon a Council when the safety of the Church urgently called for one, then the Church could exercise its intrinsic power to preserve its own being and could proceed against the person of a pontiff who had betrayed his office in this fashion. But they also held that, in normal circumstances, when a true pope existed, one who used his powers for the 'edification' of the Church, not for its 'destruction',[51] supreme authority in the Church resided in a General Council that included the Pope as its head. The Conciliarists intended that future Popes, as individuals, should be bound by the reform decrees of such General Councils. In similar fashion, in later English constitutional thought, the king as an individual could be held bound by the statutes of King-in-Parliament.

At the Council of Basle it became evident that the members of the Council, isolated from and hostile to the Pope, could achieve no significant reform on their own. And the next hundred years showed that the Pope alone could not reform the Church without the support of a Council. The eventual outcome, as I wrote in the last words of *Foundations*, was 'a new and more disastrous schism'.

Some questions still remain. What was the significance—if any—of medieval Conciliarism for modern ecclesiology? Did Vatican Council II really succeed in achieving a synthesis of Vatican Council I with the Council of Constance, as Cardinal König suggested it might? It may still be too early to answer such questions. Exegesis of the texts of Vatican Council II is an ongoing process. I think, though, that if we could transport a moderate Conciliarist from Constance to our own era he would tell us that Vatican Council II had promulgated only an imperfect or at best an incomplete ecclesiology.

The decree *Lumen gentium* of the modern Council was a compromise measure just as *Haec sancta* was. No one at Vatican Council II wanted to abandon the ancient doctrine of papal headship in the church. But the more conservative prelates would have been content to repeat the formulations of 1870, while the more progressive ones wanted to redefine papal primacy in a way that would include the

---

had explained that the papal power devolved to the Council when a Pope was lacking 'through natural or civil death'.

[51] This language of Paul (2 Cor. 10.8; 2 Cor. 13.10) was often cited by the Conciliarists.

Council members also 'in the expression of the plenitude of power' (to borrow a phrase from a medieval canonist). The outcome was that both definitions were promulgated side by side without any real attempt to harmonize them. *Lumen gentium* declared that '[T]he Roman Pontiff has full, supreme, and universal power over the church. And he can always exercise this power freely'. Then it added a collegial definition. 'Together with its head, the Roman Pontiff, and never without this head, the episcopal order is the subject of supreme and full power over the universal Church. But this power can be exercised only with the consent of the Roman Pontiff'.[52] At first the decree seems to define two distinct 'subjects' of supreme power; but really the first definition in a way cancels out the second one. The Pope is always supreme, with or without a Council of bishops. Taken together the two definitions are inconsistent with a central concept of the medieval canonists and Conciliarists: 'The Pope with a Council is greater than the Pope without a Council'. Moreover, the reiterated phrase 'and never without this head'[53] seems to exclude an exercise of collegial authority during a breakdown of papal government, the situation that had actually existed at Constance. I can imagine our hypothetical Conciliarist complaining to us in this fashion: 'You people seem to have forgotten all about our Great Schism or you imagine that such a thing can never happen again in all the centuries to come. And yet you are *still* in schism with the Greeks, mainly because you will keep on promulgating puffed up pronouncements about papal power. At *our* Council, the Cardinal of Cambrai told us that we should not diminish the power of the Pope too much nor exaggerate it so as to enervate the power of the Council,[54] and we tried to follow his advice; but the Church still doesn't seem able to strike a right balance after more than five hundred years'.

Avery Dulles has observed, that, although Vatican Council II did not succeed in harmonizing the two definitions of supreme power in the Church that it presented, theologians must continue to seek 'a coherent synthesis that does justice to both'.[55] It will not be an easy task. Some theologians, notably Karl Rahner, have argued that, when-

---

[52] W. M. Abbott, ed., *The Documents of Vatican II* (New York, 1966), p. 43.
[53] The phrase was repeated in the *Decree on Bishops*, p. 399.
[54] Von der Hardt, VI, col. 16.
[55] A. Dulles, 'Catholic Ecclesiology since Vatican II', *Concilium*, 188 (1986), pp. 3–13 at p. 12.

ever the Pope exercises his supreme power, he acts in a collegial fashion, since he always acts in his capacity as head of the college of bishops. But this argument has no force when the Pope explicitly reserves decisions to himself alone; and, since Vatican Council II, the issues that have evoked most public concern among the Catholic faithful—birth control, marriage law, clerical celibacy, the role of women in the church—have all been excluded from collegial decision and reserved for the sole judgment of the supreme pontiff. The decisions handed down from Rome have, however, provoked widespread dissent. One of the wiser Conciliarists at Basle wrote that the more a Pope consults and is seen to consult the more authority he enjoys. A modern corollary is that the less a Pope consults and is seen to consult the less authority his pronouncements command.

The objectives of the Conciliarists at Constance and of the more reform-minded prelates at Vatican Council II were in some ways very similar. They wanted to define the conciliar or collegial nature of the Church and then establish a constitutional structure in accord with the Church's understanding of its own intrinsic nature. Both groups wanted to diminish the centralized power of the Roman curia. They envisaged a program of ongoing reform to be carried out through regular meetings of the Pope with the members of a General Council or a representative synod of bishops.

The undesired aftermaths of the two Councils can also be seen as similar—in both cases a return to papal centralization and a cessation of reform. I think that our Conciliarist from Constance would be a little rueful about the style of governance that had emerged in the church thirty years after the close of Vatican Council II. But then he would perhaps remember the underlying belief that animated all the reformers of his generation. The Church is founded on a divine promise, he would recall. It cannot be without the power to sustain its own life and correct its own failings. Perhaps our Conciliarist would still find grounds for optimism as the Church faces a new millennium.

B. T.
Ithaca, N.Y.
20 March, 1997

ACKNOWLEDGMENT

I would like to thank Professor Heiko A. Oberman for encouraging me to reflect again on the history of conciliar thought and for graciously accepting this work into his distinguished series, *Studies in the History of Christian Thought.*

PREFACE

I have tried, in the title and subtitle of this book, to describe accurately its scope and nature. It is not a complete account of medieval canonistic theories on Church government, for it emphasizes only those elements in canonistic thought that contributed to the growth of the Conciliar Theory; it is not, on the other hand, a complete history of conciliar thought down to the time of the Great Schism, for it does not deal with the well-known publicistic literature of the fourteenth century. There is, inevitably, a certain artificiality in studying the development of a group of ideas with such far-reaching ramifications in medieval life and thought through the medium of one selected class of sources. Yet the limitations involved are less in evidence when one studies the works of the jurists than when one turns to the other relevant types of medieval source material, the publicistic treatises on Church government and the records of papal and episcopal administration. The medieval canonist was often actively engaged in the operations of the system of Church government whose basis and organization he sought to explain; his works reflected an intimate familiarity with the practical realities of medieval ecclesiastical life as well as a capacity for abstract reasoning about them. As Maitland observed, 'Law was the point where life and logic met'. It is necessary, therefore, that the rich canonistic material should be explored and assimilated before any broader synthesis can profitably be attempted; and this may be true, not only for the study of the Conciliar Movement in the Church, but for the history of medieval representative institutions in general.

My thanks are due, above all, to Dr Walter Ullmann. It was he who, several years ago, called attention to the importance of the canonistic sources for the investigation of conciliar ideas, and he has helped me with advice and criticism at all stages in the writing of this book. Only Dr Ullmann's students can appreciate to the full that generous enthusiasm which gives significance and life to a field of study that, in the teaching of a less sympathetic exponent, might seem marked by a certain aridity. All workers in the field of medieval canon law owe a debt to Dr Stephan Kuttner, but, again, mine is an unusually personal one. Dr Kuttner has been very patient in discussing with me various problems raised in the following pages, and in helping me in those matters where his own learning is unexcelled. I am grateful too to Professor E. F. Jacob who read an early draft of the manuscript and made valuable criticisms; and it is through the interest and encouragement of Professor Knowles that publication of the work in the present series has been made possible. When one has received so much generous help it seems necessary to add— as something more than a mere formality—that the writer alone is responsible for the opinions expressed in his work, and for the errors that remain.

It is a pleasant duty to express my thanks to Mr H. M. Adams, Librarian of Trinity College, Cambridge, and his staff, and to the staff of the Anderson Room in the University Library, Cambridge, for their unfailing courtesy and helpfulness during the preparation of this work. I am also grateful to the Librarians of Pembroke College, Cambridge, Gonville and Caius College, Cambridge, Trinity Hall, Cambridge, and the Fitzwilliam Museum for permission to consult books and manuscripts in their care; to Canon W. H. Kynaston for making available a manuscript of Lincoln Cathedral Chapter Library; and to Mgr A. Pelzer for supplying photostats of a manuscript in the Biblioteca Vaticana. Finally, I would like to express my thanks to the editors of the *Catholic Historical Review* and of the *Journal of the History of Ideas* for permission to include in the present work material that was originally published in those journals.

B.T.

WASHINGTON, D.C.
7 April 1954

LIST OF ABBREVIATIONS[1]

A.K.K.R.	*Archiv für katholisches Kirchenrecht.*
Kuttner, *Repertorium*	*Repertorium der Kanonistik* (1140–1234), (Città del Vaticano, 1937).
MS. C.17	MS. 17 of Gonville and Caius College, Cambridge.
MS. C.676	MS. 676 of Gonville and Caius College, Cambridge.
MS. F.XI.605	MS. xi.605 of Sankt Florian, Stiftsbibliothek.
MS. LC.2	MS. 2 of Lincoln Cathedral Chapter Library.
MS. P.72	MS. 72 of Pembroke College, Cambridge.
MS. Pal.Lat.658	MS. Pal.Lat.658 of the Biblioteca Vaticana.
MS. T.O.5.17	MS. O.5.17 of Trinity College, Cambridge.
MS. T.O.10.2	MS. O.10.2 of Trinity College, Cambridge.
Schulte, *Zur Geschichte*, I, II, III	'Zur Geschichte der Literatur über das Dekret Gratians', I, *Sitzungsberichte der kaiserlichen Akademie der Wissenschaften in Wien* (Phil.-Hist. Kl.), LXIII (Wien, 1869); II, *idem*, LXIV, 1870; III, *idem*, LXV, 1870.
Schulte, *Die Glosse zum Dekret*	'Die Glosse zum Dekret Gratians von ihren Anfängen bis auf die jüngsten Ausgaben', *Denkschriften der kaiserlichen Akademie der Wissenschaften* (Phil.-Hist. Kl.), XXI (Wien, 1872).
Schulte, *Quellen*	*Die Geschichte der Quellen und Literatur des canonischen Rechts von Gratian bis auf die Gegenwart* (Stuttgart, 1875–1880).
Van Hove, *Prolegomena*	*Prolegomena* (*Commentarium Lovaniense in Codicem Iuris Canonici*, I, i) (Mechliniae-Romae, 1945).
Z.S.S.R.	*Zeitschrift der Savigny-Stiftung für Rechtsgeschichte (Kanonistische Abteilung).*

---

[1] Abbreviations not listed are considered self-explanatory. Full titles are given in the 'List of Works Cited', pp. 264 ff.

INTRODUCTORY: THE CONCILIAR THEORY
AND THE CANONISTS

Two major problems concerning the nature and limits of ecclesiastical authority dominated the speculations of political philosophers in the later Middle Ages. The first problem was the centuries-old conflict of *regnum* and *sacerdotium*. The second, whose origins and development we shall try to elucidate, was concerned rather with the internal structure of the Church, with the authority of its head and the proper interrelationship of its various members. The two problems were often intimately associated in the course of their historical development, for the partisans of successive princes—of Frederick II, Philip the Fair, Lewis the Bavarian—all found it expedient to couple their claims on behalf of the secular power with appeals to the College of Cardinals or the General Council as embodying an authority superior to that of any individual Pope within the Church. But logically the problems were quite distinct from one another, and there was a sharp divergence in the modes of their eventual solutions. The first one, indeed, could find no clear-cut solution in the polity of the late Middle Ages, for the medieval dream of an ultimate unity achieved through hierarchical organization was becoming ever more remote from the real world of nascent nationalism, and the trend of political events ensured that the rival doctrines of papalists and imperialists should die away before either of them could face the crucial test of practical implementation. In a quite contrary fashion the opposing theories concerning the internal constitution of the Church were forced by the pressure of events to a final crisis in which the partisans of papal absolutism and of conciliar supremacy were engaged, no longer merely on the plane of doctrinaire pamphleteering, but as real contestants for the practical control of the machinery of Church government.

The event which precipitated this crisis was the schism of 1378. In April of that year, on a morning of confused rioting and popular tumult, the cardinals elected as Pope Bartholomew Prignani, Archbishop of Bari, and subsequently they assisted at his coronation, accepted benefices from him, and publicly acknowledged him as a true Pope. However, the conduct of the new pontiff, Urban VI, soon gave the cardinals reason to regret their choice and, four months later, having put themselves outside the immediate power of the Pope at Anagni, they declared the election of 8 April invalid on the ground that it had been made under duress, and called upon Urban to recognize the fact. When he refused the cardinals themselves declared the Holy See vacant, and proceeded to the election of a new Pope who took the name of Clement VII. The events of the next year showed that neither Pope could command universal allegiance. Urban was able to maintain himself at Rome and Clement established a rival curia at Avignon; the nations of Europe attached themselves to the obediences of the rival pontiffs, and the Church faced all the degrading scandal, the chaos and corruption of a prolonged schism.[1]

The subsequent development of the situation that now faced Christendom was influenced profoundly by the theories of Church government that had grown up during the preceding centuries. The prevailing doctrine of papal authority made it peculiarly difficult to reconcile the contending Popes, since any disposition on the part of either of them to submit the dispute to arbitration could have been interpreted as a tacit abandonment of the claim to be a true Pope, subject to no human judgement. Hence, in the dreary deadlock that ensued after 1378, many minds turned to alternative theories which had emphasized the ultimate authority of the whole Church and which had held that no one, not even a Pope, could lawfully act against the well-being of the Church. The propaganda of the Spiritual Franciscans and of the imperial publicists earlier in the fourteenth century had familiarized Christendom with the idea of a General Council as a panacea for all the ills of the Church, and accordingly it was to a Council that many looked for a deliverance from these latest evils. In the end it was in fact a General Council, convoked at first by an anti-pope, and claiming to legislate in virtue of its own inherent authority, that restored unity to the Church after forty years of embittered schism.

Those years had seen a remarkable profusion of speculations on Church government which soon went far beyond the immediate problem of healing the schism to probe deeply into fundamental questions concerning the nature of ecclesiastical authority and the machinery of Church government by which such authority should be manifested. The clash of personalities involved in the struggle between Urban

---

[1] The most recent account of the events leading up to the outbreak of the Great Schism is that of W. Ullmann, *Origins of the Great Schism* (London, 1948), pp. 9–56.

and Clement gave way to a clash of principles, and the original dispute of the rival Popes broadened into a constitutional crisis in which
the most important problem to be resolved was no longer which of
the rival claimants should be Pope but whether the Papacy itself
should continue to govern the Church in the old way. The ferment of
intellectual activity was confined to no one country or class. Among
the most eminent theorists of the Conciliar Movement were Conrad
of Gelnhausen, Henry of Langenstein, and Dietrich of Niem from
Germany, Jean Gerson and Pierre d'Ailly of France, the Spaniard
Andreas Randulf and the Italian cardinal, Zabarella. Naturally their
views were not always identical. Each tended to approach the problems at issue from his own special viewpoint as lawyer, administrator
or theologian, and there were many shades of opinion concerning
the relative authority of Pope and Council, and especially concerning
the role to be attributed to the College of Cardinals. In strict accuracy, no doubt, one should speak of a collection of conciliar proposals
rather than of 'the Conciliar Theory'; and yet there was sufficient
underlying unity of thought among the various writers to render the
latter expression significant and useful.

Their various systems of Church government were all based on
one fundamental doctrine concerning the nature of the Church, which
was already formulated clearly in the *Epistola Concordiae* of Conrad of
Gelnhausen, the first major work of conciliar scholarship to appear
after the outbreak of the Schism. Its central feature was a sharp
distinction between the Universal Church (the whole *congregatio fidelium*)
and the Roman church (understood as Pope and cardinals), together
with an uncompromising assertion that the former was superior to
the latter. Christ had promised that his Church would never fail,
that he would always protect it and maintain the integrity of its faith;
but Conrad of Gelnhausen argued that the Church which enjoyed
this divine guidance and protection could not be any particular local
church, for even in the Roman church individual Popes had erred
in the past. Moreover, Conrad brushed aside the argument that the
Roman See, understood as the corporate aggregate of Pope and
cardinals, might be identified with the unfailing Church established
by Christ, for to argue thus, he protested, was to set the College of
Cardinals above that first college of the Apostles whose faith had
wavered at the time of the Passion. He concluded that, since only
the Church as a whole could be certain of receiving Christ's unfailing guidance, the authority of the Universal Church was superior to

that of any organ of ecclesiastical government within it, including
the Papacy.[2]

The appeal to the underlying authority of the Church, understood
as the *congregatio fidelium*, was the very essence of the conciliar position. Around this central principle the later Conciliarists built up a
complex group of theories concerning the relationship of the Church
in this broad sense to the Pope and the Roman curia. It had often
been held in the past, even by the more extreme papal publicists,
that the Pope represented the Church in the sense that he personified the Church and so embodied in himself the whole of its authority; but to the conciliar thinkers the idea of representation came to
mean something more than mere personification. It implied also an
actual bestowal of authority upon the representative by those whom
he was to represent, with the corollary that such authority could be
withdrawn in case of abuse.[3] Even the Pope, therefore, was held to
possess only a derivative and limited right of government conferred
on him by the Church; far from possessing absolute power, responsible to no human tribunal, he could exercise only such authority as

---

[2] Conrad of Gelnhausen, *Epistola Concordiae* in Martène and Durand, *Thesaurus
Novus Anecdotorum*, II, cols. 1200–26 at cols. 1208–10. On the ultimate authority of
the whole Church see also Henry of Langenstein in Gerson, *Opera*, ed. Du Pin
(Antwerpiae, 1706), II, cols. 822–6; Dietrich of Niem, *De Modis Uniendi et Reformandi
Ecclesiam in Concillo Universali*, ed. Heimpel (Leipzig, 1933), pp. 9, 39; Zabarella, *Tractatus
de Schismate* in Schardius, *De Iurisdictione, Auctoritate et Praeeminentia Imperiali* (Basileae,
1566), pp. 702–3, 708–9; Andreas Randulf, *De Modis Uniendi . . . Ecclesiam in Concilio Universali* in Gerson, *Opera*, II, cols. 161–5; Pierre d'Ailly, *De Ecclesiae . . . Auctoritate* in Gerson,
Opera, II, cols. 949 ff.

[3] The idea was expressed most clearly at the very end of the conciliar period by
Nicolaus Cusanus in his *De Concordantia Catholica*, in *Opera* (Basileae, 1565), XVIII,
p. 741, '. . . quanto particularior est praesidentia, tanto certior est repraesentatio. . . .
Isti autem rectores per consensum iure divino et naturali constitui deberent et ut
Avitius papa dixit, tunc opportet ut qui omnibus praeesse debet ab omnibus eligatur. . . .' Earlier, Zabarella had argued that the Church could take away the
Pope's authority precisely because it had conferred that authority in the first place
(p. 708), and further, borrowing a familiar argument from Roman law, he held that
in conferring powers on the Pope the *congregatio fidelium* could not irrevocably alienate
its own inherent authority. (The more usual view among the jurists, however, was
that the Roman people did irrevocably alienate its powers to the Emperor. On this
see C. N. S. Woolf, *Bartolus of Sassoferrato* (Cambridge, 1913), pp. 35–7, and W. Ullmann, *Medieval Idea of Law* (London, 1946), pp. 48–9.) Pierre d'Ailly also applied to
all grades of the ecclesiastical hierarchy the idea that an official was a representative of his community. See Gerson, *Opera*, II, col. 942 (here closely following John
of Paris). One must view with reserve de Lagarde's statement, 'Jamais le Moyen
Âge n'a lié l'idée de représentation à celle d'une délégation populaire', *La naissance
de l'esprit laïque* (Paris, 1934–46), IV, p. 118. Sometimes in the later Middle Ages the
two ideas were very closely associated.

was necessary for the 'edification' of the Church;[4] if his rule tended rather to its 'destruction' he could be corrected and even deposed by a General Council exercising the superior authority inherent in the Church as a whole. The principle of conciliar supremacy was nowhere more clearly expressed than in the decree *Sacrosancta* of the Council of Constance, which Dr Figgis referred to as 'the most revolutionary document in the history of the world':

> Concilium generale faciens et ecclesiam catholicam repraesentans, potestatem a Christo immediate habet, cui quilibet cuiuscunque status vel dignitatis, etiamsi papalis existat, obedire tenetur in his quae pertinent ad fidem.[5]

From whatever point of view the Conciliarists approached their problems their underlying assumption was always the same. The whole Christian community was superior to any prelate, however exalted; the Pope was to be a servant of the Church rather than its master.

Accompanying these claims on behalf of the General Council in the conciliar works were speculations concerning the position of the cardinals in the Church. It was sometimes argued that the cardinals acted on behalf of the whole Church in the act of electing a Pope, and there were even suggestions that the cardinals themselves should be elected by the Church. Again, it was commonly held that even

---

[4] Zabarella, *De Schismate*, Schardius, p. 703, '... potestatis plenitudo est in papa ita tamen quod non errat, sed cum errat habet corrigere concilium'; Pierre d'Ailly, *De Jurisdictione Ecclesiastica* in von der Hardt, *Concilium Constantiense* (Frankfort, 1697–1700), VI, p. 44, '(papa) non habet sibi collatam potestatem super bonis ipsis nisi ad necessitatem vel communem Ecclesiae utilitatem' (again closely following John of Paris); Dietrich of Niem, *De Modis*, pp. 15–16, 'Omnes ergo constitutiones Apostolicae intelliguntur ... ubi respublica ecclesiastica ... detrimento aut divisioni non videtur subesse.' Dietrich further held that an unjust Pope should be resisted like a 'bestia' in his *De Schismate*, ed. Erler (Leipzig, 1890), III, xl, p. 224. On his views see H. Heimpel, *Dietrich von Niem* (Münster-in-Westf. 1932), pp. 123–53; E. F. Jacob, *Essays in the Conciliar Epoch* (2nd ed. Manchester, 1953), pp. 24–43; H. Jedin, *Geschichte des Konzils von Trient* (Freiburg, 1949), pp. 9–11. See also Gerson in *Opera*, II, cols. 83 ff., 92 ff., 205, and the various opinions cited by B. Hübler, *Die Constanzer Reformation* (Leipzig, 1867), pp. 369–71.

[5] Cf. the definition of a General Council given by Conrad of Gelnhausen in *Epistola Concordiae*, col. 1217, 'Concilium generale est multarum vel plurium personarum rite convocaturum repraesentantium vel gerentium vicem diversorum statuum, ordinum et sexuum et personarum totius christianitatis, venire aut mittere valentium aut potentium, ad tractandum de bono communi universalis ecclesiae in unum locum communem et idoneum conventio seu congregatio'. See also Gerson in *Opera*, II, col. 824, and Zabarella in Schardius, p. 689, '... ipsam ecclesiam universalem quae representatur per concilium generale ...', and again, '... universalis ecclesia, i.e. concilium'.

the somewhat limited authority attributed to the Roman See did not
inhere in the Pope alone but was vested in the corporate association
of Pope and cardinals. It was the task of the cardinals, therefore, to
restrain an erring Pope and, above all, to summon a General Council if, in an emergency, the Pope refused to do so.[6] Evidently the
conciliar thinkers were not content to give the Church a new head;
they were determined to give it a new constitution as well.

It is generally agreed that the theories of the Conciliarists themselves were not unprecedented novelties, invented at the end of the
fourteenth century to solve the urgent problems of the Great Schism.[7]
Yet, although the conciliar doctrines provide an important field of study
for the political theorist as well as for the Church historian, there
has been no wholly adequate account of their origins and early development. The earlier works concentrated almost entirely upon the
immediate problems raised by the Schism itself. In 1893 Dr A. Kneer
showed how the ideas of Conrad of Gelnhausen and Henry of
Langenstein grew out of their attempts to solve these problems,[8] and,
ten years later, Franz Bliemetzrieder, while severely criticizing some
of Kneer's judgements, also dealt with the conciliar theories only in
relation to the immediate context of events.[9] Bliemetzrieder produced
a valuable account of the various stages in the development of conciliar ideas during the years of the Schism, but he himself acknowledged that any really adequate investigation of their origins would
necessitate an inquiry into the theological and canonistic traditions
of the preceding centuries. A year earlier (1903), K. Hirsch had pointed
out that, long before the Great Schism, the ideas of such writers as
Conrad of Gelnhausen and Henry of Langenstein had been anticipated in the works of Marsiglio of Padua and William of Ockham,
and also that the Joachimite doctrines of the Spiritual Franciscans

---

[6] Henry of Langenstein, *Consilium Pacis* in Gerson, *Opera*, II, cols. 831–2; Pierre
d'Ailly, *De Ecclesiae et Cardinalium Auctoritate* in Gerson, *Opera*, II, pp. 937, 946; Zabarella
in Schardius, pp. 690, 698–701, 711; Gerson, *Opera*, II, p. 110; Nicolaus Cusanus,
De Concordantia Catholica, Opera, pp. 731–2.

[7] Thus Professor McIlwain, dismissing the Conciliar Movement in half a dozen
pages, remarks, 'The space here allotted to the conciliar period is wholly incom-
mensurate with its great importance, but greater brevity seemed possible because
there is so little really new in the essentials of the theory advanced at the time',
Growth of Political Thought in the West (New York, 1932), p. 349 n. 1.

[8] A. Kneer, 'Die Entstehung der konziliaren Theorie', *Römische Quartalschrift* (Erstes
Supplementheft), 1893, pp. 48–60.

[9] F. Bliemetzrieder, *Das Generalkonzil im grossen abendländischen Schisma* (Paderborn,
1904).

played a considerable part in undermining the prestige of the Papacy at the beginning of the fourteenth century.[10]

A few years later H.-X. Arquillière was led by his researches into the origins of Gallicanism to postulate a still earlier starting-point for the theory of conciliar supremacy.[11] He called attention to the importance of the Decretist text, *Dist.* 40 c. 6, which laid down that, although normally a Pope was immune from human judgement, this immunity did not extend to a Pope who became a heretic: '. . . cunctos ipse iudicaturus a nemine est iudicandus, *nisi deprehendatur a fide devius*'. Arquillière cited various sources, including pronouncements in some of Innocent III's sermons,[12] to show that this Decretist doctrine reflected an orthodox and established tradition of the Church. He then described how this loophole in the papal defences was skillfully exploited in the reign of Boniface VIII by Nogaret and his followers, who were able to confuse and almost to convince the prelates of France in the assembly of 1303, since the charges they brought against the Pope were indeed technically admissible in canon law. Nogaret's claims were based on the assumption that Boniface as a heretic had ceased automatically to be Pope and so, in Arquillière's view, there was still at this time no claim that the General Council was superior to a true Pope. Nevertheless, the very assumption that a Council was competent to pronounce upon the orthodoxy of a pontiff who was actually occupying the See of Peter encouraged the growth of a more extreme doctrine of conciliar supremacy, and this, Arquillière thought, was first explicitly proclaimed by the Spiritual Franciscans at the court of Lewis of Bavaria.[13]

---

[10] K. Hirsch, *Die Ausbildung der konziliaren Theorie* (Wien, 1903).

[11] H.-X. Arquillière, 'L'origine des théories conciliaires', *Séances et Travaux de l'Académie des Sciences Morales et Politiques*, CLXXV (1911), pp. 573–86, and also 'L'appel au concile sous Philippe le Bel et la genèse des théories conciliaires', *Revue des questions historiques*, XLV (1911), pp. 23–55.

[12] 'L'appel au concile', p. 52, referring to Migne, *Patrologia Latina*, CCXVII, col. 656.

[13] *Art. cit.* pp. 54–5. Although Arquillière was the first to consider in detail in this context the importance of the canonistic doctrine concerning a heretical Pope, Gierke had called attention to the same point some years earlier, *Political Theories of the Middle Age*, transl. Maitland (Cambridge, 1900), p. 50, '. . . the doctrine, hardly doubted in the Middle Age, that in matters of faith only the Church is infallible and the Pope can err and be deposed, led to the opinion expressed by many canonists that in this exceptional case the Pope is subjected to the judgement of the Whole Church'. A considerable number of early canonistic texts relating to the deposition of a Pope was collected by J. F. v. Schulte in his polemical treatise, *Die Stellung der Concilien, Päpste und Bischöfe* (Prague, 1871).

More recently these views of Arquillière have been accepted and developed by Mgr Martin in a series of articles on the origins of the Conciliar Theory.[14] Martin not only quoted Gratian's *Dist.* 40 c. 6 but also pointed out that certain canonists of the twelfth century extended the application of this text by adding other crimes to the one offence of heresy for which alone a Pope could be judged according to the letter of the law. Huguccio, he noted, even went so far as to assert that a Pope could be judged for any notorious crime whatsoever.[15] Nevertheless, insisted Martin, in all this there was still no hint that the General Council was actually superior to the Pope. According to the unanimous opinion of the canonists the Pope was the supreme authority within the Church, and a heretical 'Pope' was liable to judgement simply because, by reason of his heresy, he had ceased automatically to be Pope.[16] Following Arquillière, he cited the Franciscan theologian Pietro Olivi to show that this doctrine concerning a heretical Pope was still current at the end of the thirteenth century, and repeated that Nogaret's appeal to the Council was based on the assumption that the Apostolic See had become vacant as a result of Boniface's heresy.

It was in the revolutionary theories of Marsiglio and Ockham that Martin discerned the first deliberate abandonment of the ancient doctrine concerning the supremacy of the Papacy, and it was their works, and especially those of Ockham that he thought were most influential at the time of the Schism. The canonists had said that a heretical Pope could be deposed, and they had also mentioned schism as a crime tantamount to heresy, but in 1378 the essential problem was to determine which of the contending Popes was in fact schismatic. To resolve this difficulty it was necessary that a Council should have jurisdiction over both Popes, and so the Conciliarists rejected the teaching of the canonists and resuscitated the heretical doctrines of the imperial publicists.[17] For Martin the Conciliar Theory was a radical departure from the theological and canonistic tradition of the Church.

---

[14] V. Martin, 'Comment s'est formée la doctrine de la supériorité du concile sur le pape', *Revue des sciences religieuses*, XVII (1937), pp. 121–43, 261–89, 404–27. See also Martin's *Origines du Gallicanisme* (Paris, 1939), II, pp. 9–17.

[15] *Art. cit.* p. 127. Martin was here following Schulte.

[16] *Art. cit.* p. 129, 'La sentence de l'Église n'est qu'une constatation, une déclaration', p. 130, 'Au moment même où il devient hérétique le pape cesse nécessairement de représenter l'Église, il cesse d'être pape.'

[17] *Art. cit.* pp. 132–6.

It was born of the Great Schism and its prophets were the con-demned heretics Marsiglio and Ockham.[18]

This account of the genesis of the Conciliar Theory leaves much to be explained. It may be doubted whether even the circumstances of the Schism could have induced so many devout and distinguished churchmen from so many countries to subscribe to doctrines invented by known heretics a couple of generations earlier. Moreover, if it is in fact true that the main conciliar ideas were derived from Ockham, then clearly any account of the earlier stages in the development of the Conciliar Theory should consist primarily of an analysis of the sources of Ockham's thought. Here Martin failed to exploit to the full the promising line of inquiry opened up by Arquillière, for he made little attempt to relate the early doctrine concerning a hereti-cal Pope to the general background of canonistic thought in the twelfth century. Had he done so he might have encountered significant anticipations of doctrines whose origin he was content to attribute to the imperial publicists of more than a century later.

A point of view rather different from that of Mgr Martin was put forward by Dr Figgis in his very stimulating Birkbeck Lecture on the Conciliar Theory.[19] While recognizing the contributions of Ockham and Marsiglio and the importance of the Schism itself, Dr Figgis suggested that the real source of conciliar thought was to be found in the constitutional developments that had taken place in various secular kingdoms during the preceding two centuries. He thought that the Conciliarists seemed 'to have discerned more clearly than their predecessors the meaning of the constitutional experiments . . . to have thought out the principles that underlay them . . . to have discovered that arguments applicable to government in general could not be inapplicable to the Church'.[20] The Conciliar Movement, he concluded, eventually failed because these merely academic principles were unable to sustain themselves in the face of the deep-rooted tradition of papal monarchy which re-asserted itself once the scandal of the Schism was ended.

---

[18] ·Art. cit. pp. 420–3.

[19] J. N. Figgis, *From Gerson to Grotius*, 2nd ed. (Cambridge, 1916), pp. 41–70.

[20] *Op. cit.* p. 47. Cf. Gierke, *Political Theories*, p. 49, 'More and more distinctly and sharply men were conceiving the Church as "a Polity", and it was natural therefore that they should employ the scheme of categories which had in the first instance been applied to the temporal State. Indeed in the end the Church was regarded as charged with the mission of realizing the ideal of a perfect political Constitution.'

It has since been pointed out that in one sense all medieval thought
was academic, and that in another sense the great conciliar writers
were by no means all mere academes;[21] but, while one may view
with reserve the theory that conciliar thought was inspired mainly by
experiments in secular government, it remains true that, in the later
Middle Ages, there were certain constitutional problems that were
common to the Church and to other societies. Administrative centralization tended to stimulate local protests. Representative assemblies,
at first summoned to enhance the authority of the ruler, could learn
to give a corporate expression to such protests and might eventually
take advantage of some constitutional crisis, such as a disputed succession, to assert for themselves a position of supremacy. Again, the
process of centralization itself normally encouraged the growth of a
bureaucratic council which could acquire corporate rights tending to
limit the free exercise of authority by the ruler.

In the growth of the papal monarchy from the twelfth century
onwards it was natural that such problems should have been encountered and their existence reflected in the growing law of the Church
and the voluminous writings of the canonists. Indeed, the essential
point that Dr Figgis overlooked was that, when the conciliar writers
surveyed their problems, they would naturally turn for guidance, not
to the customs of France, or the laws of England, or the constitutional practices of Spain, but rather to the great mass of ecclesiastical jurisprudence, to the common law of the Universal Church and
the works of its great interpreters.[22] Considering the men they were,
their training and background, it is hardly thinkable that they would
have turned elsewhere. Yet, although one can hardly turn a page of
any major conciliar treatise without noticing references to *Decretum*
and Decretals, we are still told that the conciliar arguments rested
'on appeals partly to Aristotle and partly to the Mosaic system', and,
apart from the penetrating suggestion of Arquillière, and the limited
application of it by Martin, there has been little attempt to explore

---

[21] E. F. Jacob, *op. cit.* pp. 1–7.

[22] One might indeed argue that the resemblances between the conciliar theories
and the constitutional experiments of secular states were due partly to canonistic
influence in the secular sphere. This whole subject is being opened up in the important articles of Gaines Post, 'Roman law and early representation in Spain and
Italy', *Speculum*, XVIII (1943), pp. 211–32; 'Plena potestas and consent in medieval
assemblies', *Traditio*, I (1943), pp. 355–408; 'A Romano-canonical maxim, "quod
omnes tangit", in Bracton', *Traditio*, IV (1946), pp. 197–251; 'The theory of public
law and the state in the thirteenth century', *Seminar*, VI (1948), pp. 42–59.

the canonistic sources that especially interested the Conciliarists them-selves.[23] It seems, therefore, that an investigation of the juristic basis of their theories might contribute significantly to our understanding of the origins and growth of conciliar thought. This is the task that has been attempted in the present work.

The absence of any adequate study of the canonistic writings as sources for conciliar ideas is understandable, for the medieval canonists have usually been associated with the doctrines of extreme papalism that were put forward in the conflict of *regnum* and *sacerdotium*. It is true that the canonists normally maintained that the spiritual power was in some sense superior to the temporal, and that in the thirteenth and fourteenth centuries they pressed on to an ever more extreme formulation of this doctrine. It is also true that, in one sense, for a medieval canonist, there could be no disputing about the 'constitu-tion' of the spiritual hierarchy itself. The government of the churches was by bishops, and the unity of the Church was ensured by the communion of all its members with a single head, the Papacy. So much was agreed. But, within the bounds of that common doctrine, there was room for a variety of theories on the nature of the powers implied by the papal primacy, on the relationship between Pope and Universal Church, and on the internal structure of the Roman church itself. The widespread assumption that there was one single canonistic theory of Church government which was adequately reflected in the works of such publicists as Giles of Rome or Augustinus Triumphus does scant justice to the richness and diversity of canonistic specula-tion in this field. The theories of the more extreme papal publicists do indeed reflect one trend of canonistic thought, but the conciliar arguments in favour of a limitation of papal authority by Council and cardinals reflect another; both parties alike drew their weapons from the canonists' armoury.[24]

---

[23] The early canonistic views on the deposition of a Pope were mentioned by J. Rivière, *Le problème de l'église et de l'état au temps de Philippe le Bel* (Louvain, 1926), p. 111, and by J. Lecler, 'Les théories démocratiques au moyen âge', *Études*, CCXXV (1935), pp. 5–26, 168–89 at p. 170, but without any detailed investigation of their significance. Only Gierke realized to the full the importance of the canonistic sources. His few pages on the Conciliar Theory provide a most penetrating analysis of its main features (*Political Theories*, pp. 49–57), but Gierke did not attempt any detailed history of the growth of conciliar thought before the fourteenth century.

[24] This is true in spite of the fact that some of the well-known conciliar publicists attacked the canonists as a class (having in mind the contemporary jurists whom they regarded as the most formidable exponents of the principle of papal sover-eignty); even a theologian like Gerson, who was exceptional in that he seldom quoted

The neglect of canonistic sources by most writers on the origins of the Conciliar Theory may also arise from a mistaken approach to the early history of conciliar thought. There has been a tendency to treat the Conciliar Movement as something accidental or external, thrust upon the Church from outside, rather than as a logical culmination of ideas that were embedded in the law and doctrine of the Church itself. Kneer and Bliemetzrieder emphasized the fortuitous disaster of the Schism, Figgis directed our attention to the examples of the secular kingdoms, Hirsch and Martin pointed to the *Streitschriften* of the imperial publicists. But to understand the origins of a constitutional crisis in the Church we must surely turn to the background of constitutional law from which all parties in the crisis sought to defend their claims. Without a study of the canonists we can never hope to understand in all its complexity the polity of the medieval Church, for, to sketch in outline the growth of the *Corpus Iuris Canonici* from the appearance of Gratian's *Decretum* to the outbreak of the Great Schism is, in effect, to record the process by which the Church became a body politic, subject to one head and manifesting an external unity of organization. If the ancient doctrine of papal primacy was the corner-stone of ecclesiastical unity in the Middle Ages, the canon law was the cement, which, it was hoped, would bind together the whole vast fabric of prelates and peoples and princes.

The appearance of Gratian's *Decretum* may be taken as the starting-point of the whole process of legal integration.[25] Gratian's work was of course only one in a distinguished series of canonistic compilations, but it was so manifestly superior in quality as to become actually different in kind from its predecessors. The earlier collections had been handbooks of practical information, designed for particular purposes, and sometimes influenced by local requirements. Gratian produced a treatise that could serve the needs of the whole Church,

---

directly from canonistic sources, frequently used arguments derived from fourteenth-century publicists whose views in turn were based on a solid foundation of earlier canonistic work. See my 'Ockham, the Conciliar Theory, and the Canonists', *Journal of the History of Ideas*, xv (1954), pp. 40–70.

[25] Gratian's work appeared *c.* 1140. It is certain that Gratian's own title for it was *Concordia Discordantium Canonum*, though it was known to later canonists simply as the *Decreta*. Cf. R. Köstler, 'Zum Titel des Gratianischen Dekrets', *Z.S.S.R.* LII (1932), pp. 370–3 and 'Noch einmal zum Titel des Gratianischen Dekrets', *ibid.* LIV (1934), pp. 378–80; S. Kuttner, 'The father of the science of Canon Law', *The Jurist*, I (1941), p. 15 n. 29. An important collection of papers on various aspects of Gratian's work is to be presented in the forthcoming volume of *Studia Gratiana*.

and though his work was a private compilation without any official sanction, it came to be universally accepted in the schools as a necessary basis for canonistic studies.[26] Thus Christendom knew for the first time not only codes of law, but a Common Law.

The *Decretum* was at once a synthesis of all that was most valuable in the earlier canonistic collections and a point of departure for new inquiries into the law and institutional structure of the Church. During the next half-century the task of harmonizing its discordant texts, which Gratian himself had begun, was carried forward in a spate of Glosses, *Summae* and *Quaestiones* on the *Decretum* produced by 'una folta schiera cosmopolitica di giuristi'.[27] Among the earlier Decretists were numbered two future Popes, Rolandus Bandinelli and Albertus,[28] as well as Laborans who became a cardinal, and numerous future bishops including Paucapalea, Joannes Faventinus, Stephanus Tornacensis and Sicardus Cremonensis.[29] Perhaps the greatest of all these twelfth-century Decretists was Huguccio, Bishop of Pisa, whose very able *Summa* on the *Decretum*, written *c.* 1190, reviewed, in the light of the author's own searching intelligence, the substantial achievements of the preceding half-century of canonistic scholarship.

Gratian's private collection had established the foundations of a universal law for the Church, but the subsequent growth of that law was to be moulded by the legislative activity of the Popes. In the twelfth century Alexander III in particular poured forth a flood of decretals, clarifying points that had been left obscure by Gratian and

---

[26] On this point see especially S. Kuttner, 'Quelques observations sur l'autorité des collections canoniques dans le droit classique de l'Église', *Actes du Congrès de Droit Canonique* (Paris, 1947), pp. 303–12.

[27] S. Mochi Onory, *Fonti canonistiche dell'Idea moderna dello Stato* (Milan, 1951), p. 36. Mochi Onory presents a lively description of the diffusion of Decretist thought in the twelfth century. For general surveys of the canonistic literature of the period see J. F. v. Schulte, *Die Geschichte der Quellen und Literatur des canonischen Rechts*, I (Stuttgart, 1875); Stephan Kuttner, *Repertorium der Kanonistik*, I (Città del Vaticano, 1937); A. Van Hove, *Prolegomena* (*Commentarium Lovaniense in Codicem Iuris Canonici*, I, i, Mechliniae-Romae, 1945).

[28] Rolandus ruled as Alexander III and Albertus as Gregory VIII. The importance of this latter Pope, whose reign lasted only eight weeks, has been pointed out by W. Holtzmann, 'Die Dekretalen Gregors VIII' in *Festschrift für Leo Santifäller* (*Mitteilungen des österr. Instituts für Geschichtsforschung*, LVIII (1950), pp. 113–24). See also S. Kuttner, 'Bernardus Compostellanus Antiquus', *Traditio*, I (1943), pp. 277–340 at p. 282 n. 19, correcting some earlier attributions of Schulte.

[29] For notes on the various canonists and anonymous works mentioned in the text see Appendix II, and, for additional literature concerning them, Van Hove, *Prolegomena*.

providing remedies for new problems and old abuses,[30] while the Third Lateran Council of 1179 enacted a substantial body of legislation for the whole Church. The growth of ecclesiastical law was accelerated under Innocent III and, since the new legislation often modified the conclusions of Gratian, it became necessary to supplement his work with collections of the new decretals and canons. Among the most important productions in this sphere were the compilations of the Englishmen, Gilbertus and Alanus,[31] the *Compilatio Romana* of Bernardus Compostellanus,[32] and, above all, the collections known as the *Quinque Compilationes Antiquae*.[33]

For about twenty years after the appearance of Huguccio's *Summa* the canonists were principally occupied in the task of codifying and glossing the new legislation. From about 1210, however, a new series of important apparatuses on the *Decretum* began to appear,[34] culminating in the eclectic *Glossa Ordinaria* of Joannes Teutonicus, a work that was to prove a very fruitful source of arguments in many sub-

---

[30] W. Holtzmann, 'Über eine Ausgabe der päpstlichen Dekretalen des 12 Jahrhunderts', *Nachrichten der Akademie der Wissenschaften in Göttingen* (Phil. Hist. Kl.), 1945, pp. 15 ff.; *idem*, 'Die Register Alexanders III in den Händen der Kanonisten', *Quellen und Forschungen aus ital. Archiven*, XXX (1940), pp. 13 ff.; S. Kuttner, 'On a projected corpus etc.', *Traditio*, VI (1948), pp. 345 ff. Cf. also W. Holtzmann, 'Die Benutzung Gratians in der päpstlichen Kanslei' in *Studia Gratiana* (Bologna, 1954), I, 323–49.

[31] Completed in 1202 and 1206 respectively. Kuttner, *Repertorium*, pp. 310–13; Van Hove, *Prolegomena*, p. 354.

[32] Kuttner, *Repertorium*, pp. 317–19 and *art. cit.* (n. 27), pp. 327–33; *Prolegomena*, p. 355.

[33] The *Compilatio Prima* of Bernardus Papiensis (1191) was especially important, for it adopted the method of classification by subject-matter into five books that was followed in all the subsequent collections (Kuttner, *Repertorium*, pp. 324–44 and *art. cit.* pp. 310–20; Van Hove, *Prolegomena*, p. 356). The *Compilatio Tertia* was the first official collection of decretals. It was produced *c.* 1210 at the command of Innocent III by his Vice-Chancellor, Petrus Collivaccinus (*Repertorium*, p. 355; *Prolegomena*, pp. 356–7). The *Compilatio Secunda* of Joannes Galensis was so called because it was made up of earlier pre-Innocentian decretals though it appeared after the work of Petrus Collivaccinus (*Repertorium*, pp. 345–54; *Prolegomena*, p. 356). The *Compilatio Quarta* of Joannes Teutonicus (1216) consisted in large part of the canons of the Fourth Lateran Council (*Repertorium*, pp. 372–3, 457–62; *Prolegomena*, p. 357; S. Kuttner, 'Johannes Teutonicus, das vierte Laterankonzil und die Compilatio quarta', *Miscellenea Giovanni Mercati* (Città del Vaticano, 1946), V, pp. 608–34). The *Compilatio Quinta* was a second official compilation produced in 1226 at the command of Honorius III (*Repertorium*, pp. 382–5; *Prolegomena*, p. 357). These collections were edited by E. Friedberg, *Quinque Compilationes Antiquae* (Lipsiae, 1882).

[34] Among the most important we may mention the apparatuses *Ecce Vicit Leo, Ius Naturale* and the *Glossa Palatina* (*Repertorium*, pp. 59–80). In each case the author is unknown. Guido de Baysio in his *Rosarium* (1300) attributed all his quotations from the *Glossa Palatina* to Laurentius, but on this question see Kuttner, *art. cit.* (supra p. 15 n. 2), pp. 288–91, 309.

sequent disputes on questions of Church government.[35] The age of Innocent III was indeed a period of very high achievement in both main branches of canonistic activity, Decretist and Decretalist.

The next important phase of canonistic development began in 1234 when Gregory IX promulgated a systematic collection of all the decretals and canons not included in Gratian's *Decretum* which he wished to be preserved as laws of universal validity.[36] This work superseded all the earlier Decretalist compilations and, since it was regarded by the canonists as supplementary to the *Decretum*, it was usually referred to as the *Liber Extra* (i.e. additional to the *Decretum*).[37] Gregory's collection was quickly provided with a *Glossa Ordinaria* by Bernardus Parmensis,[38] while Goffredus Tranensis produced an influential *Summa Super Titulos Decretalium* between 1241 and 1243, and for the next two generations the main work of the canonists lay in interpreting the texts assembled in the *Liber Extra*. The works of the mid-thirteenth-century Decretalists, especially of the two greatest, Sinibald Fieschi (Innocent IV) and Hostiensis (Henricus de Segusio, Cardinal-bishop of Ostia), were perhaps the supreme achievements of medieval canonistic science. These two great masters, whose forceful and sometimes conflicting views on ecclesiastical authority dominated the canonistic speculations of the second half of the thirteenth century, retained the attractive vitality and intellectual adventurousness of their predecessors but combined these qualities with a more mature scholarship which gave an added depth and precision to their works. No inquiry into medieval theories of Church government can afford to neglect the views of such eminent and influential masters.

Innocent IV, like Alexander III before him, was important not only as a glossator but as a legislator too,[39] and many of his decretals, together with canons of the First and Second Councils of Lyons,

---

[35] The *Glossa Ordinaria* was completed after the Fourth Lateran Council (1215) and probably before the *Compilatio Quarta* (1217) (Kuttner, *Repertorium*, pp. 93–9 and *art. cit.* pp. 291–2; *Prolegomena*, pp. 430–2).

[36] The work was compiled by Raymundus de Pennaforte at the command of Gregory IX (*Prolegomena*, pp. 357–61).

[37] Sometimes abbreviated simply to the *siglum* 'X'. This form of reference has been used in subsequent notes.

[38] For dates of the various recensions of the *Glossa Ordinaria* see S. Kuttner and B. Smalley, 'The *Glossa Ordinaria* to the Gregorian Decretals', *English Historical Review*, LX (1945), pp. 97–105.

[39] He promulgated three collections of decretals and canons in 1245, 1246 and 1253. Gregory X (1274) and Nicholas III (1280) promulgated additional collections before the *Liber Sextus*, A. Van Hove, *Prolegomena*, pp. 361–3.

were incorporated in the *Liber Sextus*, another official compilation promulgated by Boniface VIII in 1298.[40] The final official volume of the *Corpus Iuris Canonici* was the *Clementinae*,[41] which appeared in 1317, though unofficial collections (the *Extravagantes Joannis XXII* and *Extravagantes Communes*) were made later in the fourteenth century. Important glosses on the new compilations and also on the *Gregoriana* continued to appear, prominent among them the works of Guido de Baysio, Joannes Monachus, Joannes Calderinus, Zenzellinus de Cassanis, Joannes Lignano and especially of Joannes Andreae, 'the fount and trumpet of the canon law'. In general the fourteenth-century canonists displayed an unprecedented erudition, but sometimes one misses in their works both the originality and clarity that had characterized the writings of their greatest predecessors. Nevertheless, these later canonists laid down the accepted interpretations of ecclesiastical law in the age of the Great Schism itself, and so their glosses provide an indispensable background for any real understanding of the problems raised by the Schism and of the proposals put forward for their solution.

Through the eventful centuries that elapsed between the appearance of Gratian's *Decretum* and the outbreak of the Great Schism there was no aspect of ecclesiastical life and organization that remained untouched by the work of the great jurists who followed one another in unbroken succession from Rolandus Bandinelli to Franciscus Zabarella, and their influence was rendered the more direct and penetrating by the fact that the greatest exponents of canonistic doctrine were ecclesiastical statesmen as well as scholars.[42] The canon law provided not only a theoretical foundation for the constitution of the Church but a discipline which moulded its greatest leaders.

Inevitably it was to this great ocean of material that the Conciliarists turned for many of their most effective arguments, and the assimilation of earlier canonistic material in their works raises interesting

---

[40] Compiled by Guilielmus de Mandagato, Berengarius Fredoli and Richardus Petronius de Senis, *Prolegomena*, pp. 363–5.

[41] Embodying the canons of the Council of Vienne (1312). The collection was made by order of Clement V, but promulgated by John XXII after Clement's death.

[42] On the importance of the canonists for general medieval studies see W. Ullmann, *Medieval Papalism* (London, 1949), pp. 1–26; S. Kuttner, 'The scientific investigation of medieval canon law; the need and the opportunity', *Speculum*, xxiv (1949), pp. 493–501; and my paper, 'The canonists and the mediaeval state', *Review of Politics*, xv (1953), pp. 378–88. A convenient guide to the growth of ecclesiastical law relating to Church institutions (with copious bibliographical notes) is provided by H. E. Feine, *Kirchliche Rechtsgeschichte*, i, *Die Katholische Kirche* (Weimar, 1950).

problems for the historian of ideas. It would, for instance, be possible
to extract from the canonistic treatises written around the year 1200
a series of assertions that seem to anticipate all the characteristic propositions of the Conciliar Theory. But, obviously enough, the leading canonists of the age of Innocent III were not really Conciliarists
in the fourteenth-century sense of the word. Nor would it be true to
suggest that the Conciliarists themselves, who drew support from these
sources, deliberately distorted their meaning. They approached the
works of the twelfth and thirteenth centuries with minds formed in
a later tradition of canonistic thought, which led them almost inevitably to see in the early texts shades of meaning different from those
that the original authors had intended. A presentation of the canonistic
contribution to the growth of conciliar thought must attempt, therefore, not only to indicate the canonistic glosses that the Conciliarists
found most useful, but also to assess the significance of those glosses
in their original contexts and to explain how the subsequent development of canonistic thought led to their re-interpretation in the
changed circumstances of the fourteenth century.

The mass of material available for such a task is overwhelming,
and it has been possible to consider only a few of the most important canonists in each generation and to present only an outline of
those elements in their thought that contributed to the growth of conciliar ideas. Nevertheless, even in such an outline it is possible to trace
the inception and growth of patterns of canonistic thought anti-
thetical to the prevailing doctrines of papal power, to discuss some
of the problems raised by the assimilation of such concepts into the
canonistic theories of the fourteenth century, and so, it is hoped, to
throw new light on the sources of conciliar thought.[43]

---

[43] Since the canonistic sources have not previously been explored with this object
in view it has seemed desirable to provide fairly copious citations from them in text
and notes. It is difficult, and sometimes impossible, to translate accurately the technical language of the canonists, but the sense of the Latin extracts is normally conveyed in the English context, and the argument will seem coherent, it is hoped,
even if the reader omits the quotations.

PART ONE

DECRETIST THEORIES OF CHURCH GOVERNMENT
(1140–1220)

CHAPTER ONE

POPE AND CHURCH

One of the most fruitful subjects of medieval debate in the sphere of constitutional theory was the problem of defining the proper relationship between the powers of a monarch and the rights of the community he governed. The issue was essentially a juristic one, and the canonists, no less than the exponents of Roman law or common law, had their own distinctive contribution to make to its discussion. For them the question arose from the problems of institutional growth that were common to the Church and to other medieval societies, and also from certain characteristics that were believed to inhere in the Church alone. The Papacy was indeed a monarchy, the greatest of the medieval world, but it could not be conceived of in just the same way as other monarchies; its heritage of Christian doctrine was not precisely comparable to the folk law or feudal customs that might limit the competence of a secular ruler. Christ had promised that his Church would never fail, that he would sustain it through all the ages; he had also set over the Church a single head, so that the Papacy could claim a divine institution more immediate than that of any other monarchy. Hence, when the problem of a conflict between ruler and community arose in the Church, it presented itself in a peculiarly intransigent form—the status of the ruler was more exalted, but the welfare of the community was more sacrosanct than in any other society.

Moreover, disputes about the government of the Church tended to involve deeper ambiguities concerning the nature of the Church itself, for, always, in medieval thought, one finds interwoven two different conceptions of the Church; on the one hand the idea of the Church as a community of believers, a *societas perfecta* infused with the Holy Spirit and sustaining an unfailing corporate life; on the other hand, the idea of the Church as a system of clerical offices deriving their authority from above, from outside the community. The two conceptions were not in themselves mutually exclusive— any adequate system of ecclesiology must surely find room for both of them—but there were always possibilities of conflict between them if either were distorted or exaggerated at the expense of the other. It seems incorrect, moreover, to regard the latter concept as the distinctively 'legalistic' one; both of them found juristic expression in the works of the canonists. It was, indeed, because both could be expressed in terms of law and institutions that their eventual opposition became a practical issue of constitutional organization as well as an abstract issue of ecclesiological theory.

At the end of the fourteenth century the crisis of the Great Schism had made such issues matters of urgent public debate. Two centuries earlier the Papacy was passing through another critical period of change, a period of constructive development rather than of threatened disintegration, and in the stimulating atmosphere of that age the problems that later faced the leaders of the Conciliar Movement were often debated with subtlety and vigour in the glosses of the canonists. These early canonists, however, were led to consider such problems by motives very different from those of the Conciliarists. When, for instance, a publicist of around the year 1400 enquired whether the authority of a General Council was superior to that of a Pope he was dealing with a problem of desperate practical urgency; when a canonist, around 1200, discussed the same question he was concerned only with a theoretical problem of legal dialectics. No doubt the developments that were actually taking place in the days of Alexander III and Innocent III did help to stimulate discussion on questions of papal authority, but the immediate occasion for most such debate was provided, not by the exigencies of contemporary ecclesiastical politics, but by the continuing problem of reconciling the discordant texts of Gratian's *Decretum*. Hence the most lively discussions on problems of Church government are usually found in commentaries on the *Decretum* rather than in glosses on the new collections of Decretals, for in these latter works the same problems seldom arose. The *Decretum* was radically different in structure from the later parts of the *Corpus Iuris Canonici*. They were codes of authoritative law. The *Decretum* was a running argument; and it displayed to the full that essential characteristic of a good argument, the judicious citation of texts on both sides of all questions discussed—including questions of Church government.

The Decretists, for their part, showed considerable ingenuity in pursuing all the implications of the texts cited. At times they even seem to have been more interested in elaborating the possible corollaries of conflicting texts than in producing a final reconciliation, a characteristic which gives an engaging air of spontaneity and vitality to their works, but which did not facilitate the construction of a closely knit, systematic theory of Church government. An examination of their arguments will suggest that the Decretists did not indeed produce any such coherent theory, that their achievement was rather to assemble the raw materials from which later theorists of all schools could build their opposing systems.

1. Tu es Petrus

The ambiguity concerning the nature of the Church which runs through medieval writings was already implied in the most famous of Petrine texts, Matthew xvi. 18–19, which was cited repeatedly in the *Decretum* as the basis of papal authority in the Church.[1] The Decretists' exegesis of this text makes an interesting minor chapter in the long and controversial history of its interpretation, and provides a convenient introduction to their ways of thinking about the Church and its head:

> Tu es Petrus et super hanc petram aedificabo ecclesiam meam et portae inferi non praevalebunt adversus eam. Et tibi dabo claves regni caelorum. Et quodcumque ligaveris super terram erit ligatum et in caelis, et quodcumque solveris super terram erit solutum et in caelis.

It was to Peter that Christ gave the 'keys of the Kingdom of Heaven'; but it was to the Church that he promised unfailing protection against the 'gates of Hell'.[2] Exegesis of the passage could accordingly emphasize

---

[1] The text was cited or referred to at *Dist.* 12 c. 2, *Dist.* 19 c. 9, *Dist.* 21 cc. 2, 3, *Dist.* 50 c. 54, C. 9 q. 3 c. 14, C. 11 q. 1 c. 14, C. 24 q. 1 cc. 15, 18, 20, 22. Cf. G. Le Bras, 'Les écritures dans le Décret Gratien', *Z.S.S.R.* LVIII (1938), pp. 47–80 at pp. 77 ff., and H. Rahner, 'Navicula Petri', *Zeitschrift für katholische Theologie*, LXXIX (1947), pp. 5 ff.

[2] According to the canonists these words signified either mortal sin in general or the sin of heresy in particular, e.g. Rufinus, *Summa ad Dist.* 19 c. 7, '*Porte inferi*, i.e. heretice pravitates que ad infernum trahunt' (*Die Summa Decretorum des Magister Rufinus*, ed. H. Singer (Paderborn, 1902), p. 43); Stephanus Tornacensis, *Summa ad Dist.* 19 c. 7, '*Porte inferi*, i.e. mortalia peccata per que introitus patet ad inferos' (*Die Summa des Stephanus Tornacensis*, ed. J. F. v. Schulte (Giessen, 1891), p. 29); Huguccio, *Summa ad Dist.* 19 c. 7, MS. P.72 fol. 128vb, '*Porte inferi*, vitia et peccata mortalia . . . vel porte inferi dicuntur hereses et schismata'. The *Glossa Palatina*, *Glossa Ordinaria* and Gloss *Ecce Vicit Leo*, commenting on this same chapter, all followed Huguccio in mentioning both sin and heresy. Cf. F. Gillmann, 'Zur scholastischen Auslegung von Mt 16, 18', *A.K.K.R.* CIV (1924), pp. 41–53.

either the unique position of Peter among the Apostles or the indefectibility of the Church as a whole; and the Decretists, as was their
wont, did not neglect either aspect of the text but developed all its
potentialities to the full.

They followed the well-worn grooves of patristic controversy in
discussing the precise connotation of the words *super hanc petram*.
Stephanus Tornacensis and Simon de Bisignano thought that the Rock
on which the Church was founded must be either Christ himself or
the unshakable faith that Peter had displayed. Joannes Faventinus
added to these interpretations the suggestion that the Rock might be
Peter himself, and the *Summa Parisiensis* explained that the Church
was founded principally on Christ, secondarily on Peter.[3] This point
was developed by Huguccio in a lengthy gloss which summarized
the various earlier opinions; the Rock might be either Christ or Peter
or Peter's faith, and although the Church was founded on Christ
principaliter et tanquam auctorem, it could be regarded as founded on
Peter *secundario et quasi ministrum*.[4] In the next generation the *Glossa*

---

[3] Rufinus, *Summa ad Dist.* 19 c. 7, p. 43, '*voluit nominari*, i.e. denominari, Petrum
scil., ab eo *quod ipse erat*, videl. petra'. This merely repeats the ambiguity of the
Decretist text itself; Stephanus, *Summa ad Dist.* 19 c. 7, p. 29, '*super hanc petram*, i.e.
super hanc fidei tue soliditatem, vel super me, qui sum petra, de qua dicit apostolus,
Petra autem erat Christus'; Simon de Bisignano ad C. 24 q. 1 c. 20 (Gillmann, *art. cit.*
p. 44 n. 2), '*supra petram*, i.e. super Christum per petram significatum. Petra autem
teste apostolo erat Christus. Vel supra soliditatem fidei ipsius Petri'; Joannes Faventinus
ad Dist. 19 c. 7 (*art. cit.* p. 43 n. 4), '*id voluit nominari*, i.e. denominari, Petrum scil.,
ab eo quod ipse erat, videlicet petra, vel *id quod ipse*, scil. Christus *erat*, i.e. Petrus, quod
sonat firmus ut petra. *super hanc petram*, i.e. super hanc fidei tue soliditatem, vel *super
me, qui sum petra*, de qua dicit apostolus, *Petra autem erat Christus*'; *Summa Parisiensis ad
Dist.* 19 c. 7, '*quod ipse*, ut Petrus diceretur sicut ipse *supra quam*, i.e. supra petram
secundario, super se principaliter', *ad Dist.* 50 c. 54, 'Cum aliter exponatur *et super
hanc petram etc* hic tamen dicitur Petrus fundamentum ecclesiae, quia primus praedicavit
gentibus' (*The Summa Parisiensis on the Decretum Gratiani*, ed. T. P. McLaughlin (Toronto,
1952), pp. 19, 47).

[4] *Summa ad Dist.* 19 c. 7, MS. P.72 fol. 128 vb, discussing the words 'Hunc enim
in consortium individuae unitatis assumptum id quod ipse erat voluit nominari dicendo,
Tu es Petrus et super hanc petram. . . .' Huguccio commented, '*Dominus voluit nominari id*,
i.e. ab eo *quod ipse* scil. Christus *erat*. Nam a petra dictus est Petrus, de qua petra
dicitur, *Petra autem erat Christus*. *Tu es Petrus*, dictus es a me petra, *et super hanc petram*,
i.e. super me, *edificabo ecclesiam meam*, principaliter, quasi super me principaliter et
tanquam auctorem edificabo ecclesiam, non super te principaliter quasi auctorem,
sed secundario et quasi ministrum. Vel sic, *nominari id*, i.e. ab eo *quod ipse* Petrus *erat*.
Ipse enim firmus erat et ideo dictus est Petrus a petra, i.e. firmitate.' Later in the
same gloss he referred to the faith of Peter, 'Vel super me, i.e. super fidem habitam
a me et de me et non super te vel fidem habitam a te vel de te, et tamen dicitur
ecclesia fundata super fidem petri quia ad instar fidei Petri salvantur omnes fideles
et quia ipse primus posuit fundamentum fidei in gentibus et quia tanquam saxum
immobile ecclesiam contineat.'

Palatina and the gloss *Ecce Vicit Leo* identified the Rock with Christ him-self,[5] while Joannes Teutonicus, in his *Glossa Ordinaria*, stated emphat-ically his opinion that it was best understood as the article of faith that Peter had enunciated.

> *Et super hanc petram.* Per hanc dictionem non credo Dominum aliud demonstrasse quam haec verba quae Petrus respondit Domino cum dixit, *Tu es Christus, filius Dei vivi*, quia super illo articulo fidei fundata est ecclesia.[6]

The various explanations of St Matthew's text other than that which identifies the Rock with Peter himself are sometimes referred to as 'Protestant' interpretations; but the twelfth-century canonist saw no incongruity in preferring one of the alternative expositions while at the same time deriving from the text a most exalted conception of the papal dignity and powers. Even if Christ himself was the true Rock, it could still be held that Peter alone was named after the Rock and so was singled out for a position of special eminence among the Apostles; and even though the Church was held to be founded ultimately on Christ, still Peter could be regarded as its founder in a secondary sense, *quasi minister*, as the chosen instrument of the heav-enly Founder. The sections of the *Decretum* which quoted the words *Tu es Petrus* commonly associated them with the concept of papal headship in the Church,[7] and, though the Decretists showed little disposition to identify Peter with the Rock, they expressed no doubts about the headship of the Papacy. Immediately upon election the chosen candidate became *verus papa et caput ecclesiae*, wrote Huguccio,[8] expressing the common opinion of the time.[9]

---

[5] *Glossa Palatina ad Dist.* 19 c. 7, MS. Pal.Lat.658 fol. 5ra; Gloss *Ecce Vicit Leo ad Dist.* 19 c. 7, MS. F.XI.605 fol. 8ra.

[6] *Glossa Ordinaria ad Dist.* 19 c. 7

[7] *Dist.* 12 c. 2, *Dist.* 19 c. 7, C. 9 q. 3 c. 14, C. 11 q. 1 c. 14, C. 24 q. 1 c. 15.

[8] *Summa ad Dist.* 79 c. 9, MS. LC.2 fol. 141va.

[9] The Pope, the Apostolic See and the Roman church were all referred to as 'head'; e.g. Gratian, C. 25 q. 1 *post* c. 16, 'Sacrosancta romana ecclesia . . . quae caput est et cardo omnium ecclesiarum'; Paucapalea, *Summa ad Dist.* 3, 'Apostolica sedes caput est omnium ecclesiarum' (*Die Summa des Paucapalea*, ed. Schulte (Giessen, 1890), p. 9); Huguccio, *Summa ad Dist.* 21 *ante* c. 1, MS. P.72 fol. 129vb, 'ipse (Petrus) solus cephas, i.e. caput dictus est'; *Ecce Vicit Leo ad Dist.* 21 c. 3, MS. F.XI.605 fol. 8vb, 'Hic dicitur quod romana ecclesia est capud aliarum'; *idem ad Dist.* 22 c. 1, fol. 9vb, 'In heresim, ergo videtur quod sint heretici qui non habent romanam ecclesiam pro capite et sic quod sint excommunicati ipso iure. . . . Quid ergo de grecis dicetur, qui non habent eam pro capite? Suntne excommunicati ipso Iure? Non credo et ideo expono *in heresim*, i.e. in peccatum quia peccat talis sed non est hereticus', *Glossa Ordinaria ad Dist.* 19 c. 5, 'intellige quod hic dicitur quod qui dicit Romanam ecclesiam non esse caput nec posse condere canones iste est hereticus'.

Moreover, the texts of the *Decretum* which mentioned the papal headship in connexion with the words *Tu es Petrus* did not refer merely to a vague primacy of honour but claimed for the Pope supreme authority, both legislative and judicial, over the whole Church. The power of the Pope to establish general laws for the Church was set out most systematically in *Dist.* 12, which emphasized the subordination of all the local churches to Rome, and at *Dist.* 19, which was concerned specifically with the universal validity of papal decretals.[10] Gratian concluded that such decretals were equal in authority to the canons of General Councils;[11] and, though the Decretists sometimes suggested that there might be a right to disobey papal commands in exceptional circumstances,[12] the principle that the Papacy was normally endowed with authority to legislate for the whole Church was universally accepted. The position of the Pope as supreme judge of the Church was presented with equal emphasis and, again, in the texts of the *Decretum*, this position was associated with the concept of papal headship and with the text *Tu es Petrus*. As head of the Church, the Pope exercised a supreme appellate jurisdiction—*praefuit in appellatione quia ipse solus cephas, i.e. caput dictus est.*[13] From his sentences there was no appeal; he could judge all and was himself to be judged by no man.[14] The Pope was also a judge of first instance, having sole

---

[10] E.g. *Dist.* 12 c. 1, 'Nulli vero dubium est, quod Apostolica ecclesia mater est omnium ecclesiarum, a cuius vos regulis nullatenus convenit deviare...'; c. 2, 'Praeceptis Apostolicis non dura superbia resistatur...'; *Dist.* 19 c. 1, '... decretales epistolae Romanorum Pontificum sunt recipiendae etiam si non sint codici canonum compaginatae'; c. 2, 'Sic omnes Apostolicae sedis sanctiones accipiendae sunt, tanquam ipsius divini Petri voce firmatae sint'; c. 4, '... ab omnibus quidquid statuit, quidquid ordinat (Romana ecclesia) perpetuo et irrefragibiliter observandum est'; c. 5, 'Nulli fas est vel velle, vel posse transgredi Apostolicae sedis praecepta.'

[11] *Dictum Gratiani ad Dist.* 20 *ante* c. 1, 'Decretales itaque epistolae canonibus conciliorum pari iure exequantur.'

[12] The doctrine of the legislative authority of the Papacy set out in *Dist.* 19 was usually accepted by the canonists with little comment. However, the wording of *Dist.* 12 c. 1, which laid down that no one should resist the Roman church *sine discretione iustitiae* suggested to some of the canonists that in the exceptional case, *cum discretione*, it might be legitimate to resist. A number of opinions on the point was cited by Guido de Baysio in his *Rosarium ad Dist.* 12 c. 1, c. 2.

[13] Huguccio, *Summa ad Dist.* 20 *ante* c. 1, MS. P.72 fol. 129*vb*. The right of appeal to Rome was set out most fully at C. 2 q. 6 cc. 3–17, e.g. c. 4, 'Si quis vestrum pulsatus fuerit in aliqua adversitate licenter hanc sanctam et Apostolicam sedem appellet...'; c. 5, 'Omnes episcopi qui in quibusdam graviores pulsantur... libere Apostolicam appellent sedem...'; c. 8, 'Ad Romanam ecclesiam ab onmibus, maxime tamen ab oppressis appellandum est....'

[14] *Dist.* 17 c. 5, C. 9 q. 3 cc. 10, 13, 14, 17, C. 17 q. 14 c. 30, *Dicta Gratiani ad Dist.* 17 *post* c. 6 and *ad Dist.* 79 *post* c. 10.

cognizance of certain specified cases, the so-called *causae maiores*, among which were mentioned most prominently cases involving the deposition of bishops, and cases involving the decision of disputed articles of faith.[15]

It is evident that the citations of the words *Tu es Petrus* in the *Decretum* led to the acceptance of far-reaching claims for the Papacy in spite of the fact that there was no clear identification of Peter with the Rock. Rather different problems, and very interesting ones, are raised by the Decretists' treatment of the second part of Matthew's text,

> Tibi dabo claves regni caelorum. Et quodcumque ligaveris super terram erit ligatum et in caelis, et quodcumque solveris super terram erit solutum et in caelis.

In later controversies this gift of the keys to Peter became the basis of extreme claims on behalf of the Papacy; but several texts of the *Decretum* suggested that the words *Tibi datro claves . . .* were not spoken to Peter alone, but to all the Apostles, who all received with him an equal power of binding and loosing.[16] In any case the 'power of the keys' was commonly identified in the twelfth century with the sacerdotal power of absolution which was certainly conferred on all the Apostles by Christ on another occasion, when he said to them, *Quorum remiseritis peccata remissa sunt et quorum retinueritis retenta sunt;*[17] and in later ages this power was obviously not limited to the Papacy but was diffused throughout the whole Church. Hence, the interpretation

---

[15] Various types of cases affecting bishops in which the Papacy claimed sole jurisdiction are mentioned at C. 2 q. 6 c. 10, C. 6 q. 3 c. 3, C. 7 q. 1 c. 34, C. 9 q. 3 c. 7, c. 9. On the supreme authority of the Papacy in cases touching articles of faith see C. 24 q. 1 cc. 9–18.

[16] *Dist.* 21 c. 2, 'Caeteri vero Apostoli cum eodem pari consortio honorem et potestatem acceperunt, ipsumque principem eorum esse voluerunt . . .'; *Dictum Gratiani ad* C. 24 q. 1 *post* c. 1, 'Unde cum omnibus discipulis parem ligandi atque solvendi potestatem daret, Petro pro omnibus et prae omnibus claves regni caelorum se daturum promisit dicens, *Tibi dabo claves regni caelorum.*' See also the view of Augustine at C. 24 q. 1 c. 6 cited *infra*, p. 34.

[17] John xx. 22–3. Cf. M. Van de Kerckhove, *La notion de juridiction dans la doctrine des Décrétistes et des premiers Décrétalistes* (Assissi, 1937), p. 23, 'Gratien a interprété le texte de Math. xvi. 18: Tu es Petrus, etc. . . . , dans un sens beaucoup plus étendu que le sens dans lequel l'employaient communément les théologiens et les canonistes du temps. Car le texte en question était alors considéré surtout comme parallèle à celui de Jean xx. 22–23. . . . Par suite l'expression "pouvoir des clefs" ne s'appliquait qu'aux matières pénitentielles et donc se rapportait directement et de façon exclusive à l'exercice à du pouvoir d'ordre.'

of the words *Tibi dabo claves* could involve the whole question of the relationship between the authority inhering in the Universal Church and the powers attributed to its earthly head, the Pope.

Gratian himself used the phrase *potestas ligandi et solvendi* in two quite different senses. In one context it was clearly identified with the power of remitting sins conferred on all the Apostles.[18] Elsewhere it was treated as a power of jurisdiction inhering in the Papacy, for Gratian argued that, in the decision of legal cases, the decrees of a Pope were to be preferred to the opinions of revered theologians like Augustine and Jerome precisely because the Pope possessed that power of binding and loosing conferred by the words, *Tibi dabo claves regni caelorum.*

> In negotiis definiendis non solum est necessaria scientia sed etiam potestas. Unde Christus dicturus Petro, *Quodcumque ligaveris super terram erit ligatum et in caelis etc.* prius dedit ei claves regni caelorum, in altera dans sibi scientiam discernendi inter lepram et lepram in altera dans sibi potestatem eiciendi aliquos ab ecclesia vel recipiendi.[19]

Here Gratian was evidently referring to something other than a sacramental power to remit sins. The power of binding and loosing attributed to the Pope was a public authority, the power to bind all the faithful by his judicial decisions; it was a power to be exercised in the *forum externum* as distinct from the *forum internum* of the sacrament of penance.[20] Very occasionally one finds a Decretist text which, commenting on this passage, developed Gratian's view of the power of the keys as a public authority inhering in the Papacy.[21] Much

---

[18] C. 24 q. 1 *dictum Gratiani post* c. 4, 'Ligandi namque vel solvendi potestas veris non falsis sacerdotibus a Domino tradita est. Apostolis enim dicturus *Quorum remiseritis peccata* etc. praemisit *Accipite Spiritum Sanctum. . . .*'

[19] *Dist.* 20 *dictum Gratiani ante* c. 1.

[20] Cf. Van de Kerckhove, *op. cit.* p. 22, 'Ces derniers mots "sed etiam potestas" se réfèrent évidemment au pouvoir du for externe, qui, selon toute la Dist. xx du Décret consiste dans le pouvoir des clefs reçu par Pierre. . . .'

[21] The *Summa Coloniensis* explained that the writings of the Fathers lacked authority compared to papal decretals because, 'altera clavium, i.e. generalis potestas eis deficit' (Van de Kerckhove, *op. cit.* p. 25), and this same *Summa* referred to, 'Mater nostra Romana ecclesia (quae) superlativam in omnibus auctoritatem gerit et claves iuris habet' (Schulte, *Zur Geschichte*, II, p. 97). The *Summa Et Est Sciendum* associated the power of binding and loosing with the papal *plenitudo potestatis*, 'Si hodie Apostolus viveret posset a Lucio solvi et ligari qui Petro in *plenitudinem potestatis* successit' (Gillmann, 'Die Dekretglossen des Cod. Stuttgart. hist. f. 419', *A.K.K.R.* CVII (1927), pp. 192–250 at p. 197). The Gloss *Ecce Vicit Leo*, without referring explicitly to the supreme power of the Papacy, clearly treated the power of the keys as a power of

more frequently the canonists accepted Gratian's opinion with little
or no comment and went on, without any apparent sense of incongruity, to discuss various technical problems connected with the power
of the keys considered as the sacerdotal power of absolution.[22] The
detailed discussions of these problems are of interest only to the student of the theology of penance.[23] Their significance from our point
of view is that they led to an explicit recognition that there were two
different types of authority comprised in the sacerdotal power of the
keys—a sacramental power to remit sins and a power of jurisdiction
which was necessary for the excommunication of a sinner or for the
imposition of penance.[24] This in turn made it possible for the canonists
readily to accept Gratian's double use of the term as applied to the
Pope. The sacramental power was absolute, the same in a Pope or

---

the *forum externum*, an authority to decide legal cases, MS. F.XI.605 fol. 8r*b ad Dist.*
20 *ante* c. 1, '*Non solum est necessaria scientia*, ergo patet quod utraque est necessaria et
scientia et potestas. Unde fatuis et indiscretis iudicibus cause non debent committi.'

[22] They inquired, for instance, whether 'knowledge' could really be called a 'key';
whether perhaps the two keys were simply the power of binding and the power of
loosing; whether, if there was a 'key of knowledge' it was possessed by all priests or
only by prudent ones; whether a priest received the power of the keys at his ordination or only at his institution in an office with cure of souls. Huguccio provides
a typical example *Summa ad Dist.* 20 *ante* c. I, MS. P.72 fol. 129r*b*, 'In causis decidendis
prevalet auctoritas romanorum pontificum, nam in diffiniendo et decidendo causas
non solum scientia sed et potestas est necessaria . . . potestas, i.e. jurisdictio. . . . *In
altera*, videtur quod sint due claves, scilicet scientia vel discretio et potestas. Scientia
scilicet discernendi inter lepram et lepram, potestas ligandi et solvendi, et sic non
omnes sacerdotes habent ambas nec omnibus presbyteris in sua ordinatione dantur.
Imperitis non datur nisi potestas ligandi et solvendi. Discretis et peritis dantur ambe,
scilicet potestas ligandi et solvendi et scientia. . . . Sed verius dicatur quod non nisi
sit una clavis sacerdotalis, scilicet potestas ligandi et solvendi et hic est ordo
sacerdotalis.'

[23] On these questions see Paul Anciaux, *La théologie du sacrement de pénitence au XII*[e]
siècle (Universitas Catholica Lovaniensis: Dissertationes ad gradum magistri in Facultate
Theologica vel in Facultate Iuris Canonici consequendum conscriptae. Series II,
Tomus 41) (Louvain-Gembloux, 1949). Anciaux provides a good selection of canonistic
texts as well as theological ones relating to the sacerdotal power of the keys. Among
the canonistic works of the early thirteenth century which he did not use the Gloss
Ecce Vicit Leo offered a particularly detailed discussion of the subject. The author
thought the suggestion that there was only one key an attractive one, 'Hec opinio
satis pulchra est si esset vera', but he concluded that there was in fact a *clavis scientiae*
as well as a *clavis potestatis*, and that all priests could possess both of them, for all
priests possessed some traces of wisdom, 'Habet enim aliquantulam scientiam que
est ei clavis.' He was particularly insistent that the power of the keys was conferred
on a priest only by his appointment to an office with jurisdiction, not by ordination
alone, 'non dantur claves in ordinatione sed tantum in iurisdictione'. MS. F.XI.605
fol. 8r*b ad Dist.* 20 *ante* c. 1 and fol. 93r*b*–93v*a ad* C. 24 q. 1 c. 6.

[24] See Van de Kerckhove, *op. cit.* pp. 21–34; Anciaux, *op. cit.* pp. 548–9, 606.

a simple priest, but each prelate could participate in the power of jurisdiction in proportion to his status in the ecclesiastical hierarchy.[25] To a parish priest jurisdiction might mean no more than the right to exercise his power of absolution with the necessary sanctions; for a bishop, successor of the Apostles, it included broad powers of government over his diocese; and in the Pope, successor of Peter himself and head of the Church, it constituted a general authority to bind all the faithful by his decisions. By relying on this argument the Decretists were able to expound satisfactorily those texts of the *Decretum* which claimed for all the Apostles a power of binding and loosing equal to that of Peter, while also accepting Gratian's allusion to the power of the keys as a unique authority belonging to the Popes. The Apostles were equal to Peter, it was maintained, in the sacramental power of orders, but in the powers of government—*jurisdictio, administratio, dispensatio*—Peter was superior to all the others:

> *Pares* ... illi pares fuerunt quo ad ordinem, quia quecumque ordines habuit Petrus habuit et quilibet aliorum sed Petrus prefuit illis in dignitate prelationis, in administratione, in iurisdictione. . . .[26]

The formula adopted by the canonists to define the relationship established between Peter and the other Apostles, the first bishops of the Church, by the powers that Christ conferred on them all, would prove of the utmost importance in the subsequent development of theories of Church government. According to one text of the *Decretum* (a quotation from Cyprian), Peter's unique position consisted in the fact that Christ designated him as the centre of unity in the Church by

---

[25] The word *jurisdictio* itself acquired an ever broader connotation in canonistic works until in the first half of the thirteenth century it was being used in that general sense in which it occurs in the modern Code of Canon Law—*potestas regiminis quae ex divina institutione est in ecclesia* (Van de Kerckhove, *op. cit.* pp. 30, 35).

[26] Huguccio, *Summa ad Dist.* 21 *ante* c. 1, MS. P.72 fol. 129*vb*. Similarly Rufinus, *Summa ad Dist.* 21 c. 2, 'Petrus igitur ex prerogativa consecrationis apostolorum primorum neminem excellebat quia omnes in pontificatus apicem consecrati sunt. . . . Ex dispensationis autem dignitate apostolos ceteros anteibat, quia ipse aliis predicandi officium et alia huiuscemodi dispensabat . . .'; Stephanus, *Summa ad Dist.* 21 c. 2, 'Sic et Petrus aliis praefuit apostolis administratione non consecratione vel ordine'; Gloss *Ecce Vicit Leo ad Dist.* 21 *ante* c. 1, MS. F.XI.605 fol. 8*va*, '. . . omnes apostolici fuerunt eiusdem ordinis sed non pares quo ad dignitatem, quia dignitate Petrus prefuit'; *Glossa Palatina ad* C. 24 q. 1 c. 18, MS. T.O.10.2 fol. 28*va*, '*pari*, in ordine et dignitate consecrationis secus in administrationis plenitudine quia satis differt ab aliis . . .'; *Glossa Ordinaria ad* C. 24 q. 1 c. 18, 'Puto verum esse quod pares fuerunt in ordine et dignitate consecrationis, secus in administrationis plenitudine quae satis differt ab aliis.'

conferring upon him alone at first the same powers that the other Apostles received after the Resurrection with the words, *Quorum remiseritis peccata remissa sunt.*[27] Gratian thought that the earlier words, *Quodcumque ligaveris . . .* themselves conferred authority on all the Apostles, but that Peter's primacy was indicated by the fact that Christ chose to address him on behalf of them all.[28] Moreover, he cited a very influential text of Augustine which explained further the relationship between Pope and Church implied in this interpretation of Christ's words. It suggested that, when Peter received the keys, he 'signified' the Church:

> Quodcumque ligaveris super terram erit ligatum et in caelo. Si hoc Petro tantum dictum est non hoc facit ecclesia. Si autem in ecclesia fit, uti quae in terra ligantur in caelo ligantur. . . . Si ergo hoc in ecclesia fit, Petrus quando claves accepit ecclesiam sanctam significavit.[29]

Any attempt to explain Augustine's or Cyprian's own ideas on Church government would require another book—or many books—and, moreover, such an analysis would add little to our understanding of medieval canonistic thought.[30] The Decretists were not interested in relating such fragments of patristic doctrine to their original contexts, but rather to the context of the *Decretum* itself, and Augustine's definition of the Pope's position in relation to the Church acquired a considerable significance for later medieval theories of ecclesiastical authority mainly because it was assimilated by the Decretists and developed by them in their own fashion. In the idea that Peter 'signified' the Church or stood *in figura ecclesiae* (another Augustinian expression borrowed by the canonists) they found a unifying concept in terms of which all parts of Matthew's text could be interpreted, Peter's declaration of faith and the promise of indefectibility to the Church as well as the gift of the keys. Whether or not Peter's declaration of faith was regarded as the Rock on which the Church was

---

[27] C. 24 q. 1 c. 18.

[28] *Dist.* 21 *dictum Gratiani ante* c. 1, 'Petrum vero quasi in summum sacerdotem elegit dum ei prae omnibus et pro omnibus claves regni caelorum tribuit.'

[29] C. 24 q. 1 c. 6.

[30] A review of the literature concerning St Augustine's position is provided by H. Grabowski, 'St Augustine and the primacy of the Church of Rome', *Traditio*, IV (1946), pp. 89–113. For a recent exposition of St Cyprian's views see G. G. Willis, *Saint Augustine and the Donatist Heresy* (London, 1950), pp. 99 ff., 110–12. See also E. Caspar, *Geschichte des Papsttums* (Tübingen, 1930), 1, pp. 76–83; F. Heiler, *Altkirchliche Autonomie und päpstlicher Zentralismus* (Munich, 1941), pp. 13–44.

founded, it could certainly be held that the faith he declared was
that of the whole Church—*ad instar fidei Petri salvantur omnes fideles*;
and when Christ said to Peter on another occasion, *Ego rogavi pro te
Petre ut non deficiat fides tua*, it was commonly held that Peter again
stood *in figura ecclesiae*. In praying for him, Christ was renewing his
promise that the faith of the whole Church would never fail. Peter
symbolized the Church in the faith that he held as well as in the
power of the keys that he received.[31] The Decretists' exegesis of
Matthew xvi. 16–18 thus led them to a doctrine of the Pope as head
of the Church, supreme exponent of the power of jurisdiction conferred on the Church, symbol of the Church's enduring faith.

2. Romana Ecclesia

In all these arguments there may seem little concern with the rights
of the Church as a community, only an emphatic assertion of the
Pope's unique position as its head. But, in fact, the Augustinian
definition of the Pope's status, so widely diffused in the Decretist
glosses, was thoroughly ambiguous in its constitutional implications,
and, as we have said, the Decretists liked to explore all sides of any
ambiguity. The idea that Peter represented the Church, stood in *figura
ecclesiae*, might mean that all ecclesiastical authority was epitomized
in the person of the Pope who accordingly exercised a unique and
illimitable power over the Church; it might also, however, be taken
to mean that the Pope possessed only a limited exercise of a power
that in its original and plenary form was inherent in the Church as

---

[31] Rufinus, *Summa ad* C. 24 q. 1 c. 8, 'Petrus autem omnium sacerdotum figuram
tenebat'; Simon de Bisignano, *Summa ad* C. 24 q. 1 c. 6, 'Et nota quod in persona
Petri universe ecclesie Dominus loquebatur' (cited by Anciaux, *op. cit.* p. 500);
Huguccio, *Summa ad Dist.* 19 c. 7, MS. P.72 fol. 128v*b*, '. . . in figura ecclesie dixit
Christus Petro, *Ego rogavi pro te Petre ut non deficiat fides tua*'; *Summa ad Dist.* 21 *ante*
c. 1, fol. 129v*b*, '. . . in eius persona enim universalis ecclesia significabatur . . . in
persona Petri intelligebatur ecclesia, in fide Petri fides universalis ecclesie que nunquam
in totum deficit vel deficiet usque in diem iuditii'; Wolfenbüttel MS. Helmst. 33 *ad*
C. 24 q. 1 c. 9, '. . . in evangelio Christus oraverit dicens, *Ego rogavi pro te Petre ut non
deficiat fides tua*. . . . In Petro quippe significatur ecclesia, ut supra, eadem quaestione,
quicunque' (cited by Schulte, *Die Glosse zum Dekret*, p. 11); the *Glossa Palatina* has the
same comment, MS. T.O.10.2 fol. 28r*b ad* C. 24 q. 1 c. 9, '. . . in Petro quippe
significatur ecclesia ut supra eadem questione, *quodcumque*'; Gloss *Ecce Vicit Leo ad
Dist.* 20 *ante* c. 1, MS. F.XI.605 fol. 8v*a*, '*ut non deficiat fides tua*, i.e. ecclesiae que est
tua fides. . . .'

a whole, even that he was accountable to the Church for his manner of exercising it. Eventually the idea of the Pope *in figura ecclesiae* was to play an important part in the most mature and harmonious of the conciliar theories, that of Nicolaus Cusanus;[32] and, already in the Decretist glosses, there existed elements of thought from which this latter interpretation could be derived.

When the Decretists considered the Pope as judge or legislator his authority could be presented as embracing that of the whole Church, for to him, as a symbol of the Church, was committed the supreme exercise of the Church's jurisdiction. It was when they discussed the Pope's position as exponent of the faith of the Church that significant reservations appeared. The Decretists held that the faith of the whole Church could never fail; they also held that, within the Church, the Pope was the supreme judge in cases involving articles of faith; but they did not maintain—what might perhaps seem a logical corollary of these premises—that the Pope's decisions were to be regarded as necessarily unerring statements of the unfailing faith of the Church. The absence of such a doctrine left in the formulation of their theory of papal authority a very real weakness that was eventually to be exploited in a fashion that the Decretists themselves could hardly have foreseen.

Gratian's teaching on this question was set out most fully in a text that has already been mentioned. In his *dictum ad Dist. 20 ante* c. 1, he laid down that, in the decision of judicial cases, the decrees of a Pope were to be preferred to the opinions expressed in patristic writings. He also maintained in the course of the same chapter, however, that in the interpretation of the Scriptures, the opinions of an Augustine or a Jerome were to be preferred to those of a Pope:

> ... apparet quod divinarum scripturarum tractatores etsi scientia Pontificibus praemineant, tamen, quia dignitatis eorum apicem non sunt adepti, in sacrarum scripturarum expositionibus eis praeponuntur, in causis vero diffiniendis, secundum post eos locum merentur.[33]

---

[32] In the theory of Nicolaus Cusanus the Pope 'figured' the Church only imperfectly, the General Council more adequately. 'Deinde ex hoc patet quod sicut Petrus unice et confusissime figurat ecclesiam qui deviabilis est ... non dubium quanto illa Synodus minus confuse, plus tenendo in veritate repraesentat...', *De Concordantia Catholica* in *Opera Omnia*, XVIII (Basileae, 1566), p. 741.

[33] The *Summa Parisiensis* added that the authority of a Pope was greater than that of one of the Fathers in the decision of a disputed article of faith, but that if the Pope and Augustine, each in his private room, wrote a book of theological exposition,

Here, as elsewhere in the *Decretum*, the Pope's power to decide doctrinal disputes was strongly upheld, but it was treated solely as an outgrowth of his judicial supremacy. His decisions commanded the assent of the Church as the sentences of a supreme judge, not as the teachings of an infallible doctor.[34] The failure to claim for the Pope that final attribute is the more striking since there were a number of texts in the *Decretum* which did explicitly declare that the Roman church had never erred from the path of the true faith, that it had always remained free from the stain of sin and heresy.[35] The Decretists were apparently deterred from building any doctrine of papal infallibility on the basis of such texts by other passages in the *Decretum* which implied quite clearly that a Pope could be guilty of heresy, and which even cited specific examples of Popes who were alleged to have erred in matters of faith. Pope Marcellinus was said to have committed idolatry, and, according to Gratian, even Peter himself had fallen into error;[36] but the case that was most frequently quoted in Decretist discussions was that of Pope Anastasius II:

> Anastasius secundus, natione Romanus fuit temporibus Theodorici regis. Eodem tempore multi clerici et presbyteri se a communione ipsius abegerunt, eo quod communicasset sine concilio episcoporum vel presbyterorum et cleri cunctae ecclesiae catholicae diacono Thessalonicensi, nomine Photino qui communicaverit Acacio, et quia voluit occulte revocare Acacium et non potuit, nutu divino percussus est.[37]

---

that of Augustine would be preferred to the Pope's. 'Sed si alias in camera librum expositionis suae componat dominus papa, componat et Augustinus, praecellit et Augustini' (*Ad Dist.* 20 *ante* c. 1).

[34] Huguccio considered the case of a Pope who was himself a revered *expositor*, like Gregory I, and concluded that Gregory's status as Pope gave no additional authority to the opinions he expressed *ut expositor*. *Summa ad Dist.* 20 *ante* c. 1 MS. P.72 fol. 129r*b*, 'Sed ecce Gregorius fuit expositor et papa, et in aliquo articulo invenitur diversus vel contrarius alicui aliorum expositorum, cui magis creditur? Respondeo, si dixerunt diversa utriusque credendum est, si contraria tunc in his que ut papa dixit ... et huiusmodi magis credendum est, in his vero que ut expositor dixit videtur non magis ei esse credendum quia papa, sed forte magis consonanter rationi dixit vel quia maioris scientie, sanctitatis, vel auctoritatis habetur.'

[35] C. 24 q. 1 cc. 9–18.

[36] C. 2 q. 7 *dictum Gratiani post* c. 39, 'Petrus cogebat gentes iudaizare et a veritate Evangelii recedere. . . .' The case of Pope Marcellinus was recorded at *Dist.* 21 c. 7. See also *Dist.* 40 c. 6, '(papa) a nemine est iudicandus, nisi deprehendatur a fide devius'.

[37] *Dist.* 19 c. 9. Döllinger long ago pointed out that Anastasius acquired a legendary reputation in the Middle Ages (and a place in Dante's *Inferno*) on the strength of this quotation of Gratian from the *Liber Pontificalis*. See his *Fables Respecting the Popes of the Middle Ages* (transl. A. Plummer, London, 1871), pp. 207–20.

Repeatedly, when the question of the indefectibility of the Roman church arose, the Decretists cited the case of Anastasius to prove that, whatever the relevant texts might mean, they could not mean that the Pope personally was divinely preserved from error. Anastasius had been deserted by the Church and smitten by God precisely because he had erred. It would have been quite within his competence, as Huguccio pointed out, to have declared that Photinus was not guilty of the heresy charged against him; the Pope's offence was that he entered into communion with Photinus knowing him to be guilty and so condoned his heresy.[38]

In the texts that he assembled Gratian thus bequeathed to his successors an unresolved antithesis between an unerring Roman church and a Pope who might be a heretic. If one approached the problem with more recent controversies in mind, one might expect to find it resolved by a series of carefully drawn distinctions between the Pope's private opinions and his public teachings, between his pronouncements as head of the Universal Church and his decisions as a local pastor. Such distinctions were certainly not unknown to the Decretists;[39] but, in their attempts to define the sense in which the Roman church was unerring, they adopted an approach quite different from that of later theologians. Instead of undertaking a refined analysis of the various modes of exercise of papal authority, they preferred rather to investigate the different connotations of the term *Romana ecclesia* itself; and, in doing so, they reached conclusions of great importance for the whole tradition of thought that culminated in the conciliar doctrines of the fourteenth century.

---

[38] *Summa ad Dist.* 19 c. 9 MS. P.72 fol. 129r*b*, 'Nota quod si voluisset ostendere quod ille nunquam fuisset in alia heresi et quod ecclesia decepta eum inde damnaverit et ita eum post mortem revocare ad ecclesie communionem, non esset malus . . . sed hoc noluit ipse facere, sed voluit eum in errore suo defendere. . . .'

[39] It seems incorrect to assert as does Van Leeuwen in a generally very perceptive article, that the theologians and canonists of the earlier Middle Ages 'ne connaissaient pas de distinction entre les opinions personnelles du pape et ses déclarations officielles' (A. Van Leeuwen, 'L'église, règle de foi chez Occam', *Ephemerides Theologiae Lovanienses*, XI (1934), pp. 249–88 at p. 279). The canonists were quite familiar with the distinction between a Pope's personal remarks and his official decrees. Cf. Mochi Onory, *Fonti Canonistiche*, pp. 30, 74–5, citing Albertus 'sic audivi papam innoc. exponentem, non sententiando tamen, set disserendo'; Huguccio, 'hanc non esse decretalem, vel si est locutus est ut magister, non ut papa . . .' (see also *supra* p. 37, n. 2); Joannes Galensis, 'suam opinionem hic dominus papa videtur recitare, non ius commune constituere. . . .' They could also distinguish between his actions as Head of the Church and as a local patriarch, e.g. *Summa Parisiensis ad Dist.* 65 c. 6, p. 57.

Most frequently, in the *Decretum*, the words *Romana ecclesia* were used to describe the local church of the city of Rome, the episcopal see over which Peter had presided and which the Popes, since his day, had ruled as bishops. In the Decretist commentaries the words were often used in the same sense. Sometimes, for instance, there were comparisons between the customs of the Roman church and those of the other local churches,[40] and, occasionally, discussions as to whether a custom of the Roman church was more worthy of emulation than a general custom of all the other churches.[41] But another quite different sense of the term *Romana ecclesia* was suggested by those passages of the *Decretum* which emphasized the unity of faith between the Roman church and the Church as a whole. Thus the *Summa Parisiensis* commented in rather obscure fashion on C. 24 q. 1 c. 25:

> *ubicumque fuerit corpus,* i.e. ex eo congregantur electi qui membra sunt ecclesiae, ubi fuerit corpus, soliditas ecclesiae fidei. Vel corpus propter veritatem (unitatem?) fidei Romanam appellat ecclesiam. . . . Propter veritatem igitur fidei corpus Romanam vocat ecclesiam quae apud eam praecipue viget.[42]

---

[40] *Summa Parisiensis ad Dist.* 11 c. 11, p. 11, 'Invenitur quaedam consuetudo, quae aliter hodie in Francia, aliter in ecclesia Romana observatur. . . . Et adhuc quid sit melius ignoratur'; *ad* c. 2 q. 7, p. 7, p. 113, 'Hoc est consuetudo Romanae ecclesiae sed Gallicana ecclesia in nulla causa civili criminali recipit laicos adversus clericos.' Cf. Mochi Onory, *Fonti Canonistiche*, p. 29.

[41] In this context Jerome's phrase *Orbis maior est urbe*, a favourite quotation of the Conciliarists, was sometimes cited (it appeared in the *Decretum* at Dist. 93 c. 24); but in the Decretist works it was usually maintained that, while a general custom might be preferred to the Roman usage, this did not imply any right to disobey the direct commands of Rome. Cf. Huguccio, *Summa ad Dist.* 12 c. 1, MS. P.72 fol. 124ra, '. . . licet ergo cum discretione aliter agere quam romana ecclesia teneat, sed nec cum discretione nec sine discretione licet agere contra disciplinam eius', and *ad Dist.* 93 c. 24, MS. LC.2 fol. 165va, '. . . cum maior sit orbis quam roma, maior est auctoritas orbis quam rome, qui presbyteros preponit quam roma que diaconos, et licet altera sit consuetudo orbis et altera urbis et illa maior quam haec non tamen altera est reprobanda. . . . Sed nonne totus orbis tenetur obedire romane ecclesie . . . sic ad observationem si precipiat aliquid observari. Sed illud de diaconis non vult observari nisi romana ecclesia.' The English gloss of Caius MS. 676 discussed the relations between the Roman church and the local churches at several points, e.g. *ad Dist.* 11 c. 11 fol. 5ra, 'Romana ecclesia conficit in azimis sicut et nos, orientalis autem ecclesia in fermentatis. Item in orientali ecclesia sacerdos licite contrahet matrimonium, in occidentali nequaquam. Sed non videtur orientalis ecclesia a romana (recedere), quoniam has eius consuetudines approbat romana ecclesia'; *ad Dist.* 12 c. 1 fol. 5ra, 'Vel aliquid est contra disciplinam eius (romane ecclesie), i.e. contra quod docet, quod non licet, aliquid contra consuetudinem, quod licet'; *ad Dist.* 93 c. 24 fol. 55va, '. . . universalis ecclesie consuetudo imitanda est potius quam romane ecclesie consuetudo particularis'.

[42] *Summa Parisiensis ad* C. 24 q. 1 c. 25.

Here the Roman church seems identified with the whole body of the faithful. The *Summa Et Est Sciendum* stated the same view much more clearly—*nomine romana ecclesia accipitur interdum universalis ecclesia;*[43] and Huguccio, commenting on Jerome's phrase *Orbis maior est urbe,* observed, *una et eadem est et ecclesia romane urbis et ecclesia totius mundi.*[44]

It would seem, then, that the term *Romana ecclesia* could be used in at least two different senses, to describe either the Universal Church or a particular local church having primacy over the others. A noteworthy feature of Huguccio's *Summa* was the skill with which he brought into play the two different concepts; and, in doing so, he made it clear that, where matters of faith were concerned, any theory of ecclesiastical authority consistent with the texts of the *Decretum* would have to be based on a clear distinction between the powers inherent in the whole *congregatio fidelium* and the authority that could be exercised by the local *Romana ecclesia.* Above all, he emphasized that, in this sphere at least, the fact that Peter stood *in figura ecclesiae* did not mean that the Pope possessed in his own person all the gifts that Christ had conferred on the Church. To Huguccio it seemed as obvious as to any fourteenth-century Conciliarist that the Roman church, understood as the Pope or the Pope and curia, could not be that *ecclesia* that was to endure for ever, unerring in faith and unstained by sin, *sine macula et ruga.* He expressed this opinion somewhat tartly, insisting that if the *Romana ecclesia* were identified with any particular local church, then 'you will not find a Roman church in which there are not plenty of stains and wrinkles':

> *Maculam* ... ergo ubicumque sunt boni fideles ibi est romana ecclesia, aliter non invenies romanam ecclesiam in qua non sint multe macule et multe ruge.[45]

And again,

> ... dicitur quod romana ecclesia non habet maculam vel rugam ... sed in romana ecclesia intelligitur universitas fidelium.[46]

The case of the erring Pope Anastasius presented no difficulties to a canonist equipped with this definition of the Roman church as the

---

[43] Cited by Gillmann, 'Die Dekretglossen des Cod. Stuttgart. hist. f. 419', *A.K.K.R.* CVII (1927), pp. 192–250 at p. 224.

[44] *Summa ad Dist.* 93 c. 24, MS. LC.2 fol. 165va.

[45] *Summa ad Dist.* 21 c. 3, MS. P.72 fol. 130va.

[46] *Summa ad Dist.* 23 c. 1, MS. P.72 fol. 132ra.

universitas fidelium. Moreover, in commenting on the critical text, *Dist.* 19 c. 9 *Anastasius,* Huguccio found it convenient to introduce another distinction, for there was a double ambiguity in the term *Romana ecclesia. Romana* as used in the *Decretum* had two meanings, but *ecclesia* had at least half a dozen. It might refer to the head of a church or to all its members or to a variety of intermediate groups. Several such meanings were listed by Joannes Teutonicus in the *Glossa Ordinaria,*[47] and, a generation earlier, Huguccio applied the same type of distinction to the definition of the unerring *Romana ecclesia.* Not only did the word *Romana* not necessarily refer to a particular local church, but the word *ecclesia* did not necessarily refer to the head of that church:

> Ecclesia romana dicitur nunquam in fide errasse... sed dico quod romana ecclesia dicitur tota catholica ecclesia quod nunquam in toto erraverit, vel romana ecclesia dicitur papa et cardinales et licet iste erraverit non tamen cardinales, vel saltem non omnes romani....[48]

The Pope, although head of the ecclesiastical hierarchy with no individual superior, did not embody in his own person the unfailing faith of the Church. The Roman church, understood as Pope and cardinals together, provided a more certain authority, but the only *Romana ecclesia* that was divinely preserved from all error was the whole body of the faithful.

Huguccio's interpretation was widely accepted, and the distinction between the authority of the Pope in matters of faith and that of the whole Church became a commonplace of Decretist thought in the next generation. The subject usually arose either in discussions on the case of Anastasius or in glosses on C. 24 q. 1 c. 9, a text of the *Decretum* which claimed that the Roman church had never erred from the path of the true faith. Thus the Wolfenbüttel gloss observed on the case of Anastasius that,

---

[47] *Glossa Ordinaria* ad C. 7 q. 1 c. 3, 'Hic dicitur ecclesia episcopus, alibi est idem quod ecclesiastici viri... alibi ponitur pro maiori parte... quandoque pro congregatione fidelium. Et dic per exempla varias significationes.' He was commenting on the words of Cyprian, 'Scire debes episcopum in ecclesia esse et ecclesiam in episcopo....'

[48] *Summa ad Dist.* 19 c. 9, MS. P.72 fol. 129rb. Cf. *Summa Et Est Sciendum, ad Dist.* 21 c. 3, 'Nota, quod nomine romana ecclesia accipitur interdum universalis ecclesia, que a romani pontificis sententia non discordat, que dicitur esse sine macula heresis et ruga duplicitatis.... Dicitur etiam romana ecclesia ipsa sedes et ecclesia petri, in qua acceptione accipitur illud, quod res romane ecclesie, i.e. beati petri, non possunt nisi centenaria prescriptione prescribi... accipitur etiam pro capite et membris, i.e. papa et cardinalium collegio ut hic, et interdum pro solo papa, ut cum dicitur, "Apello romanam sedem", i.e. papam' (Gillmann, *art. cit.* p. 224).

Ecclesia romana dicitur quandoque collectio iustorum, aliquando papa
cum suis cardinalibus.[49]

And the point was repeated and much amplified in the gloss of this
same work on C. 24 q. 1 c. 9. There the case of Anastasius was again
brought forward as a proof that the Roman church could not be
unerring, and again the difficulty was resolved by an analysis of the
different senses of the term *Romana ecclesia.* It might mean the Pope
alone, or the Pope and cardinals, or the whole *congregatio fidelium*; and
only in this last sense was the Roman church preserved from error.
Christ's promise to the Church and his prayer for Peter's faith ensured
that the Church would never err in its whole body, but any particular
individual, even the Pope, might well fall into error.

> *Errasse.* Supra di. xix, anathasius (Anastasius) contra ar. Solutio: auc-
> tor huius capituli fuit antipapa anathasii vel apostolica ecclesia non dici-
> tur tantum papa sed papa et cardinales. Vel dicitur ecclesia Christi
> congregatio fidelium ... quare ecclesia nunquam in universo corpore
> errat, licet quandoque in aliqua persona erret. Argumentum ut non
> dicatur ab ecclesia factum quod ab ipsa universitate non fit ut dist. xxi
> § decretis; sed licet papa erraverit, qui et per haeresim iudicari potest
> ut di. xl si papa, non tamen ecclesia Romana sive apostolica errat
> quae catholicorum collectio intelligitur ... id est ea quae utique nulla
> esse non potest, ut *infra eadem, pudenda* (c. 33 *ibid.*), praesertim cum in
> evangelio Christus oraverit dicens, *Ego rogavi pro te Petre ut non deficiat fides
> tua* ut di. xxi § 1. In Petro quippe significatur ecclesia. . . .[50]

The latter part of this gloss was reproduced almost verbatim in the
Glossa Palatina,[51] and the Gloss *Ecce Vicit Leo* presented a similar argument in a particularly interesting form.

> *Nunquam errasse probatur*: sed nonne invenitur de papa quod fuit hereticus
> ut in contrario, supra *dist.* xix, *Anastasius.* Item et ipse Petrus dum
> negavit. . . . Solvo: hic vocatur ecclesia non quidem collectio cardinalium
> sed fidelium. Semper enim fuit (fides) in ecclesia vel aliquibus, unde in
> beata virgine fuit in morte domini quamvis omnes discipuli tempore
> tunc peccassent et ita semper est ecclesia sine macula.[52]

The reference to the Blessed Virgin, which occurs again in the same
sense in another passage of this work,[53] calls to mind the familiar

[49] Schulte, *Die Glosse zum Dekret,* p. 11.
[50] Schulte, *Die Glosse zum Dekret,* p. 11.
[51] Gloss *ad* C. 24 q. 1 c. 9, MS. T.O.10.2 fol. 28rb.
[52] Gloss *ad* C. 24 q. 1 c. 9, MS. F.XI.605 fol. 93va.
[53] Gloss *ad Dist.* 20 *ante* c. 1, MS. F.XI.605 fol. 8va, 'ut non deficiat fides tua, i.e.

view of Ockham that the true faith might be preserved 'even in women', since it had survived in Mary alone at the time of the Passion.[54] It is not surprising in itself to find this doctrine put forward in a gloss of the early thirteenth century, for the idea of Mary as unique guardian of the faith was not unfamiliar to the theologians of the time.[55] The interesting feature of the gloss is that the Marian doctrine was not employed, as was usual, in a devotional sense, but in the precise manner of the more radical fourteenth-century Conciliarists, as an argument to demonstrate the defectibility of the Pope and the Roman church.

The most influential expression of this common Decretist opinion was that of Joannes Teutonicus, not because his views were more extreme or more explicitly stated than those of his contemporaries but simply because, in the fourteenth century, his *Glossa Ordinaria* was much the best known of the early Decretist works:

> Quaero de qua ecclesia intelligas quod dicitur quod non possit errare. Si de ipso papa qui ecclesia dicitur supra eadem *quodcumque* et 7 q. 1 *scire debes*, sed certum est quod papa errare potest ut 19 *dist. Anastasius* et 40 *dist. si papa*. Respondeo: ipsa congregatio fidelium hic dicitur ecclesia . . . et talis ecclesia non potest non esse. . . . Nam ipse Dominus oravit pro ecclesia, 21 *dist.* § 1, et voluntate labiorum suorum non fraudabitur.[56]

The promise of unfailing faith to the Church was not associated by these writers with the institution of an unerring teaching authority. It meant only that the Church would never be totally polluted by heresy. And the fact that Peter 'signified' the Church did not mean in these contexts that Peter enjoyed the supreme exercise of all the powers committed to the Church; rather the contrary, that the promise of unfailing faith made to Peter applied only to the whole Church, not specifically to Peter himself or to his successors in the Papacy.

---

ecclesie que ese tua fides, ecclesia enim nunquam deficit quia etiam in morte domini fuit saltem in beata virgine. Ecclesia enim parva esse potest, nulla esse non potest.'

[54] Cf. Ockham, *Dialogus* in Goldast, *Monarchia Sancti Romani Imperii*, II (Francofordiae, 1641), p. 492, '. . . dicunt quidam (fidem) posse salvari in mulieribus quemadmodum tempore passionis Christi salvata fuit in sola matre Christi', and p. 503, '. . . tempore passionis Christi . . . tota fides Christianae ecclesiae in matre Christi remansit'.

[55] On the origins and diffusion of this belief see Y. M.-J. Congar, 'Incidence ecclésiologique d'un thème de dévotion mariale', *Mélanges de science religieuse*, VIII (1951), pp. 277–92.

[56] Gloss *ad* C. 24 q. 1 c. 9.

In reading passages of this sort one seems to be moving in a world of ideas more usually associated with the conciliar epoch than with the age of Innocent III, and it is certainly true that the fundamental distinction between the local *Romana ecclesia* and the Roman Church understood as the whole *universitas fidelium*—often regarded as a contribution of Ockham to conciliar thought—was no invention of the fourteenth century publicists. Yet the attitude of the Decretists was by no means identical with that of the Conciliarists who would later exploit their doctrines. The Decretists' teaching on unerring authority in the Church may seem substantially similar to that of Ockham, but they did not develop it in quite the same spirit as the fourteenth-century Franciscan who envisaged with cheerful enthusiasm, and in great detail, the failure of faith in all the responsible men of the Church, and its survival in women, children or idiots. Again, the Decretist distinction between the authority of the Roman church and that of the whole *congregatio fidelium* in matters of faith was of the essence of later conciliar thought; the whole end of the Church was to guide men to salvation by nourishing them with true doctrine, and the claim to indefectibility would eventually, and perhaps inevitably, become associated with pretensions to sovereignty. But the Decretists themselves never explicitly argued that because the *congregatio fidelium* was unerring it possessed an active power of governing superior to that of the Papacy (though they did make important claims on behalf of the General Council which have still to be considered). The Conciliarists were to treat the quality of indefectibility as a positive authority inhering in the Church which could be turned against even the Pope if necessary; the Decretists saw it rather as a kind of negative capacity in the Church, an inability to err simultaneously in all its parts.

This was the common attitude of the Decretists. There was, however, one sentence in the *Glossa Palatina* which already implied a radically different approach to the whole question:

> Arg. ut non dicatur ab ecclesia factum quod ab ipsa universitate non factum, *ff de reg. iu., aliud* § 1 . . . sed licet papa erraverit . . . non tamen ecclesia romana sive apostolica erraverit, quae collatio catholicorum intelligitur.[57]

---

[57] *Glossa Palatina ad* C. 24 q. 1 c. 9, MS. T.O.10.2 fol. 28rb. The same words occur in the Wolfenbüttel gloss cited supra p. 43 but without the Roman law reference.

The Roman law reference was to a text of the Digest, stating that, 'What is done publicly by a majority is held to be done by all.'[58] Here the unfailing faith of the Church was treated, not as a heritage surviving in some unspecified individuals, but as an attribute of the Church considered as a corporate body, and capable of being expressed by the Church acting in a corporate capacity, *ab ipsa universitate*. If this line of argument were to be developed it could indeed lead to doctrines of Church government very different from those that were to prevail in the thirteenth century. The words of the *Glossa Palatina* are no more than a hint; but they hint at the whole conciliar system of thought.

---

[58] *De Diversis Regulis Iuris Antiqui*, 160 (i), 'Refertur ad universos quod publice fit per maiorem partem.'

CHAPTER TWO

POPE AND GENERAL COUNCIL

The doctrine that only the whole Church was unerring in faith was an essential element in the theories of Church government eventually to be elaborated by the Conciliarists; but, none the less, the Conciliar Theory was by no means an inevitable corollary of that doctrine. The Conciliarists assumed, not only that the authority diffused throughout the whole community was only partly embodied in the person of the Pope, but, further, that it could be expressed more perfectly in other institutions of Church government, especially in a General Council, which, accordingly, could correct an erring Pope and even depose a contumacious one. The Decretists made significant contributions to the growth of these constitutional doctrines as well as to the emergence of the underlying principle which Gierke defined as 'the Sovereignty of the Ecclesiastical Community'.

In the reign of Innocent III the composition of a General Council was modified so that it did indeed become 'representative' of the Church, in the Conciliarists' sense of the word. The Fourth Lateran Council might have served as the model for Conrad of Gelnhausen's definition of what a General Council should be; it was not simply a synod of bishops but an 'assembly of estates' to which all the constituent elements of the Church were summoned either in person or through representatives.[1] One does not, however, encounter in the works of the Decretists any theoretical analysis of the concept of representation nor any attempt to define with precision the relationship between a General Council and the Universal Church. None of them, indeed, seems to have thought it necessary to draw any distinction between the powers inherent in the Church and those that

---

[1] The importance of this development in the growth of conciliar ideas was emphasized by A. Hauck, 'Die Rezeption und Umbildung der allgemeinen Synode im Mittelalter', *Historische Vierteljahrschrift*, x (1907), pp. 465–82. 'Es scheint mir unbestreitbar: die Vorstellung von Universalsynode, die der sogen. konziliaren Theorie des 15. Jahrhunderts zugrunde liegt, stammt nicht von Konrad von Gelnhausen, auch nicht von Occam, sondern ihre Wurzeln führen zurück zu dem grossten Papste des Mittelalters' (p. 470). Cf. also J. Lecler, 'Les théories démocratiques au moyen âge', *Études*, ccxxv (1935), pp. 168–89 at pp. 168–9.

could be exercised by a Council.[2] For them the question was satisfactorily resolved by the wording of *Dist.* 15 c. 2 of the *Decretum,* a
text of Pope Gregory I which laid down that the decisions of the
first four General Councils should always be held inviolate since they
were established 'by universal consent'.

> ... quia dum universali sunt consensu constituta, se et non illa destruit
> quisquis praesumit aut solvere quos religant aut ligare quos solvunt.[3]

Yet in these same Decretist works the Pope also was held to represent the Church, to exercise the authority of the whole Church. This
would seem to raise two further questions; the theoretical question—
how to define the relationship between the two types of representation embodied in Pope and Council; and the practical question—
which authority should in fact be preferred if the decisions of a Pope
conflicted with those of a Council? The Decretists had almost nothing
to say about the theoretical question but they did rather frequently
consider the practical one, and the views they expressed in discussing it were to have an enduring influence in the later Middle Ages.

Gratian himself offered a long discussion of the whole problem
and decisively rejected the arguments in favour of a limitation of papal
authority by the canons of Councils:

> Sacrosancta romana ecclesia ius et auctoritatem sacris canonibus imper-
> titur, sed non eis alligatur. . . .[4]

His successors, however, insisted that there were important exceptions to this general principle, and, above all, there was a persistent
tendency to assert for the General Council a position of superiority
in the definition of articles of faith. The Roman law principle, 'Quod
omnes tangit ab omnibus iudicetur', was frequently adduced to prove
that in the decision of articles of faith even laymen should be repre-

---

[2] The question does not seem to have been discussed at all. The *Summa Parisiensis*
defined a General Council as 'ecclesia tota sub praesentia domini papae' (*ad Dist.* 3
post c. 2, p. 4). Joannes Teutonicus derived from Jerome's phrase, Orbis maior est
urbe', an argument in favour of the General Council against the Pope, *Glossa Ordinaria
ad Dist.* 93 c. 24, 'Et est hic argumentum quod statutum concilii praeiudicat sententiae
papae si contradicant', and again *ad Dist.* 15, c. 2, 'Videtur ergo quod Papa non
possit destruere statuta concilii quia orbis maior est urbe. . . .'
[3] On this Huguccio commented, '*Universali consensu* . . . arg. pro universitate et
quod nulli a canonico et communi consensu sui capituli vel collegii vel civitatis
recedere (licet) . . .' (MS. P.72 fol. 125v*b*).
[4] *Dictum Gratiani,* C. 25 q. 1 *post* c. 16.

sented[5] since, according to one text of the *Decretum*, the maintenance of the true faith was a matter

> quae universalis est, quae omnium communis est, quae non solum ad clericos verum etiam ad laicos et ad omnes omnino pertinet Christianos.[6]

Accordingly, it was commonly held that a Pope was not empowered to reject the decision of a General Council in any matter touching articles of faith. This principle was already stated in the *Summa Parisiensis*,[7] was widely accepted by later Decretists, and several times repeated in the *Glossa Ordinaria*.[8] The Pope, it was often said, was the supreme judge in cases involving articles of faith, but the Pope himself was required to judge in accordance with the canons of the General Councils. One is reminded of the common medieval assumption that a ruler, although supreme judge, was nevertheless 'under the law'. The canonists' position certainly did imply that they attributed to the General Council a superior authority for they always held that an equal could not bind an equal—*par in parem non habet imperium*. And Joannes Teutonicus, in discussing the inevitable case of Pope Anastasius, was led to formulate explicitly this principle of conciliar supremacy,

> Videtur ergo quod papa teneatur requirere concilium episcoporum quod verum est ubi de fide agitur et tunc *synodus maior est papa*.[9]

---

[5] Huguccio, *Glossa Palatina, Glossa Ordinaria*, all commenting on *Dist*. 96 c. 4. Similarly Richard de Lacy, cited by W. Ullmann, *Medieval Papalism*, p. 214.

[6] *Dist.* 96 c. 4.

[7] *Ad* C. 25 q. 1, p. 230, 'Quaedam sunt quae in octo conciliis sunt celebrata, quae profitetur summus pontifex usque ad unum iota servaturum, et illa similiter Romana ecclesia non potest mutare. . . . Illa igitur decreta quae dicunt summum pontificem decessorum suorum statuta mutare non posse, intelligenda sunt de illis quae ad fidem specialiter pertinent, sine quibus haberi salus aeterna non potest.'

[8] It was often mentioned in discussions on *Dist.* 15 c. 2, where Gregory the Great laid down that the first four. Councils were to be respected 'like the four Gospels'. Huguccio commented 'Verum sit quo ad articulos fidei' (MS. P.72 fol. 125vb). Similarly the *Glossa Palatina* (MS. Pal.Lat.658 fol. 4ra), *Ecce Vicit Leo*, 'nec enim potest ire contra haec concilia in hiis scilicet quae ad fidem pertinent vel bonos mores' (MS. T.O.5.17 fol. 5vb); *Glossa Ordinaria*, 'Videtur ergo quod papa non possit destruere statuta concilii quia orbis maior est urbe, 93 *Dist. legimus*, unde et requirit Papa consensum concilii, 19 *Dist. Anastasius*. Arg. contra, 17 Dist. § hinc etiam et *ext. i. de elec. significasti* ubi dicitur quod concilium non potest Papae legem imponere et 35 q. 9 *veniam*. Sed intellige quod hic dicitur circa articulos fidei.' See also *Glossa Palatina ad* C. 25 q. 1 cc. 3, 6, 7 (MS. T.O.10.2 fol. 35vb) and *Glossa Ordinaria ad Dist.* 19 c. 9, C. 25 q. 1 c. 3, C. 25 q. 2 c. 17.

[9] *Dist.* 19 c. 9.

In this same context the *Summa Et Est Sciendum* maintained that it was forbidden to a Pope to communicate with a man whom a Council had condemned;[10] and the *Glossa Palatina* remarked, 'periculosum erat fidem nostram committere arbitrio unius hominis'.[11]

There were, moreover, other matters in which, according to the Decretists, a Pope was bound by the decisions of General Councils. It was commonly held that he could not dispense against the decree of a Council in any matter that affected the general well-being of the Church; and the Decretists' elaboration of this doctrine concerning the *generalis status ecclesiae* was one of their more important contributions to later theories of Church government.[12] The very word *status* calls to mind a host of unresolved problems concerning the medieval conception of sovereignty and the growth of the idea of the state. Not only political thought but political action could be influenced by the development of such concepts, for medieval monarchs were able to enforce the claim that the maintenance of the *status regni*, the common welfare of the realm, could justify extraordinary measures, and especially extraordinary taxation, beyond what was

---

[10] 'Per hoc habes, quod non debet papa ei communicare, cui concilium censuit non communicandum' (Gillmann, 'Die Dekretglossen des Cod. Stuttgart. hist. f. 419', *A.K.K.R.* cvii (1927), pp. 192–250 at p. 216).

[11] 'Arguitur hic quod in causa fidei maior est synodus quam papa, ar. xv *di. sicut* in fi., ar. xciii *di. legimus*, nam periculosum erat fidem nostram committere arbitrio unius hominis. b. dicit contra, xxiiii q. i *haec est . . .*' (MS. Pal.Lat.658 fol. 5ra). Dr Kuttner has shown that in this gloss the siglum 'b' refers to Bernardus Compostellanus Antiquus ('Bernardus Compostellanus Antiquus', *Traditio*, i (1943), pp. 277–340). The English gloss in Caius MS. 676 maintained that a Council was necessary to condemn a new heresy, 'Ergo synodo opus est in dampnatione nove hereticis(!)' (*ad* C. 24 q. 1 c. 3, fol. 165va). The *Summa Permissio Quedam* noted that a Pope incurred anathema in going against the statutes of the 'four Councils', 'Sed quaeritur: si autem emanaverint statuta datae sententiae scil. ut qui contra venerit anathema sit, an in eam incidat dominus papa, si contra venerit? Ad quod potest responderi, quod si huiusmodi statuta emanaverint a veteri testamento vel scriptura evangeliorum vel ab apostolis vel a supradictis IIIIor conciliis, dominus papa veniens contra eo ipso est excommunicatus. Si aliunde, poterit papa contra venire et ea immutare' (Schulte, *Zur Geschichte*, iii, p. 76).

[12] The conciliar principle that papal authority could not be used to injure the Church was very familiar to the thirteenth-century canonists. It was upheld not only by the moderate Decretists but even by the later Decretalists who have usually been regarded as uncompromising defenders of papal authority. E.g. by Tancred *ad comp. III*, ii.vi.3 (MS. C.17 fol. 197vb); Bernardus Parmensis, *Glossa Ordinaria ad* X. ii.xiii.3 and iii.viii.4; Innocentius IV, *Commentaria ad* X. i.iv.4 and i.xxi.2; Hostiensis, *Summa, De Constitutionibus*, fol. 19ra. Evidently Dr Figgis was rather astray when he wrote that the Conciliarists found in the principle *salus populi suprema lex* 'a necessary bulwark against the Canonist theory of sovereignty (substantially the same as Austin's)'.

permitted by the normal law of the land. From such usages grew the Renaissance 'reason of state' and Machiavelli's concept of *lo stato*.[13]

The Decretists had a clearly formulated idea that the maintenance of the *status ecclesiae* was an overriding consideration in all matters of ecclesiastical policy, but the constitutional implications which they derived from this proposition were very different from those deduced later by the secular kings, and, indeed, by the Popes themselves. In the Decretist writings (as in the Conciliarist works of two centuries later) the necessity to preserve the *status ecclesiae* was always presented as imposing a limit on papal authority rather than as a ground for extending it. The question of the *status ecclesiae* was most commonly considered in discussions on the limitation of papal authority by a General Council, and it is this that gives to the Decretists' claims their special significance. For them the 'state of the Church' was not a vague indefinable concept which might be used to justify any extra-ordinary action of the Church's ruler, but was rather a living reality, closely identified with the rules of ecclesiastical life laid down in the laws of General Councils and confirmed 'by universal consent'. This view was most clearly expressed by Rufinus:

> Non autem istam derogationem generaliter intelligas in omnibus decretis; antiquorum enim patrum et venerabiliorum statuta, que pro omnium ecclesiarum statu conservando plena auctoritate sunt promulgata et totius pene mundi iam consecrata reverentia, sicut canones Niceni, et his similes ... illa inquam, neque auctoritate apostolici neque more utentium aliter valent evacuari.[14]

A Pope might disregard those decisions of a General Council that were of merely local or temporary significance, but the statutes that were of universal application were held to touch the 'general state of the Church' and so to be inviolable. Hence in subsequent discussions on the Pope's authority to dispense from the decrees of Councils the terms *generalis status ecclesiae* and *generale statutum ecclesiae* were used indifferently to express the same idea.[15] Sometimes hybrid forms

---

[13] Some suggestions towards a reassessment of the contributions made by the canonists and legists in this field, criticizing the views of Gierke, Kern, Lousse and de Lagarde, are made by Professor Gaines Post, 'The theory of public law and the state in the thirteenth century', *Seminar*, VI (1948), pp. 42–59.

[14] Rufinus, *Summa ad Dist.* 4, p. 13.

[15] On *generalis status ecclesiae* and *generale statutum ecclesiae* as factors limiting the dispensatory authority of the Pope see J. Brys, *De Dispensatione in Iure Canonico* (Brugis, 1925), pp. 132–4, 195–8.

occur in the manuscripts so that it is difficult to be certain what the author actually wrote.[16] *Generalis status* is the more common form, but occasionally the context makes it clear that *generale statutum* was intended. Joannes Teutonicus, for instance, held that the Pope could not grant privileges against the decrees of Councils in matters 'quae sunt de generali ecclesiae statu'[17] but he also clearly maintained that the Pope was also bound by a 'general statute of the Church':

> Ex hoc patet quod papa non potest contra generale ecclesiae statutum dispensare nec contra articulos fidei . . . sed contra statutum ecclesiae quod non est ita generale, sicut de continentia sacerdotum, bene potest dispensare.

Upon which Bartholomaeus Brixiensis observed,

> Quidquid dicat Joannes quandoque dispensat papa contra generale statutum ecclesiae sicut fecit in Lateranensi concilio Innocentius.[18]

It seems that, in the earlier opinion, the identification between a General Council and the whole Church was so complete that a canon of a Council relating to the whole Church was assumed to be necessarily beneficial to the Church; or, at least, it was supposed that normally the interests of the Church would be more effectively safeguarded in the statutes of a Council than in the decrees of a Pope;

----

[16] The Pembroke MS. of Huguccio's *Summa* has 'generalem(!) statutum ecclesie' at *Dist.* 15 c. 2 (fol. 125v*b*) and again at *Dist.* 16 c. 9 (fol. 126r*b*). In both cases the Lincoln MS. has 'generalem statum ecclesie' (fol. 21v*b* and fol. 23r*a*). At *Dist.* 40 c. 6 both have '. . . si papa esset hereticus publice et inde non posset accusari tota periclitaretur ecclesia et confunderetur generalis statutus(!) ecclesie. Sed non credo eum posse constituere aliquid in prejudicium generalis statutus(!) ecclesie ut xv dist. *sicut*' (MS. P.72 fol. 147v*b*; MS. LC.2 fol. 73v*b*). In view of the great importance of the concept *status regni* in later constitutional disputes a detailed investigation of the canonistic usage of the word *status* might prove valuable. Such a work could hardly be undertaken, however, until many more canonistic manuscripts have been collated and edited.

[17] Gloss *ad* C. 25 q. 2 c. 17.

[18] Gloss *ad* C. 25 q. 1 c. 3 and *additio* Bartholomaei Brixiensis *ad* C. 25 q. 1 c. 6. Cf. Tancred, *ad Comp. III*, II.vi.3, MS. C.17 fol. 197v*b*, 'Papa potest dispensare in omnibus quae non sunt contra articulos fidei vel generale statutum ecclesie, arg. xv dist. *sicut*.' It would seem that a 'general statute', a law applying to the whole Church, need not necessarily have been a canon of a General Council, but the Decretists seem not to have distinguished the two concepts. Both Joannes Teutonicus and Tancred supported their assertions that a Pope was bound by a 'general statute' with a reference to *Dist.* 15 c. 2 *'Sicut'*, which referred to the authority of the first four Councils. By the middle of the thirteenth century the doctrine that a Pope was bound by a 'general statute' had died away. Innocent IV and Hostiensis refer only to the 'state of the Church'.

and hence papal action against a general statute was condemned as prejudicial to the state of the Church.

In Decretist thought there were thus at least two institutions through which the inherent authority of the whole Church could be expressed, the Papacy and the General Council; and in questions of faith and other matters which affected the well-being of the whole Church, the authority of the Council was preferred to that of the Pope. The Pope indeed 'signified' the Church, he stood *in figura ecclesiae*, but the decisions of a General Council were established 'by universal consent', and this apparently gave to such decrees overriding authority. The Decretists pressed their theoretical analysis no further. They never attempted any discussion of the various problems raised by the concept of representation, and they certainly did not produce any elaborate theory such as that eventually to be propounded by Nicolaus Cusanus concerning 'immediacy' of representation. But although they produced no adequate theoretical justification of their position, some of the conclusions they reached seem substantially the same as his own.

There is, however, one important distinction to be emphasized between the Decretists' ideas on the supremacy of a General Council and those of the more radical Conciliarists. When the Decretists wrote that the Pope was bound by the laws of a Council or that in matters of faith a Council was greater than a Pope, although their language was ambiguous, they seem only to have meant that a Pope surrounded by the fathers of a Council possessed a greater authority than a Pope acting alone. In their view, it was of the essence of a General Council that the Pope or his legate should preside over it. Joannes Teutonicus indeed proclaimed, *Synodus maior est papa*, but he also held that if a difference arose between the Roman church on the one hand and all the remaining churches on the other it was the opinion of Rome that should be preferred:[19]

> Arg. quod sententia totius ecclesiae preferenda est Romae si in aliquo sibi contradicant . . . sed tamen contrario credo . . . nisi erraret Romana ecclesia quod non credo posse fieri quia Dominus non permitteret.[20]

---

[19] This passage towards the end of his work (*ad* C. 24 q. 1 c. 6) seems to reflect Joannes's final considered view on this point. He returned to the question again and again in the course of his gloss. See especially his comments on *Dist.* 4 c. 3, *Dist.* 15 c. 2, *Dist.* 19 c. 9, *Dist.* 93 c. 24, C. 9 q. 3 c. 14.

[20] Just a few lines further on (*ad* C. 24 q. 1 c. 9) he went on to assert that the only unerring *ecclesia* was the Universal Church, the *congregatio fidelium*. But, since the Decretists' doctrine of indefectibility asserted only that somewhere within the Universal

The superiority of a General Council consisted in the union of all the churches with the Roman church, not in an association of other churches acting against Rome. Huguccio therefore denied that the judgement of a Council in opposition to the Pope carried greater weight than that of the Pope himself:

> ... si in eadem questione discordat concilium a sententia pape, maior est sententia concilii quam pape. Quod non credo. Sed potius credo contrarium.[21]

The transition from the idea of a superiority inherent in Pope-and-Council to that of a superiority in the Council acting against the Pope is one of the most important developments in conciliar theory between the twelfth century and the fourteenth; and there were certain elements in early canonistic thought that could encourage the growth of this later doctrine though it was not usually held by the canonists themselves. Rather surprisingly, in view of their frequent references to the divine origin of papal authority and the clear statement in *Dist.* 21 c. 3 of the *Decretum* that the authority of the Roman church was *nullis synodicis constitutis sed evangelica voce Domini*, the extreme view that papal authority was in some sense derived from Councils was quite familiar to the Decretists and even found some measure of support in their works. The suggestion was usually made in discussions on the relative positions of Pope and Emperor, and it was stated most clearly by Huguccio:

> Omne enim ius condendi leges vel canones populus contulit in imperatorem et ecclesia in apostolicum....[22]

Church the true faith would survive, Joannes could quite reasonably maintain that it would more probably survive in the Roman church than in the others. He does seem inconsistent in asserting that God would not permit the Roman church to err, here clearly using the words *Romana ecclesia* to describe a local church. But he was careful to state also that Rome was to be followed *nisi erraret*. Joannes hoped and expected that the Roman church would not err, but there could be no final certainty on that point; it was not unusual in canonistic writings for an author to envisage some dire contingency, to declare firmly that he did not believe God would ever allow this to happen, and then to go on to discuss the implications of the ensuing situation if it did happen after all.

[21] *Summa ad Dist.* 19 c. 9, MS. P.72 fol. 129rb. At least one of his contemporaries took the opposite point of view, however, anticipating more closely the later trends of thought. *Summa Et Est Sciendum ad Dist.* 19 c. 9, 'Si in questionibus, que in concilio proponuntur, a sententia pape discordat concilium maior est sententia concilii quam pape' (Gillman, *art. cit.* p. 216). See also A. Stickler, 'Sacerdotium et Regnum nei Decretisti e Primi Decretalisti', *Salesianum*, xv (1953), pp. 575–612 at p. 610.

[22] *Summa ad Dist.* 4 *post* c. 3, MS. P.72 fol. 119ra.

In another context, however, Huguccio explained that the Roman church received its authority principally from God, only 'secondarily' from Councils, and this view was repeated in the *Glossa Ordinaria*.[23] Laurentius introduced a rather more subtle distinction, and one that was to have a considerable future in conciliar writings. The powers inhering in the office of Pope or Emperor were of divine institution, he maintained, but it was human authority that, in the act of election, designated the particular individuals who were to exercise those powers.[24] While the Decretists' terminology was sometimes equivocal it seems most probable that their comments in this matter were intended to buttress the papal authority, not to undermine it. One need not suppose that the application of the *lex regia* to the power of the Pope carried any democratic implications in the days of Frederick Barbarossa and Henry VI; to claim for the Pope, as a supplement to his divinely ordained authority, a source of power that Roman law claimed for the Emperor was not to diminish his authority but to enhance it.

A more significant anticipation of later trends of conciliar thought—one that requires detailed analysis—was the Decretist teaching concerning the deposition of a Pope. There was a steady development of this doctrine from the time of Gratian to the composition of the *Glossa Ordinaria* and, eventually, a widespread belief that the Pope could be brought to trial and deposed for any notorious crime that gave scandal to the Church. The fact that the Decretists were prepared to develop such far-reaching claims from a very slender basis of positive law seems in itself to indicate a climate of opinion markedly different from that which would come to prevail by the middle of the thirteenth century.

The *Decretum* itself contained several categorical assertions that the Pope stood above all human judgement, even that of a General Council:

---

[23] Huguccio *ad Dist.* 17 *post* c. 6, MS. P.72 fol. 126v*b*, '. . . ibi enim dicitur quod ecclesia romana habuit primatum a domino et non a conciliis, sed dico quod a domino principaliter et per auctoritatem habuit, a conciliis vero secundario et per voluntariam concessionem se illi sumitendo'. Similarly *Glossa Ordinaria ad Dist.* 17 *post* c. 6, C. 3 q. 6 c. 9. Joannes Faventinus held that conciliar approval served only to make manifest a power conferred by God. For his opinion see Guido de Baysio, *Rosarium ad Dist.* 17 *post* c. 6.

[24] '. . . set dic quod alia est ipsa iurisdictio per se inspecta, que a Deo processit, et aliud, quod ipsius iurisdictionis executionem consequatur aliquis per populum. . . . Nam populus per electionem facit imperatorem, set non imperium, sicut cardinales per electionem preferunt aliquem sibi ad iurisdictionem, que a Deo data est, exercendam' (cited by Mochi Onory, *Fonti Canonistiche*, p. 196).

Neque ab Augusto neque ab omni clero neque a regibus neque a populo iudex iudicatur. . . .[25]

Gratian indeed cited five cases of Popes who had in one way or another submitted to judgement, but he always maintained that the submission was made voluntarily, and never admitted that any man or group of men had the right to condemn an erring Pope.[26] There was only one text in the *Decretum* which implied a different point of view, but upon this was to be built a formidable edifice of canonistic speculation. The critical text was at *Dist.* 40 c. 6:

(Papa) a nemine est iudicandus, *nisi deprehendatur a fide devius.*[27]

This left the way open for the admission of charges against the Pope in the one case of heresy. In the *Summa* of Rufinus schism was coupled with heresy as a crime for which a Pope might be deposed, since prolonged schism always produced heresy.[28] Moreover Rufinus, and also the *Summa Parisiensis*, reported a much more radical doctrine current in the middle of the twelfth century,

Item dominus papa potest judicari ab ecclesia tota sed cum hac distinctione, si in fide erraverit. Alii ita distinguunt: in ea causa quae totam ecclesiam contingit judicari potest papa ab ecclesia, sed in ea quae unam personam contingit vel plures non.[29]

---

[25] C. 9 q. 3 c. 13. See also *Dist.* 17 *post* c. 6; *Dist.* 21 cc. 4, 7; *Dist.* 79 *post* c. 10, C. 9 q. 3 cc. 10–18, C. 17 q. 4 c. 30.

[26] Marcellinus (*Dist.* 21, c. 7), Symmachus (*Dist.* 17 c. 6 and C. 2 q. 7 *post* c. 41), Sixtus III (C. 2 q. 5 c. 10), Damasus (C. 2 q. 7 *post* c. 41), Leo IV (C. 2 q. 7 c. 41).

[27] This text was attributed by Gratian to St Boniface. In fact the old principle of papal immunity was first formulated in this precise form by Cardinal Humbert. The text of the *Decretum* is in literal agreement with Humbert's *Fragmentum A*, identified by A. Michel (cited by Percy Schramm, *Kaiser, Rom und Renovatio* (Leipzig-Berlin, 1929), II, pp. 128–9. Cf. also *ibid.* I, pp. 239–46; II, pp. 120–33). Michel at first suggested that 'nisi deprehendatur devius' might refer to 'nemine' (so that the general sense would be, 'no one except a man erring in faith would presume to judge the Pope'), but he has since rejected this interpretation which, incidentally, was never suggested by the canonists. See his *Die Sentenzen des Kardinals Humbert* (Leipzig, 1943), p. 32, n. 1, and 'Die folgenschweren Ideen des Kardinals Humbert und ihr Einfluss auf Gregor VII', *Studi Gregoriani*, I (1947), pp. 65–92. An important new interpretation has been put forward by W. Ullmann, 'Cardinal Humbert and the Ecclesia Romana', *Studi Gregoriani*, IV, pp. 111–27. Dr Ullmann sees a conscious distinction by Humbert between the jurisdictional primacy of the Roman church (understood as Pope and cardinals) and the personal immunity of the Pope, which was subject to limitation where matters of faith were concerned.

[28] *Summa ad Dist.* 40 c. 6, p. 96, '. . . schisma autem, quamvis heresis proprie non sit, tamen sine comite heresi non permanet'.

[29] *Summa Parisiensis ad Dist.* 21 *post* c. 3, p. 21. Similarly Rufinus *ad Dist.* 21 c. 4, p. 46.

Once again it was the overriding necessity for protecting the well-being of the whole Church that was stressed, and the further development of the Decretists' theory concerning a Pope's liability to judgement tended to emphasize still more this aspect of their thought. Stephanus Tornacensis, for instance, not only mentioned heresy and schism as crimes for which a Pope could be deposed, but also suggested that he could be brought to trial for dissipating the goods of the Church and he added, significantly, that the Pope was not to exercise the powers of his office while awaiting trial lest the Church should suffer further harm.[30]

However, it seems that we must turn to Huguccio for the first really detailed discussion of the whole question for, in place of the scattered comments of his predecessors, he presented a long and complex gloss reviewing every aspect of the problems involved in the trial and deposition of a Pope.[31] Most important of all he posed the very pertinent question of why heresy should be mentioned as the one crime that could be brought against a Pope, and in reply he quoted the generally accepted opinion that heresy in the Pope was peculiarly injurious to the Church as a whole:

> ... si papa esset hereticus non sibi soli noceret sed toti mundo, praesertim quia simplices et idiote facile sequerentur illam heresim cum credent non esse heresim.

Huguccio, however, did not agree that heresy was the only crime of the Pope that was likely to injure the whole Church, and he went on to present a catalogue of all the most heinous offenses that could occur to a twelfth century bishop—notorious fornication, robbery, sacrilege. Was all this to be tolerated in a Pope?

> ... nunquid non accusabitur ... nunquid sic scandalizare ecclesiam non est quasi heresim commitere? Preterea contumacia est crimen ydolatrie et quasi heresis ... unde et contumax dicitur infidelis ut *Dist.* xxxvii, *nullus*. Et sic idem est in alio crimine notorio quasi heresi. ...

---

[30] Thus anticipating by more than a century the similar claim of John of Paris (ed. Leclercq, p. 188.6), *Summa Stephani ad* C. 3 q. 1 p. 189, 'Item si (papa) fuerit expulsus propter dilapidationem bonorum ecclesiae non est restituendus ne consumat interim bona ecclesiae, scil. antequam veniat ad causam.'

[31] MS. P.72, fol. 147va/147vb. The whole of Huguccio's gloss on the words *nisi deprehendatur a fide devius* is quoted in Appendix I (pp. 248–50), so that the passages cited in the text may be considered in relation to their context. This gloss was also printed by Schulte, *Stellung der Concilien, Päpste und Bischöfe*, pp. 262–4, from the München MS. (Staatsbibl. 10247, cf. *Repertorium*, p. 156).

In Huguccio's view, to scandalize the Church by contumacious persistence in notorious crimes was tantamount to heresy and could be punished as such. There remained the fact that heresy alone was mentioned in the text of the *Decretum*. Huguccio suggested that heresy was mentioned by way of example or perhaps because the Pope could be accused of that crime even when it was not notorious. At the end of the gloss he stated quite explicitly that the underlying reason why the Pope's immunity from judgement could not extend to this sort of crime was that the welfare of the whole Church was at stake:

> . . . generale enim et regulare erat, quod crimina punirentur in quolibet, ergo in papa, sed illam generalitatem circa papam restrinxit constituendo privilegium ut non posset accusari de quolibet crimine, sed *propter periculum ecclesie vitandum et propter confusionem generalem ecclesie vitandum* noluit per illud privilegium removere heresim vel notorium crimen.

Huguccio's presentation of this aspect of the problem was so clear and decisive that the subject aroused little comment in later Decretist glosses; but to provide a careful explanation of why it was necessary that the Pope should be held accountable for certain types of offence was only one part of his task. He also set himself to unravel all the intricate problems of legal procedure involved in bringing a Pope to trial. In explaining why the normal rule which permitted accusations for secret crimes could not be applied to the Pope, Huguccio stated with crisp clarity the central problem that faced the canonists in their attempts to frame a consistent doctrine which would protect the Church against the abuses of an evil Pope:

> illa regula . . . non habet locum circa papam propter defectum iudicis coram quo conveniretur.

In virtue of his office the Pope stood above all human judgement. *Dist.* 40 c. 6 of the *Decretum* certainly withheld the privilege of immunity from a heretical Pope, but several other texts of the same compilation stated without any reservation that the Pope had no judicial superior, that, accordingly, no court was competent to try him. It was also laid down in the *Decretum* that an inferior could not even bring an accusation against a superior, and, of course, all men were held to be inferior to the Pope.

It has sometimes been suggested in modern works that Huguccio solved all these problems at a blow by pointing out that a Pope who fell into heresy ceased automatically to be Pope and so became liable to judgement as a private individual; and accordingly it has been held that the Decretist theories involved no real breach in the traditional doctrine of papal immunity from judgement. This seems an over-simplification of a complex issue. In itself the assertion that a heretic necessarily ceased to be Pope solved none of the legal problems involved in bringing to trial a Pope suspected of heresy; for it provided no answer to the really important question—who was to decide whether the Pope was in fact a heretic or not? Once a Pope had been elected by the vote of two-thirds of the cardinals no *exceptio* could be brought against him; even if it was proved that the election had been brought about by simony he was still a true Pope in the eyes of the canonists.[32] He remained Pope until a charge of heresy against him was legally established, and if, therefore, the Pope himself denied the charge it would seem that no court was competent to sit in judgement on it. The principle of papal immunity, if it were to be strictly upheld, could lead to a logical impasse. A Pope could only be brought to trial if he were a heretic; but the fact of his heresy could normally only be established in the course of a trial.

Huguccio was naturally aware of all these difficulties, and in attempting to dispose of them he was led to define the precise circumstances in which action could be taken against a Pope for heresy and to recognize severe limitations to the exercise of this right. A Pope could be deposed, according to Huguccio, only when he publicly announced his adherence to a known heresy and refused to abandon his heretical

---

[32] Although the Decretists held the Pope liable to accusation for any notorious crime on the ground that 'contumacia est quasi heresis', they did not accept the more familiar identification 'simoniaca heresis' (cf. J. Leclercq, 'Simoniaca heresis', *Studi Gregoriani*, I, 523–30) as a valid basis for a charge of simony against a Pope, e.g. *Glossa Ordinaria ad Dist.* 79 c. 9, 'Videtur per principium huius cap. quod papa de simonia accusari possit quia non est apostolicus sed apostaticus et quia simonia heresis est, I q. 1 *eos qui* et c. *fertur* et *liqueat* et per primum cap. huius distinctionis. Quod non credo. Et loquitur hic de illo qui per simoniam electus est ab illis qui non habebant potestatem eligendi, non a cardinalibus. Simonia autem large dicitur heresis, non secundum quod Papa de heresi potest accusari, cum scilicet errat aliquis in articulis fidei.' In this context Huguccio (MS. LC.2 fol. 141va) and the *Glossa Palatina* (MS. Pal.Lat.658 fol. 19va) expressed the same point of view. (If the simony was notorious then of course the Pope could be accused of it as of any other notorious crime.) All three glosses went on to discuss the delicate case of a man who was elected Pope in the belief that his wife was dead. What was to be done if she returned and demanded restitution of conjugal rights? It was agreed that if there was any doubt in the matter, then once again the Pope could not be compelled to submit the case to trial. If the woman was manifestly his wife he should renounce the papacy and return to her. A more desirable solution, however, would be for the wife to take a vow of continence. See Gillmann, 'Die simonistische Papstwahl nach Huguccio', *A.K.K.R.* LXXXIX (1909), pp. 606–11.

opinions after due admonition. If the Pope propounded a new doctrine that was suspected as heretical, no action could be taken against
him; if he held in secret a heresy already condemned, but denied the
charge, then again no accusation could be brought against him. For
a Pope to become liable to accusation it was necessary that his heresy should be 'public' and any other crime 'notorious'; he could never
be accused for an 'occult' crime;

> ... de crimine heresis potest papa accusari si heresim publice predicat
> et non vult desistere quamvis tale crimen non sit notorium, sed de alio
> crimine non potest accusari nisi sit notorium. Ergo de occulto crimine
> non potest accusari.

Huguccio was attempting to avoid the difficulty that no court was
competent to try a Pope by eliminating any necessity for the trial of
a Pope as such. The juristic problem was to define the circumstances
in which a Pope could be presumed guilty of heresy, and so no
longer a true Pope, without any trial being held. Huguccio solved the
problem by applying in careful detail to the Papacy a series of doctrines that Gratian himself had formulated in considering the legal
status of lesser prelates.[33] Gratian held that an inferior could not
condemn a superior, but he also pointed out that no condemnation
was necessary in the case of a man who followed a heresy already
condemned, for such a man was held to have wilfully included himself in the previous condemnation[34]—hence Huguccio's insistence that
the charge brought against a Pope must be one of adherence to a
known heresy. Moreover, Gratian had also considered the question

---

[33] In this closely following the method of the text he was glossing. Dr Ullmann
(*art. cit.* pp. 118–19) points out that the novel feature in Humbert's formulation of
the doctrine of papal immunity was that he applied to the Papacy for the first time
a reservation that Isidore and Pseudo-Isidore had applied to other prelates.

[34] C. 24 q. 1 *ante* c. 1, 'Qui vero heresim iam damnatam sequitur eius damnationis
se particem facit.' The question was often discussed in canonistic and theological
works of the twelfth century whether a prelate who became a heretic thereby lost
the powers of his office, especially the power to excommunicate. In this connexion
the distinction between a new heresy and an old one was frequently raised. It was
commonly held that the man who invented a new heresy retained his powers until
he was formally condemned by the Church, but the follower of an old heresy was
ipso facto excommunicated. The *Summa Parisiensis* put the point very clearly, *ad* C. 24
q. 1, p. 222, 'Qui novam haeresim confingit quoadusque sententia excommunicationis
notetur, potestatem habet ligandi atque solvendi, et quaecumque geruntur rata sunt
et firma, dum tamen in forma ecclesiae sunt. Qui vero jam damnatam sequitur, jam
damnatus est, neque expectandum est ut nova sententia prodeat in istum quia jam
lata sententia est. Iste talis alios excommunicare non potest. . . .'

of accusations made by inferiors against superiors and had concluded that, although normally such accusations were inadmissible, in the one case of heresy they might be accepted, since in matters of faith the heretic was lower than the worst Catholic.[35] But in a later discussion he insisted that this principle was not to be invoked to justify accusations by all and sundry against a prelate of good repute who did not admit himself to be a heretic—it could only be applied in cases of acknowledged heresy.[36] Huguccio, therefore, was following Gratian's doctrine with scrupulous fidelity when he asserted that a Pope could not be accused of secret heresy but only when he 'publicly preached heresy'. The deposition of any prelate who was thus self-convicted of heresy would not involve any breach of the principle that a superior could not be condemned by an inferior, for, as Huguccio pointed out when discussing this point in another context, even a Pope who adhered to a condemned heresy became *ipso facto* inferior to any true Catholic:

> Cum papa cadit in heresim non iam maior sed minor quolibet catholico intelligitur.[37]

It will be seen that the effect of Huguccio's analysis was to augment considerably the number of charges admissible against a Pope, since all notorious crimes were treated as tantamount to heresy, but also to limit severely the circumstances in which the charge of heresy itself could be brought. It is also apparent that his various reservations concerning this latter point were not insignificant technicalities but were essential to his whole position. If the canonists wished to adhere strictly to the principle that a man who was legally Pope stood above all human judgement they could only hold him liable to deposition for heresy in the circumstances that Huguccio had described.

---

[35] C. 2 q. 7 *post* c. 26, 'In quo hereticus inferior est, videlicet in regula fidei, in eo a malo catholico accusari potest', and again, C. 6 q. 1 c. 20, '... hereticus catholico minor sit'.

[36] C. 6 q. 1 *post* c. 21, 'Verum hoc ... de his intelligendum est, quos constat esse hereticos, non de his qui se negant in heresim lapsos.'

[37] *Summa ad Dist.* 21 c. 4, MS. P.72, fol. 130va, 'Prima est inferior superiorem non potest solvere vel ligare, nisi talibus casibus quos Jo. notavit, scilicet cum sua sponte se subicit arbitrio minoris ... et cum inferior ex delegatione obtinet vicem superioris ... et cum papa incurrit heresim, quo casu potest iudicari a subditis ut *dist.* xl *si papa*. Sed dico quod nulla fuit facienda exceptio, quia sive quis ex arbitrio sive ex delegatione cognoscat maior est in illa causa illis quorum causam tractat. ... Item cum papa cadit in heresim non iam maior sed minor quolibet catholico intelligitur. Ergo in quolibet tali casu maior iudicat minorem.'

In fact, though, the Decretists of the next generation accepted without question Huguccio's view that a Pope could be deposed for any notorious crime, but they rejected or ignored the careful reservations concerning the charge of heresy through which Huguccio had defended the principle of papal immunity.

The Gloss *Ecce Vicit Leo* followed Huguccio quite closely on several points. It noted that, since a heretical Pope was *minor quolibet catholico*, the deposition of a Pope for heresy did not constitute an exception to the rule that inferiors could not judge superiors.[38] The author of this gloss also observed that a Pope who followed a heresy already condemned was automatically excommunicated.[39] But he made no suggestion that the cases in which a Pope could be accused of heresy were limited to these occasions of automatic excommunication.[40] More explicitly, the *Glossa Palatina* cited Huguccio's views and deliberately rejected them.

> H(uguccio) dicit quod potest de quolibet crimine (accusari) si ammonitus non cessat . . . sed alii prelati accusantur etiam de occultis, papa non, etiam de heresi nisi constaret prius id quod facit vel dicit heresim esse. Mihi videtur quod . . . de heresi accusari possit etiam si occulta sit, de aliis non nisi sint manifesta. . . . Sed nunquid illa regula *Si peccaverit in te etc.* habet locum circa papam. Dicit H(uguccio) quod non propter iudicis defectum, sed non credo hanc esse causam, nam credo papa iudicem habere certum cardinalem (cetum cardinalium?).[41]

Huguccio had maintained that no accusations could be brought against a Pope except when his own admissions provided a basis for presuming him legally guilty in accordance with Gratian's doctrines. The *Glossa Palatina* held that he could be accused without any such self-incriminating evidence, and made no suggestion that the man brought to trial had ceased to be Pope before he had been found guilty. Indeed, where Huguccio carefully explained that a condemned Pope was not a superior since he was *minor quolibet catholico*, the *Glossa Palatina*

---

[38] MS. F.XI.605 fol. 8*vb ad Dist.* 21 c. 4.

[39] MS. F.XI.605 fol. 17*va ad Dist.* 40 c. 6, 'Item si papa incidit (in) heresim dampnatam estne excommunicatus? Videtur quod si incidit in talem heresim quod ipso iure excommunicatus est. . . .'

[40] MS. F.XI.605 fol. 17*rb ad Dist.* 40 c. 6, 'Sed nunquid de alio crimine quam de heresi potest accusari? Dicunt quidam quod non nec enim potest cogi ad purgationem, sed de heresi potest accusari que potest probari. Melius est quod dicatur quod de heresi occulta potest cogi ad purgationem, de aliis autem nullo modo impeti potest nisi sint notoria. . . .'

[41] MS. Pal.Lat.658 fol. 10*va ad Dist.* 40 c. 6.

simply noted that, if the charge was heresy, a Pope could be both accused and condemned by his inferiors.[42]

Joannes Teutonicus, thoroughly familiar with Huguccio's *Summa* and with the *Glossa Palatina*, discreetly refrained from raising the point at all in that context. He did, however, put forward his views on the deposition of a Pope in commenting on the critical *Dist.* 40 c. 6. There he held that a Pope could be deposed for any notorious crime and for heresy even if it was secret.[43] He drew no distinction between old heresies and new ones. Huguccio's subtle reservations were simply ignored. The *Glossa Ordinaria*, the most influential of these Decretist works in forming fourteenth-century opinion, was also the most ambiguous of them in its treatment of this whole topic. Joannes Teutonicus closely associated the judicial immunity normally conceded to the Pope with the doctrine that normally the Pope's decisions could stand against the opposition of the whole world.[44] But he also proclaimed more outspokenly than the other Decretists that in the exceptional case where articles of faith were involved a Council was superior to a Pope, *ubi de fide agitur . . . tunc synodus maior est papa.* He may have believed that, accordingly, a Council possessed a superior jurisdiction in matters of faith empowering it to judge a Pope on a charge of heresy. Ockham certainly understood the *Glossa Ordinaria*

---

[42] MS. Pal.Lat.658 fol. 5va *ad Dist.* 21 c. 4. In posing exceptions to the rule that an inferior cannot judge a superior the author writes, '. . . vel cum superior heresim incurrit. Hoc enim casu etiam papa ab inferioribus suis et accusari et condempnari posset ut *dist.* xl *si papa.*'

[43] *Glossa Ordinaria ad Dist.* 40 c. 6, 'Certe credo quod si notorium est crimen eius quandocumque, et inde scandalizatur ecclesia et incorrigibilis sit, quod inde possit accusari. . . . Hic tamen specialiter fit mentio de haeresi ideo quia et si occulta esset haeresis de illa posset accusari. Sed de alio occulto crimine non posset.'

[44] Indeed, he thoroughly confused the two elements that Cardinal Humbert, according to Dr Ullmann, was particularly anxious to separate, the personal immunity of the Pope on the one hand, and, on the other, the judicial primary of the Roman church, the fact that no authority was competent to reverse the judgements of Rome. This appears already in the gloss on *Dist.* 15 c. 2, 'Videtur ergo quod papa non possit destruere statuta concilii . . . arg. contra, 17 *dist.* § *hinc etiam.* . . .' 17 *Dist.* § *hinc etiam* (*post* c. 4) referred to a case in which a Pope was held immune from judgement by a Council. The association of the two concepts is still more clear in the gloss on C. 9 q. 3 c. 13, '*Neque ab omni clero*, Arg. quod concilium non potest Papam iudicare . . . unde si totus mundus sententiaret in aliquo negotio contra Papam videtur quod sententiae Papae standum esset.' In the article, 'Ockham, the Conciliar Theory and the Canonists', *Journal of the History of Ideas*, XIV (1954), pp. 40–70, I argued that Joannes did support the idea of a judicial superiority of the Council in matters of faith. The relevant glosses are assembled in Appendix II, so that the reader may form his own judgement.

in this sense.[45] If Joannes did suppose that the Pope's liability to deposition for heresy rested on the superior authority of a General Council in this matter (and not on any self-condemnation or automatic degradation) he would have been justified in ignoring the distinction between an old heresy and a new one and in holding the Pope liable to accusation for secret heresy. But it would also seem, in this case, that Joannes himself had confused the authority of a General Council, understood as the Pope surrounded by the fathers of the Council, with the authority of the fathers alone acting against the Pope. He may well have done so. A canonist of a later age rightly observed that Joannes's glosses were fertile and 'full of juice':[46] but, for all that, precision of terminology was not one of his virtues. What is at any rate certain is that the *Glossa Ordinaria* to the *Decretum* provided a useful source of arguments for later thinkers whose views were more radical than those of Joannes Teutonicus himself.

In reading the Decretist sources one cannot escape the impression that these writers were far more interested in defending the Church against abuses of papal power than in upholding at all costs the doctrine of papal immunity from judgement. Their arguments did open up an important breach in the principle of papal supremacy. With very little support from the texts of the *Decretum* they built up the theory that a Pope could be deposed for any conduct prejudicial to the welfare of the whole Church; and, though Huguccio constructed an ingenious argument to explain how the deposition could be brought about without any trial of a man who was presumed to be a true Pope at the time of his indictment, his views were rejected by the next generation of canonists and remained an example of isolated ingenuity, not the foundation of an enduring canonistic tradition. The Decretists themselves did not explicitly formulate the doctrine of a judicial supremacy of the Council over the Pope,[47] but their asser-

---

[45] *Opus Nonaginta Dierum*, ed. R. F. Bennett and J. G. Sikes in *Guillelmi de Ockham Opera Politica* (Mancunii, 1940), I, pp. 295–6, '. . . sed papa in causa haeresis habet iudicem superiorem, nam papa potest pro haeresi iudicari, di. xl, c. *si papa.* . . . Qui autem potest de haeresi accusari et etiam iudicari, habet superiorem a quo poterit iudicari; ergo papa habet in causa haeresis superiorem, quod glossa di. xix, c. *Anastasius*, asserit manifeste, dicens quod *ubi de fide agitur, synodus maior est papa*; ergo a papa pro causa haeresis est licitum appelare.'

[46] Baptista de S. Blasio, 'Sunt enim breves sed succo plenae et utiliores ac fertiliores quam sint glossae aliorum voluminum utriusque iuris', *Repetitiones in Universas fere Iuris Canonici Partes* (Venetiis, 1587), I, fol. 2vb n. 6.

[47] After this chapter had gone to press Dr Kuttner called my attention to the

tions that the Pope could be judged *a tota ecclesia* and their views concerning the superiority of a Council in matters of faith could quite easily lend themselves to the conciliar interpretation—that the whole Church was possessed of an authority superior to the Pope's, and that the mind of the Church was most perfectly expressed by a General Council acting, if necessary, even against the Pope.

---

following passage of Alanus in MS. Ross. 595 of the Biblioteca Vaticana (fol. 28r*b* *ad Dist.* 19). '*Sine concilio*: arg. quod in questione fidei maior est synodus quam papa. arg. s(upra) d. XV *sicut* et d. XVI *sancta*, quod firmatum est tenendum. Unde accidit ex tali causa quod sinodus potest papa(m) iudicare et dampnare. Unde accidit quod incidit in excommunicationem latam super heresi, ut hic, quod non accideret si papa maior esset sinodo vel equalis....' Thus at least one of the Decretists did explicitly assert that a Council could exercise judicial authority over the Pope where articles of faith were involved.

CHAPTER THREE

POPE AND CARDINALS

In the pattern of fourteenth-century conciliar thought two strands of argument were closely interwoven. Any adequate theory of Church government required in the first place a clear definition of the relationship between the *Romana ecclesia* (understood as a local church) and that other *ecclesia* of the canonists, the *congregatio fidelium* of the Church Universal; but, once this was accomplished, there remained the further task of explaining the constitutional structure of the Roman church itself. In more concrete terms, it was necessary to define not only the relationship between the General Council and the Pope, but also between Pope and cardinals, and, again, between the cardinals and the whole Church. Moreover, a really harmonious theory would need to present all these relationships as logically interdependent aspects of the same underlying principles of Church government.

Such a synthesis was in large measure achieved in the work of Cardinal Zabarella. It was made possible by the canonistic adaptation in the preceding centuries of two separate theories concerning the authority of a General Council and the privileges of the College of Cardinals, which in earlier times seemed quite unconnected and even at times incompatible. In upholding the authority of a General Council the Decretists could appeal to the examples of the early Church and to various patristic texts that had been incorporated in Gratian's *Decretum*. The claims of the cardinals, on the other hand, were based on their practical participation in the government of the Church, a quite recent development which had as yet found little expression in positive canon law. The authority of the Council rested on ancient precedent, that of the cardinals on contemporary institutional growth. There was no common juristic basis for the claims of both bodies, and it was not until much later that the canonists were able to explain the status of the two institutions in terms of a single coherent theory of ecclesiastical authority. In the Decretist works one finds an early formulation of several claims on behalf of the Sacred College that were to be of considerable importance in subsequent constitutional disputes, but little attempt to relate these claims to any comprehensive theory of Church government.

The name *cardinalis* was applied to certain members of the Roman clergy as early as the eighth century,[1] but it did not at first indicate any 'cardinal' importance of the title churches nor a specially close attachment of the cardinals to the Papacy (the *caput et cardo* of the whole Church).[2] The title merely referred to their incardinated status in the performance of liturgical functions in the five great basilicas.[3] It was the great reform movement of the eleventh century that transformed the College of Cardinals into an institution that was to become, at the zenith of the papal power, at once a most effective instrument of Roman centralization and the most serious rival to the absolute personal authority of the Pope. The reassertion of authority by the Papacy was accompanied by a deliberate development of the Sacred College into a standing body of the Pope's most intimate counsellors, a process that was facilitated by Leo IX's policy of including among his cardinals distinguished representatives of the reform movement from abroad who were obviously not brought to Rome 'for the sake of the cardinals' hebdomadary functions'. The new importance of the Sacred College was confirmed by the famous decree of Nicholas II on papal elections (1059),[4] and further enhanced by the circumstances of the schism of 1080–1100, when both Pope and anti-Pope found it expedient to increase the cardinals' authority in bidding for their support.

At this period too we find the first expressions of the curialist doctrines that later became so important.[5] Peter Damian described the cardinals as *spirituales ecclesiae universalis senatores*,[6] and Cardinal Deusdedit, always a staunch supporter of their privileges, wrote that they were the 'hinges' which ruled and guided the whole Church.[7] More

---

[1] P. Hinschius, *Das Kirchenrecht der Katholiken und Protestanten* (Berlin, 1869–97), I, p. 326 n. 9. On the early history of the cardinals see J. B. Sägmüller, *Die Thätigkeit und Stellung der Kardinäle bis Papst Bonifaz VIII* (Freiburg, 1896), pp. 12 ff.; H. W. Klewitz, 'Die Entstehung des Kardinalcollegiums', *Z.S.S.R.* LVI (1936), pp. 115–221; K. Jordan, 'Die Entstehung der römischen Kurie', *Z.S.S.R.* LIX (1939), pp. 97–152; M. Andrieu, 'L'origine du titre de cardinal dans l'église romaine', *Miscellanea Giovanni Mercati* (Città del Vaticano, 1946), V, pp. 113–44; and especially S. Kuttner, 'Cardinalis, the history of a canonical concept', *Traditio*, III (1945), pp. 129–214.

[2] A phrase of Pseudo-Isidore incorporated in the *Decretum* at Dist. 22 c. 6.

[3] This was established beyond doubt by Kuttner, *art. cit.*

[4] Cited in the *Decretum* at Dist. 23 c. 1.

[5] On this see especially W. Ullmann, 'Cardinal Humbert and the Ecclesia Romana', *Studi Gregoriani*, IV, pp. 111–27.

[6] *Contra Phylargyriam* in Migne, *Patrologia Latina*, CVL, col. 540.

[7] W. V. Glanvell, *Die Kanonessamlung des Kardinals Deusdedit* (Paderborn, 1905), p. 268. See Kuttner, *art. cit.* p. 176 n. 110 for other references by Deusdedit to the

important than these rhetorical expressions was a manifesto issued
by a group of dissident cardinals in 1084 which asserted that the
cardinals shared in the divinely ordained authority of the Roman see,
and could lawfully restrain an erring Pope. In support of these claims
they cited the inevitable case of Pope Anastasius:

> Ecce filii patrem ligaverunt, quorum sententiam ipsi coeli firmaverunt
> iuxta verbum domini dicentis Petro et per Petrum Romanae sedi,
> 'Quodcumque ligaveris etc.' ut evidenter appareat privilegium Petri totius
> Romane sedis esse potius quam solius pontificis.[8]

The next century saw a rapid consolidation of the cardinals' position.
They headed the great papal departments of state, represented the
Pope as *legati a latere*, and most important of all, became his constant
and intimate counsellors. In the twelfth century the consistory finally
replaced the old Roman synod, and in consistory were handled all
major questions of Church government—the administration of papal
justice and finance, questions of faith, the affairs of papal fiefs, important disciplinary matters, and all those *causae arduae* concerning bishops
and dioceses that were by law reserved to the Apostolic See.[9]

The cardinals gradually acquired a right of subscription to papal
decrees, and laws were often issued with the formula, *de consilio fratrum
nostrorum*, but the precise legal significance of these usages remained
obscure,[10] and neither the texts of Gratian's *Decretum* nor his *dicta*
gave any satisfactory answer to the fundamental question raised by the
schismatic cardinals in 1084. Did the cardinals participate as of right
in the authority divinely conferred on the Apostolic See or were they,

---

cardinals. Leo IX held that the Pope himself was the *cardo* of the whole Church and
that the cardinals' name was derived from their close association with him, Mansi,
Sacrorum Conciliorum Nova et Amplissima Collectio, XIX, col. 653B.

[8] Quoted by Sägmüller, *op. cit.* p. 235. Two years earlier, during Henry's first
siege of Rome, a council of cardinals and Roman clergy refused to consent to the
pawning of the treasures of the Church to finance the defence of the city. They
insisted on a rigid observance of the law forbidding alienation of Church property.
See D. B. Zema, 'The houses of Tuscany and Pierleone in the crisis of Rome',
Traditio, II (1944), p. 160.

[9] Sägmüller, *op. cit.* pp. 215 ff.

[10] H. Bresslau, *Handbuch der Urkundenlehre* (2nd ed. Leipzig-Berlin, 1912–31), II, pp.
52, 54, 56–61. Tancred, and following him Bernardus Parmensis, suggested that subscription implied consent, gloss *ad* X. III.xiii.6. Bernardus also maintained that subscription was necessary for papal privileges but not for other papal documents. Joannes
Teutonicus discussed the necessity for subscription to papal decrees but without stating
any definite conclusion, *Glossa Ordinaria ad* C. 12 q. 1 c. 68 and *ad Comp. III*, II.xii.1
(MS. C.17 fol. 205va).

for all their dignity and prestige, in essence mere agents of the Pope?

The reticence of Gratian on this point did not embarrass his glossators, but rather left them a clear field for speculation, and we have already seen how, in defining the term *Romana ecclesia*, they were in the habit of putting forward *papa et cardinales* as one commonly accepted definition.[11] Huguccio thought that Pope and cardinals together provided a more certain guide in matters of faith than the Pope alone, and the English gloss in Caius MS. 676, discussing once again the case of the unfortunate Anastasius, suggested that though normally all Catholics should remain in communion with the Pope 'qui sedet pro Petro', nevertheless, in this particular case 'Anastasius non fuit de societate Petri, *sed cardinales erant*.'[12] However, the frequent mention of the cardinals in connexion with the definition of the unerring *Romana ecclesia* does not provide any conclusive evidence for assessing their position in relation to the Pope, for in these contexts the canonists invariably went on to point out that the cardinals too could err, and, without any further clarification of their position, explained that the unerring *Romana ecclesia* could only be the *congregatio fidelium*. Hence these texts provide a clear distinction between the universal Roman church and the local Roman church, but tell us little about the constitutional relationships within the local church itself. To discover how far, in the opinion of the Decretists, the cardinals could exercise the authority of the Roman See in association with the Pope or without the Pope or even against the Pope, we must turn to certain specific problems concerning the authority of the Sacred College which were often discussed in their works.

Since the one right of the cardinals that was unambiguously recognized in the *Decretum* was that of electing a new Pope, it was natural that the Decretist discussions should be centred mainly on the cardinals' role as electors, and on their powers during a papal vacancy. This latter point especially interested them. Bazianus maintained that the cardinals themselves did not enjoy the exercise of the powers that they conferred on the Pope,

> Collige cardinales dare apostolico executionem potestatis quam ipsi exercere non possunt,[13]

---

[11] See the various texts cited *supra* pp. 42–4.

[12] Gloss *ad* C. 24 q. 1 c. 27.

[13] Cited by J. Juncker, 'Die Summa des Simon von Bisignano', *Z.S.S.R.* XLVI (1926), pp. 326–500 at p. 495.

but this seems to evade the real issue, for even during a papal vacancy the administration of the Church had to be carried on, and in
practice none but the cardinals could be responsible for the day-to-
day control of affairs. The question that particularly interested the
Decretists was whether, in these circumstances, the Sacred College
could properly be described as 'head' of the Church, for the answer
to this question involved the whole theory of the nature of papal
authority. It was not only that the cardinals, if they were 'head' of
the Church, could promulgate laws, confirm and depose bishops, even
defer the election of a new Pope, but also that they would then
appear as the true inheritors of the divine authority that Christ had
bestowed on Peter; and thus the whole theory of an absolute authority, limited to the persons of Peter and his successors, would be prejudiced. If it were held that the cardinals merely delegated to some
selected individual an authority of which they themselves enjoyed
the full exercise, then the Pope might indeed come to appear, in a
more technical sense that would have appealed to the thirteenth-
century pontiffs, a *servus servorum Dei*. These issues came fully to light
only a century later, when the position of the cardinals during a
vacancy had become a matter of embittered controversy, but one
may suppose that the sagacious Huguccio was not wholly unaware
of the broader implications of his question when he asked,

> Defuncto papa et alio nondum electo quis est caput ecclesie?[14]

His answer was shrewd and cautious,

> Dicunt quidam cardinales, *sed non est verum*, quia quomodo tot homines
> esse possent unum caput. . . . Est ergo ecclesia acephala et sine capite.
> Funguntur tamen vice capitis tunc cardinales. . . .[15]

Thus Huguccio concluded that the cardinals were not head but that
they acted in place of a head, which seems at first sight a sufficiently in-

---

[14] MS. LC.2, fol. 141va *ad Dist.* 79 c. 7.

[15] He continues, 'Sed nunquid possunt deponere episcopum quia . . . in multis
funguntur vice papa? ar. *di.* xlv, *si forte*, similiter et canonici mortuo episcopo possunt
excommunicare et absolvere et remissiones facere et quod cardinales talia possunt
mortuo papa erg. est eadem, *si quis papam.*' The reference to *Dist.* 45 should read
Dist. 65 *si forte*. This chapter stated that when there was only one bishop left in a
province and he neglected to summon other bishops to make consecrations, then
the people themselves should do so. In later controversies the chapter became a
standard argument for proving that the cardinals could summon a General Council
if the Pope neglected to do so. Huguccio seems to have been the first to apply it to
the Sacred College.

genious and satisfactory formula. It was repeated by Joannes Teutonicus,

> Dic ergo ecclesiam tunc vivere et tamen carere capite. Arg. tamen est quod cardinales suppleant defectum mortui papae infra, eadem distinctione, *si quis*.[16]

Yet the argument that several men could not be one head could not have seemed altogether convincing to contemporaries, for the idea of corporate headship was not unfamiliar to medieval writers. This objection was advanced in a most interesting passage of the gloss *Ecce Vicit Leo*.

> . . . sed estne ecclesia acephala mortuo papa? Potest dici quod non, quia quamvis revera caput non habet quia non potest dici quod cardinales sunt eius caput quia tunc haberet plura capita, tamen vice capitis habet eos. *Vel posset dici quod cardinales sunt caput* ita quod nullus sicut universitatis dona ita quod nullius, xii q. ii *qui manumittitur*, vel debitor ita quod nullus, *ff quod cuiusque universitas, l. sicut* § i . . . unde credimus quod possint episcopum deponere, arg. *dist. lxv c. ult.* Similiter mortuo episcopo devolvit ius ad capitulum, arg. ex. *De hereticis, ad abolendum*.[17]

---

[16] Gloss *ad Dist.* 79 c. 7, 'Sed nunquid mortuo papa ecclesia erit monstrum sine capite vel nunquid universitas cardinalium erit caput? Si hoc dicas, cardinales tunc temporis possunt deponere episcopum, eadem ratione canonici mortuo episcopo possunt deponere clericum aliquem. Dic ergo et ecclesiam tunc vivere et tamen carere capite. . . .'

[17] MS. T.O.5.17 fol. 28ra *ad Dist.* 79 c. 7. There are several scribal slips in this passage. The manuscript has 'iure capitis' for 'vice capitis', and the last sentence runs, 'unde credimus quod possint episcopum *episcopum* deponere . . . similiter mortuo episcopo *disvolvit* ius ad capitulum'. The words *Qui manumittitur* are the opening words of a sentence in the middle of one of Gratian's *dicta*, and the passage might more normally be cited as C. 12 q. 2 *Libertus etiam* (or in modern fashion, C. 12 q. 2 *dictum Gratiani post* c. 58). It refers to the Roman law doctrine that a freed slave 'owed reverence' to his former master, pointing out that a slave released by a corporation did not 'owe reverence' to all the members of it as individuals. The St Florian manuscript of *Ecce Vicit Leo* does not contain the reference to a corporate headship of the cardinals. It runs, '. . . sed estne ecclesia acephala mortuo papa? Potest dici quod non quia quamvis revere capud non habet, quia (non) potest dici quod cardinales sunt eius capud quia sic habeantur plura capita, tamen vice capitis habet eos. Unde credimus quod possunt episcopum deponere, ar. lxv *ult.*' (fol. 28va). One does find precisely the same reference to corporation doctrines in the St Florian MS. in a quite different context. In discussing the ownership of Church property the author suggested that the ownership could be vested in an ecclesiastical corporation but not in the individuals who made up the corporation. 'Ecce quod res ecclesie dicunter communes sed cuius vel quorum est proprietas illarum rerum? Solutio, dicunt quod universitatis ita quod nullius de universitate quia potest esse aliquid universitatis ita quod nullius ut inf. e.q. *qui manumittitur*. Unde redditus parochialis ecclesie erit

Just as the gift of a corporation was not the gift of any single member of it, and a debt owed to a corporation was not owed to the individual members, so the College of Cardinals could be head of the Church, not as a group of individuals who would be *plura capita*, but as a single corporate body. The chapter of the Digest cited in support of this view laid down that the powers of a corporation could be exercised by any members of it who survived; and clearly the writer of the gloss intended to convey that the powers of the Roman See were vested, not in the Pope alone, but in a corporate association of Pope and cardinals, so that during a vacancy the full authority of the See could be exercised by the cardinals alone (hence their power to depose a bishop, a function normally reserved to the Pope). This is very reminiscent of the claim of the dissident cardinals in 1084. The particular significance of the passage is that the author invoked the technicalities of corporation law to claim for the cardinals as a corporate group an authority that he acknowledged they could not possess as individuals. In this it provides an interesting anticipation of later doctrines, and may indeed be regarded as the starting-point of a tradition of canonistic thought that can be traced through the next two centuries to its culmination in the work of Zabarella.

Arising directly out of the cardinals' right to elect the Pope was the question of their jurisdiction in cases where the validity of a papal election was disputed, as was to happen in 1378. The opinion generally accepted among the Decretists held quite rigorously that once a candidate had obtained the necessary two-thirds vote of the cardinals (as required by Alexander III's election decree of 1179) no subsequent proceedings could invalidate the election. Even if the electing cardinals were proved to have acted simoniacally their nominee was still Pope, and a text that seemed to assert the contrary view, that a Pope who was elected by bribery or coercion should be expelled from his see as *non apostolicus sed apostaticus*, was interpreted as referring only to a 'Pope' who had been elected by some group other than the cardinals:

---

proprietas conventus episcopalis ecclesie' (*ad* C. 12 q. 1 c. 13, fol. 61v*b*). Dr Ullmann regarded the glosses in the Trinity MS. and in the St Florian MS. as separate though related works. Dr Kuttner prefers to classify them as variants of the same apparatus. See Ullmann, *Medieval Papalism*, p. 208; Kuttner, *Repertorium*, pp. 59–66; and Kuttner and Rathbone, 'Anglo-Norman Canonists'. *Traditio*, VII (1949–51), pp. 279–358 at p. 328.

... loquitur hic de illo qui per simoniam electus est ab illis qui non habebant potestatem eligendi, non a cardinalibus.[18]

The Decretist teaching on this point serves only to emphasize how very flimsy was the legal basis for the claims of the cardinals in 1378. There was, however, another passage in the same section of the *Decretum* which evoked more divergent opinions among its glossators:

> Si duo forte contra fas ... fuerint ordinati ... illum solum in sede apostolica permansurum, quem ex numero clericorum, nova ordinatione, divinum iudicium, et universitatis consensus elegerit.[19]

The chapter was not perhaps of great significance in itself. It was merely one of a series of texts which inveighed, conventionally enough, against schism and simony in the Sacred College. Its real importance lies in the fact that it stimulated Huguccio to ask the all-important question—who should be judge of whether an election was in fact *contra fas*. He replied that the cardinals had cognizance of such a case, but that if they disagreed a Council should be summoned to decide the issue, *de auctoritate cardinalium universitatis*:

> Forte loquitur de manifesto, vel ad cardinales spectat hoc cognoscere, vel si cardinales adeo dissentiunt debebit concilium convocari auctoritate cardinalium universitatis.[20]

The *Glossa Palatina* simply observed that such a case should be decided by General Council and cardinals,[21] but Joannes Teutonicus took a different view. He seldom displayed any sympathy with the cardinals' pretensions, and he characteristically held that in this matter they could exercise no jurisdiction, since for them to do so would be to act as judges in their own case. Accordingly he too suggested that a Council be summoned:

> Sed quis erit iudex de hoc an electio sit contra fas? Non ipsi cardinales quia si sic essent iudices in proprio facto ... dic istud cap. locum habere quando neuter est electus a duabus partibus. Vel dic concilium convocabitur.[22]

---

[18] *Glossa Ordinaria ad Dist.* 79 c. 9. Similarly Huguccio and *Glossa Palatina* in the same context.

[19] *Dist.* 79 c. 8.

[20] MS. LC.2 fol. 141va *ad Dist.* 79 c. 8, 'Sed cuius examinationi committitur haec causa utrum ita sint electi vel non? Forte loquitur de manifesto. . . .'

[21] MS. Pal.Lat.658 fol. 19va *ad Dist.* 79 c. 8, 'Sed cuius discussioni hoc committetur? Synodo generali et cardinalibus.'

[22] *Glossa Ordinaria ad Dist.* 79 c. 8.

The striking feature of these glosses is that none of the authors even troubled to discuss the question about which the later Conciliarists argued with such desperate ingenuity—whether the cardinals really had any right to summon a General Council. The principle that only a Pope could summon a General Council was laid down quite unambiguously in the *Decretum*, and Joannes and Huguccio and the author of the *Glossa Palatina* all wrote glosses on the relevant chapters without envisaging any exception whatsoever to the canonical rule.[23] Yet all of them assumed without question that when a Council was urgently needed to provide a head for the Universal Church it could be summoned, if necessary, by an alternative method. And the assumption seems a natural corollary of their underlying conviction that the maintenance of the *status ecclesiae* was more important than any other consideration whatsoever. The fourteenth-century Conciliarists were not original in relying on a doctrine of *epieikeia* and 'necessity' to justify extra-legal actions, but only in thinking that the explicit formulation of such a doctrine was indispensable to their case. The Decretists seem to have taken their *epieikeia* for granted.[24]

Our main concern is with the significance of these Decretist doctrines for the later traditions of canonistic thought that helped to shape conciliar ideas in the age of the Great Schism; but it is interesting to observe in passing that, even in the first half of the thirteenth century, their influence was not confined to a narrow circle of academic jurists. This can be illustrated from the writings of another lawyer of Bologna, more famous than any of those hitherto mentioned, but one who has not usually been remembered for his canonistic skill and learning. We refer to Petrus de Vinea, Chancellor of the Emperor Frederick II, and particularly to the series of letters written on behalf of Frederick and against Pope Gregory IX in March and April 1239.[25] At that time Frederick lay at Capua under threat of papal interdict, and since a formal excommunication seemed likely to imperil his already precarious position in Italy, he sought to avert the sentence by an appeal to the Sacred College. The first letter

---

[23] *Dist.* 17 cc. 1–6.

[24] Joannes Teutonicus did remark that laws should be interpreted equitably and in accordance with the intention of the legislator, gloss *ad* C. 23 q. 1 c. 2, 'Arg. quod non debemus inhaerere verbis sed potius menti . . . verba enim in rescriptis posita vel in lege conformare debemus aequitati. . . .'

[25] On the style and authorship of these letters see H. Wieruszowski, *Vom Imperium zum Nationalen Königtum* (München-Berlin, 1933), pp. 58 ff.

drafted by Petrus de Vinea was dated 10 March 1239, and in it was set forth the principle that the cardinals shared in the authority of the Apostolic See and that, accordingly, they should be admitted to *equa participatio* in the transaction of Church business.[26] The next letter urged the cardinals to avert the threatened sentence, and added an appeal in the vaguest terms to God, to a General Council, and to the whole Christian world.[27] But in spite of these efforts the sentence of excommunication was duly promulgated by Gregory IX, and Frederick, having no longer anything to gain by restraint, retaliated with a full-blooded personal attack on the Pope in the manifesto, *Levate*.[28] He expressed his reverence for the papal office but declared that Gregory was unfit to hold that office,[29] and he now demanded that the cardinals should summon a General Council, before which he was prepared to prove his charges against the Pope:

> ... sacrosancte Romane ecclesie cardinales ... generale concilium prelatorum et aliorum Christi fidelium debeant evocare ... in quorum presencia nos ipsi presentes cuncta que diximus sumus hostendere et probare parati et his etiam duriora.

These letters have been variously interpreted. Mgr Martin could not see in them an appeal to the Council at all 'in the juridical sense of the term',[30] but B. Sütterlin, who submitted the relevant documents to a more searching analysis, found in the claims on behalf of the cardinals, and especially in the claim that the cardinals could summon a General Council, a remarkable anticipation of later conciliar theories, and he 'wondered at the genius with which Frederick brought the idea to life'.[31] A study of the earlier canonistic writings leaves no doubt that Petrus de Vinea meant his appeal to be 'juridical' in the fullest sense of the word, but also removes any 'wonder' at the

---

[26] P. Huillard-Bréholles, *Historia Diplomatica Friderici Secundi* (Paris, 1852–61), v, i, p. 282, '... ad singula que presidens Sedi Petri proponit statuere, vel denuncianda decreverit, equa participatio vos admittat. ...'

[27] *M.G.H., Constitutiones*, ii, p. 289, 'ad Deum vivum ... et deinde ad futurum summum pontificem, ad generalem synodum, ad principes Alamaniae et generaliter ad universos reges et principes orbis terrae ac ceteros christianos. ...'

[28] 20 April 1239, *M.G.H. Const.* ii, p. 296.

[29] '... non in contemptu papalis officii vel apostolice dignitatis ... set persone prevaricationem arguimus'.

[30] 'La doctrine de la supériorité du concile sur le pape', *Revue des sciences religieuses*, xvii (1937), pp. 119–43.

[31] *Die Politik Kaiser Friedrichs II und die römischen Kardinäle 1239–1250* (Heidelberg, 1929), p. 24.

originality of his arguments. He was in fact simply restating a series of Decretist doctrines that had been debated at Bologna in the earlier years of the century when he was a student there.[32] The distinction between the person of the Pope and the dignity of the Apostolic See upon which he based his claims had been clearly expounded by Huguccio himself,

> Hoc non fit ratione pape sed propter auctoritatem sedis unde caute dixit apostolice sedis, et non dixit apostolici.[33]

The claim that the cardinals were competent to summon a General Council could also find support in the work of Huguccio. Most important of all, Petrus de Vinea showed a clear understanding that the demand for a General Council had to be based on an alleged threat to the Church as a whole, understood as the *congregatio fidelium*, and not on any private injury, even though it was the Emperor himself who suffered, for this was the heart of the earlier doctrine on the deposition of a Pope. He was careful to state that the whole Church was menaced by Gregory's conduct in the sentence immediately following his call for a General Council;

> Vos, igitur, dilecti principes, non nobis solum sed ecclesie que congregatio est omnium Christi fidelium, condolete. . . .[34]

Frederick's great chancellor was renowned in his own day as a master of rhetoric as well as of law, and the colourful language of his epistles, far removed from the technical jargon of the lawyers, has tended to obscure the canonistic basis of his thought. Nevertheless, his letters provide an interesting indication that the Decretist ideas could influence the practical politics of their own age as well as the theoretical speculations of a later epoch.[35]

---

[32] On his studies at Bologna see M. Sarti-Fattorini, *De Claris Archigymnasii Bononiensis Professoribus* (Bononiae, 1888), I, pp. 143–4, 'Accessit legum et canonum scientia qua etiam excelluit.' Huillard-Bréholles thought that Petrus de Vinea was born in 1190 and that he certainly entered the Emperor's service in 1221. It would seem probable therefore that he was pursuing his legal studies between 1210 and 1220—just the time of the revival in Decretist scholarship at Bologna.

[33] MS. P.72 fol. 128r*b ad Dist.* 19 c. 2, commenting on the words 'omnes apostolice sedis sanctiones accipiende sunt'.

[34] *M.G.H. Const.* II, p. 296.

[35] Indeed the writings of Petrus de Vinea formed one channel through which some of the more radical Decretist ideas became known to controversialists of the fourteenth century, for the chanceries of both Philip the Fair and Lewis the Bavarian made copious use of his letters. See H. Wieruszowski, *op. cit.* pp. 58 ff.

Hitherto we have considered the canonists' views on the authority of the Sacred College only in connexion with those exceptional cases when there was no Pope or no agreement as to who was the true Pope. Petrus de Vinea's demand for *equa participatio* of the cardinals in framing the policies of the Apostolic See during the reign of a vigorous pontiff may serve to remind us of this still more important problem. It was one that the Decretists on the whole neglected. They acknowledged that the cardinals did form a corporation, comparable to the chapter of a cathedral church (an analogy suggested by the cardinals' role as electors of the bishop of the Roman See), but only the gloss *Ecce Vicit Leo* showed how this could provide a basis for defining the status of the Sacred College during a vacancy; and even this work did not press the analogy any further by attempting to define the relationship of the cardinals to a reigning Pope in terms of the corporation law that it had cited. Indeed, the canonistic theory of corporation structure at this time was hardly sufficiently formulated to permit such a complete synthesis. Since the Decretists were in the habit of defining the Roman church in its more limited sense as *papa et cardinales*, it would seem that they did regard the cardinals as 'participating' in some way in the authority of the Apostolic See;[36] but they did not show themselves at all anxious to explore the constitutional implications of this participation by inquiring how far his association with the cardinals could limit the authority of a reigning Pope. Huguccio, indeed, observed that papal laws ought to be discussed *in consistorio* before promulgation,

> Multa enim consilii consideratione et compatientie maturitate debet discuti et decoqui in consistorio apostolici vel imperatoris lex ante constitutionem.[37]

But he did not inquire whether laws made without such consultation were invalid. The *Glossa Ordinaria* and the gloss *Ecce Vicit Leo* seem not to have discussed the question at all. Nor did the earlier Decretists, Paucapalea, Rolandus, Rufinus, or Stephanus.

There was one exception, however, to this general indifference.

---

[36] This seems especially clear in the *Summa Et Est Sciendum ad Dist.* 21 c. 3, '... accipitur etiam (romana ecclesia) pro capite et membris, i.e. papa et cardinalium collegio *ut hic.* ...' The passage of the *Decretum* under discussion referred to the primacy of the Roman church.

[37] MS. P.72 fol. 118vb *ad Dist.* 4 c. 3.

The texts of the *Glossa Palatina* on this question form a veritable manifesto in favour of the cardinals. Whereas Huguccio merely wrote that laws ought to be considered in consistory, the author of the *Glossa Palatina* laid down quite uncompromisingly that the Pope alone was actually incompetent to establish a general law for the whole Church, that such enactments were valid only when approved by the cardinals. The legislative authority of the Roman See resided in them as well as in the Pope,

> Quero utrum solus papa possit condere canones. Videtur quod sic, ar. xcvi in palea *Constantinus*. . . . Solutio, generalem legem de universali statu ecclesie non potest sine cardinalibus condere.[38]

He maintained the same point of view in considering the Pope's judicial supremacy. Joannes Teutonicus pointed out that a judicial sentence of the Pope carried an indisputable authority, that it could stand against the whole world. The *Glossa Palatina* accepted this claim only when the Pope's opinion was supported by a majority of the cardinals, since 'power of this sort was given to him with the cardinals':

> Videtur quod si papa sentiat contra omnem clerum standum potius sit eius sententie quam aliorum . . . hoc credo verum cum omnes cardinales vel maior pars idem sentiunt, nam cum cardinalibus intelligo huiusmodi potestatem ei concessam.[39]

These assertions that the cardinals should be associated with the Pope in the government of the Church were sweeping claims in themselves, but the *Glossa Palatina* went even further. Already by the time of Stephanus Tornacensis the idea had appeared that the cardinal-bishops' function as 'metropolitans' in a papal election might give them jurisdiction over a reigning Pope;[40] and Stephanus himself, and several of the Decretists of the next generation, thought it necessary to deny the proposition that the cardinals were greater than the Pope

---

[38] MS. T.O.10.2 fol. 35v*b* *ad* C. 25 q. 1 c. 6. Cf. also MS. Pal.Lat.658 fol. 1v*b* *ad Dist.* 4 c. 3, 'Non ergo solus potest papa vel imperator legem decernere vel condere. . . .'

[39] MS. Pal.Lat.658 fol. 44r*b* *ad* C. 9 q. 3 c. 13.

[40] *Summa ad* C. 3 q. 1, p. 190, 'Quo casu dicunt quidam male distinguere hic Gratianum, et aiunt cardinales eum locum obtinere in electione summi pontificis quem metropolitanus obtinet in electione cuiuslibet episcopi, et ideo quod iudices esse posse ipsius. Ad quod respondetur quia tenent locum metropolitani in confirmatione electionis, non in potestate iudicii.' Stephanus had in mind the wording of the election decree of 1059, '. . . cardinales episcopi procul dubio metropolitani vice funguntur. . . .'

because of the part they played in his consecration.[41] Sicardus and Huguccio did regard the cardinals as competent to depose a heretical Pope, but neither of them suggested that this implied any superior authority of the Sacred College in normal circumstances.[42] The *Glossa Palatina*, on the other hand, clearly asserted that the cardinals were not only the indispensable associates of the Pope but were collectively superior to him:

> *Universali.* arg. quod si omnes cardinales faciunt in aliquo contra papam eorum debet sententia prevalere cum plures sint, arg. xciii dist. *legimus,* nam ibi dicitur quad orbis maior est urbe. . . .[43]

This may explain why the author of the *Glossa Palatina* felt able to dispense with Huguccio's legal subtleties concerning the deposition of a Pope, for the belief that in the College of Cardinals there was an authority superior to that of the Pope would remove the central difficulty that had provoked Huguccio's cautious reservations.

These doctrines put forward in the *Glossa Palatina* could find no shred of support in the texts of the *Decretum*, and one naturally looks for some alternative theoretical basis for such extreme claims. In this, however, the *Glossa Palatina* proves disappointing, and tantalizingly so, since it implies without explicitly stating a theory that was to assume considerable importance in later conciliar thought, namely, that the cardinals could limit the authority of a Pope by reason of the fact that they represented the whole Church. The idea appears most clearly at *Dist.* 15 c. 2, in the passage just quoted, where the words *universali consensu* (which in the text refer quite unambiguously to a General Council) are taken, though without any explanation, as an argument in favour of the cardinals. In the same passage Jerome's famous phrase, *Orbis maior est urbe,* also appears as an argument for the cardinals, but again without any explanation of how they epito-mized the authority of 'the world'.[44] The *Glossa Palatina* seems to hint

---

[41] E.g. Rufinus, Huguccio, Joannes Teutonicus *ad Dist.* 23 c. 1.

[42] Huguccio *ad Dist.* 63 c. 23, 'Nam et cardinales possunt deponere papam pro heresi. Non tamen ipsi sunt maiores quam papa' (MS. LC.2, fol. 121va). Sicardus *ad Dist.* 23, 'Nam si iudex est ordinarius in nullo negotio judicabit maiorem, nisi in casu cum cardinales deponunt apostolicum haereticum' (Schulte, *Zur Geschichte,* p. 348).

[43] MS. Pal.Lat.658 fol. 4ra, *ad Dist.* 15 c. 2.

[44] In the glosses on C. 25 q. 1 c. 6 and C. 9 q. 3 c. 13 (cited in text) there is the same hint of a relationship between the cardinals and the whole Church. In the first case it was a law *de universali statu ecclesie* that required the cardinals' approval.

at a novel and important theory concerning the relationship of the cardinals to the whole Church, but fails to develop the subject, leaving the reader to draw his own inferences.

In putting forward such bold and far-reaching claims with a minimum of theoretical justification the *Glossa Palatina* provides a typical example of the Decretist approach to problems of ecclesiastical authority. These early canonists were often bold but they were not always consistent. They displayed a freshness and vitality of thought that at first sight contrast very favourably with the laboured erudition of the fourteenth-century glossators, and, outlining in a few crisp sentences basic doctrines on Church government that later thinkers were to expand into elaborate theories, they laid the foundations of much future speculation on problems of authority within the Church. Yet these early writers, in many ways so attractive, lacked certain qualities that the later canonists were able to supply, especially a capacity for patient systematization and for painstaking analysis of abstract concepts. One can find in their works many ideas that the Conciliarists were to adopt and fuse into coherent systems of thought; but the Decretists maintained them in isolation from one another, and in association with other doctrines that could form the basis of very different theories of Church government. Their claims on behalf of Council and cardinals were never satisfactorily reconciled with that other doctrine of the Pope's personal authority as successor of St Peter, which also found vigorous expression in their works. They were perhaps groping towards some such theory as that to be propounded eventually by Gerson, in which authority was held to reside in the whole Church *formaliter et absolute* and in the Pope *quoad exercitium et usum*. The Decretists did not attempt any such precise distinctions, but instead, by relying on the device of attributing different connotations to the term *Romana ecclesia* according to the context, permitted themselves a flexibility of terminology that occasionally produces an air of confusion in their works. They never really came to grips with the concept of representation involved in their presentation of the relationship between Pope and Universal Church; nor did they attempt any sufficiently refined analysis of the structure of corporations to explain their views on the positions of the cardinals within the Roman church. A more systematic presentation of the conciliar elements in

---

In the second the cardinals' support was necessary to sustain a judgement against *omnem clerum*.

their thought became possible only after the much more detailed analysis of such concepts that was undertaken by the thirteenth-century Decretalists, who, somewhat paradoxically, are usually remembered only for their extreme papalism. These canonists in fact forged the links between the speculations of the Decretists and the more coherent conciliar theories of the fourteenth century. It is their works that must next claim our attention.

PART TWO

ASPECTS OF THIRTEENTH-CENTURY ECCLESIOLOGY

CHAPTER ONE

CHANGING VIEWS ON CHURCH GOVERNMENT

1. *Papal Monarchy*

During the pontificate of Innocent III two opposing conceptions of Church government existed side by side in the works of the canonists—on the one hand the predilection for schemes of limited monarchy that can be discerned in some of the Decretist works, on the other the uncompromising doctrine of papal sovereignty that was presented in most of the Decretalist writings. It would be improper to press too far the distinction between Decretist and Decretalist sources, for in the first two decades of the thirteenth century some of the most eminent canonists were equally active in both spheres. (Joannes Teutonicus was the compiler and glossator of the *Compilatio Quarta* as well as the author of the *Glossa Ordinaria* on the *Decretum*.) Yet it remains true that writers who held 'oligarchic' or 'democratic' views on certain aspects of Church government found it convenient to express them in their commentaries on the *Decretum*, and that the more rigorous monarchical position was most consistently expounded in glosses on the new *compilationes* and especially on the *Gregoriana*. Certainly, when one turns from the moderate if muddled constitutionalism of the Decretist glosses to the Decretalist works of writers like Tancred and Bernardus Parmensis, a sharp change of tone is at once apparent, for in these works the hesitations and reservations suggested by Gratian's conflicting texts were replaced by uncompromising assertions of that doctrine of absolute papal monarchy which has often been described, and usually deplored, as characteristic of all canonistic thought. The attitude of Innocent III and of his successors ensured that these views were to be decisive for the future, that, as the canonists became more and more preoccupied with the codification and interpretation of contemporary papal legislation, the moderate doctrines of the Decretists should be half forgotten for a time, and almost wholly ignored.

In the Decretalist writings the Pope was presented as a vicegerent of God in the most literal sense, as the wielder of a *plenitudo potestatis* that set him above all human law and conferred on him absolute authority in every sphere of Church government.[1] His very will, without any rational justification, was sufficient to establish a binding law,[2] and even his unjust commands were to be obeyed[3] for no one on earth could say to him, cur *ita facis?* Innocent IV maintained not only that Christ had in fact bestowed *plenitudo potestatis* on Peter and his successors, but that the institution of any other form of Church government would have implied a defect in the divine wisdom and love.[4] *De iure* the Pope possessed all the powers of Christ on earth, and when Innocent admitted that he could not always exercise them *de facto* it was only to make the point that he could legitimately call on the temporal power to enforce his commands.[5]

Yet in spite of all these claims even the more extreme of the Decretalists recognized certain loopholes in the Pope's armour of absolute authority. Although they acknowledged him as an absolute ruler in the sense that he was above all human restraint they did not admit that he could *de iure* exercise his authority in an altogether arbitrary fashion. The idea that the powers conferred on Peter and his successors, however extensive, were bestowed only for the good of the Church and could not be used for its destruction was never wholly forgotten. Even Innocent IV admitted, though grudgingly, that papal authority could not be exercised in a manner prejudicial to the 'general state of the Church'.[6] Moreover, it was generally agreed

---

[1] Tancred *ad Comp. III*, I.v.3, MS. C.17 fol. 147va, '*Vices:* in iis gerit vicem dei quia sedet in loco Jesu Christi qui est verus deus et verus homo ... item de nichilo facit aliquid ... item in iis gerit vicem dei quia plenitudinem potestatis habet in rebus ecclesiasticis ... item quia potest dispensare supra ius et contra ius ... item quia de iusticia potest facere iniusticiam corrigendo ius et mutando ... nec est qui dicat ei, cur ita facis. ...' Similarly, Bernardus Parmensis *ad* X. I.vii.3. Innocent IV repeatedly stressed the supreme authority exercised by the Pope in virtue of his *plenitudo potestatis*, e.g. *Commentaria ad* X. I.v.4, II.ii.10, II.xxiv.20, II.xxiii.55, III.xxxiv.8, V.xxiii.24.

[2] Bernardus Parmensis *ad* X. I.vii.3, 'In his quae vult ei est pro ratione voluntas. ...'

[3] This was the opinion of Innocent IV, *Commentaria ad* X. v.xxxix.44. Bernardus Parmensis, however, held that a manifestly unjust command was not to be obeyed (*ad* X. I.xxxiii.2). Goffredus Tranensis repeated a view common among the Decretists, that unjust sentences were binding as regards the Church Militant, but not as regards the Church Triumphant. *Summa in Titulos Decretalium*, fol. 236 n. 17.

[4] *Commentaria ad* X. II.xxvii.27, 'non videretur discretus dominus fuisse ... nisi unicum post se talem vicarium reliquisset qui haec omnia potest', and again *ad* X. III.xxxiv.8, '... non videretur diligens paterfamilias nisi vicario suo ... plenam potestatem super omnes dimisisset'.

[5] *Commentaria ad* X. III.xxxiv.8.

[6] *Commentaria ad* I.xxi.2, 'Dicendum est quod non dispensat papa contra Apostolum

that the Pope had no power to dispense against articles of faith—though he could dispense against any precepts of the Bible that were not actual commands or prohibitions,[7] against the Apostle Paul (since Peter was greater in administration),[8] and, in general, according to Innocent IV, against the letter of the Scriptures though not against the spirit.[9] Some of the Decretalists recognized other limits to the Pope's dispensatory authority. Tancred and Bernardus Parmensis pointed out that he could not dissolve a consummated marriage,[10] and for half a century a vigorous controversy was maintained concerning the precise limits of the Pope's powers in other matters that were regarded as pertaining to natural law.[11] The issue most discussed in this connexion was the right of the Pope to dispense from oaths and vows, obviously a matter of the greatest practical importance in the Middle Ages. Huguccio's view that the Pope had no power in such cases was cited by Laurentius but rejected,[12] and the more common opinion held that the Pope could dispense from any vow 'with just cause'.[13] Certain exceptions to the rule were noted

---

in his quae pertinent ad articulos fidei et forte in his quae pertinent ad generalem statum ecclesiae.' Elsewhere, though, Innocent IV wrote that the Pope could dispense against the general state of the Church provided that he acted with just cause. Cf. *Commentaria ad* I.iv.4 and *ad* III.xxxv.6. And he could dispense against positive law even without cause. '. . . quidam dicunt et forte non male quod licet in his quae sunt contra votum . . . et contra Evangelium non prosit dispensatio nisi ex cause fiat, et forte idem intelligendum est si dispensatur in his quae sunt contra generalem statum ecclesiae, non tamen hoc est verum in his dispensationibus quae fiunt contra ius positivum tantum' (III.xxxv.6).

[7] W. Ullmann, *Medieval Papalism*, p. 52.

[8] Tancred *ad Comp. I*, I.xiii.2, MS. C.17 fol. 13va; Goffredus Tranensis, *Summa*, fol. 4 n. 6 and fol. 37 n. 11. Innocent IV *Commentaria ad* X. I.xxi.2.

[9] *Commentaria ad* X. I.ix.11, following the opinion of Joannes Teutonicus *ad Comp. III*, I.viii.5, MS. C.17 fol. 169ra, 'Dispensat enim contra verba evangelii sed non contra mentem.'

[10] Tancred *ad Comp. III*, I.v.2, MS. C.17 fol. 147ra, '. . . carnale (vinculum) fortius est quia dissolvi non potest etiam si interveniat consensus pape et ipsorum coniugium . . . nisi in unico casu, scilicet ante carnis coniunctionem'. Similarly, Bernardus Parmensis *ad* X. I.vii.2. However, Innocent IV, commenting on the same chapter, held that the Pope could dissolve both carnal and spiritual marriage.

[11] On the whole question see J. Brys, *De Dispensatione in Iure Canonico* (Brugis, 1925), pp. 201–26; W. Ullmann, *Medieval Papalism*, pp. 50–7.

[12] Laurentius *ad Comp. III*, II.xv.4, MS. C.17 fol. 213vb, 'Hoc tamen negat H(uguccio), et omnia quecumque dicunt vel innuunt papam absolvere a sacramento posse, vel intelligentur de illicito, vel potius sunt radenda quam legenda, quia in hiis quae sunt de iure naturali ut voto, iuramento, papa non dispensat. Quod non admitto. . . .'

[13] Thus Laurentius, *loc. cit.*; Bernardus Parmensis *ad* X. II.xxiv.18; Innocent IV *ad* X. III.xxv.6.

however. Tancred thought there could be no dispensation from a vow of chastity, since there was nothing worthier to which such a vow could be commuted, and this opinion was accepted in the *Glossa Ordinaria* on Gregory's *Decretales*.[14] Again the monastic vow of poverty provoked complex discussions even before the added complications of the Franciscan disputes had given the question a heightened significance.[15]

When one reads these discussions, often protracted into intricate detail, on the Pope's dispensatory authority it may seem that there has been no change from the earlier, moderate attitude, that the Decretalists too were determined to set precise limits to the legitimate authority of the Pope. But there were in fact important changes in the canonistic treatment of such issues during the first half of the thirteenth century. The really significant feature in the Decretists' arguments was not that they recognized certain theoretical limitations to the Pope's competence—it would be hard to find any medieval apologist who held otherwise—but that they envisaged, even if confusedly, an institutional structure to make those limitations effective. If, for instance, the *Glossa Palatina's* claims on behalf of the cardinals and those of Joannes Teutonicus on behalf of the General Council had been realized in practice, the Church in the thirteenth century might have grown into just such a 'mixed monarchy' as Gerson and d'Ailly were to advocate in the age of the Schism.

There is little trace of any such practical restraints in the Decretalist works down to the end of Innocent IV's pontificate. The Pope could

---

[14] Tancred *ad Comp. III*, III.xxvii.2, MS. C.17 fol. 271ra; Bernardus Parmensis *ad* X. III.xxv.6.

[15] The most extreme point of view maintained that the Pope, by virtue of his *plenitudo potestatis*, could dispense that a monk should hold property without renouncing the monastic life. Tancred stated this opinion without accepting it, *ad Comp. III*, III.xxvii.2, MS. C.17 fol. 271ra, 'Quad dicitur hic papam dispensare non posse quod monachus habeat proprium de plano concedo, quia abdicatio proprietatis est de substantia monachatus. . . . Sed de monacho potest facere non monachum. Alii dicunt quod papa de plenitudine potestatis sue potest facere quod monachus existens monachus habeat proprium quoniam potest papa auferre substantiam rei.' The more usual opinion was that of Tancred, that the Pope could permit a monk to leave his Order and subsequently acquire property, but that he could not authorize him to have possessions while remaining a monk. Innocent IV, however, asserted that poverty and celibacy were attached to the monastic state by positive law only, and so fell within the scope of the Pope's dispensatory authority. *Commentaria ad* X. III.xxxv.6, 'Haec autem sunt annexa ordini a iure positivo quod probo. Monachus autem nihil est quam solitarius tristis, 16 q. 1 *placuit* . . . ex hoc patet quod papa potest dispensare cum monacho quod habeat proprium vel coniugem.'

not dispense against articles of faith indeed, but in the last resort it was left to the Pope himself to determine whether an article of faith was involved in any particular case. He could not act against the well-being of the Church; but it was for the Pope himself to decide how the interests of the Church were best served. Naturally enough, in view of this more rigorous attitude, nothing more was heard of the Decretists' assertions that the Pope's power, like the Emperor's, was based partly on popular consent (*habuit auctoritatem secundario a conciliis*). Instead, the position of the Pope as a direct recipient of divine authority was contrasted with that of the Emperor, who received power only from the people.[16] Again, the attempts of moderate Decretists like Huguccio to distinguish between the personal power of the Pope and the authority of the Apostolic See were abandoned, and for the Decretalists, as for the Gratian, the terms *papa, apostolica sedes, romana ecclesia,* became interchangeable expressions.[17] When Innocent IV wrote that the Pope received the power of the keys *in persona ecclesiae* the words no longer conveyed any hint of a superior power residing in the Church as a whole.[18] They meant simply that all ecclesiastical authority was epitomized in the Pope, that, in a real sense, Peter was the Church.

The idea that Council or cardinals might limit the Pope's powers was not so much refuted as ignored, but if any suggestion of conciliar supremacy did arise it could be demolished by a convenient pronouncement of Paschal II which was not included in Gratian's collection but incorporated in the *Compilatio Prima* and subsequently in the *Gregoriana*:

> Aiunt in conciliis statutum non inveniri quasi Romane ecclesie legem concilia ulla praefixerint, cum omnia concilia per Romane ecclesie

---

[16] Tancred (*ad Comp. I,* I.iv.18, MS. C.17 fol. 5*vb*); Vincentitis (*ad Comp. I,* I.i.4, MS. C.17 fol. 1*rb*) and *ad Comp. III,* I.xi.1, fol. 171*vb*); Bernardus Parmensis (*ad* X. I.vii.1, I.xxxiii.6); and Innocent IV (*Commentaria ad* X. I.vii.1, II.ii.10, I.xv.1, II.xxvii.27, v.xxxix.49) all discussed the source of papal authority and all emphasized its divine origin.

[17] E.g. Innocent III, X. I.vii.1, 'Cum ex illo generali privilegio quod *beato Petro* et per eum *ecclesiae Romanae* Dominus indulsit, canonica postmodum manaverint instituta continentia maiores ecclesiae causas ad *Sedem Apostolicam* perferendas....' Similarly, Bernardus Parmensis ad X. I.ii.3, 'Cum (*apostolica sedes*) sit iudex ordinarius omnium Christianorum ... et omnes dignitates ordinis cuiuscumque *ecclesia romana* constituit ... idem est in sententia *papae* quia sicut ipse iudicat alii iudicare debent.' Cf. Gratian, C. 24 q. 1 *dictum post* c. 16.

[18] *Commentaria ad* v.xxxix.49, 'Hoc enim privilegium Christus Petro in persona ecclesiae concesserit.'

auctoritatem et facta sint et robur acceperint, et in eorum statutis Romani pontificis patenter excipiatur auctoritas.[19]

The Decretalists never seem to have conceded that the legislation of a Council was superior to that of a Pope alone even when such an argument could have provided a convenient solution to a difficult problem. For instance, in the Lateran Council of 1215 Innocent III revoked the existing legislation on prohibited degrees of consanguinity and laid down that the impediment extended only to the fourth degree. This was a necessary and humane decision, but Gregory the Great had written, *Qui dissolvit haec genera affinitatis negat verbum Dei in aeternum manere.* How then could Innocent's decision be justified? A Decretist writer might have explained that the enactment of a General Council possessed a peculiar force that could override any papal pronouncement, but Bernardus Parmensis, in his *Glossa Ordinaria* on the Decretals, was content with the explanation that Gregory's very forceful words forbade only unnecessary modifications in the prohibited degrees and that they did not apply to his own successors.[20]

For the Decretalists, indeed, the canon of a General Council possessed binding force simply because it was supported by the authority of the Roman church (*omnia concilia per Romane ecclesie auctoritatem . . . robur acceperunt*). The promulgation of the *Gregoriana* itself provides an obvious example of this principle, for there we have quotations from the Fathers and from ecclesiastical histories, canons of Councils and decrees of Popes all possessing the same legal force by virtue of the papal bull that introduced them—a bull that was not itself authorized by any Council. The point is again illustrated by certain comments on the case of Anastasius, cardinal-priest of the title of St Marcellus, who was deposed by a Council during the pontificate of Leo IX:

> In hac synodo Anastasius, presbyter cardinalis beati Marcelli *ab omnibus* est depositus. . . .[21]

---

[19] *Comp. I,* i.iv.18; X, i.vi.4.

[20] Bernardus Parmensis *ad* X. iv.xiv.8, 'Gregorius tamen dicit, Qui dissolvit haec genera affinitatis negat verbum Dei in aeternum manere, 35 q. 10 *fraternitatis . . .* qualiter ergo Innocentius dissolvit? Hoc intellige sine causa, et ab alio quam a successore Gregorii.'

[21] *Comp. I,* iii.iv.2 and X. iii.iv.2. The passage is taken from the *Vita Leonis IX* (Mansi, *Sacrorum Conciliorum . . . collectio,* xiv, p. 398). On this work see H. Tritz, 'Die hagiographischen Quellen zur Geschichte Papst Leos IX', *Studi Gregoriani* iv, (Rome, 1952), pp. 191–364.

The text states quite clearly that Anastasius was deposed by the whole Council, and when it was first glossed in the 1190's the fact was not queried.[22] In the early years of the thirteenth century, however, Alanus put forward the view that the Pope alone deposed Anastasius, the other members of the Council merely signifying their approval:

> *Omnibus*, i.e. omnibus approbantibus quia solus papa ipsum deposuit.[23]

The importance of this opinion did not escape Tancred, who repeated it in his *Glossa Ordinaria* on the *Compilatio Prima*, and from there it passed into the *Glossa Ordinaria* on the Decretals.[24] Alanus's opinion was perhaps accepted the more readily since his conception of the Pope's role in a General Council corresponded quite closely to the actual practice of his great contemporary, Innocent III. Richard of St Germano has left a lively eyewitness account of Innocent's actions in the Lateran Council of 1215, when the important decision to confirm the imperial election of Frederick II was taken. When the subject came up for discussion a violent quarrel broke out between the Count of Monteferrato and the delegates of Milan. In the midst of the uproar Innocent flung up his hand for silence and stalked out of the assembly. At the next session of the Council, without further discussion, he presented to the Fathers his judgement in the case of Frederick together with other decisions. The confirmation of Frederick's election was evidently decided on by the Pope, not by the Council as a whole.[25]

The canonists' assertion that Leo IX alone deposed Cardinal Anastasius would seem to indicate that they exalted the Pope's personal

---

[22] E.g. the twelfth-century apparatus on the *Comp. I* in MS. 162 of the Cistercian monastery at Zwettl, Austria, made no comment on the rights of the Council or the Pope.

[23] Apparatus on the *Comp. I ad* III.iv.2, fol. 21va of MS. Cod. Aug. XL of the Badische Landesbibliothek, Karlsruhe.

[24] Tancred *ad Comp.* I. III.iv.2, MS. C.17 fol. 55rb; Bernardus Parmensis *ad* X. III.iv.2.

[25] 'Quod cum egre nimium ferrent Mediolanenses, ipsi marchionem ipsum mentitum fuisse, ceteris audientibus, alta voce clamantes, quia pars utraque in contumeliam prorumpebat, dominus papa manu innuit et, egredientibus ceteris, ipse ecclesiam est eggressus. De vero lune ultimo mensis Novembris . . . tertio se manifestavit dominus papa. . . . Ipso prius loquente prout spiritus dabat eloqui illi, et mentionem de comite sancti Egidii qui lapsus fuerat in heresim faciente . . . librum Johacim seu tratatum dampnavit . . . predicti etiam regis Frederici electionem per principes Alamannie factam legitime in imperatorem romanum approbans confirmavit. Et sancta synodus LXX capitula promulgavit.' *Chronica Regni Siciliae*, ed. Gaudenzi, *Monumenta Storici della Società Napoletana di Storia Patria, Serie Prima* (Napoli, 1888).

authority at the expense of the College of Cardinals as well as of the General Council. Certainly the extreme claims of the *Glossa Palatina* found no echo in the works of the earlier Decretalists, but the position was complicated by the fact that in actual practice the cardinals were playing an ever-increasing part in the government of the Church. The very centralization of ecclesiastical authority threw heavier responsibilities on these intimate counsellors of the Pope and administrators of his departments of state. Their enhanced authority was acknowledged in a letter of Innocent III, included in the *Gregoriana*, which at last provided a basis in legal theory for what had long been a matter of constitutional fact—namely, that the proper business of the cardinals was to assist in governing the affairs of the Universal Church:

> ... consideramus vero quod eiusdem Cardinalis presentia utilior sit non solum Romane sed etiam ecclesie generali apud apostolicam sedem quam apud ecclesiam Ravennatem.[26]

But this decretal did not in any way clarify the position of the cardinals in relation to the Pope; nor did the canonists' glosses on it. The most distinguished among the earlier commentators on the *Gregoriana* seem to have been somewhat embarrassed by the necessity for reconciling the undoubted constitutional importance of the cardinals with their rigid theory of papal monarchy and so fell into contradictions or took refuge in evasions. Goffredus Tranensis stated that the authority competent to found general constitutions was *papa cum fratribus suis*,[27] but elsewhere, applying to the legislative authority of the Pope an old Roman adage, he wrote *omnia autem iura sunt in pectore papae*.[28] Bernardus Parmensis asserted that the cardinals were *pars corporis domini papae*, but apparently used the phrase without technical significance, applying it to other members of the curia as well.[29] Innocent IV declared on one occasion that the business of the cardinals was the care of all the churches,[30] but elsewhere time and again reiterated that the Pope personally possessed *plenitudo potestatis*.

---

[26] *Comp. III*, I.iv.3 and X. I.v.3.

[27] *Summa*, fol. 2 n. 8. Goffredus, a cardinal himself, also declared that the Sacred College had the power, during a vacancy, to reject Alexander's election decree and to choose a new Pope by any method they pleased, *Summa*, fol. 16 n. 14.

[28] *Ibid.* fol. 2 n. 15. On this expression see F. Gillmann, 'Romanus pontifex iura omnia in scrinio pectoris sui censetur habere', *A.K.K.R.* XCII (1912), pp. 3 ff.

[29] *Ad* X. I.xxx.9, II.xl.14.

[30] *Commentaria ad* I.v.3.

The cardinals were always referred to with the utmost respect, but there was no clear-cut statement that the Pope was compelled even to consult them, still less to accept their advice.

2. *Decretalist Corporation Concepts*

The Decretalists were apparently quite happy to discuss in the abstract the theoretical limits of the Pope's powers but extremely reluctant to admit that there could be any human authority competent to enforce such limitations in practice. Their really important contribution to the growth of conciliar thought must therefore be sought in a quite different department of their work. It is to be found in their technical discussions on the structure of ecclesiastical corporations, a subject which at first sight seems altogether remote from the great issues of Church government. The Decretalists themselves, down to Innocent IV, certainly had no intention of providing arguments for critics of papal sovereignty; but in fact a more detailed analysis of the structure of corporate groups was precisely what was necessary to provide a sounder juristic basis for the rather vague 'constitutional' ideas that occur in the Decretist works. At every point where the Decretist arguments ended in an ambiguity a coherent theory of corporation law could help to clarify their implications. For instance, some of the Decretist glosses suggested that there was a power to maintain the true faith diffused throughout the whole Church which could be exercised *ab ipsa universitate*; the whole relevance of the suggestion for problems of Church government would depend on the agency by which the powers of a *universitas* could be exercised in canonistic doctrine—by the head or by the members? Again, if the General Council were considered as a corporate body with the Pope as its head—as was usual in the fourteenth century—then the law of corporations might be applied to define the relationship between the Pope and the Fathers of the Council, a matter of the greatest importance that was never adequately discussed by the Decretists. The same is most obviously true of the relationship between Pope and cardinals. The cardinals were compared to a bishop's chapter but, in the Decretist works, the analogy failed to provide a satisfactory definition of their constitutional status precisely because there was no adequate theory explaining the corporate structure of a cathedral church.

There were urgent practical reasons to lead the canonists to an increasing preoccupation with the problems of corporation law during the thirteenth century. In spite of the persistent tendency towards papal centralization, the whole Church, no less than the secular states, remained in a sense a federation of semi-autonomous units, a union of innumerable greater or lesser corporate bodies. Bishoprics, abbeys and priories, colleges, chantries and guilds, religious orders, congregations and confraternities all contributed to the life of the Church and, equipped with their privileges and immunities, exercised substantial rights of self-government. These lesser corporations had their constitutional problems no less than the all-embracing *universitas* of the whole Church, and the rising flood of litigation in the high Middle Ages made the solution of such problems a matter of pressing necessity. Moreover, the growth of new forms of corporate life in the Church, especially the universities and the orders of friars with their intricate systems of representative government, both reflected the half-formed juristic ideas of the age and stimulated the canonists to clarify those ideas, and to apply them to other ecclesiastical communities.

Questions of this sort were constantly arising on the level of practical litigation. Where did authority in a church reside, in the head or in all the members? And who were the 'members' of a church in this sense? Could a bishop act in the affairs of his diocese without consulting his canons? If so, in what types of business? If not, did he need the consent of the canons or only their counsel? Could an abbot take an oath on behalf of his whole convent of monks? Did he require consent of the monks to act as their representative in so doing? What was the source of a prelate's jurisdiction? How could a bishop be prevented from acting against the interests of his church? If he did act thus in bad faith, was his action binding on the church? Did the rights of a bishop devolve to his canons during an episcopal vacancy? Did they so devolve when the bishop was negligent?[31] In discussing such subjects the canonists displayed great subtlety of thought, and their analyses of the structure of a church, of the different elements in a prelate's authority, and of the relationship between the individual churches and the Church as a whole, together with the

---

[31] One has only to substitute the words, 'Pope', 'Cardinals', 'Council' for 'bishop', 'canons', 'convent' in such questions to realize how relevant the discussion of them might prove for the major problems of Church government. The circumstances of the fourteenth century were to encourage just such a transposition.

associated development of a more explicit doctrine of representation, provided indispensable elements in the construction of later theories of ecclesiastical authority.

The contribution of the thirteenth-century Decretalists to the development of corporation theory has been a subject of much technical controversy among modern scholars, and so a consideration of some modern accounts of the canonists' theories, and, still more important, of the canonists' own attitude to their problems seems desirable as a preliminary to an examination of the actual doctrines they evolved. Of particular importance from our point of view was the work of the great German jurist Gierke, for he especially emphasized the importance of canonistic corporation concepts for the general history of medieval political theory and ecclesiology. His own account of the canonists' doctrines was influenced by its presentation in the course of a large-scale synthesis of medieval juristic and political ideas.[32] In his monumental work, *Das Deutsche Genossenschaftsrecht*, Gierke was primarily concerned to trace the growth of the Germanic law of association, based on the concept of the organized group as a *Genossenschaft*, and so his section on the medieval canonists was mainly devoted to expounding the distinction between this Germanic idea of a 'corporation' (*Genossenschaft*) and the opposing (canonistic) concept of an 'institution' (*Anstalt*). In a corporation, according to Gierke, the principle of unity resided in the actual members who voluntarily came together to achieve an end determined by themselves. In an institution, on the other hand, the principle of unity, the end of the association, was imposed 'from outside and above'. This external principle—in the case of the Church it would be God himself—was, moreover, the true 'right-subject' (*Rechts-subjekt*) of the institution, its physical members being mere representatives of the transcendent authority that infused into them unity and a semblance of corporate life. Gierke thought that the doctrines of the canonists were by no means lacking in traces of the 'true corporation spirit' which was especially evident in their definition of the whole Church as a *universitas fidelium*, but that these tendencies were quickly overwhelmed by the 'institution ideas' that the canonists applied alike to the whole Church and to the individual churches. He described the process as 'a canonistic re-coining of the corporation idea'.

Closely associated in Gierke's theory with the distinction between

---

[32] *Das Deutsche Genossenschaftsrecht* (Berlin, 1868–1913), III, pp. 243–351.

Genossenschaft and *Anstalt* was a contrast between two opposed theories of corporate personality. The Germanic, 'properly medieval' doctrine recognized in the corporation a real group personality and a group will distinct from the personalities and wills of its individual members, and the canonists, Gierke thought, progressed some way towards this conception since they did tend to personify the individual churches. However, this progress was thwarted by the acceptance of Innocent IV's doctrine that the corporate personality was to be defined as a mere *persona ficta*, a fiction of the law. The failure of the medieval corporation doctrines to issue in a recognition of the real personality of the group was, in the eyes of Gierke, a central defect in medieval thought that left the way open for the absolutist doctrines of the Renaissance.

Gierke's immense erudition and remarkable synthetic powers have always commanded respect, but his point of view has not found universal acceptance. De Wulf vigorously assailed the philosophical foundations of his theory, and E. Lewis has criticized his interpretation of the 'organic' tendencies of the medieval publicists.[33] His account of the canonists' theories has been carefully examined by P. Gillet, who concluded that the texts cited by Gierke would not bear the interpretation he imposed on them, that the canonists did not really envisage an 'abstract right-subject' standing 'outside of and above' the corporation, but endowed the actual physical members of a corporation with true right-subjectivity.[34]

On the other hand, de Lagarde's continuing survey of the process of medieval disintegration seems to be essentially a resuscitation of Gierke's thesis, emphasizing a fundamental conflict in the Middle Ages between an 'organic' and an 'atomistic' theory of corporations, and the triumph of the latter view in the fourteenth century.[35] It

---

[33] M. de Wulf, 'L'individu et le groupe dans la scolastique du XIIIe siècle', *Revue néo-Scolastique de philosophie*, XXII (1920), pp. 341 ff.; E. Lewis, 'Organic tendencies in medieval political thought', *American Political Science Revue*, XXXII (1938), pp. 849–76. See also P. Duff, *Personality in Roman Private Law* (Cambridge, 1938), pp. 206–36; F. Brendan Brown, 'Canonical juristic personality', *The Jurist*, I (1941), pp. 66–73; W. Ullmann, 'Delictal responsibility of medieval corporations', *Law Quarterly Review*, LXIV (1948), pp. 79–96.

[34] P. Gillet, *La personnalité juridique en droit ecclésiastique spécialement chez les Décrétistes et les Décrétalistes et dans le Code de droit canonique* (Malines, 1927). Gillet gives a useful bibliography of the extensive earlier literature on theories of corporate personality.

[35] G. de Lagarde, *La naissance de l'esprit laïque au déclin du moyen âge* (Paris, 1934–1946). J. N. Figgis also showed himself sympathetic to Gierke's viewpoint. See his *Churches in the Modern State* (London, 1913), pp. 58–86.

seems, though, that Ockham is to take the place of Innocent IV as the chief intellectual agent of the disintegrative process.

It is not our purpose to take sides in these controversies, but rather to suggest that the preoccupation with the issues raised by Gierke has tended to distract attention from other no less important aspects of canonistic corporation doctrines. Gierke was one of those great scholars whose work in his chosen field forms an indispensable start-ing-point for later students, even for those who would reject his conclusions. Moreover, as Maitland pointed out, the last charge that could be brought against him was that of 'aimless medievalism'. On the contrary, he was convinced that his researches were directly rel-evant to the juristic and political problems of his own day. Hence there has been an almost inevitable tendency among some of his disciples—and his critics—to approach the problems of medieval thought with habits of mind engendered by modern controversies, a circumstance that does not make for a clear understanding of the purposes of the medieval writers themselves.

One feels, for instance, that in discussing the sociological ideas of the thirteenth century de Lagarde allows himself to be excessively influenced at times by the modern antithesis between the individual and the organized state.[36] When one turns from the broad issues of political speculation to the more technical problems of jurisprudence the same tendency is still more apparent. The partisans of both the Fiction Theory and the Realist Theory of corporations look for sup-port to the doctrines of the medieval jurists, and both parties even-tually find it necessary to deplore the 'inconsistencies' of canonists and civilians alike. But this is only another way of admitting that modern categories of thought do not provide an appropriate instru-ment for exploring the ideas of medieval lawyers. Gierke's own an-tithesis between *Genossenschaft* and *Anstalt*, the foundation of all his discussion on canonistic corporation doctrines, hardly seems to have been apparent at all to the medieval canonists themselves. They were not interested in discussing whether God had implanted authority in the Church, but in determining where he had implanted it. And the conclusion that exclusive authority was conferred on 'God's earthly representative', the Pope, was by no means so inevitable a

---

[36] He stresses the subordination of the medieval citizen to a society which pur-sued a 'common good' radically distinct from the sum of individual goods, e.g. *La naissance de l'esprit laïque* . . ., IV, pp. 170–89.

corollary of their thought as Gierke at this point in his work seemed
to suppose.

It would seem, then, that the particular emphases in Gierke's work,
entirely understandable in view of his own special purpose, have tended
to focus the attention of his successors on aspects of the canonistic
theories that might not have seemed of the first importance to the
canonists themselves.[37] They were not primarily interested in the
philosophical problems of a corporation's essence around which most
modern interest seems to centre, and none of the thirteenth-century
canonists thought it necessary to fabricate a metaphysical basis for
his theories.[38] In the fourteenth century Zabarella pointed out that
the theory of the real personality of the group could be defended
only in terms of an extreme Platonism, but he dismissed the whole
subject in a manner that seems to sum up adequately the attitude
prevailing among the canonists:

> ... tamen opinio Platonis salvatur a multis theologis ad sanum intel-
> lectum; quod pro nunc dimittamus eorum disputationi.[39]

The canonists usually regarded such problems as outside their own
special province. For every obscure reference in their works to the
underlying philosophical problem of the relationship between part
and whole, between individual and group, there are dozens of
pages of close argumentation concerning the constitutional *structure* of
a corporation, the actual distribution of authority between head
and members; and it was their treatment of such problems that was

---

[37] Gierke and Gillet, defending their different theories of group personality, produce very few texts of the canonists themselves which explicitly discuss this question.
They usually argue by citing series of texts relating to corporation structure which,
by a considerable effort of interpretative skill, can be presented as supporting one or
the other theory of corporate personality.

[38] The characteristic teaching of the canonists that real personality belonged only
to the individual seems sufficiently in accordance with the prevailing metaphysical
doctrine of 'moderate realism'—there was no need for the canonists to elaborate a
philosophical defence of such a generally accepted principle. On this see Gillet,
op. cit. pp. 146–9, criticizing the views of Clunet and Saleilles. At the beginning of
the fourteenth century Bartolus bracketed together 'omnes philosophi et canonistae'
as believing that 'totum non differt realiter a suis partibus'. Cited by W. Ullmann,
art. cit. p. 86 n. 5.

[39] Zabarella, *Commentaria ad* X. v.iii.28, fol. 50v*b* n. 6, 'Quidam dicunt quod
(universitas) non est aliud quam singuli de universitate ... pro quo est quia universalia
non sunt aliquid reale extra animam, unde reprobat Philosophus Platonem, ponentem
ideas universalium extra animam. Tamen opinio Platonis salvatur a multis theologis
ad sanum intellectum; quod pro nunc dimittamus eorum disputationi'.

to prove of special importance for the future theories of Church government.

Moreover, it seems possible to present an analysis of the canonists' theories of corporation structure without any further reference to the modern speculations concerning their concept of group personality, for the canonistic doctrines were not dependent on the acceptance or rejection (even implicitly) of such a concept. On the contrary, the same laws of corporation structure have been regarded as illustrating quite different theories of corporate personality. It was, for instance, a common opinion among the canonists that the head of a corporation was required to consult its members in certain types of business, and that some of the powers of the head devolved to the members during a vacancy. In Gierke's view we have here a case of an 'abstract right-subject' which is partially represented by the head of a corporation, but more completely by head and members together, while during a vacancy the task of representation falls on the members alone. But Gillet sees in the same constitutional provisions only an example of the rule that all the physical members of a corporation possess true right-subjectivity.[40] Whichever theory we accept, the constitutional fact remains that, within a corporation, authority could be exercised by the members as well as by the head—and it was facts of that sort upon which the conciliar thinkers were to build.

Again, the canonists' tendency to personify the individual churches, to discuss the problems of their internal structure in terms of anthropomorphic imagery, did not influence the actual content of their doctrines so much as is sometimes supposed. The head-and-body metaphor could so easily be adapted to support any constitutional solution suggested by the exigencies of a particular case. It was cited to prove that the head could not act without the members or, on the other hand, that the members were dependent on the head; that neither part of the corporation could act without the other or, alternatively (and precisely because of the intimate connexion between them), that authority could easily devolve from one part to the other. The anthropomorphic imagery provided the canonists with a vocabulary in terms of which such problems could be discussed conveniently, but neither metaphysical nor—as Maitland has it—metaphysiological theories really determined the content of their thought.

---

[40] Gierke, *op. cit.* pp. 303–11; Gillet, *op. cit.* pp. 156–62.

There is more of a case for supposing that their conclusions rested on a foundation of Roman law, for the canonists did indeed borrow certain important ideas from the Digest. Nevertheless, to them, the Roman texts were useful auxiliaries, to be accepted or rejected according to their suitability in a particular case, rather than prefabricated solutions that imposed themselves with obligatory force. The general method of the canonists is well illustrated in a passage of Bernardus Parmensis dealing with the question whether a bishop could sue or answer a charge in a court of law without consent of his chapter.[41] He first put forward the inevitable organic metaphor—prelate and chapter could not act separately since they were one body:

> ... nec prelatus sine consensu capituli, nec capitulum sine consensu prelati potest iudicium exercere, nec conveniri ... cum omnes unum corpus intelliguntur.

But he went on to cite a whole series of Roman law texts that would seem to point to the opposite conclusion:

> Sed contra videtur quod solus prelatus convenire et conveniri possit *ff quod cuiusque univer. l. ulti.* ubi dicit utilis actio administratori civitatis debetur, et *ff de cond. et demon. municipibus,* et *ff ad muni. municipes* et *C. de iura. ca. l.* ii § *hoc etiam, in fin.* ....

Then he proceeded to his own conclusion, suggesting that the prelate could act alone only in certain types of cases where the interests of his church could not possibly be injured, and remarking incidentally that the rules of Roman law were not binding in ecclesiastical cases:

> Nec in rebus ecclesiasticis stamus legibus illis sed canonibus. ...

He put forward the Roman law tenets as if to show that the organic metaphor did not provide the only way of approaching the problem, but then forged ahead to the solution that seemed to him most likely to promote the well-being of the Church.

This takes us to the heart of the canonists' achievement. They were determined that in these questions of corporation structure their doctrines should be genuinely responsive to the needs of the time, that they should provide effective guidance in the circumstances actually encountered in practice. The ultimate sanction of their prin-

---

[41] Gloss *ad* X. I.xxxviii.1.

ciples is to be found, not in contemporary philosophy nor even in Roman law, but in the applicability of those principles to the concrete problems of diocesan administration. The maintenance of orderly life in the Church—nothing less—was the real task that the canonists faced in dealing with the flood of litigation, usually petty in itself, concerning the authority of ecclesiastical corporations and the rights of their various members. It was a considerable intellectual achievement that they both solved the immediate problems and, in the process, evolved a subtle and harmonious theory of corporation structure. They themselves were not usually aware of the wider implications that their doctrines would acquire in later theories of Church government, but, when one considers the growth of such theories, it is important to bear in mind that the fundamental assumptions on which they rested were not abstract formulas, derived from external sources and imposed on the Church by doctrinaire reformers. They were rather principles of ecclesiastical authority that had grown up within the Church itself, engendered by the daily exigencies of medieval life.

The work of the thirteenth-century Decretalists presents us with something of a paradox. In the conflict of *regnum* and *sacerdotium* they were, almost without exception, extreme papalists. The greatest of them even find a place in the standard histories of political thought—a rare distinction for a medieval canonist—for precisely that reason. They were also staunch upholders of the Pope's sovereignty within the ecclesiastical hierarchy. And yet, working in a field that at first seemed remote from the great issues of Church government, they evolved doctrines which subsequently proved very valuable to the authors of anti-papal systems of ecclesiastical authority. The conciliar theories of the fourteenth century were nearly all, in greater or less degree, dependent upon the canonistic corporation doctrines of the preceding century. An analysis of those doctrines will help to illustrate the nature of the dependence.

CHAPTER TWO

THE STRUCTURE OF A MEDIEVAL
ECCLESIASTICAL CORPORATION

The study of Decretalist corporation theories, a somewhat tedious
and intricate task in itself, is enlivened by the insight it affords into
the minds of two of the most distinguished among medieval canonists.
These were Innocent IV, 'the greatest lawyer that ever sat upon the
chair of St Peter',[1] and Henricus de Segusio (Hostiensis), Cardinal-
bishop of Ostia, 'fons et monarcha iuris ... lumen lucidissimum
decretorum'.[2] Superficially their careers were not dissimilar. Both
studied at Bologna and afterwards lectured in canon law there, both
entered the service of the Roman curia, and each of them became
eventually bishop, cardinal and papal legate. Innocent, indeed,
achieved the supreme dignity of the Papacy, but Hostiensis might
well have attained even that eminence but for ill-health at the conclave
of 1270. The two great prelates had little else in common however.
Innocent is usually portrayed, and perhaps with reason, as the very
embodiment of that harsh legalism that was to fetter the life of the
Church in the later Middle Ages, while Hostiensis was remembered
at Bologna as a doctor who loved justice more than the law,[3] and
who tempered in a spirit of equity Innocent's harsh decisions.[4]

Nowhere are the attitudes of the two great canonists more clearly
exemplified than in their discussions on corporation structure. On
the central issue, the location of jurisdiction in a corporation, the
view of Innocent was as forceful and uncompromising as the character of the man himself, and, as one might expect, favoured a strict
authoritarianism:

---

[1] F. W. Maitland, *Selected Essays* (Cambridge, 1936), p. 228.

[2] M. Sarti, *De Claris Archigymnasii Bononiensis Professoribus*, ed. M. Fattorini (Bononiae,
1888), I, p. 443.

[3] Sarti apparently viewed this characteristic with suspicion, '... erat aequitatis magis
quam summi juris amator, sed verear ne iste aequitatis amor in juris canonici minus
laudabilis sit quam in iuris civilis interprete', *op. cit.* I, p. 444.

[4] G. Panciroli, *De Claris Legum Interpretibus* (Venetiis, 1655), 'Aequitatis amator,
duras Innocentii opiniones libenter damnat. ...'

> Et est notandum quod rectores assumpti ab universitatibus habent iuris-
> dictionem et non ipsae universitates. Aliqui tamen dicunt quod universi-
> tates deficientibus rectoribus possunt exercere iurisdictionem, sicut rectores,
> quod non credo. . . .[5]

The theory of Hostiensis was at once more subtle and more comprehensive. For him the authority of a corporation resided, not only in
its head, but in all its members as well, and he cited the opinion of
Innocent only to counter it with an emphatic denial.

> Quod reprobat (Innocentius) verius est licet difficilius.[6]

In their discussions on the various detailed problems that arose each
canonist was naturally influenced by his own doctrine, but there is
not the same sharp opposition in the working out of each particular
issue as on the underlying principle involved, for both, after all, were
free to speculate only within the framework of positive law established by the Decretals. This inevitably led Innocent to depart from
his declared position in considering particular cases. He often found
opportunities to emphasize the authority of a prelate over his Church,
but the canons themselves laid down that the members of an ecclesiastical corporation should play a considerable part in managing its
affairs and that they could exercise important rights of jurisdiction
during a vacancy.[7] Hostiensis, for his part, was no extreme radical,
and he was often content to borrow arguments that had been first
formulated by Innocent, to whom he always referred with great respect.[8] But his words were well chosen when he described his own
position as *verius licet difficilius*. Innocent's picture of a corporation was
simplicity itself; but it happened not to correspond either with the
facts of ecclesiastical life or with the recent decretals that had sought
to regulate that life. Hostiensis's view opened the way to all kinds of
difficulties and complexities, but, unlike Innocent's, it could serve as
a basis for a coherent and workable theory of the distribution of
authority within a corporation; and, accordingly, it was the position

---

[5] *Commentaria ad* X. i.ii.8.

[6] *Lectura ad* i.ii.8 fol. 6v*b*.

[7] Doctrines that Innocent necessarily accepted, but without reconciling them with
the general principle of corporation structure stated above, e.g. *Commentaria ad* X.
i.xxxiii.11, 'Episcopo enim mortuo, potestas iurisdictionis transfertur in capitulum . . .';
X. i.ii.8, '. . . in magnis negotiis capituli consensus requiritur. Item in alienationibus
voluntariis semper est necessarius consensus episcopi et capituli.'

[8] He did not usually refer to Innocent by name, but cited him simply as d.n.
(dominus noster).

of Hostiensis that found general acceptance among later generations of canonists. The various detailed problems that he discussed may be conveniently considered in three main groups: those concerning the status of the members of a corporation when they acted in association with the head, those dealing with the role of a prelate as representative of his corporation, and those relating to the authority of a corporation when it lacked a head.

1. *Head and Members*

It was laid down in the *Decretum* that a bishop needed the co-operation of his chapter in conferring benefices and privileges, in alienating church property, and also in judging cases.[9] These provisions were confirmed and extended in two letters of Alexander III which decreed that counsel of the canons was generally necessary in the conduct of the affairs of a church, and that privileges conferred without their approval were to be held invalid. These Alexandrian decretals formed the basis of much future discussion on the rights of the canons, but in them the terms *de consilio, de consensu* and *subscriptione* were used without any clear definition,[10] so that, as a preliminary to any further clarification of the canons' status, it was necessary to determine the precise significance of these words. Tancred held that subscription always implied consent when the subscriber signed with full knowledge and in his own name, and Bernardus Parmensis and Innocent IV followed him in this opinion.[11] However, the more important issue was to define the terms 'counsel' and 'consent', for at first there was a marked tendency to confuse the two expressions. Joannes Teutonicus even wrote that where *assensus* was required mere consultation might suffice—it was sufficient that consent had been sought even though it was not obtained;[12] and half a century later

---

[9] *Dist.* 24 c. 6, C. 10 q. 2 c. 1, C. 12 q. 2 c. 53, C. 15 q. 7 c. 6. Cf. *Glossa Ordinaria ad Dist.* 24 c. 6, 'Requiritur ergo consensus canonicorum in ordinibus conferendis . . . item in causarum diffinitionibus . . . item in conferendis beneficiis . . . item in privilegiis conferendis et aliis negotiis.'

[10] X. III.x.3, III.x.4, '. . . non decet te omissis membris aliorum *consilio* in ecclesiae tuae negotiis uti'. Cf. X. III.x.1, 'Irrita erit episcoporum donatio . . . absque collaudatione et *subscriptione* clericorum', and X. III.x.6, '. . . si constiterit conventus vel maioris et sanioris partis non affuisse *consensum*, institutiones huiusmodi convenit evacuari'.

[11] Bernardus Parmensis, citing Tancred, *ad* X. III.xiii.6; Innocent *ad* X. III.x.4.

[12] Gloss *ad Dist.* 63 c. 35, 'Videtur quod non tantum consilium religiosorum sed

Hostiensis could still refer to contemporaries who used the two terms indifferently.[13] In the meantime, however, Innocent IV had called attention to the distinction between them, and Hostiensis himself defined it quite clearly, emphasizing that the phrase *de consilio* did not imply any necessity for actual consent:

> Ubi consensus requiritur non valet quod agitur nisi consensus habeatur ... ubi vero consilium exigitur potest sequi consilium si vult is qui ipsum requirit, si non vult non habet necesse.[14]

Hostiensis was very anxious that the taking of counsel should not be merely 'derisory', and that a prelate should really respect the advice of his canons,[15] but none the less his definition does seem to rob Alexander's decretals of much of their force. His distinction, however, served only as an introduction to the real problem, to define the class of cases in which consultation would not suffice and actual consent was necessary.

This problem was greatly complicated by the growth within each ecclesiastical corporation of different spheres of rights.[16] The canonists had to take into account not only the rights of the corporation as such, and those of its members considered solely as individuals, but also a whole class of what might be termed intermediate rights, which Innocent IV defined as belonging to the *res ecclesiae singulariter ad quemlibet canonicum pertinentes*.[17] For instance, the revenues of a prebend belonged in a sense to the church, but more immediately to the particular individual who held the prebend; and there was a specially strong tendency for the chapter as a whole to acquire rights quite distinct

---

etiam consensus requirendus est ... si tamen fuit habitum consilium et non consensus tenet electio ... et expone consensu requisito licet non habito.'

[13] *Summa, De his quae fiunt ab episcopo*, col. 802, 'Alii dicunt quod consilium requiritur, i.e. consensus et his verbis consilio et consensu promiscue utuntur et secundum ipsos nulla est differentia inter consensum et consilium ... sed tales intelligunt sicut placet.' See also *Lectura ad* X. I.xliii.7. fol. 191rb, III.x.3 fol. 44ra, III.x.4 fol. 43vb; III.x.5 fol. 44va; and V.xxxi.1 fol. 69vb.

[14] Innocent, *Commentaria ad* X. III.x.4; Hostiensis, *Summa, De his quae fiunt ab episcopo*, col. 801.

[15] *Ibid.* 'Ex quo ipsum sequi non tenetur hoc videtur frustratorium et derisorium. Respondeo, licet non teneatur sequi tamen possit quod consilium capituli traheret praelatum ad se ... et breviter, sine consilio fratrum parum aut nihil facere debet praelatus.' Cf. *Summa, De officio ordinarii*, col. 298, 'Omnia fac cum consilio et tunc non poenitebis.'

[16] On this development see Gierke, *Das Deutsche Genossenschaftsrecht*, III, pp. 262–7, and Gillet, *La personnalité juridique*, pp. 160–2.

[17] *Commentaria ad* X. III.xi.4. Cf. Gierke, *op. cit.* pp. 297–8.

from those that the prelate possessed as head. Hence there could be no simple and general rule explaining when the consent of the canons was required in the conduct of the corporation's affairs, since their degree of responsibility varied according to the circumstances of the particular case. Moreover, it seemed to most of the canonists an oversimplification to suggest that prelate and chapter should each be solely responsible for actions touching their own particular rights. Certain rights did, indeed, pertain especially to specific individuals or groups within the corporation, but the whole corporation had an interest in seeing that such rights were not abused.[18] The aim of the canonists, therefore, was to associate all the members of a corporation in all its business while ensuring that the special interests of particular members were not unduly compromised.

Bernardus Parmensis devised an ingenious formula for this purpose which was later accepted by Hostiensis. He pointed out that there were three different types of corporation rights to be considered: those that pertained specially to the prelate, those that pertained specially to the chapter, and those that were held in common by prelate and chapter together. He suggested therefore that a syndic, actor or proctor for any case should be appointed:

> . . . ab ipso praelato de consensu capituli . . . et hoc cum negotium principaliter tangat praelatum . . . et si negotia principaliter tangant capitulum ab ipso capitulo constituatur de auctoritate praelati . . . et haec locum habent quando negotia capituli et praelati sunt discreta. . . . Si vero sunt communia, praelatus de consensu capituli constituit syndicum.[19]

The doctrine that consent of the canons should be required when any vital interest of the whole corporation was involved was the basis of Hostiensis's more elaborate statement of their position. In discussing the question of alienations he pointed out that their consent was necessary even in the case of property pertaining specially to the bishop, since bishop and chapter together formed a single corporate body which suffered as a whole from any loss,[20] but this insistence

---

[18] Thus Innocent IV argued that an abbot had a legitimate interest even in those revenues that pertained specially to the convent, '. . . nec haec possunt dici bona conventus discreta . . . cum multum iuris habeat (abbas) in eis, scil. administrationem, licet fructus dispensentur in usum monachorum tantum'. *Commentaria ad* X. I.iii.21.

[19] Gloss *ad* X. I.iii.21.

[20] *Lectura ad* X. III.x.4 fol. 44rb, 'Si quaeras rationem quare in alienatione rerum episcopalium requiritur consensus canonicorum, haec potest reddi, quia interest cuiuslibet canonici quod possessiones ecclesiae sive capituli non alienentur, et aeque

on the corporate unity of bishop and chapter raised further problems. Granted that consent of the whole body—head and members together—was required in matters touching the common welfare, there remained the question of how that consent was to be expressed. Did it require the unanimous opinion of the canons in support of the bishop? Or a majority of those present including the bishop? Or the *maior et sanior pars* as in an episcopal election? And if the decision rested with the *maior et sanior pars* what weight did the voice of the bishop carry in the assembly? How many canons had to support him to form a party of greater weight than the opposition? These were eminently practical questions that had to be answered in any adequate theory of corporation structure.

Their discussion was further complicated by the fact that in some churches the bishop had the right to sit in chapter in two different capacities, either *ut prelatus* or *ut canonicus.*[21] The distinction was discussed in some detail by Joannes Teutonicus, who launched himself into a sea of complexities when considering the apparently simple and sensible provision that a bishop should take it upon himself to correct an erring canon if the chapter possessed the right to do so but was negligent in exercising it. The question was one of considerable importance in the life of the local churches, since, as the canonists were quick to realize, the arguments involved could be applied to the conferment of prebends in the gift of the chapter as well as to the exercise of jurisdiction. Joannes argued that a right could not devolve from chapter to bishop through negligence, since the bishop, as head, was always a part of the chapter, and so shared

---

bene dicuntur possessiones ecclesiae illae quae pertinent ad episcopatum sicut illae quae pertinent ad canonicos sive capitulum. . . . Et idem forte dicendum, scilicet consensum canonicorum requirendum esse ubicumque eorum interest. . . . Tu dicas quod illa est ratio quare in alienatione rei episcopatus consensus canonicorum requiritur quia episcopus et canonici unum corpus constituunt.' Innocent IV presented a similar argument, *Commentaria ad* X. III.x.4.

[21] The canonists often pointed out that the different local churches followed their own particular traditions in such matters—*in diversis ecclesiis diversae sunt consuetudines.* The doctrines evolved by the canonists provided an influential norm which could be appealed to in doubtful cases, but to discover the actual practice in any medieval diocese on points of detail it is necessary to consult the records of that particular church. (For bibliography see Feine, *Kirchliche Rechtsgeschichte,* I, pp. 313–23.) Kathleen Edwards has provided a particularly interesting analysis of the relations between bishop and chapter in a group of English cathedral churches, *The English Secular Cathedrals in the Middle Ages* (Manchester, 1949), pp. 97–135. Her description of the actual practice in these churches seems to correspond quite closely with the canonistic theories discussed in this chapter.

in its negligence. And to conceive of the chapter acting without a head would be monstrous, he thought.[22] His eventual solution hardly seems to dispose of this difficulty. In spite of his opening arguments he concluded by admitting that, where such a custom existed, jurisdiction could be exercised by the chapter without its head. The question then was whether in such circumstances the bishop had a vote in the chapter not as head but as one of the canons. If so he shared in its negligence and no right could devolve to him; but if he were not 'of the chapter' then a right which the chapter neglected to exercise could devolve to him as bishop.[23]

The subsequent discussion of this problem proliferated into a sort of juristic jungle. Bernardus Parmensis took Joannes Teutonicus to task for his careless terminology. The bishop, he maintained, was always 'of the chapter'. The point was that he might be of the chapter in two different capacities, either *ut prelatus* or *ut canonicus*. If he shared a right with the canons in his capacity *ut prelatus* and neglected to exercise it, then it passed to a superior; but if he shared in the right *ut canonicus* then, although the whole chapter was negligent, the bishop was not negligent in his capacity *ut prelatus*, and the right could devolve to him as such.[24] Innocent IV (who seems to have been rather adept at inventing fictitious legal entities) accepted this point of view and added that when the bishop had the right of sitting *ut canonicus* he should be regarded as possessing two legal personalities—*fingitur gerere duas personas*.[25] He also pointed out that when

---

[22] Gloss *ad Comp. III*, I.xiii.1, MS. C.17 fol. 339vb, '. . . quomodo devolvitur haec potestas iudicandi de capitulo ad episcopum cum episcopus sit de illo capitulo, est enim caput capituli. . . . Si enim episcopus non esset de capitulo sequeretur quod capitulum esset monstrum non habens caput. . . .'

[23] *Ibid.* 'Ego credo ubicumque est episcopus de capitulo, si episcopus est negligens cum aliis, devolvitur ius eligendi vel corrigendi ad metropolitanum. Quandoque episcopus non est de capitulo . . . et tunc devolvitur potestas de capitulo ad episcopum.'

[24] Gloss *ad* X. I.xxxi.13, 'Nec videtur rationem habere, quod dicit Joannes, quod episcopus quandoque de tali capitulo sit, quandoque non; quandoque tamen episcopus interest electionibus non tanquam episcopus sed tanquam canonicus, et est specialis consuetudo in quibusdam ecclesiis, in quibus episcopus retinet ius canoniae et praeter redditus suos percipit aliquid de capitulo, et tunc est in electionibus tanquam canonicus . . . et tunc simpliciter transfertur potestas ad ipsum episcopum nisi malitiam adhibeat.' Bernardus added that when a right of correction devolved from chapter to bishop he should still exercise it with counsel of the canons because 'licet perdiderint ius corrigendi non perdiderunt ius commune quo debent cum episcopo in talibus interesse'.

[25] *Commentaria ad* X. I.xxxi.13, 'Nos dicimus quod si episcopus interest capitulo non tanquam episcopus sed quodam iure segregato tanquam canonicus . . . ita fingitur gerere duas personas.'

the bishop sat in chapter *ut canonicus* the meeting was only an assembly of canons, and so could transact only such business as pertained specially to the canons' affairs, and he suggested that the status of the bishop at any particular meeting could be determined from the weight that his voice carried in the discussion.[26]

In spite of these earlier speculations it was left for Hostiensis to attempt a systematic explanation of a prelate's authority in these two different capacities, and to relate the result to the existing doctrine on counsel and consent. It will be seen that in any final systematization there were two sets of factors to be included: first, the type of business being discussed (whether it touched especially the rights of the prelate, or the chapter, or of both parties equally), and secondly, the status of the prelate (whether he sat *ut prelatus* or *ut canonicus*). Hostiensis disposed of one case without difficulty by laying down that when corporation business touching the rights of the canons alone was under discussion the bishop could sit *ut canonicus*, with a vote that was only equal to that of each of the other canons; and, since he did not sit *ut prelatus* a right could devolve to him as bishop in case of negligence.[27] When business touching the prelate's rights was under discussion the issue was again quite straightforward. Hostiensis

---

[26] *Commentaria ad* X. III.viii.15. Innocent had a further subtlety peculiarly his own. He argued that, although when a bishop participated in the conferring of a prebend *ut prelatus* there could be no devolution of the right to him in case of neglect, nevertheless, if a dispute arose concerning the validity of the election there could be a licit appeal to him. Innocent's argument was very characteristic. The bishop, he suggested, formed *unum capitulum* with the canons in conferring the prebend, but he did not form a single body with them in the exercise of jurisdiction for that belonged to the bishop alone, the head of the corporation. '... licet episcopus et canonici faciant unum capitulum in electione non tamen est unum capitulum in iurisdictione facienda, imo cum ad solum episcopum pertineat iurisdictio, ad ipsum appellare licebit'. Hostiensis rejected this argument, *Lectura ad* v.xxxi.1 fol. 69vb.

[27] *Lectura ad* X. III.viii.15 fol. 41ra, '... diligenter est attendendum utrum episcopus intersit communibus tractatibus ut prelatus vel ut canonicus, in quo casu dicitur capitulum tantum canonicorum et non commune episcopi et canonicorum, quia episcopus sedet non ut episcopus sed ut canonicus, nec valet vox sua plus quam alterius canonici...'; fol. 41rb, '... si tanquam canonicus habet vocem a vobis ad ipsum devolvatur potestas tanquam ad superiorem....' Hostiensis' further discussion of the question provides an interesting insight into the actual workings of a cathedral corporation. He explained that a right belonging to the canons should not devolve to the bishop if he prevented them exercising it by fraud—if, for instance, he refused to attend the meeting, or influenced the one who had the duty of summoning a meeting, or used a party of favourites among the canons to prevent agreement, or himself refused to agree. But in this last case, Hostiensis pointed out, the canons could override the opposition of the bishop, since his vote was only equal to that of each canon.

suggested that then the bishop sat *ut prelatus*, and his vote was not equal to that of each of the other canons but was rather equal to that of the sum of all the canons' votes, so that the bishop with one canon could outvote the rest of the chapter. He added that even without such support the prelate's opinion was to be preferred. As Hostiensis noted, this was only a rather intricate way of restating the accepted doctrine that in some circumstances the counsel but not the consent of the chapter was required.[28]

The complexities in Hostiensis's analysis arise in his discussion of the third type of capitular assembly, in which affairs touching the common well-being of the whole corporation were considered. In this case again he maintained that the bishop normally sat *ut prelatus*,

> Hoc est de iure communi quo ad communes tractatus habendos in his quae ad episcopum et capitulum pertinent communiter quod episcopus habeat vocem in capitulo tanquam prelatus unde in talibus unus nihil debet facere sine reliquo. . . .[29]

It was all very well to write that neither party should act without the other, but if, whenever the bishop sat *ut prelatus*, he needed the vote of only one canon to make a majority, it would seem that the canons enjoyed no effective right of consent except in those relatively minor matters that concerned the chapter alone. Joannes Andreae indeed understood Hostiensis in this sense;[30] but Cardinal Zabarella rightly pointed out that he had misinterpreted the ideas of his great predecessor.[31] Although Hostiensis used ambiguous language in some of his discussions he did in fact state quite clearly that the rule of the prelate with one canon forming a majority applied only when the business under discussion was such that, *de iure communi*, merely counsel

---

[28] *Lectura ad* X. III.viii.15 fol. 41r*b*, 'Quando episcopus vocem habet in capitulo ut prelatus solus episcopus videtur habere vocem per se quantum omnes alii . . . idem in hoc casu dummodo habeat de capitulo secum duos vel unum saltem maiorem partem habet . . . et hoc considerato dicunt iura quod procedit episcopus de capituli consilio non consensu. . . .' *Ad* X. v.xxxi.1 fol. 69v*b*, '. . . in his in quibus episcopus habet vocem tanquam prelatus requiritur tam consensus episcopi quam capituli . . . verum si simul congregati discordent, episcopi est diffinitio cuius stabitur. . . .'

[29] *Lectura ad* X. III.viii.15 fol. 41ra.

[30] Gloss *ad Sext.* II.xv.11, 'Hostiensis dicit quod (episcopus) repraesentat mediam partem capituli et quod ipse et unus canonicus faciunt maiorem partem capituli . . . communis autem opinio doctorum est in contrarium.' The gloss is interesting as indicating that the *communis opinio* accepted the view that was in fact that of Hostiensis, although Joannes Andreae thought otherwise. See also his *Novella ad Sext.* II.xv.11 fol. 68 n. 3.

[31] Zabarella, *Commentaria ad* X. III.viii.15.

and not consent was required. In other matters affecting the well-being of the whole corporation the bishop could not act without consent of the chapter, or its *maior et sanior pars*, even though he sat among the canons *ut prelatus*:

> Quando episcopus vocem habet in capitulo ut prelatus solus episcopus tantam videtur habere vocem per se quantam omnes alii . . . idem in hoc casu dummodo habeat de capitulo secum duos vel unum saltem maiorem partem habet . . . sed et hoc intelligi debet quo ad collationes beneficiorum et institutiones . . . quae de iure communi *ad ipsum solum spectant*, nam in alienationibus et similibus necesse est quod *totum capitulum consentiat* vel maior et sanior pars ipsius.[32]

And in matters of this sort, since the bishop sat *ut prelatus*, there could be neither devolution of a right to him in case of negligence, nor a licit appeal in case of dispute. In both cases the matter was to be referred to a superior.[33]

Hostiensis, then, presents us with a three-fold classification. The prelate may sit *ut canonicus* with only the vote of a canon to discuss matters that belong especially to the chapter. He always sits *ut prelatus* to discuss common business, but is still unable to act without consent of the chapter. Only in considering matters that *de iure communi* belong to the prelate alone does he have an overriding authority to act even against the opposition of his canons.

One may perhaps feel a certain sympathy with a view held by some of Hostiensis's successors,

> Aequitatis amator, duras Innocentii opiniones libenter damnat, quamquam non desunt qui nimiae subtilitatis eum redarguunt.[34]

Hostiensis was indeed subtle, and in these questions of corporation structure it might seem at times over-subtle, but the quality did not arise from any mere legal obscurantism. The actual structure of a medieval corporation was very complex, and a law that could effectively regulate its internal life needed to be both intricate and flexible. If, however, we set aside the complications arising from the different 'right-complexes' within the corporation and the different roles of the prelate, and consider what Gierke called 'the pure corporation concept', a quite clear-cut and most important principle emerges from

---

[32] *Lectura ad* III.viii.15 fol. 41r*b*.
[33] *Lectura ad* V.xxxi.1 fol. 69v*b*.
[34] G. Panciroli, *De Claris Legum Interpretibus* (Lipsiae, 1721), p. 330.

the discussions of the canonists. In the first half of the thirteenth century they built up the doctrine, denied only by Innocent IV and hardly challenged after Hostiensis, that authority in a corporation was not concentrated in the head alone but resided in all the members; and as a practical consequence it followed that the prelate could not act without consent of the members in the more important matters affecting the well-being of the whole corporation. It is not difficult to appreciate the possible relevance of this principle to wider issues of Church government than those involved in diocesan squabbles. To take only the most obvious of several possible applications—if the corporation doctrines that have been discussed were applied to the College of Cardinals (a corporate body with the Pope as its head charged with the government of the whole Church) then they could provide a firm juristic basis for most of the claims on behalf of the Sacred College that had been put forward, though without any such foundation, in earlier works like the *Glossa Palatina*. But before we turn to these further developments it is necessary to describe certain other aspects of Hostiensis's corporation theory that were to prove even more important for the future.

2. *The Prelate as Proctor*

In the cases that have been discussed the bishop always appears (whether *ut prelatus* or *ut canonicus*) as an integral part of his corporation, sharing with the canons the responsibility for guiding its affairs. There remains, however, a whole category of cases in which he played a somewhat different part, when he acted alone in a legal suit on behalf of his church, charged with the task of defending the interests of the whole body over which he presided as head. When the canonists considered the position of a prelate acting in this capacity there were two main problems for them to resolve. The first was to explain how far he could proceed in such matters on his own initiative, that is to say, without express authorization from the members of the corporation. The second was to define the precise juristic relationship between prelate and corporation in such cases, to explain how one man could in fact take an oath on behalf of a whole group or bind them by his decisions. Such questions, which may seem mere legal technicalities in themselves, assumed a considerable importance in the development of thirteenth-century ecclesiology, since their discussion led to detailed inquiries into the origins and limits of a prelate's power. The inevitable starting-point for such inquiries was the accepted fact that, when a prelate appeared in a court of law on behalf of his church, it was not his own possessions that he defended; he did not possess legal *dominium* over the ecclesiastical property entrusted to his protection; his status, therefore, had to be defined as that of one who represents the interests of another party. The canonists often discussed the question where actual *dominium* did reside and usually agreed that, while God himself was the ultimate owner of all the goods of the Church, *dominium* over them in an earthly sense belonged to the ecclesiastical community. Huguccio attributed it to the *congregatio fidelium*,

> ...illa bona competant ecclesiae catholicorum, non enim parietibus sed congregationi fidelium.[35]

The *Glossa Palatina* and *Glossa Ordinaria* to the *Decretum* both held that *dominium* rested with the clergy as *dominium* over the goods of a corporation with its members,

> Dic dominium esse apud clericos sicut dominium rerum universitatis apud cives....[36]

Goffredus Tranensis defined the holder of *dominium* as the *universitas loci*,[37] a view repeated in the *Glossa Ordinaria* to the *Gregoriana*.[38] The gloss *Ecce Vicit Leo* suggested that ownership of the property of all the churches in a diocese might be vested in the chapter of the cathedral church, but found this view unacceptable, since the property of such a corporation might be inherited by a single surviving member.[39] It

---

[35] Cited by Gillet, *op. cit.* p. 101.

[36] *Glossa Ordinaria ad* C. 12 q. 1 c. 13, 'Quaeritur quis sit dominus rerum ecclesiasticarum.... Potest dici quod ecclesia sit domina... sicut haereditas est domina.... Alii dicunt quod ipse Deus.... Vel dic dominium esse apud clericos sicut dominium rerum universitatis apud cives.' *Glossa Palatina ad* C. 12 q. 1 c. 13, MS. Pal.Lat.658 fol. 49*vb*, '... ergo apud ecclesiam est dominium earum... et dicunt quidam apud ecclesiam scilicet locum illum parietibus circumclusum... alii dicunt quod dei est proprietas... tu dic dominium earum esse apud clericos sicut rerum universitatis est apud ipsos cives'.

[37] Cited by Guido de Baysio, *Rosarium ad* C. 12 q. 1 c. 13.

[38] *Ad* X. v.xl.13.

[39] MS. F.XI.605 *ad* C. 12 q. 1 c. 13 fols. 61*vb*–62*ra*, 'Ecce quod res ecclesie dicuntur communes sed cuius vel quorum est proprietas illarum rerum. Solutio; dicunt quod universitatis ita quod nullius de universitate quia potest esse aliquid universitatis ita quod nullius ut infra eadem, questio ii, *qui manumittitur*. Unde redditus parochialis ecclesie erit proprietas conventus episcopalis ecclesie. Sed secundum hoc... sequeretur quod unus si totum capitulum preter unum decesserit habeat proprietatem rerum

seems to have been an overriding consideration in the minds of the canonists that no one person should have the right to dispose of the goods of a church as his own property. To explain a prelate's right to act on behalf of his church they therefore made use of various Roman law analogies, comparing him to a *tutor, actor, administrator*, while, in the texts of both *Decretum* and Decretals, the status of a prelate in relation to the property of his church was defined as that of a *procurator*.[40] It was this idea of the prelate as proctor of his corporation that Hostiensis was to emphasize as an integral part of his theory of corporation structure.[41]

Gaines Post has observed that the earlier canonistic references to the prelate as proctor of his church do not provide evidence of true proctorial representation of a corporation—'true corporate representatives these proctors are not—they are apparently prelates acting as agents of their churches'.[42] In this connexion it is interesting to note that in the second half of the twelfth century, to define the authority which a bishop derived from election before his subsequent consecration, the canonists did sometimes use the technical terminology which Roman law applied to the definition of a proctorial mandate and which the canonists themselves were beginning to adapt for the same purpose.[43] Moreover, even if it be conceded that at that time the description of the prelate as proctor of his church was more of a metaphor than a formal juristic definition, it must be emphasized that the position changed significantly in the first half of the thirteenth

---

ecclesiasticarum et hoc esset inconveniens dicere. Ideo melius potest dici quod proprietas dei est vel pauperum . . . sed dispensatio pertinet ad episcopum et canonicos.'

[40] C. 12 q. 1 c. 26, C. 23 q. 7 c. 3, 'Non sunt illa nostra sed pauperum quorum procurationem gerimus'; X. III.xxiv.2, 'Fraternitatem tuam credimus non latere quod cum episcopus et quilibet praelatus ecclesiasticarum rerum sit procurator non dominus, conditionem ecclesiae meliorare potest, facere vero deteriorem non debet.'

[41] The description of the prelate as proctor recurs frequently in both his *Summa* and *Lectura*, e.g. *Summa, De his quae fiunt ab episcopo*, col. 800, 'Praelatus sit procurator generalis ad negotia . . . et liberam administrationem videatur habere'; *De treuga et pace*, col. 317, 'Si dicatur episcopus pater est tamen ecclesiae procurator'; *De procuratoribus*, col. 337, 'Episcopus dominus non est sed procurator'; *De rescriptis*, col. 76, 'Capitulum non dicitur procurator ecclesiae sed prelatus'; *Lectura ad* X. I.xxxvi.3 fol. 165va, '. . . prelatus procurator est habens generalem et liberam administrationem'; X. III.xxiv.2 fol. 67ra, 'Quamdiu ergo bene administrat, procurator et prelatus est.'

[42] 'Roman law and early representation in Spain and Italy', *Speculum*, XVIII (1943), pp. 211–32 at p. 214. See also *idem*, 'Parisian masters as a corporation', *Speculum*, IX (1934), pp. 421–45 at pp. 430–8.

[43] E.g. a bishop could be said to acquire *plena auctoritas* or *plena potestas*. Rufinus, *Summa ad Dist.* 23 p. 52; Huguccio, *Summa ad Dist.* 79 c. 9, MS. LC.2 fol. 141va.

century. Then the canonists found themselves obliged by new problems raised in the contemporary decretals to define with all the technical resources at their command the precise nature of the proctorial mandate conferred on a prelate and the precise extent of the powers that he could exercise by virtue of it.

It was certain at any rate that he could not go so far as to alienate the property of his church without formal approval of the canons, and Alexander III added that the chapter could repudiate a *transactio* made by the prelate without its consent, that is to say, a settlement with the opposing party in a lawsuit.[44] On the other hand a decretal of Innocent III clearly established that a prelate, by virtue of his office, could act in a suit on behalf of his whole corporation:

> Edoceri postulastis a nobis, utrum per litteras adversus abbates, nulla mentione habita de suis conventibus impetratas teneantur abbates ipsi super causis quae ad conventus pertinent ... respondere ... duximus respondendum, quod per appellationem se tueri non possunt quominus debeant auctoritate litterarum huiusmodi legitime respondere. Cum ex officio suo teneantur congregationum suarum negotia procurare. Nisi forte abbatis et conventus negotia essent omnino discreta.[45]

Innocent's decision still did not explain, however, whether the abbot was required to consult his convent before responding to the citation or how far he could proceed in the case without reference to it. On these points there was lively discussion among the canonists at the beginning of the thirteenth century.

Laurentius maintained that a bishop could not act or respond to a suit without consent of his chapter,[46] but Vincentius held that he did not require any special authorization and could act on his own initiative like a *tutor* or *actor*. He cited in support of this view certain sections of the Digest which were always a favourite source of arguments in subsequent discussions of the problem.[47] To act or respond, however, were merely procedural matters, and Vincentius acknowledged that a bishop could not carry the case to a conclusion and

---

[44] X. I.xxxvi.3.

[45] X. I.iii.21.

[46] His opinion was cited by Innocent IV, *Commentaria ad* X. I.iii.21, 'Sed nunquid si abbas egerit necessarius est consensus conventus ... Lau(rentius) dicit quod sic.'

[47] Gloss *ad Comp. I*, III.ix.4, MS. C.17 fol. 59ra, 'Quero an audiatur episcopus exercens actiones pro ecclesia sua sine litteraris capituli de rato. Et dico quod sic, sicut administrator decurionum, *ff Quod cuiusque univer. l. ult.*, et tutor non cavet de rato nisi vero dubitatur an sit tutor, *ff De admin. tu. l. vulgo*, nec actor ... *ff Quod cuiusque univer. item eorum § actor. ...*'

negotiate a settlement by virtue of his ordinary powers. To do this required a mandate of *libera et generalis administratio* for which the consent of the chapter was necessary.[48] Joannes Teutonicus seemed undecided about the nature of a prelate's proctorial power. The prelate did not have quite the *libera et generalis administratio* attributed to a *procurator Caesaris*; on the other hand, he had rather more freedom than a simple proctor, since, in spite of the general rule against alienations, he sometimes by local custom had the right of making small gifts from the property of the church.[49] Bernardus Parmensis was extremely wary and disposed to limit stringently the bishop's freedom of action. A prelate could not alienate, he held, and therefore he could not act or defend without special authority, for

> ... qui non potest alienare non potest rem in iudicium deducere.

Moreover, Bernardus thought, if prelates could embark on legal cases without reference to their chapters, they might practise collusion to the detriment of their churches.[50] He therefore recognized only a small class of cases, such as the recovery of improperly alienated property, where the prelate could act alone, since the church stood only to gain and could not suffer injury from them. Innocent IV, at the other extreme, characteristically claimed the widest powers for the prelate in his capacity as *administrator*.[51]

---

[48] *Ibid.* 'Dico quod episcopus non habet liberam administrationem nisi vero habet consensum capituli....' A decree of Alexander III (X. I.xxxvi.3) laid down that a prelate needed a special mandate from his chapter to 'transact'.

[49] Gloss *ad* C. 12 q. 1 c. 26, '...prelati dicuntur procuratores rerum ecclesiasticarum ut hic... quandoque domini dicuntur... quandoque defensores... quandoque patres... non tamen habent liberam et generalem administrationem sicut procurator Caesaris... modicum tamen donare possunt... tamen loco domini habentur cum bene administrant, loco praedonis cum male...'; *Ad* C. 23 q. 7 c. 3, '...tamen licet praelatus dicatur procurator magis habet liberam administrationem quam simplex procurator, unde aliquantulum dare potest si hoc habet consuetudo regionis'.

[50] Gloss *ad* X. I.xxxviii.1, '...colligitur evidenter quod nec praelatus sine consensu capituli, nec capitulum sine consensu praelati potest iudicium exercere nec conveniri, quia nec alienare potest alter sine reliquo nec commutare nec donare... et praeterea dicit lex quod qui non potest alienare non potest rem in iudicium deducere... si praelatus sine consensu capituli posset agere vel conveniri et praeiudicaret ecclesiae factum praelati, fraus posset fieri ecclesiae et praeiudicium: quia permitterent, immo procurarent quandoque praelati se conveniri et facerent collusionem'.

[51] *Commentaria ad* X. I.iii.21, 'Sed quid de episcopo utrum potest agere sine consensu capituli vel econverso... respondemus quod quicumque vel quaecumque habet administrationem potest agere et conveniri sine consensu alterutrius, *ff Quod cuiusque univer. l. fin.*' He went on to argue that in some circumstances a prelate could act without consent not only in common business but even in cases pertaining to the separate revenues of the convent.

Once again it was left for Hostiensis to provide a final clarification of the whole problem and to show how the more valuable elements in the views of his predecessors could be preserved and harmoniously combined with the existing doctrines on counsel and consent and on the distribution of property rights within a corporation. He realized that an adequate definition of the prelate's status must concede to him that freedom of action which was essential for the efficient transaction of day-to-day business in a litigious age, while ensuring that the authority he exercised was of a purely derivative nature and could not be used to injure the well-being of the church. He agreed, therefore, with Innocent against Bernardus Parmensis that a prelate could act in common business without a special mandate from the chapter but carefully defined the capacity in which he appeared in such a case:

> Quid si omnia habent communia . . . ibi praelatus nomine suo et capituli, etiam sine consensu ipsius, et agit et defendit . . . nisi contra ipsum orta sit suspicio . . . cum praelatus sit procurator generalis ad negotia . . . et liberam administrationem videatur habere.[52]

A *procurator generalis ad negotia* was appointed, not merely for one particular case, but with authority to act in any suits that might arise during his proctorship, and Hostiensis added that in his view such a mandate empowered a proctor to act in administrative as well as purely judicial affairs. Normally, when the mandate of a general proctor was strengthened by the formula conceding to him *libera administratio* or *plena potestas* he could conduct almost any business on behalf of his principal including alienation and 'transaction'; but, in discussing the relationship between bishop and chapter as head and members, Hostiensis had insisted on the need for consent of the canons where their own interests were involved;[53] moreover, the powers of alienation and 'transaction' were expressly denied by positive law to a prelate acting without consent of his chapter. Hostiensis therefore had to modify the civilian doctrine of proctorship to conform to the canons. He was able to do so without inconsistency by applying to

---

[52] *Summa, De his quae fiunt ab episcopo*, col. 800.

[53] Quite consistently therefore he prefaced his claim of *libera administratio* for the prelate acting as proctor with the reservation that if the special interests of the canons were likely to be prejudiced in any particular case their consent should be obtained. 'Si quaeratur de judicialibus et posset praejudicari capitulo quo ad subjectionem et limitationem consensus capituli requiritur.'

these particular cases a commonly accepted principle of Roman and canon law—that no proctorial mandate, however broad its terms, could confer on its recipient a right wilfully to injure his principal. As for alienations Hostiensis explained that,

> Per haec verba (libera administratio) non datur potestas male administrandi ... bene datur potestas aliquid conferendi ... sed non conceditur perdere ... ergo nihil alienabit in ecclesiae detrimentum.[54]

So too with 'transactions',

> ... praelatus procurator est ... habens generalem et liberam administrationem ... sed talis potest transigere ... Respondeo, liberam administrationem habet dum bene administrat, non quando ecclesiam spoliat.[55]

Alienation and transaction were treated as matters prejudicial to a church and so full powers in these matters were not included even in a mandate of *libera administratio*. The bishop was, however, free to conduct every-day legal business without constant reference to the chapter over trifles, always provided that he acted in good faith. If there was any suspicion concerning his integrity his mandate in any particular case could be revoked and his subsequent actions repudiated. A prelate could thus be held to account for any abuse of the power that he exercised on behalf of his church.[56]

This view of a prelate's authority solved not only the practical problem of how the necessary freedom of action of the prelate could be secured without endangering the interests of his church, but also the theoretical one of why the affairs of a whole community could be comprised in a summons addressed to its head alone. The most obvious and direct explanation of the fact would have been that all the power and jurisdiction of a church resided in the head; that for all practical purposes the prelate was the church. Moreover, such a view was not without support in earlier canon law. A passage of Cyprian taken into the *Decretum* had laid down that the life of a church was epitomized in its bishop,

---

[54] *Lectura ad* X. i.vi.19 fol. 40v*b*.

[55] *Lectura ad* X. i.xxxvi.3 fol. 165va.

[56] *Summa, De his quae fiunt ab episcopo*, col. 800, 'praelatus nomine suo et capituli ... et agit et defendit ... nisi contra ipsum orta sit suspicio'. In the next century Henricus de Bohic remarked, with a reference to Hostiensis, that ecclesiastical prelates could be elected for life, unlike civil magistrates, because they were not lords but proctors and so easily subject to correction. *Distinctionum Libri Quinque ad* X. iii.i.7. On the revocation of proctorial mandates see X. i.iii.33, i.xxxviii.4.

> Scire debes episcopum in ecclesia esse, et ecclesiam in episcopo, et si quis cum episcopo non sit in ecclesia non esse.[57]

As might be expected Innocent IV did cite this passage in his gloss on the decretal *Edoceri*, but he, like his predecessors, acknowledged that the word *ecclesia* did not always refer to the bishop alone.[58] Indeed, an unqualified acceptance of Cyprian's definition was hardly possible for the canonists. They could not consistently maintain that all authority in a church was concentrated in its head when, in discussing various problems of corporation structure, they had attributed to the members a considerable share in managing its affairs. Certain other analogies that were popular with the canonists throughout the Middle Ages were open to the same objection. The favourite anthropomorphic imagery presented the chapter apart from the prelate as a 'headless' being, incapable of any independent action, and the comparison of the prelate to a *tutor* or *actor* assumed that the chapter was a minor and again legally incapable. The proctorial concept as developed by Hostiensis avoided these difficulties. It provided, not merely an analogy, but a definition of the prelate's position, and a definition that explained in a clear and technically precise fashion how he could be at once an embodiment of his corporation's authority and its responsible agent—in the fullest sense of the word a representative.

Gaines Post[59] and, from a different point of view, de Legarde[60] have emphasized the importance of the canonistic doctrine of representation in the general history of medieval representative institutions; but neither has been concerned with the thirteenth-century development of the theory of the prelate as proctor of his corporation. It may be that in this refinement of the proctorial concept is to be found an important link between the earlier medieval concept of representation as mere personification and the later idea, growing ever more explicit in the fourteenth century, that a true representative needed an actual delegation of authority from his community; for it

---

[57] C. 7 q. 1 c. 9.

[58] *Commentaria ad* X. i.iii.21, 'Nomine enim praelati ecclesia intelligitur ... et ecclesia est in episcopo, 7 q. 1 *Scire*. Quandoque tamen nomine ecclesiae non designatur episcopus.' *Ad* X. v.xl.19, 'Nota per "ecclesia" hic intelligi capitulum maioris ecclesiae ... quandoque autem intelligitur tantus episcopus ... quandoque viri ecclesiastici ... quandoque quaelibet ecclesia ... quandoque congregatio fidelium. ...'

[59] *Artt. citt. supra* p. 11 n. 2.

[60] 'L'idée de représentation dans les œuvres de Guillaume d'Ockham', *Bulletin of the International Committee of Historical Sciences*, ix (1937), pp. 425–51.

was generally agreed among the canonists that the jurisdiction and administrative authority of a bishop were derived from election, not from consecration, to the episcopal order.[61] Hostiensis gave a general formulation to the principle:

> Universitas facit iudicem ordinarium eligendo ipsum ... potest igitur dici quod omnes ministri ecclesiae qui per electionem creantur iurisdictionem ordinariam habent, ex quo administrationem consequuntur.[62]

The implications that could be deduced from his position are strikingly illustrated in a case of 1313 involving the canons of Lincoln. In the course of one of the frequent disputes concerning their rights the canons found occasion to set forth their own view on the relationship between bishop and chapter. They maintained that jurisdiction was vested in the canons; that during a vacancy they exercised it; that when the see was occupied the bishop could exercise it only with their counsel or consent; and that, on his death, it returned to the chapter as to its source. And in support of these claims they cited the authority of Hostiensis:

> Quod resideat in capitulo patet quia secundum dominum Hostiensem. Capitulum habet iurisdiccionem a iure et de iure per illud sede vacante exercetur, et sede plena sine ipsius Capituli consilio vel consensu nequit per Episcopum exerceri nec sine consensu Capituli alienari, et sede iterum vacante redit ad Capitulum ut ad fontem.[63]

---

[61] E.g. Rufinus *ad Dist.* 23 p. 52, 'Quaeri solet si in electione confirmatus ante episcopalem unctionem usque adeo plenam auctoritatem possideat ... sed dicimus quod plenam auctoritatem habeat quo ad administrationem, non autem quo ad dignitatis auctoritatem ...'; Stephanus *ad Dist.* 23 p. 35, 'Habet enim electus potestatem administrationis, non auctoritatem dignitatis.' The prelate did not enter upon the full exercise of his authority until his election was confirmed, but it was commonly held that confirmation did not actually confer a new authority, but only freedom to exercise the authority already derived from election. Thus Joannes Teutonicus *ad Dist.* 63 c. 10, 'Si quaeras quale ius acquiritur electo per electionem dico quod ius praelaturae et ius administrandi sed non exercitium praelaturae vel administrationis. Per confirmationem enim nihil iuris novi acquiritur sed tantum exercitium.' According to Guido de Baysio this was also the view of Alanus, Laurentius and Huguccio, *Rosarium ad* C. 8 q. 2 c. 2, 'Dicunt quidam quod hic de confirmato loquitur ... ex sola enim electione secundum eos non efficitur quis praelatus. Sed secundum Ala., Hu., et Lau. si recte capitulum inspiciatur aperte dicitur quod ex electione efficitur quis praelatus et videtur statim habere administrationem rerum ecclesiae.' Hence, when confirmation was unavoidably delayed, it was provided in the Decretals that a prelate could exercise the powers derived from election even before his confirmation, X. I.vi.44. On the views of Huguccio see also Mochi Onory, *Fonti Canonistiche*, p. 151.

[62] *Summa, De officio ordinarii*, col. 289. Cf. Gierke, *op. cit.* III, p. 304 n. 175.

[63] *Statutes of Lincoln Cathedral*, ed. H. Bradshaw and C. Wordsworth (Cambridge, 1897), p. lxxvi. Cf. Kathleen Edwards, *op. cit.* pp. 97–8.

Maitland cautiously observed on this passage, 'I doubt whether Hostiensis would have committed himself to a statement which makes the Chapter to be "the fount" of episcopal jurisdiction.' The canons were certainly over-simplifying Hostiensis's position. He had a genuinely high conception of the episcopal dignity and would not have wished the bishop to be presented as merely subservient to the chapter. Moreover, it is proper to insist that the doctrine of a prelate acquiring authority by virtue of his election did not necessarily imply that the body making the election delegated its own authority to the chosen candidate. Yet Hostiensis's treatment of the prelate's status as proctor of his church certainly did tend to blur the rather fine distinction involved and so to open the way for the extreme position adopted by the Lincoln chapter.

3. *Episcopal Vacancies*

If the bishop's administrative and judicial authority were to be regarded as derived from the chapter the question would naturally arise of how the canons could confer an authority that they did not themselves possess. It might be replied that they did possess such authority, at least *in habitu*; but eventually the question lost most of its force for, during the thirteenth century, the doctrine gradually became established that the chapter could in fact exercise nearly all the powers conferred on a bishop by election. The canons of Lincoln in 1313 were confidently claiming that, *sede vacante*, the jurisdiction of the church could be exercised by themselves.

The decisive factors which encouraged the growth of this doctrine were the Roman law tenet that the rights of a corporation lived on in its surviving members,[64] and, more important for the canonists, a decretal of Lucius III imposing on cathedral chapters the duty of judging heretics during an episcopal vacancy.[65] Alanus realized that this was to decree in effect that the ordinary jurisdiction of a bishop could devolve to his chapter, and this fact was generally accepted by his successors, including Hostiensis.[66] There was much more discussion

---

[64] Digest, *Quod cuiusque univer. l. sicut* (III.iv.7).

[65] X. v.vii.9.

[66] Alanus *ad Comp. I*, v.vi.11, MS. C.17 fol. 115r*b*. Bernardus Parmensis *ad* X. I.xxxiii.14, v.vii.9, Innocentius IV, *Commentaria ad* X. I.xxxiii.11, v.xxx.30; Hostiensis, *Summa, De officio ordinarii*, col. 299.

concerning the administrative powers of the chapter during a vacancy, and especially concerning its right to confer prebends. The
more usual opinion during the thirteenth century held that its powers in this sphere were limited to those matters which in any case
pertained specially to the canons.[67] At the end of the century, however, Boniface VIII ruled that during a vacancy the canons alone
could make a collation that normally belonged to bishop and chapter together, and, accordingly, the fourteenth-century commentators
on the *Sext.* like Guido de Baysio and Joannes Andreae recognized
that at such times the canons possessed full administrative and jurisdictional authority in all matters that were normally dealt with by
the whole corporation.[68]

The discussions on the powers of the canons during a vacancy led
the canonists to emphasize their distinction between powers derived
from election and those conferred by ordination. Even before the
decretal of Lucius III, Rufinus had suggested that during a vacancy
the chapter should exercise all episcopal jurisdiction except that conferred by consecration.[69] Alanus added that authority pertaining to
the episcopal order devolved to a superior during a vacancy, and his
argument was repeated and expanded by Bernardus Parmensis and
Hostiensis.[70] Meanwhile Innocent IV had formulated the general rule
that when a prelate died his jurisdiction should return to the authority that had bestowed it in the first place.[71]

There were thus two quite distinct elements in a bishop's authority—
one set of powers derived from election, which devolved to inferiors

---

[67] The distinction was emphasized by Hostiensis who held that, during a vacancy,
the chapter possessed full rights of jurisdiction but powers of administration only in
those affairs pertaining specially to the chapter, *Summa, Ne sede vacante,* col. 797.

[68] *Sext.* III.viii.1, 'Si ad episcopum et capitulum communiter pertineat collatio
prebendarum, mortuo episcopo vel a beneficiorum collatione suspenso, poterit capitulum vacantes conferre prebendas etiamsi episcopus interesse habeat in collatione
huiusmodi ut praelatus.' For earlier views on the limits of the chapter's administrative
authority during a vacancy see Joannes Teutonicus *ad Dist.* 71 c. 5, C. 12 q. 2 c. 42,
C. 12 q. 2 c. 47; Bernardus Parmensis *ad* X. I.xxxiii.14, I.xxxiii.11; Goffredus Tranensis, *Summa, Ne sede vacante,* fol. 122 n. 3; Innocentius IV, *Commentaria ad* X. III.ix.1,
III.ix.2; Hostiensis, *Summa, De maioritate et obedientia,* col. 309; *Ne sede vacante,* cols. 795,
796, 797. And, after the *Sext.,* Joannes Monachus *ad Sext.* I.viii.3 fol. 128; Guido de
Baysio *ad Sext.* I.viii.3 fol. 42, I.vi.40 fol. 38, III.vi.1 fol. 93.

[69] *Summa ad Dist.* 23 c. 1, p. 52.

[70] Alanus *ad Comp. I,* v.vi.11, MS. C.17 fol. 115rb, 'Arg. clerum iurisdictionem
episcopalem habere vacante ecclesia . . . quod verum est. Ea autem que ad ordinem
episcopalem spectant ad superiorem devolvunt'; Bernardus Parmensis *ad* X. I.xxxiii.11;
Hostiensis, *Summa, ne sede vacante,* col. 797.

[71] *Commentaria ad* X. v.vii.9.

during a vacancy, and one derived from consecration which passed to a superior; and in the first category were included most of the powers essential for the practical affairs of Church government. The canonistic theory on devolution of authority from bishop to chapter acquired an added significance from the fact that it could be held to apply, not only when a prelate was actually dead, but when he was only virtually so; for instance, if he were held prisoner by infidels or if he had fallen into heresy.[72] Moreover, it was laid down in the *Decretum* that the clergy should act on behalf of their bishop if he became incapable through old age or illness,[73] and Huguccio took an important step when he transferred this doctrine concerning an incapable bishop to the case of one who was merely neglectful.[74] The basis for this transfer was provided by *Dist.* 65 c. 9, a chapter much quoted in later controversies:

> Si forte in provincia unum tantum contigerit remanere episcopum, superstes episcopus convocet episcopos vicinae provinciae et cum eis ordinet comprovinciales sibi episcopos. Quod si facere neglexerit, populi conveniant episcopos vicinae provinciae.

On the basis of this and other chapters in the *Decretum* Joannes Teutonicus formulated the general rule that whenever a prelate was negligent his inferiors could take action to remedy the harm caused by his default:

> Arguo quod si praelatus non vult vel negligit facere ea quae debet, debent suppleri per subditos, et econverso.[75]

---

[72] E.g. Goffredus Tranensis, *Summa, Ne sede vacante* fol. 122 n. 1; Hostiensis, *Summa, Ne sede vacante*, col. 796; Joannes Monachus *ad Sext.* I.viii.3; Joannes Andreae *ad Sext.* I.vii.3. It was not clear whether the clergy had the right of withdrawing allegiance from an evil or heretical bishop. In the *Comp.* I (I.iv.8) one finds, 'Plebs obsequens dominicus preceptis a peccatore preposito separare se debet. . . .' Vincentius, commenting on this passage (MS. C.17 fol. 3va), suggested that it only applied when sentence had been passed on the prelate. Laurentius laid down that the crime must be notorious but referred to a passage which laid down that condemnation was necessary to establish notoriety. Gregory IX ruled, however, that *evidentia rei* would suffice (X. III.iii.10). Bernardus Parmensis, following Joannes Teutonicus, thought that the members could recede from the head in case of heresy, schism, or notorious fornication, but should await a definitive sentence concerning any other notorious crime.

[73] C. 7 q. 1 c. 4.

[74] *Summa ad Dist.* 65 c. 9, MS. LC.2 fol. 127va, 'Arg. quod vacante ecclesia clerici possunt alios episcopos invitare ad ordinationes faciendas . . . si minor negligit facere quod debet per maiorem supplendum est et econtrario.'

[75] Gloss *ad Dist.* 89 c. 2. See also glosses *ad* C. 9 q. 3 and *ad Dist.* 65 c. 9.

This was to provide a ready-made argument for the later conciliar theorists who emphasized the 'suppletive' principle, the idea that the Church as a whole could remedy a failure in any of its organs of government—including the Papacy.

In general one may sum up the development of canonistic corporation doctrine during the thirteenth century as a gradual extension and systematization of the rights of the members of a corporation in relation to its head. By the middle of the century it was established that consent of the canons was necessary for actions touching their interests, and anything affecting the well-being of the whole corporation was held to concern them. By the end of the century the canons had acquired extensive judicial and administrative authority during an episcopal vacancy. And even when the bishop did act *ex officio* on behalf of the whole church his position could be described as that of a proctor, exercising a derivative authority with clearly defined limitations.

So far we have considered as corporations only the individual churches, and, within each one, only a small group of prelates and canons as constituting the church. Such an approach was unavoidable, since the canonists actually evolved their laws of corporation structure in discussing the affairs of such groups—it was the canons who elected a bishop, the canons who co-operated with him in ruling the church, the canons who limited his proctorial authority in case of abuse or strengthened it with letters *de rato*, the canons who succeeded to the jurisdiction of a dead prelate. Yet there always remained in the background, never wholly forgotten, the older, more catholic view that the Church was not made up of prelates and higher clergy alone, but that the word *ecclesia* in its fullest significance meant nothing less than the whole *universitas fidelium*, the Mystical Body of Christ. Moreover, for medieval theologians and jurists, the description of the Church as a *corpus mysticum* was no mere metaphor; the words were intended to denote a real, organic, juristic and corporate union of the faithful. It was possible, therefore, that the ideas of corporation law might be adapted to embrace this wider unity, to explain the internal structure, not only of the churches, but of the Church. Before this process could take place, however, it had first to be established that the *corpus mysticum* was indeed a corporation, that the *universitas fidelium* was a *universitas* in the more technical and legally precise sense of the term. Once again we can trace the growth of this concept in the glosses of the thirteenth-century canonists.

CHAPTER THREE

THE WHOLE CHURCH AS A CORPORATION

1. Corpus Mysticum

The belief that the whole society of Christians is something other than an aggregate of individuals is as old as the Church itself. Among the Apostles St Paul in particular laid great emphasis on the 'incorporation in Christ' of all the faithful, and often depicted the whole Church as a single organism, a mystical unity proceeding from the indwelling of Christ in each believer. 'Not I now, but Christ liveth in me.' Alternatively he described Christ as the 'head' to which all Christians were united as 'members', and both types of imagery served to illustrate the underlying concept that dominated his thought, the idea of a Mystical Body, a union of all the faithful in Christ. The concept was much developed in patristic writings with especial emphasis on the significance of the Eucharist as symbol of the organic unity of the Church. The consecrated Host was held not only to be the corporeal body of Christ, but to symbolize that other Mystical Body, in whose life all the faithful participated.[1] It has been claimed, moreover, that the underlying assumption of corporate unity with Christ profoundly influenced the development of other Christological doctrines even when it was not explicitly cited;[2] and certainly any detailed investigation of the doctrine of the Mystical Body leads at once to the problems of incarnation and redemption, the central mysteries of Christian faith.

It is a somewhat lower plane of thought that we have to consider. In two recent studies of the concept of the Mystical Body the view has been expressed that a dominant influence in the development of the doctrine in the thirteenth century was the legalistic spirit of the age.[3] We are not concerned, however, with any possible influence of

---

[1] E. Mersch, *Le Corps Mystique du Christ* (Paris, 1936), I, pp. 298, 431–4, 469–76, 498–507; II, pp. 24–6, 113–16.

[2] *Ibid.* II, p. 372.

[3] *Ibid.* II, p. 160, 'Not that the Scholastics were all jurists. . . . But they were men of their time. Not a few took pride in showing that the Christian doctrine could be

the canonists on theological speculations, still less with an appraisal of the doctrines of the theologians themselves, but only with the effects of the canonists' assimilation of the idea of the Mystical Body on their own juristic theories. It was inevitable that such a venerable concept should influence the formulation of their systems of ecclesiology, but, although they often described the Church as the *corpus Christi*, the canonists quite properly made little attempt to explore in detail the purely theological implications of the term. Their task was rather to adapt the doctrinal subtleties of the theologians to their own legalistic categories of thought.

This task might seem exacting enough in itself, but in fact the canonists displayed a considerable facility in attaching to the symbols and analogies of patristic lore a juristic connotation that rendered them easily assimilable within a purely legal frame of reference. For instance, the ancient description of a bishop as 'spouse' or 'father' of his church provided an occasion for deploying all the technicalities of Roman and canon law concerning marriage and the status of minors. Sometimes the method was pushed to extremes, as when the right to reinstatement in his benefice of a clerk who had been held captive was upheld by citing the parallel case of a woman who remarried under the impression that her husband had been killed in battle. If the first husband returned the woman must go back to him, and so too the clerk must be reinstated in his church, *cum ecclesia sit uxor clerici*.[4] On this case Gillet understandably remarked, 'On avouera que c'est pousser un peu loin la métaphore!'[5] Yet this is hardly one of the most fanciful examples of canonistic exegesis. An equally ingenious interpretation was evoked by a passage of Cyprian, incorporated in the *Decretum*, in which the saint, struggling to express the inexpressible, put forward metaphor after metaphor to illustrate the unity in diversity that characterized the Church. He wrote of the rays of light that shone from a single source, of the numerous branches that stemmed from one parent tree, and, finally, of the separate rivulets that flowed from the same fount. Whereupon the *Glossa Palatina*

---

expressed *ad apices iuris* as well as any other science, in terms of contracts, divine decrees, promises etc.' Cf. Henri de Lubac, *Catholicism*, transl. Sheppard (London, 1950), p. 162. On the juristic adaptation of the Pauline idea of corpus and its significance for Roman law see M. Roberti, 'Il corpus mysticum di S. Paolo nella storia della persona giuridica', *Studi in Onore di Enrico Besta* (Milan, 1939), IV, pp. 37–82.

[4] Joannes Teutonicus, gloss *ad* C. 34 q. 1 c. 1.

[5] *Op. cit.* p. 104.

solemnly cited as an appropriate elucidation a law of the Digest stating that when a community had the right to draw water from a certain source any member of the community could exercise the right.[6]

In view of this exegetical dexterity the canonists were not unduly daunted even by so subtle a concept as that of the Mystical Body, especially since, in earlier theological writings, the idea of the *corpus mysticum* had been associated with the definition of the Church as a *universitas fidelium*.[7] Even the best equipped canonist might have been a little ill at ease in face of the more refined theological nuances of an Augustine or Cyprian; but he could be quite at home in dealing with the structure of a corporation. However, the word *universitas* itself did not necessarily carry any technical juristic connotation, and some of the earlier canonists showed no disposition to invest it with a strictly legal significance. Stephanus Tornacensis referred often to the doctrine of the Mystical Body, but always in terms that owed everything to Cyprian and Augustine, and nothing to the Digest,

> Unus panis ex multis granis conficitur, sic ex multis fidelium personis Christi corpus, quod est ecclesia.[8]

And Joannes Teutonicus too was content to define the nature of the Church's unity in theological terms, referring to 'the Holy Spirit in us that makes us one body'.[9]

On the other hand may be set an opinion of Huguccio who suggested that the structure of the Church as a whole was comparable to that of the lesser corporate bodies within it. Commenting on the statement of Gregory I that decisions of General Councils were approved by the whole Church he wrote:

> *Universali consensu*, arg. pro universitate et quod nulli a canonico et communi consensu sui capituli vel collegii vel civitatis recedere. . . .[10]

---

[6] MS. T.O.10.2 fol. 28*vb ad* C. 24 q. 1 c. 18. Guilielmus Durantis, the nephew of the Speculator, used the same quotation from the Digest as an argument against excessive concentration of authority in the Papacy, *De Modo Generalis Concilii Celebrandi* (Parisiis, 1545), p. 16.

[7] Hugh of St Victor provides a typical example, 'Ecclesia sancta corpus est Christi. . . . Quid est ergo ecclesia nisi multitudo fidelium, universitas Christianorum?' Cited by Schwane, *Histoire des dogmes* (Paris, 1903), v. p. 252 n. 2.

[8] Stephanus *ad De Consecratione, Dist.* 2 c. 1, p. 269. Cf. the view of Cyprian cited by Mersch *op. cit.* II, p. 25. See also Stephanus *ad* C. 1 q. 1 c. 11 and *ad De Consecratione, Dist.* 2 cc. 22, 36, 45. Cf. *Dig.* 41.3.30 pr.

[9] Gloss *ad* C. 24 q. 1 c. 18, '. . . unus (spiritus) sanctus est in nobis quo unum corpus efficimur'.

[10] MS. P.72 fol. 125*vb ad Dist.* 15 c. 2. The idea of the whole Church as a

Thus, already by the age of Innocent III, there were apparent in the canonistic writings two different approaches to the problem of Church unity. If the purely theological terminology of Stephanus were to be retained the Mystical Body could never be to the canonists more than a pious dogma, venerated but outside the main stream of their thought. If, on the other hand, the more legalistic approach of Huguccio were to be decisive for the future, a complex process of assimilation was necessary. Just as the theologians, writing of the Mystical Body, could emphasize the headship of Christ or the intimate association of the members, so too the canonists, in their more practical sphere, had to explain both the unity of the Church and the principle of authority within it. The latter point offered little difficulty, for it could be claimed that, just as Christ was head of the whole Church, so too his earthly representative, the Pope, was head of the Church on earth or, as it was sometimes put, the Roman church was 'head of all the churches'. The more interesting question was whether the concept of mystical unity in the Church could be likewise assimilated and identified with the canonistic concept of legal incorporation, for such a development, if carried to its logical conclusion, might well lead to a consideration of the constitutional structure of the whole Church in terms of the corporation doctrines that have been described.

The implications of Huguccio's argument were not at once generally accepted. Bernardus Parmensis rejected the idea that the *congregatio fidelium* was legally a corporation, drawing a clear distinction between the technical status of incorporation and the bond of charity that united all the faithful under the headship of Christ. There were many different senses of the word *corpus*, he wrote, and added that a bishop formed a corporation with his canons but not with the lesser clergy of the diocese:

> Item episcopus cum capitulo facit unum corpus, cuius ipse est caput, sed cum clero civitatis vel diocesis non dicitur facere unum corpus. . . .[11]

Gierke attached great importance to this passage, and on the basis of it argued that, in canonistic theory, all 'right-subjectivity' in a church was vested in a divinely imposed *magisterium*, while the lesser clergy

---

corporation in the juristic sense of the word is again suggested in the passage of the *Glossa Palatina* cited *supra* p. 41.

[11] Gloss *ad* X. v.xxxi.14.

and laity were mere 'right-objects', the 'sphere of activity' within which the rights of their superiors were exercised. And he thought that, although theologians and canonists alike referred to the Church as *unum corpus*, they did not conceive of it as a true corporation because they subjected it to this super-imposed hierarchical authority.[12] Gillet, too, noted that, from the first, the principle of hierarchical organization distinguished the Church from the Roman *universitas personarum*,[13] and it is certainly quite clear that in canonistic theory the subordination of all the members to a single head was a characteristic feature of a corporation. But it need not be admitted on that account that, as Gierke suggested, the canonists abandoned all the 'fellowshiply' implications of the term *universitas* and invested it with a purely 'institutional' significance;[14] for, as we have seen, the recognition that each corporation was united under one head in no way precluded the various members from playing an active and influential part in the conduct of its affairs. Indeed, nine-tenths of all canonistic discussion on problems of corporation structure was concerned precisely with defining the relative rights of head and members. The antithesis between hierarchy and corporation does not seem really to correspond to the canonists' own categories of thought.

Moreover, the view of Bernardus Parmensis that, in a strictly legal sense, only a small group of cathedral clergy were 'members' of a church (i.e. in the sense of forming a corporation with the bishop) seems to have been only an individual opinion and one that was by no means universally accepted in the thirteenth century. It seems hard to reconcile it with the prevailing doctrine of the bishop as *procurator rerum ecclesiae*, for the canonists usually attributed *dominium* over church property either to all the clergy of the church or to the whole congregation,[15] and the old law that election of a bishop should be by *clerus et populus* was preserved in several texts of Gratian's *Decretum*.[16] It was universally agreed that the canons had acquired a

---

[12] *Das Deutsche Genossenschaftsrecht*, III, pp. 252–4.
[13] *La personnalité juridique . . .*, pp. 41–4.
[14] Gierke argued that, according to the canonists, all authority was concentrated in a restricted governing corporation, and that within that corporation all jurisdiction was attributed to the head. But the only canonists he cited in support of this opinion were Innocent IV and Joannes Andreae (who merely repeated Innocent's argument). It was in fact an exceptional point of view. *Op. cit.* p. 306 n. 1.
[15] *Supra* pp. 109–110.
[16] The whole subject was discussed in *Dist.* 62 of the *Decretum*.

valid legal right to make the election, and in discussions of the prelate's proctorship it seems often to have been assumed tacitly that he was a proctor of the canons, for it was their consent that was required for actions that lay outside his normal competence. But there was no real intention of setting up the cathedral chapter as *dominus* in a technical sense; the canons, like the bishop, were concerned in administering property of which the *dominium* resided elsewhere. Such a position seems incomprehensible if we accept the view of Bernardus Parmensis that there was a sharp discontinuity between bishop and chapter on the one hand and clergy and people on the other; it becomes quite reasonable if we suppose that the whole body of the faithful formed a corporation whose rights were normally exercised by a corporate head of bishop and chapter. If that were the case one might expect to find that, just as the bishop normally exercised the jurisdiction of the corporate head but in some matters required consent of the canons, so too, in exceptional circumstances, the co-operation of the lower grades of the hierarchy might be sought. A systematic treatment of such problems was undertaken only in the fourteenth century, and then it was the corporation of the whole Church rather than of each individual church that was usually considered, but already in the earlier canonistic works there were ideas more in accordance with this view of a church's structure than with the view of Bernardus Parmensis. Innocent IV maintained that a bishop was not only head of his cathedral church but of all the other churches in his diocese, and drew the corollaries that he could act on behalf of the lesser churches and also that he should seek counsel of their clergy in dealing with their affairs.[17] There was also the Decretist doctrine that in some circumstances the *populus* could act in place of a negligent bishop, a doctrine that was not forgotten in the thirteenth century but that was revived by Hostiensis and applied to the corporate structure of the Roman church itself.[18] Again, the lower clergy of a diocese were in practice 'subjects' of rights that could be defended at law, and they did participate at local synods in the corporate life of the church. The view that, being excluded from the governing corporation of bishop and chapter, they were mere 'objects of rights' seems inconsistent both with the actual facts of diocesan life and with the prevailing trends of canonistic thought.

[17] *Commentaria ad* X. I.ii.8, III.xxvi.16.
[18] *Infra* p. 152.

If, however, we turn from the local churches to consider the corporate structure of the Church as a whole, Gierke's view might seem much more defensible. During the thirteenth century the description of the Church as a *corpus mysticum* did come to acquire a juristic connotation in the works of the canonists, but it was always through an insistence on the subordination of all the members to a single head, not through any emphasis on the corporate solidarity of the member churches. Since Christ was head of the Mystical Body the canonists found it natural to refer to his vicar as head of the Church on earth, for it was precisely the function of the vicar to fill the place of Christ in relation to the Church militant. When, therefore, the canonists referred to the Pope as head they seemed only to be giving expression to a simple and inevitable corollary of the ancient doctrine of the Church as the Body of Christ; yet inevitably, from the very nature of the problems they dealt with, they were led to import their own legal ideas into the concept of headship. When Stephanus referred to the Church constituted *ex multis fidelium personis Christi corpus*, his thoughts were full of the symbolism of the Eucharist; when Alanus, half a century later, wrote *Est enim corpus unum ecclesia, ergo unum solum caput habere debet*, he had in mind the proper subordination of Emperor to Pope.[19] When a theologian wrote of the Mystical Body and the headship of Christ, the problems that suggested themselves were ones of sacramental and Christological theology; but when a canonist encountered a reference to the Pope as head of the Church his natural inclination was to embark on an analysis of the juristic relationship between this head and the members who together with him formed *unum corpus*.

We have already considered the general legislative and judicial authority attributed to the Pope by the Decretists in virtue of his headship.[20] In the Decretals the authority of the head was further stressed, with especial emphasis on the unity subsisting between Rome as head and the other churches as members. The relationship could be defined in the familiar anthropomorphic imagery which was sometimes pressed in extreme detail:

> Ecclesia universalis unum Christi corpus est . . . huiusmodi corporis caput est ecclesia romana. . . . Aliae vero ecclesiae ab isto capite descendentes,

---

[19] Gloss *ad Comp.* I. II.xx.7. Cf. Mochi Onory, *Fonti Canonistiche*, p. 191 n. 1; W. Ullmann, *Medieval Papalism*, pp. 147–9.

[20] *Supra* pp. 26–27.

> membra huius capitis appellantur et sicut in corpore naturali vides a
> capite membra descendere et a membris membra derivari, unde sicut
> a brachio derivato, ab ipso manus, a manu digiti ... ita a capite, id est
> romana ecclesia maiores descendunt ecclesiae et ab eis aliae a quibus
> aliae quaecumque descendunt.[21]

More significantly, there were specific legal corollaries to be drawn
from this relationship. The Decretists' view that the term *Romana
ecclesia* could be used to describe the whole *congregatio fidelium* under-
went a further development, though one without any conciliar implications, in the Decretals. There it was maintained that the congregation
of any local church, in virtue of their membership of it, could also
be called members of the Roman church since their own church was
related to it as member to head, forming one body with it. Hence,
no member of another church could plead *privilegium fori* at Rome
since Rome was a 'common homeland' of all Christians.[22] Again, it
was held that one could not object against the postulation of a prelate
of the Roman church by the chapter of another see that the prelate
was already attached to an alien church:

> Praeterea cum sedes apostolica omnium ecclesiarum caput existat ...
> quando de ipsa quis sumitur in praelatum alterius ecclesiae ei posse
> obiici non videtur propter capitis privilegium quod obtinet plenitudinem
> potestatis, quod de aliena ecclesia eligitur, cum a capite non debeant
> membra reputari aliena censeri.[23]

In such a passage the idea of headship in the Church seems devoid of
any 'mystical' overtones and appears as a concept of almost arid legality. There was certainly nothing mystical about a writ of postulation.

The juristic implications of the doctrine of the Church as a Mystical Body were explored from another point of view by Innocent IV.
In the earlier discussions on the ownership of church property that
we have considered, although there were different definitions of the
holder of *dominium*, it was generally assumed that *dominium* rested in
some sense with the local community—with the *universitas loci* as
Goffredus Tranensis put it. Innocent put forward a very influential

---

[21] Abbas Antiquus, cited by Gillet, *op. cit.* p. 171. See also Gierke, *op. cit.* III,
p. 251 n. 19, and, for further references, A.-H. Chroust, 'The corporate idea and
the body politic in the Middle Ages', *Review of Politics*, IX (1947), pp. 423–52.

[22] X. II.ii.10. The idea of Rome as 'communis patria' goes back to Cicero (*De
Lege Agraria*, ii, 86) and also occurs in Roman law. Cf. *Dig.* 27.1.6 (11) and *Dig.*
48.22.19.

[23] X. I.vi.19; I.v.3.

restatement of the doctrine, suggesting that *dominium* was vested in the whole *aggregatio fidelium*, the Body of Christ:

> Non praelatus sed Christus dominium et possessionem rerum ecclesiae habet... vel ecclesia habet possessionem et proprietatem... id est aggregatio fidelium quae est corpus Christi capitis.[24]

The argument had this implication. If *dominium* rested with the Universal Church, the *aggregatio fidelium*, then, for practical purposes, all ecclesiastical property could be regarded as at the disposal of the earthly head of the *aggregatio fidelium*, Christ's representative, the Pope. In assuming that the Church, defined as the *corpus Christi*, was an entity capable of the quite prosaic function of property ownership, Innocent was apparently regarding it as not only a *corpus mysticum* but as something closely akin to a legal corporation. And it will be remembered that in his view all the jurisdiction of a corporation was concentrated in its head, so that he could quite consistently present the whole Church as a corporation while at the same time upholding an extreme doctrine of papal monarchy in all affairs of Church government.

2. Plenitudo Potestatis

It seems undeniable that towards the middle of the thirteenth century the whole tendency of canonistic thought was to emphasize the universal authority of the Pope, and to treat the local churches as subordinate members whose unity was produced only by their common adherence to a single head—Gierke's 'institution-idea' in its purest form one might suppose. Yet it is not altogether paradoxical to treat this development as a stage in the growth of conciliar ideas. It is a

---

[24] *Commentaria ad* X. II.xii.4. Bernardus Compostellanus presented a more detailed argument on this point. He suggested that while *dominium* over ecclesiastical property rested with the whole *congregatio fidelium*, the use of such property could be attributed to the individual local churches. His views were reported by Guido de Baysio and contrasted with the opinion of Goffredus that actual *dominium* belonged to the local church. *Rosarium ad* C. 12 q. 1 c. 13, '... dicit Bernardus Hispanus quod ipsa prima collectio fidelium sit domina. Sed obiicitur, ergo res eiusdem ecclesiae sunt eiusdem cuius res illius et econverso et hoc plano concedit. Dicuntur tamen illius ecclesiae et alia eius secundum usum rerum qui ita competit clericis illius ecclesiae quod non istius et similiter pauperibus istius ecclesiae specialis quam istius.... Sed Goffredus dicit verius est quod sunt universitatis illius loci....'

commonplace of constitutional history that in the secular kingdoms theories of corporate representation could flourish only after a degree of monarchical unity had been attained. As the idea of the Church as a corporate entity in the more legalistic sense became accepted there was always the possibility that it might be restated in a form that would lay all the emphasis on the due participation of the members rather than on the unique authority of the head. The doctrine of Innocent IV on church property, for instance, could lead to the theories of John of Paris as well as to those of Giles of Rome. Such a restatement would be quite in keeping with the theories of the canonists on the corporate structure of the lesser churches, and, in spite of the prevailing climate of opinion, there did exist in the glosses of the thirteenth century doctrines concerning the Papacy and the Church as a whole that were favourable to a development of this sort.

There was the doctrine that a Pope could not legitimately act against the general well-being of the Church, and that, at least in case of heresy, he could be deposed by the Church. There was the canonistic teaching that the very rights which were the ultimate roots of all ecclesiastical authority—dominion of church property and ability to maintain the faith with certain truth—rested, not with the Pope nor with any exalted group of prelates, but with the whole *congregatio fidelium*. There was, above all, the fact that the Papacy was itself an elective office and so invited the same sort of analysis that the canonists had applied to the elected heads of other corporations. The Papacy was indeed particularly sensitive to such analysis, since the attributes in which the Pope was held superior to other bishops, his powers of jurisdiction and administration, were precisely the qualities that were usually held to be derived from election. A detailed discussion of the sources and limits of these elements in the papal authority would, moreover, involve a consideration of the concept of papal *plenitudo potestatis*, and here it could be shown that the position of the Pope was vulnerable at what seemed its strongest point, for the adaptations of this concept by the fourteenth-century papal publicists were by no means inevitable corollaries of its earlier canonistic connotations. The whole subject is of considerable importance for the understanding of conciliar thought and requires a little further examination.

The familiar doctrine of *plenitudo potestatis* presents it as a unique and all-embracing authority, pertaining solely to the Pope and conferred solely by God, radically different in kind from the power of lesser prelates since it was the source from which all other authority was derived. In some of the conciliar works, however, the concept of *plenitudo potestatis* appears in a very different sense. Zabarella built his whole theory around the assertion that the Pope possessed plenitude of power not alone but as the head of a corporation,[25] a definition that led him to the conclusion that the papal *plenitudo potestatis* was an authority limited, derivative and revocable. This seems flatly opposed to the normal sense of the words, but Zabarella was presenting a point of view solidly based on a foundation of early canonistic theory—it would be strange if it were otherwise for he was one of the most learned jurists of his generation. Indeed, the early development of this most important expression, and the connotations it acquired in fourteenth-century controversies can hardly be understood without reference to the canonistic corporation theories that have been described.

When the term *plenitudo potestatis* came into general use in the Decretist works written around 1200 it had not acquired the connotation of absolute sovereignty later associated with it. Canonistic terminology was still fluid, and *plenitudo potestatis* appears as only one of a whole group of similar expressions which were not sharply differentiated from it and which were also used to describe the papal authority. One finds, for instance, *plena potestas, plena auctoritas, plenaria potestas, plena et libera administratio,* all used to denote the administrative authority conferred by election on the head of an ecclesiastical corporation, and, *a fortiori,* on the Pope.[26] And just as these terms were applied to the Pope as well as to other prelates, so too the term *plenitudo potestatis* was used of others besides the Pope. Ambassadors and legates, indeed any representative exercising full authority on behalf of his principal, could be said to enjoy *plenitudo potestatis;* in one usage the

---

[25] *Tractatus de Schismate,* p. 703 in S. Schard, *De Jurisdictione, Auctoritate et Praeeminentia Imperiali* (Basileae, 1586). Cf. *infra* pp. 203–204.

[26] Huguccio *ad Dist.* 79 c. 9 MS. LC.2 fol. 141va, 'Ipse (papa) enim eligitur confirmando et confirmatur eligendo . . . ergo statim habet *plenam potestatem.*' *Glossa Palatina ad Dist.* 11 c. 2, MS. Pal.Lat.658 fol. 3ra, '*Plena auctoritas* dicitur quando continet preceptum et generalitatem et observantie necessitatem sicut romanus pontifex. . . .' (The gloss was commenting on a phrase of Pope Nicholas, 'Consequens est, ut quod ab huius sedis rectoribus plena auctoritate sancitur . . . firmiter et inconcusse teneatur.') Gloss *Ecce Vicit Leo ad Dist.* 79 c. 2, MS. F.XI.605 fol. 28va, 'Ecce quod statim post electionem habet papa *plenariam potestatem.* . . .' Bernardus Parmensis *ad X.* I.vi.6, 'Et ideo dum eligitur (papa) confirmatur et statim habet *plenam et liberam administrationem.*'

term was simply a variant of the formula *plena potestas* or *plena auctoritas* more commonly employed in proctorial mandates.[27]

A comparison between the type of authority exercised by a bishop and that possessed by the Pope sometimes arose in discussions on the question whether episcopal authority could be exercised immediately after election and before confirmation, for the canonists took the opportunity to point out that the problem did not arise in the case of the Pope whose election required no confirmation. But, apart from this reservation, they would use the same terms to describe the authority of Pope and bishop alike:

> Videtur quod electus in episcopum *plenam* habet *potestatem* administrandi et disponendi de rebus ecclesiae ipso actu, sed hoc speciale est in papa.... Ipse enim eligitur confirmando et confirmatur eligendo... ergo statim habet *plenam potestatem* sicut alii electi in episcopos habent post confirmationem....[28]

So, too, the term *plena auctoritas* could be used of the Pope or of other bishops; and that this everyday administrative qualification of *plena potestas* or *plena auctoritas* could be identified in the twelfth century with the *plenitudo potestatis* of the Pope that was to acquire such a mystical—one might almost say magical—significance for some later writers is suggested by a simple definition of Huguccio—*auctoritas papae dicitur plena quia plenitudinem habet potestatis.*[29]

The canonists were really using the same set of terms to express two different meanings. Phrases like *plena potestas, plena auctoritas, plenitudo potestatis* could be used to describe the authority conferred by any community on its head in the act of election, an authority that could be defined in language akin to that of a proctorial mandate. Huguccio

---

[27] For papal legates see Ullmann, *Medieval Papalism*, p. 153 n. 4. Similarly Philip of Swabia and Frederick II sent ambassadors with mandates of *plenitudo potestatis* (*M.G.H. Legum Sectio IV*, II, 17, no. 14 and *M.G.H. Constitutiones*, II, p. 303). See Gaines Post, 'Plena potestas and consent', *Traditio*, I, pp. 355–408.

[28] Huguccio, *Summa ad Dist.* 79 c. 9, MS. LC.2 fol. 141va. Similarly *Ecce Vicit Leo ad Dist.* 79 c. 2, MS. F.XI.605, '... statim post electionem habet papa plenariam potestatem, executionem, administrationem et est speciale in eo quia non habent alii Prelati nisi post confirmationem'. The election decree of 1059 and that of 1179 both stated that the papal authority was conferred at once by the act of election. Cf. F. Wasner, 'De consecratione, inthronizatione, coronatione Summi Pontificis', *Apollinaris*, VIII (1935), pp. 86–125, 248–81, 428–39 at pp. 118–21, 256–7, 269, 271; E. Eichmann, *Die Weihe und Krönung des Papstes im Mittelalter*, ed. K. Mörsdorf in *Münchener Theologische Studien*, I (1951), pp. 34–5, 48.

[29] *Summa ad Dist.* 11 c. 2, MS. P.72 fol. 123vb.

even wrote that Pope and Emperor both possessed a *plenitudo potestatis* conferred on them by the people.[30] But all these terms were also used to describe a particular attribute of the Roman church by virtue of which it was superior to all other churches. *Plena auctoritas* occurred in this sense in one of the texts of the *Decretum*,[31] Innocent III himself used *plena potestas* to describe the supreme authority of the Apostolic See,[32] and there were two pseudo-Isidorian decretals cited by Gratian which used *plenitudo potestatis* to define a distinctive characteristic of the Roman church:

> (Romana ecclesia) quae vices sues in aliis impertivit ecclesiis, ut in partem sint vocatae sollicitudinis, non in plenitudinem potestatis.[33]

In their original contexts these words had not been intended as an assertion that bishops derived their ordinary episcopal authority from the Pope, and the earlier canonists showed little disposition to interpret them in that sense. They did, of course, recognize that the Pope's authority was in some way different from that of the other bishops who were *vocati in partem sollicitudinis*. The Pope was always said to be *maior in administratione, in iurisdictione*, but, according to the Decretists, the distinction did not lie in the fact that the Pope's *plenitudo potestatis* was radically different in kind from the authority of other bishops; it was rather that the Pope's authority extended over a broader area than theirs, was not limited in a geographical sense. Huguccio held that the Pope's *plenitudo potestatis* enabled him to exercise over all the churches the same ordinary jurisdiction that each bishop exercised over his own diocese,[34] and other glosses pointed out that the essential

---

[30] *Summa ad Dist.* 4 c. 3, MS. P.72 fol. 119ra, 'Omne enim ius condendi leges vel canones populus contulit in imperatorem et ecclesia in apostolicum unde intelligitur uterque plenitudinem potestatis quo ad hoc. . . .'

[31] *Dist.* 11 c. 2.

[32] E.g. X. IV.xiii.17. So too Innocent IV *ad* X. III.xxxiv.8.

[33] C. 2 q. 6 c. 11, and, again, C. 2 q. 6 c. 12, 'Ipsa namque ecclesia quae prima est ita reliquis ecclesiis vices suas credidit largiendas, ut in partem sint vocatae sollicitudinis, non in plenitudinem potestatis.' The first formulation of this most influential phrase can be traced to Leo I, 'Vices nostras ita tuae credidimus charitati, ut in partem sis vocatus sollicitudinis, non in plenitudinem potestatis' (Migne, LIV, col. 671, ep. 1). But this letter referred to the powers exercised by a metropolitan as papal vicar, not to his ordinary episcopal jurisdiction. The texts given by Gratian were pseudo-Isidorian adaptations of Leo's words attributed to Vigilius and Gregory IV. On the whole subject see J. Rivière, 'In partem sollicitudinis . . . évolution d'une formule pontificale', *Revue des sciences religieuses*, V (1925), pp. 210–31.

[34] *Summa ad* C. 6 q. 2 c. 3, cited by Mochi Onory, *Fonti Canonistiche*, p. 166,

difference between the Pope's *plena auctoritas* and that of other bishops was that the bishop's authority lacked the quality of *generalitas*:

> Plena auctoritas dicitur quando continet preceptum, et generalitatem et observancie necessitatem . . . si ergo penes papam sunt haec tria penes quemlibet episcopum sunt primum et tertium.[35]

It would be interesting to trace in detail from this point the parallel development of the concepts of episcopal *plena potestas* and papal *plenitudo potestatis*, for the two phrases, which had come into use as closely related variants of the same expression, were to have very different careers in later writings. By the middle of the thirteenth century the *plena potestas* of a bishop had been carefully analysed and was coming to be treated as a form of proctorial mandate which conferred on its holder a wide but essentially derivative and by no means irresponsible authority. Meanwhile the cognate term *plenitudo potestatis* was undergoing a quite different course of development. In the letters of Innocent III it was not only cited time and again to vindicate the Pope's universal powers of jurisdiction and administration, his right to intervene in the affairs of all the churches,[36] but it was also presented as the source of all other authority in the Church.[37] Moreover, according to Innocent III, the Pope's *plenitudo potestatis* not only set him above all other prelates but also above the law, *supra ius*.[38] Following the example of Innocent, Tancred emphasized the

---

'. . . solus episcopus est iudex ordinarius in diocesi sua . . . metropolitanus non est iudex ordinarius nisi in parrochia sua, et licet sit iudex ordinarius suorum episcoporum non tamen illorum qui subsunt episcopis . . . in papa autem speciale est, qui est iudex ordinarius omnium, scilicet maiorum et minorum prelatorum et subditorum . . . ipse enim solus habet plenitudinem potestatis'. Elsewhere he suggested that in some matters, such as the exposition of Scripture, even the Popes were *vocati in partem sollicitudinis, Summa ad Dist.* 20 c. 1, MS. P.72 fol. 123r*b*, '. . . summis pontificibus non licet recedere ab eorum expositionibus . . . sunt in huiusmodi vocati in partem sollicitudinis, non in plenitudinem potestatis'.

[35] *Glossa Palatina ad Dist.* 11 c. 2, MS. Pal.Lat.658 fol. 3ra. Similarly Huguccio *ad Dist.* 11 c. 2, MS. P.72 fol. 123r*b*. See also Caius MS. 676 *ad Dist.* 11 c. 2, fol. 5ra, 'Plena potestas consistit in precepto, necessitate observantie, generalitate. Quilibet episcopus duo istorum habet in sua diocesi, scil. preceptum et necessitatem observantie. Summus vero pontifex habet tres, scil., preceptum, necessitatem et generalitatem.'

[36] E.g. X. i.vi.39, iii.viii.4, iv.xvii.13, v.xxxiii.23 and Migne, ccxv, col. 279 (ep. 1), col. 405 (ep. 119), col. 898 (ep. 82), col. 901 (ep. 83).

[37] *Ibid.* col. 279, '. . . vocatis caeteris in partem sollicitudinis hunc assumpsit Dominus in plenitudinem potestatis . . . Petrum caput ecclesiae . . . qui . . . in membra diffunderet ut nihil sibi penitus deperiret, quoniam in capite viget sensuum plenitudo, ad membra vero pars eorum aliqua derivatur'.

[38] X. iii.viii.4, 'Secundum plenitudinem potestatis de iure possumus supra ius dispensare.'

significance of *plenitudo potestatis* as a quite unique authority that set the Pope in an exalted sphere beyond all human reproach.[39] Innocent IV went still further, asserting that the possession of *plenitudo potestatis* enabled the Pope to exercise temporal power as well as spiritual power, and that it gave him authority over infidels as well as over Christians.[40] The ground was thus well prepared for the concept of *plenitudo potestatis* as an illimitable and all-embracing sovereignty which becomes so familiar in the writings of the fourteenth-century papal publicists.

And yet, as other trends of fourteenth-century thought were to show, the older, more moderate idea of *plenitudo potestatis* as an authority akin to the *plena potestas* of a lesser prelate was not wholly forgotten. When the problems of the age led influential thinkers to discuss the sources of papal authority in a really critical spirit, even the concept of *plenitudo potestatis* could be given a conciliar interpretation. In essence it described the jurisdiction and administrative authority conferred on a Pope by virtue of his election;[41] according to earlier theory it differed from the *plena potestas* of a bishop only in that it extended universally over the whole Church. It could readily be argued—by analogy with lesser corporations—that it was to be regarded as an authority delegated by the whole Church and subject to limitation by the Church. The fact that papal *plenitudo potestatis* was held to be of divine origin, an attribute of the Pope in his capacity as Vicar of Christ, would not seriously hinder such a development; for, after all, a bishop too could be referred to as a vicar of God, but that had not prevented the canonists from analysing minutely the human machinery by which his authority was conferred and by which it could be limited.

---

[39] Gloss *ad Comp*. III. I.v.3, MS. C.17 fol. 147va, '... gerit vicem dei quia plenitudinem potestatis habet in rebus ecclesiasticis.... Nec est qui dicat ei, cur ita facis?'

[40] *Commentaria ad* X. II.ii.10, III.xxxiv.8.

[41] Even the later canonists who magnified the papal *plenitudo potestatis* to the utmost degree insisted that it was an authority conferred on the chosen candidate solely by the act of election. Gerson, indeed, thought it necessary to take them to task for their attitude on this point. *De potestate ecclesiastica, Opera*, II, col. 239, 'Et quamvis ex electione possit aliquid jurisdictionis habere, non tamen habet ante consecrationem in Episcopum plenitudinem Ecclesiasticae potestatis tam Ordinis quam jurisdictionis utriusque; quod perspicuum est ex terminis. Hic autem consurgit aequivocatio non modica propter Dominos iuristas, qui loquentes de plenitudine potestatis Papalis solum loqui videntur de potestate iurisdictionis, ex qua locutione videtur haec absurditas sequi quod pure laicus imo et femina posset esse papa et habere plenitudinem Ecclesiasticae potestatis.'

The whole concept of *plenitudo potestatis*, regarded as a basis for the more extreme claims put forward on behalf of the Papacy, was peculiarly ill-adapted to withstand any detailed canonistic analysis; and in this it typified a general weakness in the theories of papal sovereignty evolved in the thirteenth century. The Decretalists built a great edifice of papal claims, but their underlying theories concerning the corporate structure of the Church and the origins of ecclesiastical authority provided an inadequate foundation for such an ambitious superstructure. The conciliar implications of their theories were worked out in detail only in the fourteenth century, but, in the period that we have been considering, there was already one distinguished canonist who anticipated some of the most important of the later developments. A brief account of his views will therefore serve as a preliminary illustration of the immediate relevance to the major problems of Church government of the thirteenth-century corporation theories that have been described.

3. *Hostiensis and the Roman Church*

The work of Hostiensis has a double importance in the history of conciliar thought. He not only played an important part in the shaping of canonistic corporation theory, but also showed himself prepared to apply that theory consistently to the structure of the Roman See and of the whole Church; and in doing so, he was led to formulate a doctrine of Church government significantly different from the prevailing theory of papal monarchy.[42] His whole treatment of papal authority was based on the assumption that the Roman See, like any other bishopric, was subject to the normal rules of corporation law, an assumption whose corollaries he explored in considerable detail. It had usually been taken for granted in the earlier canonistic writings that the cardinals were in fact a corporate body, but by the time of Hostiensis their corporate status had obviously been called into question, for he found it necessary to rebuke those who held that the cardinals were mere individuals,

---

[42] His views are discussed in the article, 'A conciliar theory of the thirteenth century', *Catholic Historical Review*, XXXVI (1951), pp. 415–40.

tanquam homines a diversis mundi partibus vocati et in diversis ecclesiis intitulati. . . .[43]

On the contrary, Hostiensis maintained, they formed a single body meeting together to transact the business of the whole Church in association with the Pope:

> . . . ad tractatus communes totius mundi expediendos communiter conveniunt . . . summum et excellens collegium super omnia alia unitum a Deo cum papa, quod cum ipso unum et idem est.

Their relationship to the Pope was indeed so intimate that they could be described as actually parts of himself—*tanquam sibi inviscerati*.[44] If, then, one were to apply the rules of corporation structure favoured by Hostiensis to this corporate unity of Pope and cardinals, it would seem that the authority of the Roman See resided, not in its head alone, but also in the members. Hostiensis did not leave this conclusion as merely implicit in his arguments but set out quite clearly the constitutional implications of his corporation theory:

> . . . multo magis et multo excellentius maior est unio inter papam et collegium romanae ecclesiae quam etiam inter aliquem patriarcham et capitulum suum . . . et tamen patriacha non debet ardua expedire sine consilio fratrum. . . . Multa fortius ergo decet papam consilia fratrum suorum requirere. . . . Unde et dicti sunt cardinales a cardine quasi cum papa mundum regentes . . . unde et dictum est non *iudicabis* in singulari sed *iudicabitis* in plurali, ut non solum papa sed et cardinales includerentur etiam in expressione plenitudinis potestatis.[45]

It would seem that for Hostiensis the papal *plenitudo potestatis* was not a unique authority inhering in the person of the Pope, but a power comparable to that of any other bishop which was shared with the members of his ecclesiastical corporation.

This definition enabled him to give a decisive answer to a question that his recent predecessors had been content to evade, the question of the cardinals' status during a papal vacancy. Once again the normal theory of corporations supplied a clear-cut solution that Hostiensis did not hesitate to apply to the Papacy:

> Pone papam mortuum, quaero penes quem resideret haec potestas? Respondeo utique penes Romanam ecclesiam quae mori non potest . . .

---

[43] *Lectura ad* v.vi.17 fol. 32r*b*.
[44] *Lectura ad* v.xxxiii.23, fol. 85r*a*.
[45] *Lectura ad* iv.xvii.3 fol. 38v*a*.

> sed numquid collegium cardinalium habet jurisdictionem papae et etiam exercitium ipsius . . . tu teneas quod sic.[46]

He went on to point out that this was the normal rule concerning devolution of authority in a corporation, and then adduced numerous arguments to prove that the normal rule should be applied in this particular case. He argued that the cardinals exercised authority by tradition and that good customs should be preserved; that Christ would not wish his Church to lack a pastor; that the cardinals themselves would not be without a head since Christ was always with them as their head—indeed, it was absurd and not far from heresy to suppose that the Roman church, the head of all the churches, could itself be headless. He claimed, moreover, that the cardinal-bishops were endowed with papal authority since they acted in place of metropolitans in the consecration of a new Pope, for to take the place of a metropolitan of the Roman church was in fact to take the place of the Pope. Clearly Hostiensis was determined to press into service every argument possible to prove his case, and the reason becomes evident at the end of the passage:

> Haec scribo ad confutandos illos qui potestatem cardinalium quasi adnihilare videntur.[47]

Hostiensis, a cardinal himself, was not unnaturally a zealous defender of the dignity and prestige of the Sacred College.

His view of the status of the cardinals seems defined exactly in his phrase, *cardinales includerentur in expressione plenitudinis potestatis*. They formed with the Pope a collegiate body that enjoyed the exercise of the authority divinely conferred on the Roman church. This was, in effect, to substitute for the monarchy of a single Pope the rule of a self-perpetuating oligarchy in whom all rights of government over the Church were vested by a direct act of the divine will. But Hostiensis's corporation theories could have even broader applications

---

[46] *Lectura ad* v.xxxviii.14 fol. 102ra.

[47] '. . . tunc quia alia inferiora collegia hoc habent . . . tunc et quia cardinales sic utuntur . . . nam et beata consuetudo est attendenda in talibus . . . tunc quia visibile est quod filio Dei placeat hic intellectus ne ecclesiam videtur reliquisse sine pastore . . . non obstat quod aliqui dicunt quod cardinales sunt sine capite quia hoc non est verum, immo habent caput ecclesiae proprium et generale, scilicet Christum . . . et valde est absurdum sentire quod illa ecclesia capite careat quae caput est aliarum . . . immo etiam nec est longe ab heresi . . . episcopi cardinales proculdubio vices metropolitani obtinent . . . et exponi opportet metropolitani i.e. papae quia nec alius posset esse metropolitanus Romanae ecclesiae.'

than this. In a very special sense the cardinals formed a corporate body with the Pope, but all the other members of the Universal Church were also united to him as their head.[48] The implications of this relationship became apparent when Hostiensis chose to consider the one contingency that could disrupt the continuity of authority in the Roman church. How was the government of the Church to be maintained, he asked, if the whole College of Cardinals were to become extinct during a papal vacancy? If one were to accept without qualification the idea of an immediate grant of authority from God, limited to the college of the Roman See, it would seem that nothing short of a miraculous intervention could re-establish the extinct Papacy. But Hostiensis had a very different solution:

> Quid si nullus superest? Hoc nunquam accidet Deo propicio. Dicit tamen clerus Romanus quod ad ipsum spectat.... Alii dicunt quod concilium esset congregandum et per ipsum universali ecclesiae providendum ... et clerus et populus Romanus debent concilium convocare, *arg. opt. 65 dist. Si forte.* Solvo, et si hoc secundum sit forsan iustius, primum tamen videtur levius et commodius quia periculum est in mora.[49]

His argument implied that the doctrines of corporation law were applicable, not merely to a narrow circle of governing prelates, but to all levels of the ecclesiastical hierarchy. Just as the Pope's authority devolved to the cardinals during a vacancy, so too the cardinals' authority devolved to the Roman clergy and people. They could themselves provide a Pope in case of necessity or, more properly, summon a General Council to do so, a Council that in turn represented the Universal Church. (Hostiensis explained in another context that the Church as a whole was to be regarded as the source of authority of all General Councils.)[50] He was applying to the whole Church an attitude implicit in the canonistic treatment of the structure of lesser corporations, a conviction that the hierarchical ordering of a society was not incompatible with a corporate participation of its members in the conduct of its affairs. The whole Church could

---

[48] *Lectura ad* v.xxxiii.23 fol. 85ra, '... licet Papa sit caput universalis ecclesiae et singuli fideles membra generalia est tamen speciale caput cardinalium'.

[49] *Lectura ad* i.vi.6 fol. 32vb.

[50] *Summa, De Decimis et Primitiis*, col. 974, 'Licet enim iura non loquantur de concilio generali praedicto, loquuntur tamen de consimili et necesse est ut cum ecclesia generalis illorum et istius auctrix sit, quod de uno dicitur de altero intelligitur.'

be presented as one great corporation in whose authority all the members participated in the last resort.

In this argument of Hostiensis—which was cited by eminent Conciliarists of the next century like Conrad of Gelnhausen and Cardinal Zabarella—one can find another source of the basic doctrine of the Conciliar movement, the idea of an inherent right diffused throughout the whole community. The underlying authority of the *congregatio fidelium*, which the Decretists had acknowledged but had usually treated as a negative capacity, an inability to err or a passive *dominium* over goods administered by others, now appeared as a positive power to act in the interests of the whole Church, at least in an emergency. Moreover, it was only a small step from arguing that the powers of the cardinals could devolve to the whole Church to suggesting that, in the normal exercise of their authority, the cardinals acted as representatives of the Church. Once that step was taken in the fourteenth century the conciliar ideas that had been germinating for so long began at last to appear on the surface of medieval political thought.

PART THREE

CONCILIAR IDEAS IN THE FOURTEENTH CENTURY

CHAPTER ONE

JOHN OF PARIS

The history of Boniface VIII's pontificate provides an unusually rich background for the study of that intricate pattern of ideological concepts, political exigencies and personal idiosyncrasies which moulds the content of political theories no less than the course of historical events. In the canonistic commentaries of the previous century there existed, side by side, both extreme claims for the Papacy and a group of less conspicuous doctrines which could be developed into a wholly different theory of Church government; and during the stormy reign of Boniface VIII both trends of canonistic thought were forced into prominence, so that an age which produced the most extreme demands of papal monarchy saw also the first tentative formulations of the conciliar doctrines that would reach their full development only a century later. Under the impact of contemporary events the existing canonistic ideas that were pressed into service by rival publicists acquired new shades of meaning and entered into new relationships with one another; then they in turn, modified by these early controversies, helped to determine the outcome of events in the later crisis of the Great Schism.

In the world of external affairs the most conspicuous factor operating to produce a new alignment of ideas was the embittered dispute between Boniface VIII and Philip the Fair, with its attendant appeals against the Pope to a General Council of the Church. Yet, since the accusations of heresy and notorious misconduct brought against Boniface were charges technically admissible against a Pope according to earlier canonistic doctrine, their presentation by royal lawyers like Nogaret did not involve any novel claims against the Papacy as such.[1] Indeed, Nogaret himself contributed nothing to the theoretical development of conciliar ideas; the significance for future conciliar thought of his sustained campaign against Boniface lies in the fact that it did resuscitate in the sphere of practical politics the

---

[1] Cf. H.-X. Arquillière, 'L'appel au concile sous Philippe le Bel et la genèse des théories conciliaires', *Revue des questions historiques*, XLV (1911), pp. 23–55.

issue of a Pope's liability to judgement and so stimulated the canonists to reconsider this whole question, and also in the fact that it occurred at a time when quite different problems were encouraging more fundamental inquiries into the very nature of papal authority itself. Hence the theoretical status of the Pope as head of the Church became a matter of critical investigation just when the reigning pontiff was peculiarly vulnerable to attack.

The problems which stimulated these latter speculations arose out of the resignation of Pope Celestine V and the refusal by certain discontented factions within the Church to recognize the validity of his successor's election. The Spiritual Franciscans, dismayed by the eclipse of the only Pope who had ever whole-heartedly sympathized with their ideals, lent the prestige of their sanctity to the enemies of Boniface and renewed their Joachimite demands for 'the good Pope to come'.[2] The Colonna cardinals, actuated by the very different motive of family antagonism, and influenced perhaps by the current canonistic doctrines on the powers of the Sacred College which had been formulated by Hostiensis, also condemned as illegal Celestine's renunciation, and in May 1297 they denounced Boniface as a usurper, a simoniac and a heretic, demanding, moreover, that he should be cited before a General Council to answer these charges.[3] The Colonnas were supported by some of the most influential leaders of the Spiritual Franciscans—Jacopone da Todi was one of the signatories of

---

[2] On the attitude of the Spiritual Franciscans see Decima Douie, *The Nature and Effect of the Heresy of the Fraticelli* (Manchester, 1932), pp. 43–4, 139. Pietro Olivi, however, defended the principle of papal abdication in his letter to Conrad of Offida of 14 September 1295 (*Archivum Franciscanum Historicum*, XI, p. 366) and in his tract, *De Renuntiatione Pape* (ed. P. L. Oliger, *ibid.* pp. 340 ff.). On his views see also M. Maccarrone, 'Una questione inedita dell'Olivi sull'infallibilità del papa', *Rivista di Storia della Chiesa in Italia*, III (1949), pp. 309–24.

[3] The crisis was precipitated by an attack upon a convoy of papal treasure made by Stephen Colonna on 3 May 1297. Boniface cited the two Colonna cardinals to appear before him in consistory and demanded that they answer the question 'whether he was Pope or not'. After a delay of several days the two cardinals appeared before Boniface and, according to their own account, refused to recognize him as Pope. Boniface then demanded the return of the treasure, the surrender of Stephen Colonna and the handing over of three important Colonna castles. The Colonna cardinals replied with the manifesto of 10 May issued from their fortress of Longhezza. It was followed by two other letters dated 16 May and 15 June 1297. These Colonna manifestos were printed by Denifle in *Archiv für Literatur- und Kirchengeschichte*, V (1889), pp. 493 ff. For the background of the dispute see Mohler, *Die Kardinäle Jacob und Peter Colonna* (Paderborn, 1914); Finke, *Aus den Tagen Bonifaz VIII* (Munster, 1902), pp. 108–25; T. S. R. Boase, *Boniface VIII* (London, 1933), pp. 159–85; R. Scholz, *Die Publizistik zur Zeit Philipps des Schönen und Bonifaz VIII* (Stuttgart, 1903), pp. 198–208.

their first manifesto—and they attempted also to secure the help of Philip of France. For a moment it seemed that Boniface's position might be imperilled by an alliance of all his enemies.

The situation of 1297, with a faction of cardinals in open revolt against the reigning Pope, impugning both his personal integrity and the legitimacy of his election, seems like an ominous foreshadowing of the more disastrous revolt of 1378;[4] and, as in 1378, the constitutional crisis in the Church was accompanied by significant developments in the realm of pure ideas. Their nature will become apparent if we consider briefly the arguments adduced by the dissident cardinals and their Franciscan allies. In their first manifesto, the Colonnas put forward thirteen reasons for holding that no Pope could lawfully resign, a proposition which implied that, at the time of Boniface's election, Celestine V was still a true Pope, and that, accordingly, Boniface was a mere usurper, a *pseudo-presul*. The content of their arguments can be reduced to two or three fundamental ideas, the central one being that papal power could not be taken away from the Pope by any human agency since it was conferred solely by God. No one could withdraw an authority that he was not competent to bestow and no ecclesiastical dignity could be taken away except by a superior. But the Papacy, since it was the *summa virtus creata*, had no superior, and so the Pope could be deprived of his authority by God alone. Again, even the Pope could not decree that a bishop should cease to be a bishop, and so still less could he decree that the supreme bishop should cease to be supreme bishop. The Colonnas added to these arguments various accusations of maladministration and corruption against Boniface, in the course of which they displayed a convenient familiarity with the old canonistic doctrines that a heretical Pope could be deposed by a General Council, and that not even a legitimate Pope was empowered to misuse the goods of the Church.[5]

These latter charges might have had some basis in canon law; the points concerning Celestine's renunciation had none whatsoever,[6] and

---

[4] One essential difference was that Boniface, unlike Urban, was able to retain the support of the overwhelming majority of the cardinals. Apart from the two Colonnas there were nineteen cardinals and seventeen of them signed a declaration upholding the legitimacy of Boniface's election. Denifle, *art. cit.* pp. 524–9.

[5] Denifle, *art. cit.* pp. 510 ff.

[6] The possibility of a Pope resigning had always been freely admitted. The only doubt was whether the consent of the cardinals was necessary. See *Glossa Ordinaria*

yet it was these arguments, which seem almost naïve in their confusions between person and office and between jurisdiction and orders that were to prove most important for the future. The Colonna claims could present some appearance of validity only because the extreme papalists themselves had come to present the Pope's supreme power as a mystical authority transcending all normal laws and limitations; they could be effectively answered only by applying to the Pope and his *plenitudo potestatis* the same technique of detailed analysis that the canonists had already employed in defining the relationship between other bishops and their ecclesiastical corporations. Even the friends of the Papacy were compelled to turn to such analysis. Hence, the real significance of the Colonna arguments lies in the replies that they provoked; the doctrines that were to prove really important for later Conciliarists were evolved, not by the few extremists who supported the fulminations of the Colonnas, but by moderate writers who set out to demolish their arguments and establish beyond all doubt the legitimacy of Boniface's election. Mere rhetorical exaltation of the Papacy could provide no answer to an attack which took as its starting-point an exaggerated conception of the Pope's immutable prerogatives; but it proved that the canonistic doctrines which provided the most effective refutation of the Colonna arguments were equally destructive of the theories propounded by the more extreme supporters of Boniface himself. Innocent IV had written that it was sacrilege even to dispute concerning the Pope's *plenitudo potestatis*, but from the reign of Boniface VIII the disputation never ceased.[7]

The full implications of the position were not at once apparent, for Giles of Rome, who was the first to undertake a systematic refutation of the Colonna arguments, was himself a convinced exponent of the most extreme hierocratic ideas.[8] In his tract, *De Renuntiatione Papae*, he accordingly confined his attention strictly to the immediate difficulties raised by the rebellious cardinals, and refrained from press-

---

ad Dist. 21 c. 7, *Dist.* 63 c. 23, and the views of Huguccio and Vincentius cited by the Archdeacon in his *Rosarium ad* C. 7 q. 1 c. 12. See also W. Ullmann, 'Medieval views on papal abdication', *Irish Ecclesiastical Record*, LXXI (1949), pp. 125–33.

[7] John of Paris discussed this particular point and firmly maintained that it was licit to discuss the Pope's 'state' (whether he was a true Pope or not), the extent of his powers, and their possible abuse. *De Potestate Regia et Papali*, ed. Leclercq (Paris, 1942), pp. 248–51.

[8] His tract *De Renuntiatione Papae* (in Rocaberti, *Bibliotheca Maxima Pontificia*, II, pp. 1–64) appeared in 1297. See R. Scholz, *op. cit.* p. 44 and J. Rivière, *Le problème de l'église et de l'état au temps de Philippe le Bel* (Louvain, 1926), p. 111.

ing his arguments to their logical conclusions when to have done so might have proved embarrassing. It was left for his contemporary, John of Paris, to explore systematically all the implications of the arguments that could be adduced against the Colonnas, and by doing so, to achieve a new and very important formulation of the traditional doctrine concerning papal headship in the Church.

Before we proceed to an analysis of his work, some apology may seem necessary for treating John of Paris as an exponent of canonistic thought, for though Schulte did not hesitate to classify the *De Potestate Regia et Papali* as a work of canonistic scholarship[9] John has usually been regarded simply as a theologian and a publicist.[10] Moreover, the latest interpreter of his work has tended to reject the idea of any extensive canonistic influence on the formulation of his theories.[11] Dom Leclercq acknowledges that John of Paris quoted very often from the *Decretum* and *Decretales*,[12] and also from the *Glossa Ordinaria* to each of these works, but concludes that, 'là se borne son érudition canonique', apparently because John did not often refer, with exact references, to the works of other famous canonists (although, as Dom Leclercq points out, he did mention Huguccio, Ricardus Anglicus, Goffredus Tranensis and Hostiensis as well as citing the glosses of Joannes Teutonicus and Bernardus Parmensis—a by no means negligible display of canonistic erudition). This general argument seems a little strained when we note that John of Paris also never referred explicitly to St Thomas Aquinas, whom, none the less, Dom Leclercq rightly regards as a dominant influence on his work; and some of the particular instances adduced to prove John's lack of canonistic acumen seem hardly more convincing.[13] We would maintain that,

---

[9] J. F. v. Schulte, *Quellen*, II, pp. 177–8.

[10] See R. Scholz, *op. cit.* pp. 275–333; J. Rivière, *op. cit.* pp. 281–300; A. J. Carlyle, *History of Mediaeval Political Theory*, V, pp. 422–37; M. Grabmann, *Studien zu Joannes Quidort von Paris O.P.* (Munich, 1922); J. Leclercq, *Jean de Paris et l'ecclésiologie du XIIIᵉ siècle* (Paris, 1942). This last work includes a valuable edition of the *De Potestate Regia et Papali* from which our quotations will be taken. See also F. Merzbacher, 'Wandlungen des Kirchenbegriffs im Spätmittelalter', *Z.S.S.R.* LXX (1953), pp. 274–361 at pp. 343–6.

[11] J. Leclercq, *op. cit.* pp. 65–70.

[12] In fact he quoted from these sources far more often than from any others except the Scriptures themselves.

[13] It is pointed out that John quoted from the *Summa* of Goffredus 'mais sans en indiquer le référence, ce qu'il n'omet jamais de faire quand il invoque une "autorité" dont il connaît la source'. But John not infrequently quoted his authorities without any more exact reference than the name of the relevant work; the argument would

besides reflecting the acknowledged influence of St Thomas, the work
of John of Paris displays a much greater familiarity with the early
Decretist sources and the intricacies of Decretalist corporation doctrines than its editor seems willing to concede.[14] But it remains true
that John was not a professional canonist, and we would certainly
agree with Dom Leclercq that 'L'originalité de Jean de Paris n'est
pas dans l'ampleur de son érudition canonique, mais dans la mise en
œuvre des textes.'[15] His essential contribution did indeed consist in
his manner of using canonistic texts that were familiar enough to the
other contemporary publicists; and, after all, no very profound juristic erudition was needed for the task he accomplished. A study of
the *Glossa Ordinaria* to the *Decretum* and the *Lectura* of Hostiensis—
both works which John of Paris did know and cited—could have
provided all the necessary materials for a theory of papal authority
radically different from the prevailing doctrine of the time.

It is not altogether surprising that, in the age of Boniface VIII, we
find the most enterprising manipulation of canonistic ideas in the
work of a scholar who was himself trained in a different discipline.
From the early fourteenth century onwards the technical canonistic
compilations tended to become ever more voluminous and encyclo-
paedic, the occasional grain of original thought buried under layers
of accumulated authorities whose very multiplication made for incohe-

---

seem to imply, therefore, that he did not even know the title of Goffredus Tranensis's
extremely well known and widely quoted *Summa super titulis Decretalium*. This seems
hardly likely. Again, 'Il attribue à Hostiensis une opinion qui ne se trouve pas exprimée
au lieu indiqué.' John of Paris gave a reference to the *Lectura* of Hostiensis *ad* X.
v.vii.10; the correct reference is to be found in the *Lectura ad* v.vii.9. It seems a
somewhat trivial slip upon which to base a judgement of the quality of John's canonistic scholarship. Finally, 'Il ignore le Sexte, qui lui eût cependant fourni un argument
nouveau en faveur de la renonciation de Célestin V.' But if John of Paris refrained
from citing a collection promulgated by Boniface VIII in an argument designed to
prove that that pontiff in fact possessed a legitimate authority, it might as well have
been out of a regard for the elementary rules of logic as out of mere ignorance.

[14] It is certain that John's work was filled with ideas that had been developed by
the canonists of the preceding century, and the question of whether he had become
acquainted with some of them at second-hand is perhaps not of the greatest importance. A complete study of the sources of his thought would need to determine, not
only the immediate contexts from which John drew his quotations, but also the
extent to which these sources were themselves influenced by earlier canonistic traditions. For instance, John of Paris is known to have used the *De Renuntiatione Papae*
of Giles of Rome—which in turn relied to a great extent on canonistic arguments.

[15] *Op. cit.* p. 66. Dom Leclercq also remarks with justice of John of Paris that,
'l'usage qu'il fait des textes canoniques diffère autant de l'opportunisme intéressé des
régaliens que de l'arbitraire des théocrates'.

rence. John of Paris was under no obligation to indulge in this rather
pedantic erudition which was becoming the hall-mark of professional canonistic scholarship, but could set himself instead to select
from the canonistic works of the preceding century a group of significant but hitherto unrelated doctrines and then to combine them
in a new and daring synthesis. It is this constructive element in his
work that justifies its presentation as a contribution to the main stream
of canonistic tradition rather than merely as a publicistic treatise which
showed traces of canonistic influence. After all, every publicist of the
fourteenth century quoted from canonistic sources, but John of Paris
was the only one who so thoroughly appreciated their inner logic that
he could offer a development of canonistic ideas which not only influenced subsequent publicistic arguments, but also penetrated into the
technical compilations of the canonists themselves.[16]

His theory concerning the internal structure of the Church was, in
essence, a combination of those Decretist doctrines which had emphasized the underlying authority of the whole Church with elements of

---

[16] E.g. the great canonist Joannes Andreae followed John of Paris literally in his
Novella on the *Sext. ad.* I.v.1 fol. 32 n. 2:

Joannes Andreae

Et iurisdictio sit res quod augeri et
minui potest ergo deleri vel tolli.
... dicitur papalem potestatem dupliciter considerari uno modo prout ligatos
et solutos in terra liget solvit in celo. Et
est hoc simpliciter a Deo, alio modo
prout haec potestas est in isto vel in illo
quod etiam a Deo est qui operatur omnia
in nobis Ysa. 26. Tamen in hoc vel in
illo est per co-operationem humanam scil.
per consensum eligentium et electi, et sic
esse in hoc vel illo desinere potest per operationem humanam, sic et anima ratio-
nabilis est a solo Deo per creationem
tamen quod sit in isto vel in illo cooperat
natura dispensando et organizando et
ideo per operationem naturae potest desinere naturaliter et violenter.

Et per hoc fit responsum ad quartum
quod dicebatur de summa virtute creata,
licet dici possit papatum esse equalem vel
maiorem virtutem certo casu in concilio
vel tota ecclesia. ...

John of Paris

Iurisdictio vero sicut potest augeri vel
minui, ita et deleri et tolli (p. 258.35).
... dicendum est quod potestas papalis
dupliciter potest considerari. Uno modo
secundum se, et sic est a solo Deo. ...
Alio modo potest considerari ut est in
isto vel in illo et sic est a solo Deo eo
modo quo omnia opera nostra Deo attri-
buimus. Isaie 26. ... Licet igitur papatus
sit in se a solo Deo, tamen in hac persona vel illa est per cooperationem humanam, scilicet per consensum electi et
elegentium et secundum hoc per consensum humanum potest desinere esse in isto
vel in illo sicut cum anima rationalis sit
a solo Deo per creationem tamen quod
sit in isto corpore cooperatur natura dis-
ponendo et organizando, et ideo per operationem naturae potest desinere anima
rationalis esse in isto corpore (p. 255.1).

... licet sit summa virtus creata in persona tamen est ei equalis vel maior in
collegio sive in tota ecclesia (p. 258.6).

thought derived from later canonistic corporation theories. Hostiensis had elaborated with a wealth of juristic detail a series of doctrines relating to the constitutional structure of corporate groups within the Church and had shown too, in a number of scattered glosses, how those doctrines might be applied to the Roman church and the Church as a whole. John of Paris was not interested in Hostiensis's legal refinements, but he applied the general principles which underlay them to the corporate structure of the Universal Church and to the position of the Pope as its head more systematically than the canonists themselves had ever done. In particular, his exposition was built around the principles—whose juristic elaboration we have already considered—that a prelate was to be regarded as *procurator* or *dispensator*, not as *dominus* of his church, that authority in a corporation was not concentrated in the head alone but diffused among the various members, that the power of jurisdiction, unlike the power of orders, was conferred on a prelate by human delegation in the act of election. Once these ideas had been transferred from the technical sphere of corporation theory to the publicistic literature on Church government, they became important elements in the growth of subsequent theories of conciliar authority.

The *De Potestate Regia et Papali* opened its discussion on Church government with a deceptively conservative account of the origins and nature of papal authority. Just as each diocese was a corporate unity with a bishop as its head, wrote John, so too the whole congregation of the faithful formed *unus populus* which, like any other corporate group, required a supreme head to maintain its unity.[17] In the case of the whole Church a single head was particularly necessary, since there might arise dissensions concerning articles of faith which would grow into schisms unless there were some supreme judge with authority to decide such cases;[18] and, moreover, since the property of the Church was held in common (unlike that of laymen) it was necessary that there should be some single head with general rights of administration over it.[19] Christ had foreseen these contin-

---

[17] P. 180.5, 'Et ideo sicut in qualibet diocesi est unus episcopus qui est caput ecclesie in populo illo, sic in tota ecclesia et toto populo Christiano est unus summus scilicet papa Romanus. . . .'

[18] P. 180.14, '. . . contigit interdum circa ea que fidei sunt questiones moveri in quibus per diversitatem sententiarum divideretur ecclesia . . . nisi per unius sententiam unitas servaretur'.

[19] P. 181.10, 'Sed bona ecclesiastica communitati sunt collata; ideo oportet quod

gencies and had provided for them in the special powers which he had conferred on Peter and through him on the Papacy;[20] under Christ the Pope might properly be described as head of the whole Church:

> Potest . . . dici summus pontifex caput quantum ad exteriorem ministrorum exhibitionem in quantum ipse est principalis inter ministros a quo ut a principali Christi vicario in spiritualibus totus ordo ministrorum dependet ut a hierarcho et architecto, sicut romana ecclesia indubitanter est caput omnium ecclesiarum.[21]

These quite sincere acknowledgements of the Pope's unique authority as 'head of the Church' have sometimes led to a dismissal of John's other opinions as mere minor eccentricities, provoked by the circumstances of the time, and exaggerated to suit their own purposes by later conciliar thinkers.[22] This interpretation does less than justice to the underlying consistency and coherence of John's work. The recognition of papal headship as a necessary condition of Church unity was neither a sop to convention nor a denial in advance of the more radical implications of the analysis that was to follow. It was rather an indispensable basis for the subsequent exposition in which the everyday concept of corporate unity in the Church acquired a new and surprising significance simply because John of Paris consistently assumed that the structure of the whole Church was subject to the same rules that the canonists had evolved in considering the affairs of lesser groups within it.

The assertion that the Pope's relationship to the Church was the same as that of any other prelate to his ecclesiastical corporation was repeated several times in the course of his work, introducing each new phase of the argument and unifying the whole theory. It appeared already in the first discussion on papal authority,

---

sit aliquis unus qui communitati presit ut bonorum omnium communis dispensator et dispositor communis.'

[20] P. 180.17, 'Hic autem unus principatum habens est Petrus successorque eius, non quidem synodali ordinatione sed ex ore Domini. . . .'

[21] P. 230.4.

[22] E.g. V. Martin remarked, 'Jean de Paris n'était pas un révolutionnaire', and added that when ideas inconsistent with the accepted doctrines on papal power are found in his work and that of his contemporaries, 'il s'agissait là de brèves propositions, éparses dans des traités hétérogènes, elles ne s'imposaient pas à l'attention'. 'Doctrine de la supériorité du concile sur le pape', *Revue des sciences religieuses*, XVII (1937), pp. 261–89 at p. 262.

> ... sicut in qualibet diocesi est unus episcopus qui est caput ecclesie in populo illo, sic in tota ecclesia ... est unus summus scilicet papa romanus.[23]

And it recurred when John proceeded to his very important discussion on the ownership of ecclesiastical property. It was agreed, he wrote, that ordinary prelates were not *domini* but *tutores, procuratores, dispensatores*; but, he added, some writers would claim for the Pope a quite different dignity and attribute to him actual *dominium* over ecclesiastical property.[24] This claim John refused to admit, and his subsequent analysis of the question was largely a restatement of the canonistic theories on Church property which we have already mentioned. For John of Paris, as for Huguccio and Innocent IV, *dominium* rested only with the *congregatio fidelium*,[25] and all prelates, including the Pope, were *dispensatores* to whom was entrusted only the duty of administration. But whereas a bishop was *dispensator* only of the goods of his own local church the Pope was a *universalis dispensator*,

> ... ipse tamquam caput et supremum membrum universalis ecclesie est universalis dispensator omnium generaliter bonorum ecclesiasticorum spiritualium et temporalium.[26]

John expressed himself with an unusual lack of precision in considering the old problem of the canonists, whether *dominium* did truly belong to the local church or to the Universal Church. He suggested that, in a sense, both possessed *dominium*, the Universal Church *generaliter*, the local church *in bonis sibi correspondentibus*.[27] His views on the relationship between the Pope as *universal dispensator* and the heads of the local churches were made more plain in other discussions on the structure of the ecclesiastical hierarchy; at this point in his argument he was at any rate quite clear and definite in his assertion that the Pope did not possess *dominium* over the goods of the Church. Replying to those who held that the Pope was *verus dominus*, he wrote,

> Hoc autem patet falsum esse ex predictis cum papa non sit dominus omnium ecclesiasticorum bonorum generaliter, sicut nec prelati inferiores

---

[23] P. 180.5. See also pp. 186.43, 188.18, 197.8, 254.24, 257.19.

[24] P. 174.23.

[25] P. 186.4, 'Et ideo in bonis ecclesiasticis nulla persona singularis habet proprietatem et dominium sed communitas sola. . . .'

[26] P. 186.23.

[27] P. 186.26, '. . . sola communitas universalis ecclesie est domina et proprietaria omnium bonorum generaliter, et singule communitates et ecclesie dominium habent in bonis sibi correspondentibus'.

bonorum sui collegii. Sed papa est universalis dispositor et dispensator bonorum, et amplius facit sibi fructus suos de bonis communibus pinguiores, secundum exigentiam sui status, quam prelati inferiores qui vocati sunt in partem sollicitudinis, non in plenitudinem potestatis.[28]

This was the only occasion when he used the term *plenitudo potestatis* to describe the Pope's authority, and it is interesting that it occurs in a passage whose general purpose was to emphasize, not the magnitude, but the limitations of papal power.

He went on to discuss those limitations in more concrete terms. All ecclesiastical authority was given for the 'edification' of the Church, not for its 'destruction', he pointed out, borrowing from St Paul a phrase that was to become a stock argument in later conciliar works; and to this general principle he added specific rules deduced from the Pope's status as *dispensator*. If the Pope had been *dominus* of Church property, John argued, he could have used it in any way he pleased, but since he possessed only powers of administration over goods that ultimately belonged to the whole Church, he had no authority to use them except in the interests of the Church:

> ... papa non potest ad libitum detrahere bona ecclesiastica ita quod quidquid ordinet de ipsis teneat. Hoc enim verum esset si esset dominus, sed cum sit dispensator bonorum communitatis in quo requiritur bona fides non habet sibi collatam potestatem super bonis ipsis nisi ad necessitatem vel utilitatem ecclesie communis.[29]

In a later discussion he made it clear that the same limitations applied to the Pope's spiritual authority as to his rights over Church property. In matters of doctrine the Pope possessed a right of jurisdiction, a power to determine legal cases involving questions of faith, but he did not possess in himself the absolute power that would have enabled him to add to or to alter articles of faith at his own will. He could not, for instance, define as a matter of faith that the Pope possessed jurisdiction over the property of laymen; for the Christian faith pertained to the whole Church and the highest authority for defining it was not the Pope alone but a General Council of the whole Church. This contention was supported by a series of references to the *Decretum*,

---

[28] P. 186.42. Cf. C. 12 q. 1 c. 13 '(episcopus) omnium quae habet ecclesia efficitur dispensator' and X. III.xxiv.2, '... episcopus et quilibet praelatus ecclesiasticarum rerum sit procurator non dominus'. The close correspondence between John's theory of Church property and that of the canonists was noticed by both Gierke (*Genossenschaftsrecht*, III, p. 255 n. 33) and Gillet (*Personnalité juridique*, p. 118 n. 2).
[29] P. 188.7.

> Amplius cum fides christiana sit catholica et universalis non potest
> summus pontifex hoc ponere sub fide sine concilio generali quia papa
> non potest destruere statuta concilii, xix d., *Anastasius*. Nam licet conci-
> lium non possit pape legem imponere . . . tamen non intelligitur in hiis
> que fidei sunt, eo quod orbis maius est urbe et papa cum concilio major
> est papa solo, xciii d., *Legimus*.[30]

The fact that the Pope's authority could be augmented by the co-
operation of the fathers of a Council implies another doctrine that
was an important element in John's scheme of thought, namely, that
the authority inhering in the ecclesiastical hierarchy was not concentrated in the person of the Pope but was diffused among other
members of the Church as well. He treated this theme from several
different points of view, and in other contexts developed more explicitly the idea that there existed in the Church centres of authority
whose powers were not derived from the Pope but could be used to
supplement the papal authority or even to oppose it. The question
first arose in a discussion on the Pope's relationship to secular princes.
No one, he argued, would maintain that an ordinary bishop possessed temporal authority in virtue of his episcopacy or that there
could be an appeal to him from the local prince in a secular case;
yet the bishop, as a successor of the Apostles, lacked no type of
authority which the Pope possessed, and here *Dist.* 21 of the *Decretum*
was cited to prove that all the Apostles received power equally with
Peter and directly from Christ.[31] The only difference was that the
Pope exercised over the whole Church those same powers that a
bishop possessed only in his own diocese:

> . . . sicut tunc in apostolis quidquid potuit unus sicut Petrus potuit alius,
> ita et nunc de iure communi quidquid papa potest quilibet episcopus
> potest, nisi quod papa potest ubique, ceteri vero episcopi in suis dio-
> cesibus tantum.[32]

This view of the Pope's supreme authority seems precisely in accordance with that of the Decretist sources considered in the previous

---

[30] P. 243.2.

[31] P. 196.33, 'Item eamdem potestatem acceperunt omnes Apostoli cum Petro,
Matthei xviii, et habetur xxi *Dist.*, *In Novo*, ubi dicitur quod Petrus ligandi solvendique
potestatem primus accepit, ceteri vero apostoli cum eodem, et non dicitur ab eodem,
pari consortio honorem et potestatem acceperunt, et in collatione huius non posuit
Christus aliquam restrictionem respectu aliorum a Perro, licet appareat ex modo
loquendi quod vellet Petrum esse principaliorem et quasi caput ecclesie propter
unitatem ecclesie conservandam.'

[32] P. 197.7.

chapter, and closely related to John's doctrine of the Pope as *dispensator*. The Pope did not confer authority on other bishops but only determined the boundaries within which the authority of each should normally be exercised.[33] The fact was mentioned again as an *a fortiori* argument to prove that royal authority was not derived from the Pope. It was absurd to suggest that the power of a king was obtained mediately, through the Pope, when not even the prelates of the Church obtained their power from him; the prelates' authority came from God directly and from the Christian people—*a Deo . . . immediate, et a populo eligente vel consentiente.*[34]

Moreover, John regarded the authority diffused among the members of the Church as at least equal to that which was concentrated in its head. This opinion was expressed in his answer to one of the Colonna arguments which asserted that no human authority could take away the powers of a Pope, since the Papacy was the *summa virtus creata.*

> Ad quartam rationem que videtur specialiter probare quod papa non possit deponi noluntarius quia papatus est summa virtus creata, respondeo . . . licet sit summa virtus creata in persona, tamen est ei equalis vel maior in collegio sive in tota ecclesia.[35]

Elsewhere he defined the Pope's position as *caput* and *principale membrum* of the Church, so that his theory as a whole seems a precise restatement of Hostiensis's doctrine that the 'head' of a corporation was its 'principal part', enjoying an authority greater than that of any single member of the corporation, but not greater than that of all the members together.[36]

It will be seen that John of Paris applied this argument not only to the voluntary resignation of a Pope but also to his forced deposition. He returned to this point again and again,[37] and his treatment of it is perhaps his most significant contribution to the development of conciliar ideas. All the elements of John's thought that we have

---

[33] P. 209.29.

[34] P. 199.34, 'Sed potestas prelatorum non est a Deo mediante papa sed immediate, et a populo eligente vel consentiente.'

[35] P. 258.6.

[36] P. 186.10, '. . . est aliquod membrum quod est principale et caput communitatis ut episcopus'. P. 186.20, '. . . omnes ecclesiastice congregationes habent quamdam generalem unitatem in quantum sunt una ecclesia habens connexionem ad unum principale membrum . . . scilicet dominum papam, ideo ipse tamquam caput et supremum membrum universalis ecclesie est universalis dispensator. . . .' Cf. Hostiensis, *Lectura ad* X. III.x.4, fol. 44ra, 'Prelatus est principalis pars ecclesie.'

[37] Pp. 188.18, 214.37, 215.17, 248.17, 250.26, 254.21, 257.3 and 260.19.

mentioned thus far—the Pope as universal *dispensator*, the existence of authority in the Church other than the Pope's, the derivation of a prelate's authority *a Deo . . . et a populo*—all were blended together in his discussions on the deposition of a Pope. In these discussions he relied mainly on canonistic arguments, but deployed them in such a fashion as to reach conclusions more radical than any that the canonists themselves had envisaged. According to John of Paris, a Pope could be deposed, not only for heresy or notorious crime, but even for mere incompetence; and this was true, not only because the Pope received his authority for the Church, *propter ecclesiam* (as John often pointed out), but because, in a real sense, he received it from the Church as well.

The subject was first raised in his opening discussion on *dominium* of Church property. His argument here, with its insistence that the Pope was a *dispensator . . . in quo requiritur bona fides*, recalls not only the Decretist warnings against abuse of ecclesiastical property but also, and even more closely, the later development of the doctrine of the prelate as proctor of his corporation. It will be recalled that, according to the canonists, no proctorial mandate conferred on the recipient a right to act in bad faith against the interests of his principal, nor to squander any property entrusted to him by extravagance and maladministration. Moreover, the common doctrine of Roman and canon law held that if a proctor did act in bad faith his mandate could be revoked by the corporation that he represented, and so, since the canonists had taught that a bishop was proctor of his corporation, they might logically have maintained that he could be deposed by his chapter in case of misconduct. They did not in fact press their argument to that conclusion, and the fact is not surprising. All their discussions on the prelate's proctorial status were evoked by technical problems concerning the limitations on his freedom of action in a court of law; moreover, there already existed in positive canon law detailed provisions concerning the deposition of a bishop and the procedure required was much more elaborate than a mere dismissal by the canons. Nevertheless, it was held that the bishop's status as a proctor rendered him easily liable to correction; the canons could limit his freedom of action by withholding their consent in important matters that affected the well-being of the whole Church; and in the last resort they could bring about his deposition by invoking the due process of law. John of Paris apparently regarded this as a quite satisfactory basis for arguing that the Church could bring about the deposition of a Pope who abused his powers as *dispensator*:

> Et sicut etiam monasterium posset agere ad depositionem abbatis vel
> ecclesia particularis ad depositionem episcopi si appareret quod dissipa-
> ret bona monasterii vel ecclesie ... item si appareret quod papa bona
> ecclesiarum infideliter detraheret ... deponi posset si admonitus non
> corrigeretur. d. xi (sic), capitulo *Si papa*. ...[38]

And he went on to quote the famous gloss of Joannes Teutonicus on
Dist. 40 c. 6 of the *Decretum*, in which it was maintained that a Pope
could be deposed for any notorious crime. Thus, the theoretical basis
for the deposition of a Pope was derived from John's favourite analogy with the juristic status of the heads of lesser corporations; the
actual authority for applying that analogy to the Pope in this particular instance was provided by the *Glossa Ordinaria* to the *Decretum*.
The problem of an established canonical procedure which arose in
the case of other bishops caused no difficulty when the case of the
Pope himself was under consideration, for the argument that a General Council, representing the whole Church, was competent to depose a Pope fitted in conveniently enough with the view that the
Pope was a *dispensator*, acting on behalf of the whole Church. John
also maintained, quite consistently, that a Pope who abused his spiritual powers could be deposed just like one who 'dissipated the goods
of the Church'.[39]

It is not difficult to see how these views could be developed quite
naturally out of existing canonistic doctrines, but the course of the
argument seems to have brought us to a conclusion quite inconsistent with the premisses set out at the beginning of John's work, for
there the Papacy was presented as an institution established by the
direct will of God, and so, it might seem, responsible to God alone.
This difficulty was resolved in the analysis of papal authority with
which John of Paris brought his work to a close. His last two chapters were devoted to a direct refutation of the claims of the Colonna

---

[38] P. 188.18. In another discussion on the deposition of a Pope he cited canonistic
texts suggesting that, if a bishop became of unsound mind and refused to resign, the
chapter could proceed to elect a successor. P. 257.19, 'Amplius, casu specialis ecclesie
ubi episcopus nullo tempore ad sane mentis officium redit vel si interdum redit et
requisitus cedere noluerit, potest et debet alium eligere, VII, q. 1, *Qualiter* et *Quamvis
triste* et ibidem Iohannes, et *Extra, de renunciatione, Quidam cedendi.* Ergo a simili collegium
cardinalium vice totius ecclesie poterit papam invitum deponere.'
[39] P. 215.17, 'Si vero in spiritualibus delinquat papa, beneficia simoniace con-
ferendo ... vel sentiendo vel docendo circa ea que ad fidem vel bonos mores pertinent, tunc primo monendus esset a cardinalibus qui sunt loco totius cleri. Et si
incorrigibilis esset ... tunc imperator ... deberet procedere contra ipsum ad eius
depositionem.'

cardinals, and the arguments used in them were nearly all borrowed with slight though significant modifications from the *De Renuntiatione Papae* of Giles of Rome; but, whereas in that work the arguments at times seem somewhat tendentious since Giles was obviously not prepared to explore all their implications, they provide an entirely logical and satisfying conclusion to the work of John of Paris. The difficulty for Giles of Rome was that, in proving that a Pope could voluntarily abdicate, he was in danger of proving too much, that a Pope could be compelled to resign even against his own will. For John of Paris, on the other hand, a proof that the divine origin of papal authority did not confer upon the Pope immunity from human judgement was precisely the conclusion needed to give coherence to his whole theory.

He therefore repeated towards the close of his work that papal authority was from God, but went on to apply to the Papacy the well established juristic distinction between a personified office and the individual who for the time being occupied that office. The intrinsic authority of the Papacy itself was conferred directly by God and so was immutable, but the decision as to which particular individual should exercise that authority was made by men. It was an act of God only in the sense in which all our works are attributed to God, and so, argued John, since papal authority was conferred on a given individual by human agency it could be taken away from him by human agency.[40] It was just as reasonable to suppose that God would approve the deposition of an unworthy pontiff as to assume that he confirmed the election of a worthy one;[41] and the consent of the people to the deposition of a Pope who proved unsuited to his office (not necessarily heretical or criminal) was just as efficacious in removing him as their consent, expressed through election, had been in installing him:

> ... efficacior est consensus populi in hoc casu ad deponendum eum invitum, si totaliter inutilis videatur, et ad eligendum alium, quam eius voluntas ad renunciandum populo nolente.[42]

Again, while the Papacy was of divine origin, it was not the only power in the church of divine origin—and here John brought in his

---

[40] P. 255.12, 'Licet igitur papatus sit in se a solo Deo, tamen in hac persona vel illa est per cooperationem humanam, scilicet per consensum electi et elegentium et secundum hoc per consensum humanum posset desinere esse in isto vel in illo.'
[41] P. 256.8.
[42] P. 254.25.

argument that there existed *in collegio sive in tota ecclesia* an authority
at least equal to the Pope's. As for the oft-repeated canonistic maxim
that the Pope was immune from all human judgement, John of Paris
simply remarked that to him this doctrine seemed unintelligible (*illud
non intelligo*) in view of other canonistic texts which implied quite clearly
that in some circumstances a Pope could be tried and deposed;[43]
and, when one remembers the ambiguities which had surrounded
earlier canonistic discussions of this question, it is not difficult to
understand his perplexity.

Having established that the divine origin of the Papacy did not in
itself preclude the possibility of an individual Pope being deposed,
John of Paris next proceeded to a more detailed discussion of the
sense in which a Pope derived his authority from human consent.
His argument now rested on the distinction between the power of
orders and the power of jurisdiction, a distinction which as we have
seen, had played an important part in canonistic discussions on episcopal authority during the preceding century. This familiar division
of powers had a peculiar force when applied to the Papacy, for it
was commonly held among the canonists that in the matter of orders
Peter was the equal of the other Apostles, that his primacy consisted
solely in a superior power of jurisdiction. The canonists had also
held, however, that, while the power of orders was a supernatural
and indelible gift of God, the power of jurisdiction could be conferred
solely by human election and consent. John of Paris accepted this
principle and extended its application to include even the Pope, presenting the papal jurisdiction as a mere delegation from the Church.
His conclusion was that, since the Pope's jurisdiction was conferred
by men, it could be taken away by men (though no human authority
could take away his power of orders); and, since his jurisdiction was
the distinctive characteristic of papal authority, a pontiff who was
deprived of it would cease to be Pope. He would still be a bishop
since the power of orders was indelible, but he would no longer be
the supreme bishop:

> Iurisdictio vero sicut potest augeri vel minui ita et deleri et tolli; et
> ideo amota iurisdictione, papa desinit esse papa et summus pontifex
> desinit esse summus pontifex, licet non desinit esse pontifex.[44]

---

[43] P. 257.15.
[44] P. 258.29. Cf. pp. 259.11, 260.19.

The idea that the jurisdiction of a Pope was conferred by the whole Church was an integral part of John's system of thought; but, of course, in practice the Pope was elected only by the College of Cardinals. John, however, several times asserted that the cardinals acted on behalf of the whole Church.[45] Moreover, while acknowledging that a General Council was usually regarded as the proper authority to depose a Pope, he himself expressed the view that the College of Cardinals was competent to bring about his dismissal. If their consent on behalf of the Church was effective in electing a Pope it would be equally effective in removing him:

> Credo tamen quod simpliciter sufficeret ad depositionem huiusmodi collegium cardinalium quia ex quo consensus eorum facit papam loco ecclesie, videtur similiter quod possit eum deponere....[46]

The canonistic treatment of the cardinals' status during the preceding half-century could easily have given rise to the view that they represented the whole Church. Innocent IV had revived the description of the Sacred College as Senate of the Church,[47] and the definition was widely repeated among canonists contemporary with John of Paris. Moreover, the term was not used merely as a vague title of honour, for various technicalities of Roman law relating to the Senate were used to define the authority of the cardinals;[48] and technically, according to the texts of Roman law, the senators acted on behalf of the whole Roman people.[49] It is not surprising, therefore, that John never attempted to defend his view of the cardinals as representative of the Church, but always mentioned it casually as though referring to a commonly accepted idea of the age.[50]

---

[45] The cardinals were said to be 'loco totius cleri' (p. 215.20), 'in loco totius cleri et totius populi' (p. 254.6), 'loco ecclesie' (p. 254.35), 'vice totius ecclesie' (p. 257.23).

[46] P. 254.34.

[47] Innocent IV *ad* X. II.xxvii.23.

[48] See, for example, Guido de Baysio, *Rosarium ad Dist.* 50 c. 25 C. 2 q. 3 c. 7 and C. 16 q. 1 c. 7.

[49] *Inst.* I.ii.5, 'Cum auctus esset populus romanus in eum modum ut difficile esset in unum eum convocare legis sanciendae causa, aequum visum est senatum, vice populi consuli.'

[50] Pietro Olivi in his *De Renunciatione Papae* (1297) also described the cardinals as acting on behalf of the whole Church, and in language that seems like a paraphrase of the Roman law text, 'Quod vero si in electione papae plebis assensus necessario prae-exigitur multa pericula et incommoda possent contingere, ideo congrue ordinatum est quod vicem omnium in hoc gererent aliqui praecipui qui nunc communiter cardinales vocantur' (ed. Oliger, *Archivum Franciscanum Historicum*, XI, pp. 340 ff.).

Modern interest in the writings of John of Paris has centred mainly upon his discussion of the problems of Church and State, and his work in that field was marked by such a rare maturity and integrity of judgement that there has been a tendency to neglect the really radical implications of his theories on the internal government of the Church. His work in fact provides by far the most consistent and complete formulation of conciliar doctrine before the outbreak of the Great Schism; and his arguments could be more readily assimilated than those of some later publicists (such as Marsiglio) because they were so firmly based upon well-known and generally accepted juristic principles. Indeed, in so far as it referred to the relationship between Pope and Church, John's work was simply an exercise in applied canonistic theory. All the doctrines upon which he based his arguments had been hammered out in detail by the thirteenth-century canonists; John's achievement was to publicize some of the logical corollaries that would follow from an unreserved application of those doctrines to the Papacy. But to trace the sources of his thought is not to deny the very real originality of his work. He was one of those rare and influential thinkers whose 'originality' consists simply in placing the accepted platitudes of their age in a novel setting, where they reveal unexpected facets and sparkle like new-found truths.

Looking back upon the history of fourteenth-century thought, one can see that the *De Potestate Regia et Papali*, which treated with equal emphasis the problems of Church and State and the internal problems of Church government, marked a turning-point in the development of ecclesiological theory. Until the end of the thirteenth century interest had been mainly centred upon defining the relations between the spiritual and temporal hierarchies; henceforth it was to be the problems of authority within the Church, the interrelationship of Pope, cardinals and General Council, which more and more engaged the attention of the most influential thinkers of the age.

CHAPTER TWO

CONFLICTING CRITICISMS OF PAPAL MONARCHY

John of Paris was the most shrewd and gifted of the early Conciliarists, but the scholarly detachment of his work made it untypical of an age in which speculations on ecclesiology and political philosophy were so often dominated by personal and party passions. In the early fourteenth century the discussions on purely internal problems of Church government were often no more disinterested than the vituperative attacks launched against Boniface VIII by the partisans of Philip the Fair in the conflict of Church and State, for the very process of ecclesiastical centralization was producing ambitions and resentments within the Church which gave rise to protests against the system of papal autocracy. It would be unjust no doubt to suggest that the intransigent personality of Boniface himself was responsible for provoking such a diversity of attacks on the papal policies, but it is probably true that the weakening of papal power and prestige consequent upon the struggle with Philip the Fair encouraged an open expression of grievances which, until then, had been prudently concealed.

In the curia itself the process of centralization had increased the importance of the cardinals, and, what is perhaps just as significant, it had increased their own sense of their importance; yet their legal position in relation to the Pope remained obscure and ill-defined, and the general acceptance of a theory of papal *plenitudo potestatis* such as that propounded by Giles of Rome would inevitably have reduced them to the rank of mere subordinate agents of the Pope. At the other extreme, the growth of curial power naturally aroused resentment among the diocesan bishops who felt that all real power, and especially the all-important power of patronage, was slipping from their grasp, so that they too had cause to view with suspicion the doctrine of *plenitudo potestatis* which was invoked to justify the ever-increasing papal claims.

Thus two separate schools of thought arose which differed profoundly in many respects but which were united in their hostility to the theory of papal monarchy expounded by writers like Giles of

Rome and incarnated in Boniface VIII; and in the first decade of the fourteenth century each point of view found a zealous exponent in a distinguished canonist. The curialist school was represented by Joannes Monachus, Cardinal of SS. Marcellinus and Peter,[1] while the rights of the bishops were passionately defended by Guilielmus Durantis, Bishop of Mende, a nephew of the famous Speculator.[2] Although the views of these two very influential canonists have been occasionally mentioned in works on fourteenth-century political theory there has been no systematic discussion of their ideas in relation to the earlier currents of canonistic thought and the later developments of conciliar theory. Hence the true nature of Joannes Monachus's claims on behalf of the Sacred College has never been adequately presented, while the often original ideas of Guilielmus Durantis have been overshadowed by the more radical speculations of Marsiglio and Ockham.

Both canonists were perhaps somewhat in advance of their age in that each provided a theoretical formulation of a trend of thought which reached its full maturity only much later in the fourteenth century. It has been doubted, for instance, whether the writings of Joannes Monachus and the revolt of the Colonna cardinals provide really convincing evidence of any widespread 'oligarchic' tendencies in the Sacred College during the pontificate of Boniface VIII;[3] and

---

[1] On the life and character of Joannes Monachus see F. Lajarde, *Histoire Littéraire de la France*, XVII, pp. 201–24 and Finke, *Aus den Tagen Bonifaz VIII*, pp. 126–45. T. S. R. Boase, *Boniface VIII*, pp. 324–7, describes his mission to Philip the Fair in 1302. His views on the authority of the Sacred College are discussed by R. Scholz, *Publizistik zur Zeit Philipps des Schönen*, pp. 194–8; J. Rivière, *L'église et l'état*, pp. 358–9; and especially by W. Ullmann, *Origins of the Great Schism*, pp. 204–9.

[2] See R. Scholz, *op. cit.* pp. 208–23; J. Rivière, *op. cit.* pp. 363–9; J. Haller, *Papsttum und Kirchenreform* (Berlin, 1903), I, pp. 58–73; Andreas Posch, 'Die Reformvorschläge des Wilhelm Durandus jun. auf den Konzil von Vienne', in *Mitteilungen des Öst. Instituts für Geschichtsforschung*, XI, *Ergänzungsband*, 1929, pp. 288–303; P. Torquebiau, 'Le Gallicanisme de Durand de Mende le jeune', *Acta Congressus Iuridici Internationalis*, III, 1936. (Torquebiau seems to distort the views of Durandus by emphasizing his occasionally cautious phraseology concerning the relative authority of Pope and Council), E. Müller, *Das Konzil von Vienne, 1311–1312* (Münster in Westfalen, 1934), pp. 591–607.

[3] Rivière, *op. cit.* p. 359, 'Au total, rien n'autorise à chercher l'expression d'un système moins encore la manifestation d'un parti dans les récriminations intéressés de deux mécontents ou dans les revendications platoniques des théoriciens du droit.' On the other hand, Sägmüller (*Thätigkeit der Kardinäle*, p. 221) wrote, 'Es hat nun bereits in dieser Zeit nicht an Stimmen gefehlt welche den Papst an den Rath oder die Zustimmung der Kardinäle binden, so den Parlamentarismus in die Regierung der Kirche einführen, ja an Stelle der Monarchie eine Aristokratie setzen wollten.'

certainly the overwhelming majority of the cardinals publicly supported Boniface through all the vicissitudes of his reign, while the evidence of private hostility within the curia comes, naturally enough, from sources that were prejudiced against the Pope. But, on the other hand, Boniface was a man of violent moods, impatient of restraint, whose intemperance of language rivalled that of Urban VI himself, and there seems little reason to doubt that at least one of the posthumous charges brought against him had a basis in fact. 'He did not seek counsel from the cardinals to follow it, but rather exacted consent from them for whatsoever he himself wished.'[4] Joannes Monachus certainly thought that the rights of the cardinals were being undermined and set himself to act as a spokesman in their defence. His attitude emerges very clearly from his account of a consistory held at the beginning of Boniface's reign to consider the legality of certain grants which Celestine V had made without the customary approval of the cardinals. Joannes writes, rather complacently, 'I told the Pope that he would do well to obey himself the laws that he laid down for others.'[5] This was not the sort of language that Boniface was likely to tolerate from a subordinate (one remembers his savage retort to Joannes Monachus on another occasion, 'Pig-head from Picardy, I want no advice from asses like you'),[6] and it is surprising to read on in the cardinal's further account that the Pope accepted the advice of the Sacred College on this occasion and duly revoked the grants of his predecessor. Some of the later canonists, however, flatly refused to believe the story.[7]

Like Joannes Monachus, Guilielmus Durantis was perhaps not wholly uninfluenced by personal considerations in his denunciations of ecclesiastical abuses.[8] It may be doubted whether in his day the

---

The appearance of Sägmüller's views in 1896 led to a controversy between him and Karl Wenck in several subsequent volumes of the Journal, *Theologische Quartalschrift* (see Klewitz, 'Die Entstehung des Kardinalcollegiums', *Z.S.S.R.* LVI (1936), p. 116 n. 1). The ambitions of the cardinals were mentioned by Finke, *op. cit.* pp. 77–108 and Scholz, *op. cit.* pp. 190–4. See also T. S. R. Boase, *op. cit.* pp. 123–5 and W. Ullmann, *op. cit.* p. 185 n. 1.

[4] Dupuy, *Histoire du différend d'entre le pape Boniface VIII et Philippe le Bel* (Paris, 1655), p. 339.

[5] *Glosa Aurea super sexto Decretalium libro* (Parisiis, 1535), Gloss *ad Sext.* v.ii.4, fol. 347va, 'Dixi tunc decere ut quod papa mandat in suo canone aliis, id observare non negligat.'

[6] Dupuy, *Histoire du différend*, p. 339.

[7] *Infra*, p. 187.

[8] P. Torquebiau, *art. cit.*, observes in Guilielmus Durantis '... un attachement

system of papal provisions was already arousing such widespread resentment as he would have us suppose, and it is even more doubtful if this system really was the root cause of all the evils in the Church which he so profusely deplored. But he too, by identifying his grievances with those of a whole estate of the Church, was able to infuse a glow of righteous indignation into his condemnations of papal centralization. The position he adopted was very different from that of Joannes Monachus. In general questions of Church government the French cardinal supported a system of uncompromising absolutism, with the one important qualification that the cardinals should have a major share in the illimitable authority that he attributed to the Roman See. Durantis, on the other hand, condemned the whole system of centralized administration and, while putting forward extensive claims for a General Council, expressed nothing but contempt for the *curiales* whose greed and venality, he thought, were bringing the Church to ruin.

The sharp cleavage of opinion that was already apparent in the writings of these two distinguished canonists persisted throughout the fourteenth century and helped to create the climate of thought in which the problems of the Great Schism were debated. Throughout the period of the Avignon Papacy the oligarchic ambitions of the cardinals always seemed in direct opposition to the ideals of would-be conciliar reformers; and yet, paradoxical though it seems, the curialist arguments were eventually absorbed without incongruity into the theories of such eminent conciliarists as d'Ailly and Zabarella, who were themselves both members of the Sacred College. It is extremely important, therefore, if one is to trace any coherent pattern in the complex systems of thought that arose in the years of the Schism to examine the theoretical bases of these contrasting, yet ultimately complementary traditions of thought.

It is especially interesting to consider the principles that Joannes Monachus chose as the foundations of his theory, for the legal status of the Sacred College had been somewhat modified since Hostiensis had defended the rights of the cardinals. Gregory X's decree, *Ubi Periculum*,[9] laid down new and more stringent rules for the conduct

---

passioné à ses droits, une âpreté violente à les revendiquer, une persistante rancune à l'égard de ceux qui y ont porté atteinte' (p. 287).

[9] Promulgated in the second Council of Lyons, 1274, and incorporated in the *Sext.* at I.vi.3.

of electoral conclaves, with the important additional provision that the cardinals were not to engage in any business other than the election itself except in case of grave and evident peril; and Boniface's decree condemning the Colonna cardinals also contained a clause stating that their punishment could not be revoked 'even by the College of Cardinals during a vacancy'.[10] Joannes Andreae could write that the rather extreme views of Hostiensis were 'excusable' since he could not have known of the subsequent legislation. But there was no such 'excuse' for Joannes Monachus, and so from this point of view the task of championing the cardinals' prerogatives had been made considerably more difficult. On the other hand, the increasing importance of the cardinals in the administration of the whole Church was naturally reflected in an enhanced prestige, and the claim of the Colonna cardinals that the Sacred College had been established, 'ab exordio nascentis ecclesiae . . . ad dirigendos Romanos pontifices et consulendum eisdem'[11] met with little opposition. This claim that the Sacred College was a divinely instituted part of the government of the Church was not a new one,[12] but now for the first time it found general acceptance. Papal publicists like Giles of Rome and Augustinus Triumphus conceded that the cardinals were 'successors of the Apostles',[13] and even the canonistic works which sharply rejected the extreme claims of Joannes Monachus did not hesitate to use the most exalted language in describing the dignity of the Sacred College. (The cardinals were often said to be *senatores ecclesiae, pars corporis domini, membra capitis,* or *patricii scripti in diademate principis.*)[14]

Joannes Monachus must have felt some temptation to base his whole theory on these accepted titles of honour, especially in view of the canonists' fondness for extracting legal principles from allegories

---

[10] *Sext.* v.iii.1, '. . . non possit absolvi, nec etiam per collegium Apostolicae sedis eadem sede vacante'.

[11] *Archiv für Literatur- und Kirchengeschichte*, V, p. 522. The real controversy centred around their next words, 'non ut consiliarii voluntarii, sed necessarii potius'.

[12] Already in the eleventh century Peter Damian saw the cardinals pre-figured in Old Testament imagery. Cf. Sägmüller, *op. cit.* p. 211 n. 6. Innocent III compared the cardinals to the priests of the tribe of Levites mentioned in Deuteronomy xvii, 8–12 (X. IV.xvii.13), and Frederick II described them as 'successores Apostolorum' in his letter of 10 March 1239 (Huillard-Bréholles, *Historia Diplomatica*, V, i, p. 282).

[13] Giles of Rome, *De Renuntiatione Pape* (Rocaberti, *Bibliotheca Maxima Pontificia*, II, p. 33); Augustinus Triumphus, *Summa de Potestate Ecclesiae* (Romae, 1584), Q. 8, art. 4.

[14] See, for instance, Guido de Baysio *ad Sext.* I.vi.3, s.v. *Cardinales*, I.xv.1, s.v. *officii*; Henricus Bohic *ad X.* I.xxvii.23, fol. 163 rb n. 11; Joannes Andreae, Gloss *ad Sext.* II.xiv.2, s.v. *Cardinales, Novella ad Sext.*, I.xv.1, fol. 40 n. 1; Zenzelinus de Cassanis ad *Extravagantes*, I.iii.1, s.v. *circa nos.*

and similes. He did of course use such descriptions very freely to build up a general picture of the cardinals' exalted dignity, but whenever he wished to establish their technical legal authority in a particular case, either in relation to a reigning Pope or during a papal vacancy, he chose to employ a quite different type of argument. The position he adopted then was precisely the same as that set forth by his great predecessor Hostiensis half a century earlier, and developed in his own fashion by John of Paris. It was simple, and, granted the premiss, wholly adequate—Pope and cardinals together formed a single corporate body subject to the normal rules of corporation law; the Pope stood in exactly the same relationship to the cardinals as any other bishop to his cathedral chapter:

> Papa sic se habet ad collegium cardinalium, sicut alter episcopus respectu sui collegii. . . .[15]

The importance of canonistic corporation theory in the development of Joannes Monachus's views concerning the Sacred College was long ago noticed by Sägmüller,[16] but unfortunately, in estimating its significance, he seems to have been led astray by an attempt to interpret the ideas of Joannes and other contemporary canonists in the light of certain remarks of Gierke on the medieval theory of corporations, which, whatever their general validity, were hardly relevant to this particular case. Gierke wrote, in a passage which Sägmüller quoted in discussing the structure of the Roman church, that, according to the prevailing opinion among the canonists, an ecclesiastical college, just like its prelate, merely represented a right-subject standing above prelate and college.[17] Sägmüller therefore supposed that, in the theory of Joannes Monachus, the cardinals were held to represent the Church in the sense that they represented 'a transcendent ecclesiastical right-subject', and he assumed that this was the basis of Joannes's claims on behalf of the Sacred College. But there

---

[15] Joannes Monachus, Gloss ad Sext. v.iii.1, fol. 366 n. 4.

[16] He asked on what grounds the cardinals' claims against the Pope were based and replied, 'Wie die angeführte Stelle aus Joannes Monachus beweist, vor allem auf die Parallele, die man zwischen dem Papst und den Kardinalen einer-, dem Bischof und den Domkapitularen andererseits zu ziehen pflegte. Den gemeinsamen Untergrund aber für die gleichmässige Beurtheilung dieser Verhältnisse gab der Korporationsbegriff der Kanonisten und dessen Anwendung auf Kirche und Kirchen' (Thätigkeit, p. 225).

[17] Op. cit. p. 227. A little further on, however, Sägmüller acknowledged that this doctrine could not provide an adequate basis for all Joannes's claims on behalf of the cardinals (p. 238 n. 5).

is no evidence in the work of Joannes Monachus that he thought of the cardinals as 'representing' the Church in any sense whatsoever. The more serious confusion arose when Sägmüller went on to apply this Gierkian idea of representation to John of Paris and other writers who really did believe that the cardinals 'represented' the Church; for it is quite certain that when John of Paris, and, following him, Joannes Andreae and Zabarella wrote thus of the cardinals, they meant that the cardinals represented the *congregatio fidelium*, not that they represented an 'abstract right-subject'. This was made abundantly clear by John of Paris himself who, in describing the status of the cardinals, wrote indifferently that they were *loco ecclesie* or *loco totius cleri et totius populi*. It is of some importance to clarify this point, since the idea that the cardinals exercised authority as representatives of the whole *congregatio fidelium* was of considerable significance in the formulation of later conciliar theories; and Joannes Monachus certainly did not believe that the cardinals represented the Church in this more concrete sense of the word. In general Sägmüller never sufficiently emphasized that Joannes held quite distinctive and very extreme views concerning the authority of the Sacred College, and that there was a sharp cleavage between his opinions on this subject and those of most other contemporary canonists.[18]

We shall not find the key to his thought in any abstract speculations on 'right-subjectivity', for the only corporation doctrines that influenced Joannes Monachus were the severely practical ones deal-

---

[18] Sägmüller's whole chapter, 'Die Kardinäle und der Papst' (*Thätigkeit*, pp. 215–49) must be treated with reserve in so far as it deals with the views of the canonists. In this early work Sägmüller seems to have slipped several times in presenting their doctrines. The Archdeacon is consistently presented as a supporter of the cardinals' claims against the Pope (pp. 223, 224, 232), whereas in fact he sharply rejected them (*infra* pp. 207–10). Although Sägmüller states the opposite, the Archdeacon actually held that a Pope could resign without consent of the cardinals (Gloss *ad Sext.* I.vii.1, s.v. *resignare*. In assessing the Archdeacon's views it is necessary to bear in mind that he often transcribed without comment in the *Rosarium* Decretist opinions which he clearly rejected in his gloss on the Sext.). Again, Sägmüller attributes to Huguccio and Joannes Teutonicus the opinion that the College of Cardinals 'ganz und gar in die Stelle des gestorbenen Papst einrücke' (p. 227). But neither canonist went as far as that. He writes of Huguccio and the Archdeacon that they regarded the cardinals as representatives of the Church, but there seems to be no evidence that either of them did so. He includes John of Paris among those who held that a Pope could not resign without consent of the Church (p. 232), but John's whole theory on the deposition of a Pope was based on the contrary assumption that, just as a Pope could resign when the Church was unwilling, so too he could be deposed when he himself was unwilling.

ing with corporation structure, with the actual distribution of authority in a corporation; but these were indeed essential to his theory of
the cardinals' authority. His anxiety to establish the central principle
that Pope and cardinals were subject to the same laws of corporation structure as were lesser ecclesiastical colleges was very evident in
his crucial discussion on the phrase, *de consilio fratrum nostrorum*, which
occurred in so many papal decrees:

> Quaero an haec sint verba voluntatis, congruentiae, decentiae vel
> necessitatis. Scio quod Celestinus papa V multas abbatias episcopatus
> et superiores dignitates contulit sine fratrum consilio, et coram successore
> fuit iste articulus in dubium revocatus, et dixi tunc decere ut quod
> papa mandat in suo canone aliis id observare non negligat. Mandat
> enim quod episcopi, abbates et superiores saltem ardua ecclesiarum
> suarum ordinent de consilio fratrum suorum, *alias non teneat quod agitur*.[19]

The last words are the most important ones in this passage, for every
one would have agreed that the cardinals were, as Joannes Monachus
put it,

> in hac possessione quod ardua negotia erant de eorum consilio tractanda
> et terminanda.[20]

No one denied that this was the customary and correct procedure
for transacting the business of the Roman church. The question at
issue was whether the Pope contained in his own person such an
overwhelming and exclusive *plenitudo potestatis* that he could disregard
the customary forms and, by an act of his own will, promulgate valid
edicts without any such consultation. Joannes himself had no doubt
on the question, and, pressing home his attack, he went on to cite
the well-known Roman law principle, *Princeps legibus solutus est*, which
normally provided a standard argument for his adversaries. In his
citation, however, the whole weight of emphasis fell on the second
part of the famous quotation, *tamen secundum leges ipsum vivere decet.*

> ... licet princeps sit solutus legibus, tamen secundum leges ipsum vivere
> decet ... et omnem indecentiam in principe (qui est omnium director)
> dico impossibilem saltem moris ... et Benedictus papa XI statuta quae
> dedit marchianis Bonifacii papae absque consilio fratrum, quia ardua
> tangebant, fuerunt suspensa (sic).[21]

---

[19] Gloss *ad Sext.* v.ii.4, fol. 347 n. 2.
[20] *Ibid.*
[21] *Ibid.*

The Roman law doctrine by itself could establish only a moral obligation on the part of the prince to obey his own laws, and so Joannes
Monachus skilfully interpolated it between two accounts involving
Pope Benedict and Pope Boniface in which, he alleged, papal edicts
had been held invalid because they were promulgated *absque consilio
fratrum*. Thus the Roman law doctrine that a prince ought to obey
the laws was reinforced by concrete cases in which a failure of the
Pope to do so was held to have invalidated his enactments; and so
Joannes Monachus felt justified in concluding that, in the case of a
Pope as of any lesser prelate,

> Defectus in persona facientis vel in numero necessario redit factum
> inutile.[22]

This opinion was quite inconsistent with the doctrine of a personal
plenitudo potestatis inhering in the person of the Pope alone as vicar of
Christ, and it was not generally accepted by contemporary canonists.
Yet, considered in itself, it was only an unusually emphatic reassertion
of a traditional privilege, and this fact, combined with the apparently
unqualified recognition of papal authority that can be found in other
glosses of Joannes Monachus,[23] has sometimes led to a misunderstanding of the really novel position he adopted in regard to the
personal power of the Pope. 'Jean Lemoine ne demande, lui aussi,
pour les cardinaux que le droit d'être consultés, mais il reconnaît au
pape la *plenitudo potestatis* bornée seulement par les exigences du droit
naturel et divin. . . .'[24] It is quite true that Joannes Monachus applied
the term *plenitudo potestatis* to the Pope; but there can be no understanding of fourteenth-century thought unless one bears in mind that
this term could have more than one meaning. In fact, Joannes
Monachus displayed a rare virtuosity in adapting the concept of
plenitudo potestatis to suit his own particular purposes.

In most of his discussions on papal authority the phrase was used
in the sense that had become most common, that is to say, it indicated simply a unique and illimitable absolutism. Joannes Monachus

---

[22] Only in trivial matters did Joannes Monachus think that the Pope might act
without consulting the cardinals, Gloss *ad Sext.* III.vii.8, 'Forsan in istis minoribus
non est necesse consilium requiri, quod est in maioribus.'

[23] E.g. Gloss *ad Sext., Proemium*, fol. 6 n. 1, I.iii.11 fol. 36 n. 18, I.vi.45 fol. 116
n. 1, I.viii.2 fol. 127 n. 5, I.xv.1 fol. 146 n. 1, II.ii.1 fol. 185 n. 2, III.iv.3 fol. 251
n. 6, III.iv.32 fol. 288 n. 6.

[24] Rivière, *op. cit.* p. 358.

indeed, like Hostiensis before him, insisted that this absolute authority resided in the cardinals as well as in the Pope ('in papa est principalis, in collegio subsidiaria'),[25] and that, during a vacancy, the cardinals alone enjoyed the full exercise of the Roman *plenitudo potestatis*:

> Et haec vidi fieri in electione summi Pontificis per honorabilem cetum cardinalium penes quem plenitudo potestatis (sede vacante) residet....[26]

With this one qualification he was prepared to exalt the *plenitudo potestatis* of the Papacy as enthusiastically as any of the contemporary publicists, so long as he was discussing the powers of the Roman church in relation to the other churches.

But when he turned to a closer analysis of the distribution of authority within the Roman church itself and considered the position of the Pope in relation to the cardinals, then the words *plenitudo potestatis* took on a quite different significance. The discussion arose out of Boniface's provision that not even the College of Cardinals during a vacancy could absolve the two condemned Colonna cardinals. Joannes Monachus inquired whether this was a legitimate exercise of the papal *plenitudo potestatis*, and, with characteristic boldness, he concluded by flatly refusing to accept the Pope's decision. Most important of all, in the course of his argument, he succeeded in presenting the papal *plenitudo potestatis* as a delegated authority subject to severe limitations; and thus, by exploiting the fact that this much-abused term was extremely ambiguous in its juristic implications, he was able to undermine the theory of the Pope's personal autocracy without departing from the terminology of the extreme papalists themselves:

> Hic fuit plenitudo potestatis quae subtrahere voluit potestatem aliis competentem ... item *dativa administratio data papae per cardinales non tollit legitimam* ... et papa sic se habet ad collegium cardinalium sicut alter episcopus respectu sui collegii, cum ergo episcopus non possit tollere administrationem legitimam sui capituli, nec papae licebit.[27]

This conclusion had perhaps been implicit in canonistic theory ever since Hostiensis had systematized the earlier doctrine of the prelate

---

[25] Gloss *ad Sext.* v.xi.2 fol. 399 n. 6.

[26] *Ibid.* The claim was based on the usual analogy with the rights of cathedral chapters; the gloss goes on, '... absurdum enim esset quod capitula ecclesiarum cathedralium (quorum praelati in sollicitudinis partem sunt vocati) haberent in illa partem sollicitudinis ... et cetus cardinalium in tota sollicitudinem non haberet'.

[27] Gloss *ad Sext.* v.iii.1, fol. 366 n. 3.

as proctor of his corporation, but applied thus to the Roman church it certainly produces an impression of striking novelty. In the view of Joannes Monachus, a legitimate right of administration over the Church was vested in the Sacred College. The cardinals, without alienating their own *legitima administratio*, bestowed upon the Pope a mere *potestas dativa*, a derivative authority which did not empower him to act against the interests of the cardinals themselves. The Pope was simply an agent of the cardinals—and so Joannes Monachus was indirectly exalting the power of the Sacred College even when he most vigorously stressed the absolute authority of the Pope in relation to the rest of the Church. From his point of view there seemed no danger in subjecting the whole Church to the Pope as long as the Pope, in his turn, was subject to the cardinals.

Guilielmus Durantis, on the other hand, was principally concerned to defend the rights of the local churches, and so on this central issue his views were directly opposed to those of Joannes Monachus; yet the underlying patterns of their arguments were not altogether dissimilar. Since each canonist was evidently influenced by a desire to magnify (or at least to defend) the dignity of his own office, it would not be unjust to maintain that the one essential difference between them was that Joannes was a cardinal while Guilielmus was a bishop. Naturally enough, while one sought to limit the powers of the Pope only in so far as they affected the Sacred College, the other was equally zealous for the rights of the episcopate as a whole; and since Guilielmus saw the main threat to episcopal independence in the curial system of papal provisions, he inveighed against the activities of the cardinals in this sphere as vehemently as against those of the Pope.

The fact that has always prevented a just assessment of his really very considerable contribution to the growth of conciliar thought is that he inveighed against so many other things as well. Within the short limits of his treatise he discussed with impatient irascibility every conceivable abuse in the life of the Church from sorcery to simony, and from the deplorable trends in contemporary ecclesiastical art to the inadvisability of bishops keeping hunting dogs. It is something of a task, therefore, to disentangle his fundamental views on Church government from this confused mass of criticism, and Rivière very aptly characterized his work as displaying 'un très grande luxe d'érudition canonique, mais une absence totale de composition'.[28] When

---

[28] Rivière, *op. cit.* p. 363.

one compares the turgid irrelevancies of the Bishop of Mende with the easy lucidity of John of Paris the justice of Rivière's second point becomes all too apparent; but the canonistic erudition is equally indisputable, and far more important. Guilielmus Durantis displayed a familiarity with Decretist literature exceeding that of any contemporary except Guido de Baysio, and an ingenuity in marshalling the Decretist texts in support of his own views that was quite unparalleled. Some of his most effective chapters were simply elaborate patchworks of skilfully chosen passages from the *Decretum*.

At the start of his work he set out to prove the proposition that had already provided the basis for the views of Joannes Monachus, namely, that the Pope, like any other ecclesiastical ruler, was subject to the law of the Church; but while the cardinal had approached the subject by describing recent transactions of business in the curia which he claimed to have witnessed, Durantis based his case entirely upon the texts of the *Decretum*. He cited a formidable series of canons which included pronouncements attributed to Popes Urban, Zosimus, Damasus, Gelasius and Leo IV[29] and ended with the very influential letter of Gregory the Great, *Sicut quattuor evangelii*.[30] On the basis of these quotations he concluded that no Pope could establish a new law contrary to the canons of earlier Councils without summoning a new Council for the purpose, and in support of this principle he further cited a Roman law doctrine which had long been accepted by the canonists, which had been used by some of the earlier Decretists in their discussions on conciliar authority, and which, ironically enough, had been included in Boniface's own *Liber Sextus* as a *regula iuris*:[31]

> Illud quod omnes tangit, secundum iuris utriusque regulam ab omnibus debeat communiter approbari.[32]

---

[29] Part I, Tit. 2, pp. 4–5 referring to *Dist.* 12 c. 5, *Dist.* 15 c. 2, C. 25 q. 1 cc. 1, 5, 6, 16 and C. 25 q. 2 c. 4 (*Tractatus de Modo Generalis Concilii Celebrandi* (Parisiis, 1545)).

[30] *Dist.* 15 c. 2, 'Sicut sancti evangelii quattuor libros sic quattuor concilia suscipere et venerari me fateor.'

[31] *Sext.* v, *De Reg. Iur. Reg.* xxxix.

[32] Part I, Tit. 3, pp. 10–11, 'Videretur esse salubre pro republica ... quod contra dicta concilia et iura nihil possent de novo statuere vel condere nisi generali concilio convocato. Cum illud quod omnes tangit, secundum iuris utriusque regulam ab omnibus debeat communiter approbari.'

The main purpose of Guilielmus Durantis in arguing thus that the Pope was not entirely *legibus solutus* was to justify the traditional rights of the bishops, and so, having thus prepared the ground, he went on to assert that, in particular, the Popes were bound to obey that 'general ordinance of the Universal Church' which laid down that all clergy and religious should be subject to the authority of their diocesan bishop. Once again the whole armoury of Decretist erudition was brought into play, this time to prove that the episcopal organization of the Church was of divine institution, that all of the Apostles received authority directly from Christ and transmitted that authority to their successors, the bishops of the Church. We are reminded, with a wealth of references to the *Decretum* that, according to Anacletus, all the Apostles received with Peter 'pari consortio honorem et potestatem'; that Cyprian wrote of the whole episcopate sharing in the same divinely infused authority; that, in the opinion of Augustine, the power of the keys was conferred upon the whole Church and not on Peter alone; that Paul had not hesitated to reprove Peter, which he would never have dared to do had he not known himself to be Peter's equal; that, according to Augustine again, all bishops succeeded to the authority of the Apostles.[33] All this led up to the conclusion that the Pope should not grant exemptions from episcopal authority except in cases of grave and evident necessity; and Durantis took the opportunity in passing to rebuke those monks and friars who presumed to think themselves the equals of bishops.

The expression of such views concerning the authority of the episcopate was not uncommon in the early years of the fourteenth century. The centralization of authority in the papal curia, the growing practice of papal provision to benefices, and, most especially, the privilege conceded to the friars to preach and hear confessions without permission of the local ordinaries, all aroused suspicions that the authority of the episcopate might be virtually annihilated, the effective government of the Church handed over to subordinate agents of an all-powerful Pope. John of Paris, himself a friar, had maintained that the Pope was not the source of episcopal authority. His contemporary, Jean de Pouilli,[34] who championed the rights of the secular

---

[33] Part I, Tit. 5, pp. 16–17 referring to *Dist.* 21 cc. 1, 2, C. 2 q. 7 c. 33, C. 24 q. 1 c. 6, C. 24 q. 1 c. 18.

[34] On Jean de Pouilli and his doctrines see N. Valois, *Histoire littéraire de la France,* XXXIV, pp. 220–81; Glorieux, *La littérature quodlibétique de 1260 à 1320* (Kain, 1925), pp. 223–8; J. Koch, 'Der Prozess gegen den Magister Johannes de Polliaco und

clergy, argued in the same way but carried the argument much further. He did not deny that the Pope, by reason of his universal *plenitudo potestatis* could hear any man's confession, or even that he could delegate that power to another; but he did object to the use of the papal authority in such a fashion as to subvert the hierarchical structure of the Church.[35] In particular, he maintained that a man who confessed his sins to a friar licensed by the Pope would not comply with the law of the Church unless he confessed a second time to his parish priest whose authority was derived from the local bishop; and for stubbornly maintaining that opinion, he was cited to Avignon in 1318 and duly condemned.[36]

Guilielmus Durantis avoided that particular theological morass and escaped formal censure, but his views were essentially the same as those of the condemned theologian. He too regarded the papal authority as of divine origin but not as the source of episcopal jurisdiction; he too was anxious to defend the divinely ordained status of each grade in the ecclesiastical hierarchy. Indeed in his first warm defence of the powers of the bishops, the whole traditional conception of Roman primacy seems to have been forgotten. Later on, however, he returned to the question and professed his adherence to the orthodox view of the Roman church as 'head of all the churches', the centre of unity to which all the others were joined as members.[37] Once again one finds the blending of a hierarchical view of the Church with a corporative view. The totality of all the churches formed a corporate unity of which the Roman church was 'head', but headship in such a 'body' did not imply an absorptive and absolute authority

---

seine Vorgeschichte', *Recherches de théologie ancienne et médiévale*, V (1933), 391–422; J. G. Sikes, 'John de Pouilli and Peter de la Palu', *English Historical Review*, XLIX (1934), pp. 219–81.

[35] Jean de Pouilli distinguished between the Pope's *plenitudo potestatis* and his ordinary power; the *plenitudo potestatis*, he held, should be used only to meet some special emergency, not as a normal instrument of Church government (J. G. Sikes, *art. cit.* p. 237 n. 5).

[36] The famous decree of the Fourth Lateran Council which imposed on all Catholics the obligation of annual confession stipulated that the penitent should confess to his parish priest. The basic issue at stake was thus the old one that the Decretists had discussed—whether a Pope could dispense against the statute of a General Council in a matter touching the *generalis status ecclesiae*.

[37] Part III, Tit. 1, p. 163, 'Sane quantum ad reformationem universalis ecclesiae utiliter et perseveraliter et efficaciter faciendum videtur, quod a capite ratio sit edenda, videlicet a sacrosancta Romana ecclesia quae caput est omnium aliarum. Ad quam tanquam caput et matrem omnium ecclesiarum secundum Calixtum membra omnia sequi debent.'

over all the members. In all this his thought seems reminiscent of
John of Paris, but Durantis carried the argument to still more radical conclusions. He not only maintained that each separate church
had its own proper rights which the central authority was required
to respect, but also held that all important decisions affecting the
Universal Church as a whole should be taken by head and members
together, united in a General Council. A council should therefore be
summoned,

> quandocumque aliquid esset ordinandum de tangentibus communem
> statum ecclesiae vel ius novum condendum.[38]

It is not difficult to see how such a doctrine might take shape in the
mind of a canonist steeped in the early Decretist sources, with their
insistence that a Pope could not go against the canons of existing
Councils in matters which affected the *generalis status ecclesiae*. But it
was a characteristic feature of fourteenth-century thought that the
resuscitation of ancient doctrines on Church government led almost
imperceptibly, and perhaps without conscious intent on the part of
their exponents, to the formulation of really novel claims against the
Papacy. Guilielmus Durantis seems to have overstepped the bounds
of Decretist thought in thus applying the *Quod omnes tangit* principle
to the general legislative authority of the Papacy, for Joannes Teutonicus had maintained in a quite contrary sense that to deny the
Roman See's right of establishing law for the whole Church was
heresy.[39] Only in the promulgation of articles of faith did he suggest
that a General Council was required.

The role of the General Council in the government of the Church
was discussed in each of the three parts into which the work of
Durantis was divided. In the first part he was content to establish
the principle that a Pope alone could not override the legislation of
previous Councils; in the second part he put forward this more radical
opinion that, for the future, a General Council should be summoned
whenever laws were to be promulgated touching the 'common state
of the Church'; in the third part he quite certainly went far beyond

---

[38] Part II, Tit. 41, p. 101, 'Videtur utile quod predictum concilium per Romanam
(ecclesiam) servaretur quandocumque iura condenda sunt, cum dicta iura pro tangentibus communem utilitatem sint edenda.... Et quod idem servaretur quandocumque aliquid esset ordinandum de tangentibus communem statum ecclesiae vel
ius novum condendum. Cum illud quod omnes tangit ab omnibus approbari debeat.'
[39] Gloss *ad Dist.* 19 c. 5.

anything that his predecessors had envisaged. The Council was not to be an extraordinary assembly summoned at rare intervals for some special purpose but was to meet regularly every ten years; and, moreover, the provision of revenue sufficient for the honourable upkeep of the curia was to be dependent upon its observance of the laws of the Councils:

> Item quod nulla iura generalia deinceps conderet, nisi vocato concilio generali quod de decennio in decennio vocaretur . . . Item quod de bonis ecclesiasticarum personarum superabundantibus, talis provisio fieret supradictae Romanae ecclesiae quod absque omni taxationis nota et infamia posset communiter et divisim honorabiliter vivere . . . provisa tamen quod ultra et contra praedicta et alia quae concilio rationabilia viderentur, contra divinas et humanas leges non posset absque generali concilio habenas extendere plenitudinis potestatis.[40]

These claims were indeed novel and full of significance for the future. Earlier canonists had seen in the General Council only a final court of appeal in matters of faith, or an instrument of coercion which could bring about the deposition of a Pope who proved grossly unworthy of his office. Durantis, on the other hand, wished to assign to the Council a regular constitutional role in the government of the Church, to make it the necessary channel for taxation and all important legislation.

Thus, the reform of the Church was to be brought about not only by a negative insistence on the rights of the members against the head, but also by the active participation of the members in the shaping of ecclesiastical policy. The distinctive contribution of Guilielmus Durantis was to show how the natural desire of the bishops to defend their own status, which in itself seemed likely to produce only a disruptive particularism, could be expressed in a more constructive form through their corporate association in a General Council; his work provides an interesting link between the current theories of episcopal authority and the later conciliar doctrines. Especially significant were his illustrations of the divergencies between some of the early sources of ecclesiastical law and the doctrines of papal centralization that were fashionable in his own day. The painstaking citation of every possible text in the *Decretum* that could be made to bear an anti-papal interpretation was itself an important contribution to the

---

[40] Part III, Tit. 27, pp. 190–1.

growth of conciliar ideas. Indeed, this sprawling ill-designed work, with its appeals for radical reform of the Church 'in head and members', its proposals for regular meetings of General Councils, its blistering denunciations of venality and corruption in the curia, strikes for the first time the authentic note of the Conciliar Movement properly so called.

By the time of the Council of Vienne all the separate elements of thought that were to be combined and systematized in later conciliar theories had been propounded in the works of distinguished canonists, though they had not as yet been fused into a wholly satisfactory system of Church government. Indeed, the seductions of system-building seldom attracted the professional canonists. Down to the outbreak of the Great Schism their main contribution to medieval ecclesiology continued to be what it had been in the twelfth and thirteenth centuries—not the construction of imposing doctrinal edifices but the analysis of concepts, the definition of terms, the investigation of the juristic status of particular institutions and individuals within the Church. Such work provided a mass of materials from which the publicists could construct their own theories—the publicists built the mansions of thought; the canonists made the bricks. The works of Joannes Monachus and of Guilielmus Durantis were both manifestos on behalf of particular classes in the Church rather than fully integrated theories of ecclesiastical authority, and although John of Paris had sketched in the outlines of a preliminary synthesis, it was not until after the disaster of 1378 that his doctrines were wholeheartedly accepted by some of the canonists themselves as an acceptable exposition of the law of the Church.

The years between the Council of Vienne and the outbreak of the Schism are important in the history of conciliar thought as a period in which earlier ideas were assimilated and popularized rather than for any really original contributions to the theory of Church government. Within the curia itself the 'oligarchic' tendencies reflected and defended in the work of Joannes Monachus, becoming more and more pronounced, engendered 'a long and often bitter constitutional struggle between the papacy and the college of cardinals'.[41] Before the crisis of 1378 the most striking evidence of such a struggle is provided by the election capitulations of 1352, when the cardinals

---

[41] G. Barraclough, *Papal Provisions* (Oxford, 1935), p. 75.

sought to bind the future Pope to act only with their consent in various important matters affecting their own authority.[42] Meanwhile the continuing conflicts between Popes and secular rulers led to renewed appeals from Pope to General Council, and the doctrine that ultimate ecclesiastical authority rested with the *congregatio fidelium* acquired considerable notoriety through the works of well-known publicists like Marsiglio and Ockham.[43] There remains, however, besides the pamphlets of the publicists and the records of curial administration, another whole class of literature which must be evaluated if we are to achieve a full understanding of the constitutional crisis of 1378. Just as significant as the overt publicizing of anti-papal doctrines was the gradual penetration of conciliar concepts into the glosses of respected canonists who were themselves avowedly loyal to the orthodox doctrine of papal monarchy—for it was to the writings of these men that perplexed churchmen first turned for a solution of the juristic problems raised by the Schism.

---

[42] See G. M. Souchon, *Die Papstwahlen von Bonifaz VIII bis Urban VI und die Entstehung des Schismas 1378* (Braunschweig, 1888); J. Lulvès, 'Päpstliche Wahlkapitulationen', *Quellen und Forschungen aus ital. Arch.* XII (1909), pp. 212–35; *idem.* 'Die Machtsbestrebungen des Kardinalcollegiums gegenüber dem Papsttum', *Mitteilungen des Instituts für österreichische Geschichtsforschung*, XXXV (1914), pp. 445–83; G. Mollat, 'Contribution à l'histoire du Sacré Collège de Clément V à Eugène IV', *Revue d'histoire ecclésiastique*, XLVI (1951), pp. 22–112 at pp. 100–4; H. Hofmann, *Kardinalat und Kuriale Politik* (Leipzig, 1935). At the outbreak of the Schism itself the position of the cardinals was defended most trenchantly by the canonist Peter Flandrin. On his views see F. Merzbacher, *art. cit.* pp. 346–51.

[43] The influence of canonistic ideas on these publicists is considered in my articles, 'A conciliar theory of the thirteenth century', *Catholic Historical Review*, XXXVI (1951), pp. 415–40 and 'Ockham, the Conciliar Theory and the canonists', *Journal of the History of Ideas*, XV (1954), pp. 40–70.

CHAPTER THREE

THE ATTITUDE OF THE ACADEMIC CANONISTS

Joannes Monachus and Guilielmus Durantis had this in common that they were both practical men of affairs rather than academic jurists. They were both indeed very skilled canonists, but neither was a professional teacher of the canon law, and although their intimate contact with the everyday problems of ecclesiastical administration gave unusual vigour to their theoretical works, the main traditions of fourteenth-century jurisprudence continued to be moulded by the famous doctors of law in the great universities of France and Italy. It was these men—great teachers like Guido de Baysio, Joannes Andreae, Zenzellinus de Cassanis, Henricus Bohic, Joannes de Lignano, to mention only a few of the most influential—who shaped the juristic doctrines of Church government in the years before the Schism; and one might expect, therefore, that a study of their works would shed some light on the origins of the conciliar theories that came into such prominence at the end of the fourteenth century. Yet it would certainly be misleading to suggest that these distinguished jurists contributed to the growth of conciliar thought by any deliberate advocacy of the more radical doctrines propounded by writers like Guilielmus Durantis and Joannes Monachus. In their works one finds very little of the speculative audacity that characterized the theories of the French cardinal and the irate Bishop of Mende. The academic canonists were principally concerned to defend the existing state of affairs, the centralized absolutism of the Avignon papacy, and, accordingly, all the more respected and influential of them denied that the Pope's divinely ordained authority over the whole Church as universal legislator and supreme judge could be limited by any human agency. Joannes Andreae, the most renowned of them all, was typical in his exaltation of the papal authority. For him the Pope was truly lord of the world—*Apostolicus totius orbis est dominus;*[1] his authority was from God, not from man, and so all his commands

---

[1] *Liber Sextus Decretalium Bonifacii Papae VIII* (Parisiis, 1601), Gloss *ad* v.vii.2 s.v. *mundi.*

were to be obeyed; he was not subject to the laws of Councils like lesser mortals for he gave authority to them, not they to him; he could revoke conciliar legislation of his own will by exercising his inherent plenitude of power; all were subject to his judgement and he could be judged by no one.[2] Joannes Andreae even quoted with approval the opinion that the Pope was a superhuman being, a sort of semi-deity:

> Papa stupor mundi. . . . Nec Deus est nec homo, quasi neuter est inter utrumque.[3]

Views of this sort were commonplace among the fourteenth-century canonists. Yet although their works displayed no overt sympathies with the contemporary critics of the Avignon regime the canonists did not succeed in framing a wholly satisfactory defence of the doctrine of papal monarchy that they all supported; and their failure to do so was to be a factor of some significance in the situation that developed after 1378. The canonists put forward exalted claims for the Papacy, but they did not undertake to integrate those claims into a coherent theory of ecclesiastical authority that could be applied consistently in all actual and foreseeable circumstances and that could be sustained against all the arguments of the contemporary publicists. Perhaps the materials with which they had to work made such a synthesis impossible.

The law of the Church reflected the structure of ecclesiastical

---

[2] *Novella in Sextum Decretalium* (Lugduni, 1550), ad III.iv.5 fol. 73 n. 1, '. . . cum auctoritas papae non sit ab homine sed a Deo . . . patet quod contra ipsius decretum sine ipsius consensu nil potest fieri ab homine'. Gloss *ad Sext.* I.vi.3 s.v. *concilio*, 'Et certe cum constitutio ista tam utilis approbationi tanti concilii fuerit edita, non aequum fuit quod absque requisitione concilii revocata fuerat . . . de plenitudine tamen potestatis id facere potuerat, cum sit papa super omnia concilia.' Gloss *ad* II.xiv.2 (superscriptio), 'Papa vero non subiicitur canonibus nec ab eis auctoritatem habet, sed econtra . . . ipse ergo omnes iudicat et nullus ipsum.'

[3] *Clementis Papae Quinti Constitutiones* (Parisiis, 1601), Gloss *ad Proemium* s.v. *papa*, referring to the English poet Geoffrey de Vinsauf (cf. W. Ullmann, *Medieval Papalism*, p. 153 n. 6), Gloss *ad Sext.* I.vi.17 s.v. *homini*, 'Et in hac parte Papa non est homo sed Dei vicarius.' But, even in the fourteenth century, the canonists never quite lost sight of the fact that there were some theoretical limits to the Pope's powers. Guilielmus de Monte Lauduno, for instance, displayed a commendable moderation in acknowledging that a papal command could not turn black into white, 'In his tamen quae factum nudum continent et veritatem respiciunt nullam potestatem habet (papa), quia non posset facere de albo nigrum . . . Item nec in his quae fundamentum nostrae militantis ecclesiae sustinent seu concernunt sicut decem praecepta, 12 articuli, 7 sacramenta et aliqua alia substantialia legis divinae.' Discussions on the precise limits of the Pope's dispensatory authority occurred frequently in the fourteenth-century works as in the Decretalist glosses of the thirteenth century.

institutions as well as helping to shape their development, and in the fourteenth century the structure of the Church, although it was centralized indeed, was by no means monolithic. In spite of the aspirations of the jurists and theologians the unity and stability of the Church were maintained in practice, not through a harmonious ordering of all its members under a single head, but through a tense balance of conflicting forces—the unity of a Gothic cathedral rather than a classical temple. Within the Christian community there were, most obviously, tensions between the ecclesiastical and the secular hierarchies of government; tensions again within the ecclesiastical hierarchy between papal curia and local episcopate; tensions finally within the curia itself between Pope and cardinals. It is not surprising, therefore, that in the law of the Church too there were tensions that hindered the efforts of any who sought to construct a coherent theory of Church government on the basis of its texts. The canonists, indeed, had to assimilate not only the living experience of the Church in the fourteenth century but also the juristic expression of the experience of previous centuries recorded in the *Decretum* and Decretals and their various commentaries. The fact was emphasized by the appearance in 1300 of Guido de Baysio's *Rosarium*, a vast compendium of Decretist glosses that had been half-forgotten since the days of Innocent III. Just when the circumstances of the times were giving a new urgency to the discussion of problems concerning the deposition of a Pope, the status of the cardinals, and the authority of the Church, the canonists were reminded of the stimulating if sometimes incautious speculations of writers like Huguccio, Joannes Teutonicus, and the author of the *Glossa Palatina* on these same questions; and the rather undiscriminating erudition of the fourteenth-century glossators ensured that their ample works incorporated many elements of this early canonistic thought that were hardly compatible with the theory of papal authority they sought to sustain.

Still more important, the fourteenth-century canonists inherited from their immediate predecessors and themselves further developed a conception of the Church that could lend itself just as readily to a conciliar interpretation as to their own doctrine of papal monarchy. In discussing the sources of conciliar thought Gierke observed that 'A definition which declared the Church to be "the Congregation of the Faithful" was not be to eradicated.'[4] One might go further and

---

[4] Gierke-Maitland, *Political Theories of the Middle Age*, p. 49.

say that in the fourteenth century this definition was emphasized as never before.

In discussions of the earlier thirteenth century it had been customary to offer a variety of definitions for the word *ecclesia*; the canonists explained that it might indicate the bishop alone, or the cathedral chapter, or a majority of the canons, or the clergy of the diocese and, finally, they added that it might sometimes be used to indicate the *congregatio fidelium*.[5] The glosses of the fourteenth century show a marked change of emphasis. We have noted how the term *universitas fidelium* was used by Innocent IV to define the sense in which the Church possessed *dominium* of ecclesiastical property. His definition was repeated by Joannes Monachus, Joannes Andreae and Henricus Bohic,[6] but, while these writers mentioned other groups who might be regarded as possessing *dominium*, they did not suggest that the word *ecclesia* itself had any connotation other than *congregatio fidelium*. Somewhat earlier Guilielmus Durantis (the Speculator), in his *Rationale Divinorum Officiorum*, had defined the spiritual church (as opposed to a material church building) as the *congregatio fidelium*,[7] without thinking it necessary to add any further definitions; and Guido de Baysio noted that the word *ecclesia* could be used in several senses but thought only two of them worth quoting,

> ... quandoque dicitur ecclesia sanctorum collectio ... quandoque ecclesia dicitur catholicorum collectio.[8]

Zenzellinus de Cassanis summed up the prevailing trend of thought when he remarked, after referring to the various usages of the term

---

[5] E.g. Joannes Teutonicus *ad* C. 7 q. 1 c. 7, Bernardus Parmensis and Innocent IV *ad* X. v.xl.19.

[6] Joannes Monachus, Gloss *ad Sext.* III.ix.2, 'Et sic nota quod bona ecclesiastica dicuntur esse ecclesiae et ita ecclesia habet dominium ipsorum. . . . Et intelligitur ecclesia, i.e. congregatio fidelium quae est corpus cuius caput est Christus . . . alibi vero dicitur quod sunt pauperum et ibidem quod sunt clericorum. . . . Et predicta sic concorda(nt), dicendo quod ecclesia, i.e. congregatio fidelium habet dominium istorum et etiam Christus tanquam caput. Et quod dicitur pauperum verum est quo ad sustentationem et quod dicitur clericorum verum est quo ad administrationem sive gubernationem et propter hoc clerici dicuntur procuratores non domini.' The substance of this gloss was repeated by Joannes Andreae, Gloss *ad Sext.* III.ix.2 and Henricus Bohic, *Distinctiones ad* X. v.xl.13.

[7] *Rationale Divinorum Officiorum* (Venetiis, 1609), Lib. 1 n. 1, 'Notandum est ergo quod ecclesiarum alia est corporalis . . . alia spiritualis quae est fidelium collectio.'

[8] *In Sextum Decretalium Commentaria* (Venetiis, 1577), Gloss *ad* I.vi.17, fol. 32rb.

ecclesia, 'Proprie dicitur ecclesia congregatio fidelium.'[9] Evidently it was coming to be accepted that this was the primary meaning of the word. Zabarella was only expressing the common opinion of his age when he in turn declared, 'Ecclesia nihil est aliud quam congregatio fidelium',[10] though some of the corollaries he derived from the proposition were different from any that his predecessors would have admitted.

Zabarella was quite typical of his age again in that he could use the term *corpus mysticum* to describe indifferently the relationship between a bishop and his chapter or the mystical unity which St Paul had ascribed to the whole Church,[11] for during the fourteenth century the idea of the *congregatio fidelium* as a corporate entity in the juristic sense came to be more and more taken for granted. The attitude is perhaps best exemplified in Joannes de Lignano's treatise, *De Censura Ecclesiastica*, where, in the course of a long analysis of the structure of the Church and the vicissitudes that might befall it, he compared the *corpus ecclesiae* not only to a human body in the usual fashion but also to a *universitas* or *civitas*.[12] Later in the same work he embarked on a discussion of the legal 'medicine', the system of general and local canons, through which the life of all the members of the *corpus mysticum* was healthfully regulated. After referring to the medical care of a human body he went on,

> sic ut corpus totum mysticum conservetur et partes egrote curentur a Deo prodiit scientia tradens modum conservativum huius mystici corporis, et hec est scientia canonum et legalium constitutionum. . . . Sic in corpore mystico propter varietatem regionum et circumstantiarum singularium fit ad conservandum et corrigendum singula corpora universitatum que sunt partes magni corporis mystici varia constitutionum et consuetudinum introductio; que tamen formam trahunt et fomentum a canonibus generalibus. . . .[13]

---

[9] Gloss *ad Extravagantes* I.i.2 s.v. *ecclesiis*, repeated at *Extrav.* I.iii.1 s.v. *universali* (*Extravagantes in Constitutiones Ioannis Papae XXII* (Parisiis, 1601)).

[10] *Super Quinque Libris Decretalium Commentaria* (Venetiis, 1602), Gloss ad I.i.1 fol. 11va.

[11] *Commentaria ad* X. III.x.4, 'Nota quod episcopus et capitulum sunt unum corpus scilicet mysticum . . .'; *ad* X. V.vi.17, 'In corpore mystico militantis ecclesiae omnes sumus unum corpus secundum Apostolum. . . .'

[12] *De Censura Ecclesiastica* in *Tractatus Universi Iuris* (Lugduni, 1549), XVI, fol. 228rb n. 3.

[13] *Op. cit.* fol. 229va n. 17.

One could hardly look for a more 'legalistic' presentation of the doctrine of corporate unity in the Church.[14] Some of the possible implications of such an attitude are suggested by a sequence of glosses taken from the apparatus of Zenzellinus de Cassanis on the *Extravagantes Joannis XXII*:[15]

> s.v. *Romana ecclesia* . . . licet etiam respectu habito ad locum peculiarem in urbe Romana dicatur ecclesia Romana quod verum est de illa quae membrum est universalis Ecclesiae, ipsa autem universalis Ecclesia in plura membra hodie est dispersa.
>
> s.v. *Circa nos* . . . ad instar senatorum lateri principis assistentium, de quibus et eadem ratione de dominis cardinalibus potest dici quod censentur pars corporis principis, unde sicut in illis, ita in istis crimen laesae committi dicitur majestatis.
>
> s.v. *Universali* . . . quae proprie dicitur collectio fidelium . . .
>
> s.v. *Serviendo*. . . . Not. cardinales dici servitores Ecclesiae. Nec mirum cum et papa servire ei dicatur quare se servum appellat et imperator servum ultimum Ecclesiae se vocat . . . ordo enim serviendi est in humana creatura, ut inferior superiori deserviat, aliter enim universitas nulla poterit ratione subsistere nisi ex diversitate graduum ordo diversitatem in ea servaret.

Now Zenzellinus was an out and out papalist. He condemned with robust zeal those who sought to undermine the Pope's authority, and he certainly intended no anti-papal implications in the glosses quoted.[16] Yet they are all comments which could occur without incongruity in one of the more radical conciliar treatises, and, divorced from their context, they might even be read as a programmatic statement of some characteristic conciliar theses. We find the Roman church described as merely one member of the Church Universal; the cardinals

---

[14] Another extreme example is provided by Conrad of Gelnhausen who referred to the belief that the true faith had survived only in Mary at the hour of the Crucifixion—and then adduced in support of this assertion the legal doctrine that the rights of a corporation could be retained by one surviving member, 'Unde fides christi, cum omnes discipuli eo relicto fugerunt, in sola virgine Maria creditur remansisse. Nam et ius universitatis in uno salvari potest ut notatur, *de postulatione praelatorum*, c. *gratum*' (*Epistola Concordiae* in Martène and Durand, *Thesaurus*, II, col. 1215).

[15] Glosses *ad Extrav.* i.iii.1, commenting on the words, 'Cardinalibus tamen sanctae Romanae ecclesiae qui circa nos universali Ecclesiae serviendo singularum ecclesiarum commoditatibus se impendunt. . . .'

[16] The Roman church was referred to as a member of the Universal Church only to emphasize that the Church founded on Peter and subject to the Pope was not merely the local church of Rome but the whole Church; and in spite of his respect for the cardinals Zenzellinus did not concede to them any right effectively to limit the Pope's sovereignty. Cf. *infra* p. 208.

apparently participating in the authority of the Roman church as parts of the Pope's body; the Universal Church itself defined as the *collectio fidelium*; the *collectio fidelium* compared to a *universitas* sustained by the services of its various officers, among whom are included the Pope himself. The fourteenth-century canonists, the defenders of papal authority, were operating with just the same concept of the Church that, a little later, was to form the very foundation of the conciliar theories.

It was this underlying conception of the Church as the corporate aggregate of the faithful that made it particularly difficult for them to formulate a consistent theory of Church government, for the prevailing canonistic ideas on the structure of corporations were substantially different from the doctrine of unitary absolutism that they wished to apply to the Church as a whole. Hence, in discussing specific problems of papal authority, they tended either to insist rigidly on the Pope's personal sovereignty—which proved inconsistent with their views on the corporate structure of the Roman church and of the Universal Church, or, alternatively, they allowed their corporative concepts to influence their treatment of the Pope's status in the Church— which seriously compromised their doctrine of papal monarchy.

The canonistic treatment of the authority of the Sacred College provides a good example of the first procedure. The fourteenth-century canonists held the cardinals worthy of the utmost respect and expressed it in a flattering variety of imagery and honorific titles. Joannes de Lignano could not resist the opportunity of displaying his astronomical learning[17] by comparing the cardinals to the poles around which the earth revolved, and he even managed to bring in the poles of the other heavenly bodies as well.[18] More commonly the cardinals

---

[17] Joannes de Lignano, best known for his *De bello, de represaliis et duello* (ed. T. E. Holland, Oxford, 1917), was something of a polymath. He wrote on medicine and natural philosophy as well as on civil and canon law, and his political views have attracted some interest. On these see G. Ermini, *I Trattati della Guerra e della Pace di Giovanni de Legnano* (*Studi e Memorie per la Storia dell'università de Bologna*, I, 8, Imola, 1923); G. W. Coopland, 'Un ouvrage inédit de Jean de Legnano. Le Somnium de 1372', *Actes du Congrès International d'Histoire des Religions*, II, pp. 344 ff., G. Ermini, 'Un ignoto trattato "De principatu" di Giovanni de Legnano', *Studi di Storia e Diritto in Onore di Carlo Calisse*, pp. 421 ff.; W. Ullmann, *Medieval Idea of Law* (London, 1946), pp. 173 ff. Joannes de Lignano was also the author of an important *Consilium* on the legality of Urban VI's election—see W. Ullmann, *Origins of the Great Schism* (London, 1948), pp. 147 ff. On his canonistic output see Van Hove, *Prolegomena*, pp. 495, 502, 506, 507, 509.

[18] *De Censura Ecclesiastica*, fol. 229ra, 'Hec sunt quatuor virtutes cardinales que

were described as the 'hinges' which controlled the Church, as senators, patricians, councillors of the Pope, even as parts of his body.
The canonists were prepared to concede to the Sacred College all
honour and dignity, everything in fact except the one thing that
mattered most of all—effective power against the Pope. On that point
the more common tradition of the fourteenth century was derived,
not from Joannes Monachus, but from his contemporary, Guido de
Baysio, Archdeacon of Bologna, who considered just the same problems as the French cardinal and arrived at diametrically opposed
conclusions.[19] In the opinion of Guido de Baysio the words *de consilio
fratrum nostrorum* laid down a desirable rule of procedure for the Pope
which it was proper for him to observe, but did not bind him *quantum
ad necessitatem*.[20] Guido's great pupil, Joannes Andreae, took the same
view[21] and, moreover, expressed sheer incredulity about the story of

---

debent esse in capite corporis mystici scilicet in Romani pontifice et sicut sunt quatuor
virtutes cardinales in quatuor partibus capitis, sed cardinales sunt partes non dico
solum corporis imo capitis et sunt sedes illarum virtutum vel esse debent. Vel iudicio
meo debebunt esse quatuor et non plures tracta ordine examina dictis(?) vel duo ad
instar cardinum super quibus defertur ostium vel etiam ad instar mundi cardinum
qui sunt duo, videlicet articus et antarticus et utinam quatuor veri cardinales non
deficerent ad plus si dentur cardines omnium orbium erunt xvi vel xviii ad instar
omnium sumendo. Ex quibus liquide constat quod si sumatur nomine cardinalatus
a virtutibus cardinalibus que aggregant caput papale debet esse quadruplex tantum.
Si autem a cardinalibus super quibus circumduciter porta corporis mystici, tunc
duo. Si autem a cardinibus super quibus circumvolvitur orbis, etiam duo. Si autem
a cardinibus super quibus circumvolvuntur omnes orbes, tunc autem xvi aut xviii ad
plus.' The proper number of the cardinals was of course a very delicate subject,
especially after the election capitulations of 1352, and one is tempted to see an
undertone of satire in all this rigmarole. Joannes expressed his impatience with the
curiales on another occasion, *Tractatus de Pluralitate Beneficiorum*, in *Tractatus Universi
Iuris*, XV, fol. 129va, 'Tunc erat curia contra me cum dixi quod nollem esse prelatus
et quod nollem bibere sanguinem deputatum pauperibus sed potius sudorum manuum
mearum, ex quo Deus concesserat gratiam ut viverem de labore meo.' It must have
been refreshing for the curia to hear of someone who did not want an ecclesiastical
benefice—Joannes was a layman and married.

[19] Guido de Baysio influenced subsequent fourteenth-century thought on this
question in two ways. His own views were as conservative as his position might lead
one to expect (he was usually referred to by contemporaries simply as 'the Archdeacon'). But through his *Rosarium* he gave a new currency to the view expressed in the
Glossa Palatina that the Pope could not establish general laws for the whole Church
without consulting the cardinals. This opinion was often cited in later controversies,
e.g. by Albericus de Rosate, Zabarella, Panormitanus, Andreas de Barbatia.

[20] *In Sextum Decretalium Commentaria* (Venetiis, 1577), gloss *ad* I.xvii.8 fol. 55rb, '(Papa)
habet uti consilio potissime fratrum ... sed non quantum ad necessitatem.'

[21] Gloss *ad Sext.* I.vi.17, s.v. *contingeret*, 'Non compellitur (petere consilia cardinalium),
habet enim in se celestis et terreni imperii iura.'

Boniface VIII and Benedict XI revoking privileges of their predecessors because they had been made without consent of the cardinals,

Hoc ultimum admiror et difficulter credo Bonifacium id facisse.[22]

Later on Dominicus de Sancto Gemignano said that Joannes Monachus could not be believed since, as a cardinal himself, he was an interested party in the events he described.[23] Zenzellinus de Cassanis too held that, in virtue of his plenitude of power, the Pope could dispense with the counsel of the cardinals if he so wished;[24] Joannes de Lignano was of the same opinion; and Albericus de Rosate stated that the common opinion of the doctors held that the Pope possessed the power to legislate for the Universal Church even without the cardinals.[25] It was only after the Schism that the views of Joannes Monachus again attracted considerable support among the canonists.[26]

The Archdeacon dealt rather more lengthily with the second main problem concerning the cardinals, their status during a papal vacancy. The cardinals, he acknowledged, were coadjutors of the Pope, sons of the Roman church, but he did not remember ever having read that they could succeed in place of the Pope, the Vicar of Christ. Indeed, if they could do so, there would seem no need for them to elect a Pope at all; the cardinals themselves could carry on the govern-

---

[22] *Novella ad Sext.* v.ii.4 fol. 103 n. 1. The point that Joannes Andreae doubted was that Boniface had revoked Celestine's grants on the ground that, lacking approval of the cardinals, they were invalid. He was aware of the fact that some Celestinian grants had in fact been cancelled 'quia (Celestinus) stili romane curie erat modicum expertus'. Cf. *Novella ad Sext.* III.iv.40 fol. 82 n. 1.

[23] *Lectura super Sexto Libro Decretalium* (Tridini, 1522), ad v.ii.4 fol. 245ra, 'Sibi non sit credendum quia cum esset cardinalis conabatur sustinere causam propriam.'

[24] Gloss *ad Clem.* I.iii.1 s.v. *de ipsorum consilio*, 'Consilio (cardinalium) papa utitur quia vult ... non autem ad hoc de necessitate tenetur ... vocatus enim est in plenitudine potestatis.'

[25] *Lectura super Codicem* (Lugduni, 1518), fol. 47ra, 'Utrum papa sine cardinalibus possit leges sive decretales facere. Laurentius tenet quod non generales ... communis opinio est in contrarium et etiam de facto servatur. De hoc notatur per Archidiaconum, XXV q. 1, *que ad perpetuum* et c. *sunt quidam*.'

[26] Andreas de Barbatia, reviewing the whole question in mid-fifteenth century, warmly defended the views of Joannes Monachus 'ille summus canonista' and cited in support of them Baldus, Panormitanus, Zabarella and Petrus de Ancharano. To the aspersion of Dominicus de Sancto Gemignano, he replied, 'Nec obstat cum dixit dominus Dominicanus non esse credendum Ioan. Monacho cum fuerit cardinalis ... ad hoc respondeo procedere quando solus Ioan. Monachus hoc dixisset. Sed quando habet multos illustres doctores contestes qui illud etiam affirmant, tunc ex confirmatione aliorum tollitur illa suspitio' (*De Prestantia Cardinalium, Tractatus Universi Iuris*, XIV, fol. 365va).

ment of the Church.[27] The problem possessed the same theoretical significance as in the days when the Decretists had discussed it, and a much greater practical importance since, in the late thirteenth century, vacancies lasting months and even years had actually occurred. Was the Church to be regarded as headless at such times? Guido de Baysio answered that the Church was not rendered headless by the loss of Christ's vicar, since she always retained her true Head, Christ Himself.[28] It was unnecessary to postulate a headship of the cardinals. Their authority could never be equal to that of the Pope since it was of merely human origin, delegated by the Pope, whilst the powers of the Pope himself were from God alone. Hence it was ridiculous to assert that, even during a vacancy, the cardinals could rescind a law made by the Pope:

> Ridiculum enim videtur dicere, quod illi qui utuntur potentia in eos transfusa ab homine, possint tollere et infligere quam statutum est ab eo qui utitur potentia a solo Deo infusa.

The premiss of the argument was just the opposite of that adopted by Joannes Monachus who held that it was the Pope who exercised a merely derivative power—*dativa administratio*—conferred on him by the cardinals. Guido de Baysio expressed his own views forcefully enough but acknowledged that there were arguments on the other side. The fact that Boniface VIII, in condemning the Colonna cardinals, specifically ordained that they were not to be absolved even by 'the college of the Apostolic See during a vacancy' seemed to him an argument against his position, for it implied that, if there were no such express prohibition, the cardinals could revoke the Pope's sentences.[29] He concluded by submitting his views to correction and

---

[27] Gloss *ad Sext.* I.vi.3 fol. 20ra, 'Praeterea cardinales sunt apostolici coadiutores in executione officii et etiam consultores recti et intrepidi . . . vel sunt filii ipsius ecclesie. . . . Nec unquam memini me legisse quod succedant loco Apostolici qui est Vicarius Dei . . . quod si esset frustra Papa haberet eligi cum ipsi per se sufficere viderentur.'

[28] *Ibid.* 'Si dicatur non est veresimile quod Deus velit ecclesiam esse acephalam, respondeo, absit a cordibus fidelium, sed dicam . . . ipse Christus est caput nostrum . . . unde dicitur ecclesia Christi quae est corpus ipsius . . . per quod patet quod mater nostra, quae est ecclesia nunquid potest esse acephala quamvis Christi Vicarius ab ipso revocetur a Vicariatu.'

[29] Guido explained that the power of absolution was one that normally devolved to a college lacking a prelate, so that in this case an express prohibition was necessary, 'Sed his praemissis multum obstare videtur constitutio Bonifacii . . . *ad succidendos,*

referring the reader to Hostiensis's thorough discussion of the whole problem.

Joannes Andreae also displayed a certain hesitancy in dealing with this question. In his gloss on the *Sext* he referred to the early opinions of Huguccio and Joannes Teutonicus and went on to repeat at length the points put forward by Hostiensis, concluding with the argument that the Roman church could never die, and that accordingly the cardinals could be said to possess plenitude of power *in habitu* in so far as they were considered to be the Roman church. The authority of a legate of the Apostolic See did not expire when the Pope died, but it could not endure,

> nisi collegium sedes Apostolica censeretur et posset dici quod cardinales habent potestatis plenitudinem habitu tunc in quantum Romana ecclesia censentur quae non moritur.[30]

Joannes did not accept or reject these views, but contented himself with observing that the cardinals ought not to concern themselves with matters other than the election except in cases of grave necessity—a point of view no one would have disputed.

However, in his later gloss on the Clementine decretal, *Ne Romani*, which laid down more stringent rules governing the conduct of the cardinals during a vacancy, he adopted a much firmer attitude. He no longer hesitated between the views of Guido de Baysio and those of Hostiensis. Hostiensis was 'excusable' since he did not know the recent legislation; but he was quite definitely wrong. The cardinals did not succeed to the papal authority during a vacancy, and Christ himself, not the Sacred College, was head of the Church at such a time. Hostiensis's claim that the cardinals possessed the same rights as the members of other ecclesiastical corporations was expressly denied by the provisions of *Ne Romani*.[31]

These views again found general acceptance among the canonists before the Great Schism;[32] the unique authority of the Pope was

---

ibi *nec etiam per collegium*. Sed respondi potest quod loquitur in absolutione excommunicationis, quae vacante sede ad collegium devolvebatur, nisi per sedem apostolicam fuisset interdicta potestas ... *de mai. et obed., episcopali.*'

[30] Gloss *ad Sext.* v.iii.1 s.v. *sede vacante.*

[31] Gloss *ad Clem.* I.iii.2 s.v. *non consonam.*

[32] For a review of fourteenth-century opinions see again Andreas de Barbatia, *De Prestantia Cardinalium*. In general the canonists who held that the Pope was not obliged to consult the cardinals, maintained also that the cardinals did not succeed to the papal authority during a vacancy.

thus uncompromisingly asserted. Yet the formulation of the doctrine was extremely vulnerable to attack even on the canonists' own premisses. To dispose of the claims of the cardinals they maintained that the headship of Christ alone sufficed to sustain the Church during a vacancy, but the standard canonistic argument proving that the powers of Peter descended to his successors rested precisely on the assumption that an earthly head was necessary at all times. Joannes Andreae did notice that the argument might be applied to the powers of the cardinals during a vacancy but did not explain how it should be refuted,[33] and neither he nor the Archdeacon provided an effective reply to Hostiensis's very ingenious suggestion that Christ should be regarded as the Head of the Sacred College, which in turn provided an earthly head for the Church. Again, the canonists did not deny that the cardinals formed a corporate body with the Pope as head—Joannes Andreae reaffirmed this common opinion in the gloss on *Ne Romani* itself[34]—but, when it was argued that the members of an ecclesiastical corporation possessed substantial rights of administration and jurisdiction either in association with their prelate or in his absence, they could only reply that in this particular case the law decreed otherwise. The Roman church was apparently in a class apart, its constitutional structure quite unrelated to that of the other churches—a rather unsatisfactory conclusion in view of the general belief that the Roman church should be a pattern and example for all the others;[35] and even this position was not consistently maintained,

---

[33] Gloss *ad Sext.* v.iv.1 s.v. *deseret*, '. . . per hanc litteram satis patet quod potestas Petri transivit ad posteros; alias post Petrum sine pastore remansisset Ecclesia, quod non est verum . . . et idem potest hic argui circa collegium cardinalium cum vacat sedes, ut dixi supra, *tit. proxi.* c. *unico* (v.iii.1)'.

[34] Gloss *ad Clem.* I.iii.2 s.v. *coetum*, 'Quomodo vero cardinales habent ius collegii vel capituli, nec censentur iure singulorum in diversis titulis locatorum, satis tractavit Hostiensis, *de Iudaeis, ad Liberanda.*' On the corporate unity of Pope and cardinals see also Archdeacon *ad Sext.* I.xv.1 fol. 50v*b*, '. . . pars eius corporis . . .'; Zenzellinus *ad Extrav.* I.iii.1 s.v. *sublimitatem*, '. . . pars corporis papae . . .'; Joannes de Lignano, *De Censura Ecclesiastica*, fol. 229ra, '. . . cardinales sunt partes non dico solum corporis imo capitis'; Paulus de Liazariis, '. . . sunt pars capitis, ideo non iurant obedientiam Papae' (*Repetitionum in Universas fere Iuris Canonici Partes . . . volumina sex* (Venetiis, 1587) II, fol. 222v*b*). Again, in discussing the affairs of other ecclesiastical corporations, Joannes Andreae did not dissent from the accepted view that a prelate could not act without consent of his chapter in important cases, and that his ordinary jurisdiction devolved to the chapter during a vacancy. Gloss *ad Sext.* I.viii.3 s.v. *si episcopus*, II.xv.11, *casus*, Gloss *ad Clem.* III.iv.2 s.v. *consentiente*, *Novella ad Sext.* I.xvii.1 fol. 44, II.xv.11 fol. 68.

[35] Joannes Andreae, *Novella ad Sext.* I.vi.17 fol. 24 n. 4, 'Urbs composita est ad

for both Guido de Baysio and Joannes Andreae did make use of the analogy between the cardinals and a cathedral chapter when it was convenient for the purposes of their argument to do so.[36] Not until after the Schism did Aegidius de Bellamera press the implications of *Ne Romani* to their logical conclusion by suggesting that perhaps, after all, the cardinals did not form a corporate body with the Pope;[37] his predecessors were content to affirm that they did so, but were unable to accept some of the most important juristic consequences of such a relationship.

The disharmonies that marred the canonists' presentation of their doctrine of papal authority are still more apparent when one turns to the relationship between Pope and Universal Church. The academic canonists maintained as a general principle that the Pope received sovereign authority from God and was himself the source of all inferior authority in the Church; yet in discussing particular problems they seem to have assumed tacitly that the Church as a whole was endowed with an authority in its own right which could be used, in exceptional circumstances, even against the Pope. The most obvious example is provided by the canonists' treatment of the perennial problem of the deposition of a heretical Pope. On this question there was substantial agreement concerning the form of procedure to be adopted and the judge competent to conduct the trial, and again it was a doctrine formulated by Guido de Baysio and repeated by Joannes Andreae which came to be most widely accepted. Guido followed the more common opinion of the thirteenth-century Decretalists in holding that resistance to a Pope suspected of heresy could not take the form of a procedural *exceptio* but must be expressed in

---

exemplum orbis.' Here again Joannes was following his master, Guido de Baysio, who wrote, 'Urbs composita est ad modum orbis, sed orbis maior est urbe' (*Commentaria ad Sext.* i.iv.17 fol. 32r*b*). Cf. Guilielmus Durantis, *De Modo Generalis Concilii Celebrandi*, p. 163, 'Romana ecclesia quae caput est aliarum . . . quae sicut Innocentius Papa scribit est omnibus posita in speculum et exemplum.'

[36] Guido de Baysio, *supra* p. 209 n. 2. Joannes Andreae argued that the cardinals could not create another cardinal, although they could elect a Pope, by citing the parallel case of a cathedral chapter which could elect a bishop but could not bestow a benefice in the gift of the bishop alone. Gloss *ad Clem.* i.iii.2 s.v. *potestatis*.

[37] *Commentaria in Gratiani Decreta* (Lugduni, 1550), *ad Dist.* 79 c. 7 fol. 86r*b*, 'Sed certe non eo modo se habet collegium cardinalium ad papam sicut collegium ecclesiae cathedralis ad episcopum . . . et forte ratio est quia forte papa, maxime tanquam caput universalis ecclesiae, non facit unum corpus cum cardinalibus et eorum collegio sicut facit episcopus cum capitulo suo.'

an *accusatio*;[38] that is to say, it could not be alleged that the Pope's election had been invalidated by the fact of his heresy and that consequently he had never been a true Pope; it was necessary to present a criminal indictment to be followed by a trial of the suspected Pope. As for the authority competent to try such a case, Guido de Baysio laid down firmly that it could only be a General Council. He knew of Huguccio's view that the cardinals could depose a heretical Pope, but observed that it was not supported by any law and so could not be accepted:

> ... tantus est favor fidei, quod de crimine haeresis etiam in occulto Papa potest accusari, ut patet ex eo quod leg. et not. 40 *dist. Si papa* ... et hujus criminis iudex competens est concilium generale duntaxat, ut legitur expresse 17 *dist.* § Hinc etiam.... Scias tamen quod Hugo. scripsit, 73 *dist. In synodo*, quod Cardinales possunt deponere Papam propter haeresim. Sed hoc iure aliquo non probavit et ideo non recedo ab eo quod plane dicitur in prae § *Hinc etiam*....[39]

Guido, moreover, held that it was the proper function of the Council actually to condemn the Pope, rejecting the opinion of those who held that it was for the Pope to pass sentence on himself:

> ... et quamvis tale crimen probetur in concilio contra Papam videtur quod concilium non debeat eum condemnare, sed ipse Papa contra se sententiam habeat promulgare.... Sed contra credo, et hoc clare colligitur ex praealleg. c. *Si papa*.[40]

These opinions were repeated by Joannes Andreae and Henricus Bohic,[41] and, at the end of the century, Aegidius de Bellamera reported that the *communis opinio* held the General Council to be the competent judge of a Pope accused of heresy:

> Dic ergo quod iudex erit in hoc casu, secundum communem opinionem quam sequor, concilium generale, et quod concilium generale in hoc casu sit iudex tenet Archidiaconus....[42]

---

[38] *Rosarium ad Dist.* 40 c. 6, *Commentaria ad Sext.* I.vi.3 fol. 19v*b*. According to Henricus de Bohic the opinion that an *accusatio* but not an *exceptio* could be brought against a Pope suspected of heresy had been upheld by Vincentius, Innocentius IV, Hostiensis, Bernardus Compostellanus, Abbas Antiquus, Alanus and Joannes Andreae as well as Guido de Baysio (*Distinctiones ad X.* I.vi.6 fol. 19v*a*).

[39] *Commentaria ad Sext.* v.ii.5 fol. 114r*a*.

[40] *Ibid.*

[41] Gloss *ad Sext.* II.xiv.2 s.v. *haeresi* and *Novella ad Sext.* v.ii.5 fol. 103 n. 1. Henricus Bohic, *Distinctiones ad X.* I.vi.6 fol. 19 n. 3.

[42] *Commentaria ad Dist.* 40 c. 6.

The Archdeacon did not mention crimes other than heresy and he did not explain how the General Council was to be summoned if the Pope proved obdurate, but Cardinal Petrus Bertrandi held that the cardinals could summon a Council to deal with an evil Pope even though he was not a heretic;[43] and Henricus de Bohic, following the *glossa ordinaria* to the *Decretum*, maintained that a Pope could be accused before a Council for any crime that was notorious and that gave scandal to the whole Church.[44]

On the surface, the canonists' treatment of this problem seems almost perverse in view of their own high doctrine of papal authority. They could not indeed deny the accepted doctrine that a heretical Pope was liable to deposition, and there was weighty authority for extending the case of heresy to cover all notorious crimes; but they seem to have gone out of their way to present the issue in as 'conciliar' a form as possible. There were no arguments about the automatic degradation of a heretic, no attempts to prove that the Pope had already ceased to be Pope before any proceedings against him were instituted, simply a reiterated insistence that the Pope had to be formally condemned by a General Council. Aegidius de Bellamera indeed attributed to the Archdeacon the view that the Council's jurisdiction over the Pope was based on the fact that the bishops in Council possessed an authority superior to the Pope's in the definition of articles of faith.[45] The Archdeacon never put forward that opinion, and it is doubtful whether any fourteenth-century canonist before the Great Schism would have committed himself to such a statement, but their treatment of the whole question could easily seem to imply an assumption of conciliar superiority.

---

[43] His view was cited by Pierre d'Ailly, *Utrum indoctus in iure divino possit juste praeesee* in Gerson, *Opera*, II, cols. 646–62 at col. 661, 'Et opinio Petri Bertrandi in Clementinam, Ne Romani. Ubi dicit quod *contra malum Papam non haereticum est remedium, quod Ecclesia oret pro ipso et quod Cardinales convocent Concilium generale, si Papa nolit convocare.*'

[44] *Distinctiones ad* X. I.vi.6 fol. 19 n. 3, 'Si queris utrum electus in papam a duabus partibus possit accusari et per accusationem deiici . . . refert, Aut queris utrum possit accusari et tunc aut queritur nunquid possit accusari de crimine heresis notorie vel occulte quod tamen probari potest. Dic quod sic, ut xl *dist. si papa.* Aut de alio crimine et tunc et de crimine notorio . . . et de quo scandalizatur ecclesia, et dico quod de tali potest accusari. Nam talis incorrigibilis est contumax et contumacia dicitur heresis. . . . Aut de alio crimine non notorio et de quo ecclesia non scandalizatur et de tali accusari non potest.'

[45] *Commentaria ad Dist.* 15 c. 2 fol. 20vb, 'Circa ea que fidem catholicam et articulos eius respiciunt plus valet sententia episcoporum in concilio quam sententia pape. Et patet quia si contra sententiam episcoporum papa erraret in illis, posset de hoc in concilio accusari, xl *dist. si papa* in fi. secundum Arc.'

It seems especially surprising that neither in his *Rosarium* nor in his gloss on the *Sext* did the Archdeacon reproduce the arguments of Huguccio, with which he was certainly familiar, and which would seem to have provided adequate safeguards for the principle of papal immunity. Perhaps the explanation may be found in the actual circumstances of the times, for Huguccio's view that a heretical Pope was self-condemned and automatically degraded from his office carried certain implications that could hardly have been acceptable to a defender of papal authority in the fourteenth century. In spite of all the appeals of royal and imperial publicists, there was after all no serious probability before the Great Schism of a validly convoked General Council sitting in judgement on a reigning Pope and deposing him; but there was a real danger of secular rulers denouncing the Pope as a heretic and inducing the clergy of their dominions to withdraw allegiance from him without awaiting any such formalities. Huguccio's arguments would seem to provide a justification for such a course provided that the alleged heresy was one that had been already condemned, or the alleged crime persistently repeated. There would be no difficulty in ensuring the proper degree of notoriety! In actual practice the position of the Pope was probably best defended by the canonists' insistence on a formal trial and condemnation, but their acceptance of such a procedure certainly compromised the theory of papal supremacy.

The idea of an authority diffused throughout the whole Church, normally lying dormant but able to be invoked to meet an exceptional crisis appears at other points in the fourteenth-century glosses. Henricus de Bohic reminded his readers that inerrancy in faith belonged to the *ecclesia generalis simul congregata*.[46] Joannes de Lignano described the Pope as a *dispensator* who was required to respect the public good in granting dispensations.[47] Baldus, who was no Conciliarist although he wrote in the age of the Schism, referred to the inalienable right of the Church to provide itself with a head. The cardinals might lose possession of this right which they held, not in their own name, but in the name of the whole Church; but the Church itself could never lose it.[48] Joannes Andreae raised a somewhat similar

---

[46] *Distinctiones ad* X. v.xxxix.21 fol. 131*va* n. 3.

[47] *Tractatus de Pluralitate Beneficiorum, Tractatus Universi Iuris*, XV, fol. 129ra, fol. 129va.

[48] *Baldus super Decretalibus* (Lugduni, 1547), *ad* I.ii.25 fol. 38ra, 'Sive per veros cardinales sive per falsos papa eligatur ecclesia semper retinet possessionem . . . et si expellerentur cardinales tamen quia ipsi non possident nomine suo, sed nomine totius catholice ecclesie ipsa universalis ecclesia non perdit possessionem eligendi.'

question in discussing the abdication of a Pope, and his hypothetical case has a special interest because it resembled quite closely the dilemma that actually arose in 1378.[49] He suggested that a Pope might resign and then challenge the position of his successor by denying that he had done so, thus precipitating a schism:

> Si papa post electionem successoris vel prius dum cardinales vellent eligere negat se renuntiasse, quid iuris vel quid erit iudex? Dimittamus solutionem Deo cuius vices gerit papa verus, nec est credendum quod talem casum dubium evenire permittet.[50]

But in spite of his confidence in the divine providence Joannes did not neglect to suggest a solution for the problem:

> Si tamen hunc casum permitteret evenire, et pars quelibet abundaret sequentibus non essemus sine schismate electo iam successore, ad materiam tamen vide quod scripsi *de ele. licet de vitanda.* super versi *cardinales.*

The reference was to his *Novella* on the Decretals (*ad* i.vi.6), and there he quoted the opinion of Hostiensis that, should the whole College of Cardinals become extinct during a papal vacancy, then the 'Roman clergy and people' could summon a General Council to provide the Church with a head.[51] It was this doctrine that he considered applicable in a schism where there was grave doubt as to which of two candidates was the validly elected Pope.[52] Thus it would

---

[49] At another point in his works Joannes Andreae did pose the precise issue of 1378. If a faction of cardinals claimed to have been intimidated during the course of a papal election, what was to be done, and who should judge the issue? He did not, unfortunately, answer his own question. Gloss *ad Clem.* i.iii.2 s.v. *compellant*, 'Sed quid si alii non intrantes habent iustum metum mortis ... et dicatur dominus temporalis non esse potius ad securitatem ipsorum, vel etiam tunc dicebatur; quid fiet et quis de causa metus cognoscet? Ista non decisa, nec tunc provisa adhuc egebunt provisione.' This gloss was quoted by Henry of Langenstein in his *Consilium Pacis*, Gerson, *Opera*, II, cols. 809–40 at col. 829.

[50] *Novella ad Sext.* i.vii.1 fol. 32 n. 1.

[51] '... deo propitio non accidet quod nullus (cardinalis) supersit. Sed tunc dicit clerus romanus quod ad ipsum pertineret (electio).... Alii dicunt quod tunc esset congregandum concilium et per ipsum providendum ... et convocetur per clerum et populum romanum. Dicit Host. quod licet hoc secundum videatur iustius primum videtur levius et commodius.'

[52] Baldus raised the same question in connexion with the Schism of 1378 itself, basing his argument not on Hostiensis but on Huguccio. He seems to have approved the suggestion of the cardinals summoning a General Council, but thought Huguccio very radical in suggesting that the Council thus assembled might get rid of both contending Popes and elect a third. Gloss *ad* X. i.ii.25 fol. 38ra, 'Quis ergo

seem that not only a heretical or criminal Pope, but even a true Pope might sometimes be held subject to the jurisdiction of a Council summoned by an authority other than that of the Pope himself. Moreover, in the course of this same gloss, Joannes Andreae introduced certain views of John of Paris in order to refute the Colonna arguments against the validity of a papal renunciation and so was led to the explicit conclusion that there could exist in the whole Church or in a General Council an authority at least equal to that of the Pope.[53] This was quite in accordance with the view of the Pope as head of the Universal Church, provided that the Church was regarded as a juristic corporation subject to the normal laws of corporation structure, but it was thoroughly inconsistent with the doctrine of papal *plenitudo potestatis* normally held by the fourteenth-century canonists.

It would be unreasonable to criticize the canonists for failing to present in their glosses a comprehensive and systematic treatise on the theory of Church government. The task they attempted was rather different, to expound the legal implications of all the multifarious decretals included in the collections promulgated by the Papacy. Hence they usually touched on the broader problems of Church government only incidentally when the particular decretal they were glossing raised such an issue. But it would seem reasonable to expect that the canonists should apply consistent principles of ecclesiastical authority to the different problems as they arose, that their views should be, if not systematically expounded, at least capable of systematization. Instead one finds, below the layers of accumulated erudition, a real uncertainty in the face of the fundamental problems concerning the juristic structure of the Church and the interrelation of its various organs of government. The Pope was held to stand above the laws

---

congregabit concilium? Ugutio determinat expresse in d.c. *si uno forte* ubi dicit quod ubi est dissensio inter cardinales debent concilium convocare autoritate cardinalium . . . et illud quod dicit quod concilium pertinet ad cardinales non est in glossa dicti c. *si duo forte* (i.e. *Glossa Ordinaria*) et ideo recurre ad glossam Ugutionis quia glossa Bart. Brixiensis truncata est. . . . In hac congregatione non requiritur autoritas eius qui se pretendit papam quia tractatur de sua exauatoratione et sic de causa propria. Ultimo subiicio quodam mirabile dictum Ugutionis in d.c. *si duo forte*, qui dicit quod propter scandalum vitandum uterque potest per concilium repelli, xl *dist. si papa*, et tertium eligi qui non sit eiusdem scandali prosecutor. Et in hoc advertat rex francorum ne veniat. Scribitur enim, incidit in Scyllam cupiens evitare Charybdim. Et si permititur depositio permititur eius preambula, scilicet subtractio obedienti solite. . . .'

[53] The gloss is cited *supra* p. 164 n. 1.

of the Councils; yet in certain special cases a General Council could exercise jurisdiction over a Pope and even depose him. The Sacred College was said to have the rights of a corporation—*habent ius collegii*; yet some of the most important powers that flowed from such rights were denied to the cardinals. The Pope was said to be endowed with *plenitudo potestatis*, to possess all power under Heaven; yet the authority inherent in the whole Church could be equal to or greater than the Pope's.

For an understanding of the crisis of 1378 and its aftermath these ambiguities of the canonists are as important as the systematic exposition of conciliar thought in the familiar publicistic treatises. It has often been pointed out that the prevailing doctrine of papal sovereignty formed a serious hindrance to all the various attempts at healing the Great Schism, but it should also be emphasized that the Schism could hardly have broken out at all if that doctrine had been expressed with unswerving consistency and clarity in the law of the Church and the teachings of the canonists. The original claim of the dissident cardinals that Urban's election had been invalid was flimsy enough; the subsequent confusion and controversy—with men of good will and good sense on all sides of the complicated arguments—could hardly have arisen except in an age when the whole problem of the right relationship between Pope, cardinals and General Council was enmeshed in ambiguities and in legal intricacies that the lawyers themselves could not unravel. The ideological strife which accompanied the political and religious cleavage of Europe was only the culmination of a conflict of ideas which had been reflected in even the most cautious and conservative glosses of the fourteenth century.

CHAPTER FOUR

FRANCISCUS ZABARELLA

In the preceding chapters we have traced the growth of a group of ideas concerning the structure of the Church, the authority of a General Council, and the status of the cardinals. It would be inappropriate in a survey of canonistic thought to attempt any detailed analysis of the publicistic development of these theories and of the various attempts to implement them in the age of the Conciliar Movement; yet it seems desirable to give some account of the process whereby the different elements of thought which had been scattered diffusely in the earlier glosses were consolidated into a systematic theory of Church government at the end of the fourteenth century. The work of Franciscus Zabarella provides an illustration of this conciliar synthesis most appropriate for our purpose, for the great Italian scholar was at once a cardinal, an eminent Conciliarist, and a most distinguished canonist.[1] Moreover, his *Tractatus de Schismate* was a work of pure canonistic scholarship, a comprehensive survey of all the conciliar elements in the glosses of the preceding two centuries, fusing together in one system of thought ideas which had formerly seemed unconnected or even incompatible.

The whole of the *Tractatus* was embodied in Zabarella's enormous commentary on the Decretals as a gloss to chapter i.vi.6,[2] and in that context it seems by no means incongruous, for the work was no mere controversial *tour de force* but an integral part of Zabarella's whole exposition of canonistic doctrine. He drew his arguments with equal facility from the glosses of Decretists and Decretalists; Joannes Teutonicus, Hostiensis, Joannes Monachus, Guilielmus Durantis all contributed elements of thought to Zabarella's synthesis; so too did

---

[1] On Zabarella's contributions to conciliar thought see A. Kneer, *Kardinal Zabarella: Ein Beitrag zür Geschichte des grossen abendländischen Schisma* (Münster, 1891); Enrico Carusi, *Enciclopedia Italiana* s.v. *Zabarella*; and, above all, W. Ullmann, *Origins of the Great Schism*, pp. 191–231. On his canonistic output see Van Hove, *Prolegomena*, pp. 475, 496, 502, 506, 507.

[2] *Super Primo Decretalium Commentaria* (Venetiis, 1602), fol. 107rb/110vb. The Tractatus was also printed by Schardius in his *De Iurisdictione . . . Imperiali ac Potestate Ecclesiastica* (Basileae, 1566), pp. 688–711.

John of Paris who, of all the earlier writers, most nearly anticipated his doctrines. Zabarella's views on the corporate structure of the Church seem essentially the same as those put forward by John of Paris, though in the later work the emphasis of the arguments was modified to meet the particular problems of the Schism and the whole theory was presented with a much greater wealth of juristic learning. Yet, characteristically, Zabarella made no explicit reference to the *De Potestate Regia et Papali*, since this was not a formal canonistic commentary. All his arguments were drawn from legal sources,[3] and when he made use of the ideas, or even the very words, of John of Paris he preferred to quote, not the work of John himself, but the canonistic doctrines that lay behind his work.

In the opening lines of his treatise Zabarella takes us at once to the heart of his system of thought,

> ... ille erit papa quem iudicium et universitatis consensus elegerit. Nam nomine universitatis debet intelligi universitas totius Christianitatis. ...[4]

The whole of Christendom was one great corporation over which the Pope presided in the same way as the rector of any other corporation; all the exposition that followed was a commentary on that fundamental premise. We have already noted that Zabarella used the same language to describe the theological idea of mystical unity in the Church and the canonistic concept of legal incorporation, and his emphasis throughout the *Tractatus* upon the applicability of this latter concept to the unity of the whole Church is readily understandable in view of the peculiar circumstances of his age. In the sombre years of the Schism the very foundations of medieval Catholicism seemed threatened, for the Church which for so long had sought to incarnate in a visible society the medieval aspiration to unity, now seemed irretrievably 'divided against itself'. A whole generation grew up which had known only a divided Christendom, torn by dual headship and conflicting allegiances; yet to the Catholic mind the Church was before all things a unity, '*unam* sanctam catholicam ecclesiam'. It could never be admitted that the 'seamless robe' had been rent apart, and if the hierarchical organization which should have manifested the intrinsic unity of the Church had become riven

---

[3] Except for a passing reference to Aristotle, *Commentaria*, fol. 107va (Schardius, p. 689).

[4] *Commentaria* fol. 107rb (Schardius, p. 688).

by inveterate schism, it was natural that well-intentioned churchmen should turn with new enthusiasm to the ancient doctrine of a unity inherent in the whole *congregatio fidelium*, a mystical unity that could never be compromised by the dissensions of Popes and prelates. This tendency was apparent in many of the conciliar works, and especially in those of Jean Gerson,[5] but Zabarella, always first and foremost a canonist, realized more clearly than any of his contemporaries that the essential problem was to give legal effect to this mystical unity which, they all believed, the Church had never lost.[6] The canonistic doctrine of corporations provided a most effective instrument for this purpose. It was not only that a trained canonist like Zabarella tended to envisage any organic association in terms of legal incorporation, but also that the technicalities of corporation law were peculiarly well adapted to cope with the particular problems raised by the Schism; for, as we have seen, the canonists taught that corporate unity, and the legal rights associated with it, could survive in a corporation even when it lacked an effective head.

Several of Zabarella's arguments were based on this doctrine. He maintained that the state of schism which divided the Church had produced a 'quasi-vacancy' in the Papacy, since neither Pope could effectively govern the whole Church, and that, in these circumstances, the authority of the Church could be exercised by the *congregatio fidelium*:[7]

> Est ergo ecclesia quasi-vacans.... Cum autem vacat ecclesia potestas universalis ecclesiae videtur residere in ipsa tota ecclesia quae est fidelium congregatio.[8]

And he added, with a reference to Aristotle, that this power could be exercised by the *pars valentior* of the whole *congregatio fidelium* assembled in a General Council; and within the Council again, since

---

[5] See especially his sermon delivered to the Council of Constance in *Opera*, II, col. 205.

[6] Cf. *Commentaria ad* X. I.vi.6 fol. 106va, '... non possunt esse duo apostolici quia offenderetur illa regula *unam sanctam catholicam* etc.... et posses dici quod non proprie offenderetur quia unitas conservatur in unico matrimonio inter Christum et ecclesiam ... Sed bene verum est quod esse unum Pontificem consonum est illi articulo.'

[7] It had commonly been held by earlier canonists that the laws relating to devolution of authority in a corporation were applicable, not only when the prelate was dead, but also when, for one reason or another, he was unable to discharge his functions. *Supra* pp. 118–119.

[8] *Commentaria*, fol. 107va (Schardius, p. 688).

it too was to be regarded as a corporate body, by the *pars potior* or *pars idoneior*:

> ... sic etiam dicunt philosophi quod regimen civitatis consistit penes congregationem civium, vel ipsius congregationis partem valentiorem quae sententia colligitur ab Aristotele tertio politicorum ... ita ergo et regimen universalis ecclesiae vacante papatu penes ipsam ecclesiam universalem quae repraesentatur per concilium generale, et ipso concilio congregato consistit penes ipsius concilii partem potiorem ... nam etiam ad ipsum concilium non conveniunt omnes catholici sed personae praecipuae, puta episcopi et alii praelati ecclesiastici ... et in rebus et negotiis universitatum requiruntur rectores vel pars idoneior. ...[9]

The apparent echo of Marsiglio's terminology in the use of the phrase *pars valentior* has sometimes been unduly emphasized. It will be seen that Zabarella used three similar terms rather loosely, without any attempt to define them closely, and, although one of the terms may be Marsiglio's—it was also used by William of Moerbeke in his translation of the *Politics*—the underlying thought remained essentially juristic. The idea that the whole power of a corporation could be exercised by its more substantial part was a long-established tenet of canonistic theory—the more usual legal phrase was *sanior pars* or *maior et sanior pars*[10]—and all the texts that Zabarella cited in support of this principle referred to the doctrines of Roman and canon law touching the structure of corporations. Moreover, he chose to emphasize the juristic foundations of his theory at this point by remarking that thus far his arguments were quite uncontroversial since any trained canonist would have agreed with them.[11]

Since, in a vacancy or 'quasi-vacancy', the whole power of the Church was vested in a General Council, the next problem was to decide how a Council could be summoned to deal with the existing problem of the Schism. Canon law laid down clearly enough that it

---

[9] *Commentaria*, fol. 107r*b* (Schardius, p. 688).

[10] The principle was most clearly laid down at X. III.xi.1. In his commentary on this canon (*Commentaria*, fol. 72v*b*), Zabarella repeated the view of Bernardus Parmensis that, in assessing the *maior pars*, not only numbers but 'reason' and 'piety' were to be taken into account, '... maior pars est illa quae maior ratione et pietate nititur'. Marsiglio was following a very common medieval opinion in expressing his own view, 'Valentiorem inquam partem considerata quantitate personarum et qualitate in communitate' (*Defensor Pacis*, ed. C. W. Previté-Orton (Cambridge, 1928), I, xii, p. 49). On Zabarella's use of the term *valentior pars* see W. Ullmann, *op. cit.* pp. 197–8.

[11] 'Sed in hoc non oportet instare quia periti canonum communiter in hoc conveniunt.'

was for the Pope to summon a General Council, and Zabarella thought that in the actual circumstances, the proper course was for the two rival pontiffs each to summon his own obedience. But if the pontiffs refused to do so, then, he argued, the right devolved to the cardinals.[12] If they too proved neglectful then the right of assembling to exercise their inherent authority belonged to the whole *populus*. The Emperor ought to act on behalf of the people in summoning the Council, since the powers of the *populus* had been transferred to the Emperor,[13] but if he failed to act and two parts of the Council could be brought together by any means they could call on the other members to join them and take all steps necessary to end the Schism; this argument was again based on the canonistic doctrine concerning the assembly of other corporations.[14]

Evidently, for Zabarella, the essential need was that a Council should assemble; the means by which it was brought into existence were of secondary importance, for, in his view, its authority was not derived from the convoking power but from the *congregatio fidelium*. Moreover, he did not limit his consideration of the *congregatio fidelium* as a source of ecclesiastical authority to the circumstances of a papal vacancy or schism; on the contrary, the doctrine of an underlying authority inhering in all the members of a corporation was made the basis of a detailed analysis of the position of a reigning Pope in relation to the *congregatio fidelium*, the General Council and the College of Cardinals. The heart of the whole treatise was Zabarella's definition of the idea of papal *plenitudo potestatis*. His treatment of this concept provided the final systematization of a trend of thought which had been current among the Decretists and developed in the corporation theories

---

[12] *Commentaria*, fol. 107va (Schardius, p. 690), '. . . remanet penes collegium talis potestas'.

[13] *Commentaria*, fol. 107vb (Schardius, p. 692), 'Ipse autem Imperator repraesentat totum populum Christianum cum in eum translata sit iurisdictio et potestas universi orbis.' The right of the *populus* to authorize a Council was deduced from *Dist.* 65 c. 9 which laid down that the people of a province could summon bishops from neighbouring provinces in case of necessity if their own bishop neglected to do so— the text had earlier been applied to the summoning of a General Council by Hostiensis (*supra* p. 139). Zabarella also cited at this point the view of Innocent IV, that, when the prelate whose duty it was to summon a chapter meeting failed to do so, the duty devolved to the next in seniority (Innocentius *ad* X. i.xxxiii.1). Apparently the same principle was to be applied to the summoning of a General Council.

[14] *Commentaria*, fol. 108rb (Schardius, p. 693), 'Si due partes collegii quomodocumque conveniant, ipsi possunt vocare alios, qui commode possunt vocari. Et si non veniunt, ipsi procedunt ad faciendum quod instat.'

of the Decretalists, which John of Paris had echoed, and Joannes Monachus had openly applied to the Papacy, though without exploring its full implications. This was the idea of *plenitudo potestatis* as a limited and derivative authority conferred upon the head of a corporation by its members. It is only the neglect of this whole aspect of canonistic thought which makes it seem paradoxical to find in Zabarella's definition of the Pope's authority in relation to the Church at once an epitome of the whole conciliar outlook and a recapitulation of two centuries of canonistic tradition:

> ... id quod dicitur quod papa habet plenitudinem potestatis debet intelligi non solus, sed tanquam caput universitatis ita quod ipsa potestas est in ipsa universitate tanquam in fundamento, et in papa tanquam principali ministro per quem haec potestas explicitur, ita tamen quod praecedat clave discretionis.[15]

The assertion that *plenitudo potestatis* resided in the whole Church *tanquam in fundamento* was repeated several times in other contexts,[16] and always with the purpose of emphasizing the essentially derivative and responsible nature of the *potestas* that could properly be attributed to the Pope. We have already seen that Zabarella regarded the consent of the *universitas totius Christianitatis* as the constitutive factor in the making of a Pope. His treatment of the concept of papal *plenitudo potestatis* makes it clear that he had adopted in an extreme form, and applied to the whole Church and the Papacy, an idea that earlier canonists had often hinted at in their discussions on corporation structure and had sometimes seemed to take for granted in their treatment of a prelate's status as proctor, but which they had never stated so plainly and trenchantly as did Zabarella—the idea that, when an ecclesiastical community created a prelate by election or consent, the nature of its act was to confer on the new prelate the exercise of an authority inherent in the community itself.

In the view of Zabarella, the Pope could exercise only such powers as the Church had conferred on him ('papa ... posset non quod libet sed quod licebit'),[17] and, like the proctor of any lesser corpora-

---

[15] *Commentaria*, fol. 109va (Schardius, p. 703).

[16] *Commentaria*, fol. 109va (Schardius, p. 703), '... concilium apud quod est plenitudo potestatis tanquam in fundamento ...'; fol. 110rb (p. 708), '... potestas ecclesiae est in ipsa universitate tanquam in fundamento'; '... in prima universitate est totalis plenitudo potestatis tanquam in fundamento'; fol. 110va (p. 709), 'Ipsum concilium ... habeat plenitudinem potestatis.'

[17] *Commentaria*, fol. 109va (Schardius, p. 704).

tion, he could never exercise those powers in a manner detrimental to the Church that had conferred them:

> (Universitas) totius ecclesiae non habet superiorem nisi Deum et papam *cum bene administrat.*[18]

He added that it was for the *universitas* itself to decide whether the Pope administered well or not, for, in conferring power on the Pope, the Church could not totally alienate its own inherent authority any more than could the *populus romanus* when it conferred jurisdiction on the Emperor.[19] Again, it was for the Church to undertake the correction of the Pope if it did find him erring:

> . . . potestatis plenitudo est in papa, ita tamen quod non errat sed cum errat habet corrigere Concilium, apud quod ut praedixi est plenitudo potestatis tanquam in fundamento.[20]

Zabarella had no doubt that this correction could extend even to the deposition of a Pope if necessary, and he thought that this could be brought about in two ways, either by a simple withdrawal of allegiance on the part of the Christian people, or, more properly, by the sentence of a General Council. To assert as a logical proposition that an authority conferred by the Church in the first place could be withdrawn by the Church in case of abuse was simple enough; but to establish a juristic proof of the validity of such extreme action against a Pope was a more complicated task, for Zabarella, of all men, could not be content to write 'illud non intelligo' in face of the canonistic texts asserting that a Pope was immune from all human judgement.

He raised the problem himself by inquiring how a Pope could validly be deposed when his authority was greater than that of any Council—for the law laid down that the Roman church lent authority to Councils, not the Councils to the Roman church. His first response followed a line of argument familiar to the Decretists two centuries earlier. He was not concerned, he wrote, with the 'Roman church' but with the Pope; and the term 'Roman church' did not

---

[18] *Commentaria*, fol. 110va (Schardius, p. 708). Cf. Joannes Teutonicus *ad* C. 12 q. 1 c. 28, '(Praelati) loco domini habentur *cum bene administrant*, loco praedonis cum male'; Hostiensis, *Lectura* ad X. iii.xxiv.2, 'Quamdiu ergo *bene administrat*, procurator et prelatus est.'

[19] On Zabarella's view of the relations between Emperor and *populus* see also his gloss *ad* i, vi, c. *verum*, fol. 150ra, and on the whole question of the part assigned to the Emperor in Zabarella's theory W. Ullmann, *op. cit.* pp. 220-8.

[20] *Commentaria*, fol. 109va (Schardius, p. 703).

necessarily refer to the Pope. It could have several meanings; it might, for instance, be used as equivalent to 'Apostolic See' as when one wrote that the Apostolic See was unerring in faith; but then it meant not the Pope alone nor any local church, but the whole *congregatio fidelium*:

> ... quod tamen dicitur sedem Apostolicam errare non posse videtur intelligendum accipiendo sedem pro tota ecclesia i.e. congregatione fidelium.[21]

Again, he argued, in these matters of faith a General Council was greater than a Pope according to the *Glossa Ordinaria* to the *Decretum*, and the Schism could properly be regarded as a matter of faith since its continuance imperilled the faith of the whole Church.[22] Thus, the provisions of canon law which forbade the deposition of a Pope could be circumvented by citing the one exception that they themselves admitted, the case of heresy, and by emphasizing that contumacious persistence in schism—or indeed in any notorious crime—was tantamount to heresy and could be punished as such.[23] To these arguments of the Decretists Zabarella added an effective point of his own. It had often been maintained in the past that the *plenitudo potestatis* which Christ had conferred on the Church, and which was usually treated as an attribute of the Pope, could override any enactment of positive law; but Zabarella held that *plenitudo potestatis* rested with the Church or with a General Council *tanquam in fundamento*, and so he could argue that a Council too was not bound by any positive law, not excluding *Dist.* 40 c. 6 of the *Decretum*, the law that laid down that a Pope was immune from human judgement except in case of heresy.[24] The idea of an illimitable *plenitudo potestatis* developed by the

---

[21] He went on to suggest that the term *Sedes Apostolica* could also be used to designate Pope and cardinals together. Cf. *infra* p. 211.

[22] *Commentaria*, fol. 109r*b* (Schardius, p. 701). 'Item in casu nostro agitur de fide, quae periclitaretur in hoc schismate. . . . Cum autem agitur de fide synodus est maior quam papa, 19 *Dist.* c. *Anastasius* in glossa, 15 *Dist. Sicut sancti* in glossa ultima.'

[23] The idea that schism was tantamount to heresy, which often recurs in the writings of the Conciliarists, was not invented to meet the difficulties of their own day. It was put forward as early as the twelfth century, e.g. by Rufinus, *Summa ad Dist.* 40 c. 6, 'Dioscorus . . . a fide devius extitit, dum in scisma quod heresim comitatur incidit.' Zabarella repeated Joannes Teutonicus' view that the Pope could be judged for any notorious crime at fol. 108v*a* (Schardius, p. 697). See also his gloss *ad* III.viii.4 fol. 56r*b*, 'Sed videretur quod quando persisteret (papa) impenitens possit haberi pro male sentiente in fide.'

[24] *Commentaria* fol. 110v*a* (Schardius, p. 709), 'Item ipsum concilium non subiicitur iuri positivo cum habeat plenitudinem potestatis. . . .'

more extreme supporters of the papacy was thus ingeniously turned against the position of the Pope himself. Zabarella added that, even if *Dist.* 40 c. 6 had been promulgated by a General Council, which was not in fact the case, it would still not have limited the competence of future Councils since *par in parem non habet imperium.* Once again it was an argument which hitherto had been usually employed to uphold the absolute authority of a reigning pontiff. As for the underlying theological difficulty that papal power could be taken away by no human agency since it had been conferred by God alone, he was content to quote in reply the arguments that John of Paris had helped to popularize at the beginning of the century,

> ... quando concilium privat papam, potestas non dicitur sibi auferri ab homine sed a Deo, cum dispositio concilii sit divina. . . . Item, licet potestas papae sit a Deo, tamen quod iste sit papa vel iste est immediate ab homine. . . . Unde potest ab homine tolli.[25]

There was one further objection that Zabarella took note of which might have undermined the whole structure of his argument, based as it was on a clearly defined conception of the whole Church as a corporate entity. Innocent IV had held that the jurisdiction of a corporation was not diffused throughout its whole body but was concentrated in the head alone. Zabarella replied that this argument was not necessarily valid, since, against the authority of Innocent could be set the authority of Hostiensis who maintained the contrary opinion; and in any case, their arguments applied only to corporations possessing a superior:

> Sed quidquid sit de hoc istud tamen locum habet in universitate habente superiorem, quod cessat in universitate totius ecclesiae, quae superiorem non habet.[26]

Zabarella expressed himself at this point with less than his usual lucidity. It would be incorrect to suppose that he was dismissing all previous corporation theory, the views of Hostiensis no less than those of Innocent, as inapplicable to the whole Church, for that would

---

[25] *Commentaria*, fol. 110r*b* (Schardius, p. 708). Cf. John of Paris, *ed. cit.* pp. 254.21, 258.8.

[26] *Commentaria*, fol. 110r*b* (Schardius, p. 708), 'Innocentius . . . dicit quod si universitas habet rectorem iurisdictio est penes rectorem, non penes universitatem. . . . Sed negari potest hoc, nam Hostiensis ibi tenet hoc quod universitas exerceat licet sit incommodosum. . . . Sed quidquid sit de hoc istud tamen locum habet in universitate habente superiore. . . .'

have demolished at a stroke all his more telling arguments. In fact the argument concerning a corporation with no superior was itself borrowed from Hostiensis who had maintained, with a similar apparent inconsistency, firstly, that the cardinals could exercise authority during a papal vacancy because they had the same rights as other corporations, and secondly, that their authority was exceptional since there was no superior judge to whom the power of the Apostolic See could devolve.[27] The underlying thought of Zabarella and Hostiensis seems to have been exactly the same—Innocent's view that the members of a corporation could not exercise its jurisdiction was probably incorrect in any case, but it was quite certainly inapplicable in the case of a corporation with no superior. Accordingly, Zabarella had no hesitation in affirming again and again that the whole power of the Church rested ultimately in all its members, or in citing earlier corporation law in support of that principle.

His interest in the problems of corporation structure seems to be reflected in his treatment of another most important aspect of the relations between Pope and Council. In discussing the deposition of a Pope he had extracted from the texts of Joannes Teutonicus a doctrine that Joannes himself never clearly asserted, namely, that the Pope's liability to judgement in case of heresy could be deduced from the fact that the Council possessed an authority superior to the Pope's in the definition of articles of faith. But this was to assume that the superiority in matters of faith inhered in the members of a Council separated from the Pope, indeed sitting in judgement on him. In one of his glosses on the Decretals[28] (not included in the *Tractatus de Schismate*) Zabarella did consider this central problem, the relative authority of a Pope and a Council in opposition to the Pope. He posed the problem for discussion in the language of Joannes Teutonicus, '... videtur standum sententiae papae si contradicat ecclesiae vel concilio', and the arguments he applied to its solution were nearly all taken from the *Decretum*. But to understand fully the background of his thought it seems necessary to turn aside and glance at some of his comments on the parallel problem of the structure of other ecclesiastical corporations. We have seen how Hostiensis ex-

---

[27] *Lectura ad* X. v.xxxviii.14 fol. 102r*b*, 'Sed nunquid collegium cardinalium habet iurisdictionem papae et etiam exercitium ipsius ... tu teneas quod sic ... tunc quia alia inferiora collegia hoc habent ... tunc et quia alia iudex non superest ... in quo casu multa conceduntur quae alias non concederentur.'

[28] *Commentaria ad* I.vi.4 fol. 104v*a*.

plored in considerable detail the relationship between the authority of the head and that of the members in a corporate group, and suggested that, in certain circumstances, the head could be regarded as possessing an authority equal to that of all the members together, so that his vote, with that of one member, constituted a valid majority. Zabarella reviewed this doctrine at some length, first chiding those who had misunderstood Hostiensis, and then advancing to a criticism of his own. Even if it were granted that a prelate's authority might be equal to that of his whole chapter it would still not be true, according to Zabarella, that authority could be augmented by the adherence of a minority of the canons. Prelate and chapter came together as distinct units 'at least in respect to one another', and the whole power of the chapter was expressed in the decision of its *maior pars*.[29]

In his *Tractatus* Zabarella maintained in similar fashion that the whole authority of a General Council could be expressed by its *potior pars*. Hence, when he discussed the relative authority of Pope and Council there was no question of considering the degree of support which a Pope needed among the Fathers of the Council to justify his acting on behalf of the whole body. Pope and Council came together as separate and, he seems to have assumed, co-equal entities. If they were in agreement their decision was equivalent to a declaration by the whole Church; but if the Pope differed from the *potior pars* of the Council the question to be decided was which opinion should be preferred. Zabarella replied, in effect, that this depended on the nature of the business being transacted. The general rule was that the Pope's decisions should be accepted, but it could be gathered from the *Glossa Ordinaria* to the *Decretum* that this rule did not extend to the decision of matters of faith, and Zabarella added that the determination of issues touching the general state of the Church formed another exception to it:

> Decimo oppono in eo quod dicit quod concilia accipiunt robur ab ecclesia Romana, et sic videtur standum sententiae papae si contradicat ecclesiae vel concilio, cum tamen non possit immutare universalem statum ecclesiae, 24 q. 1 c. *memor*. . . . Solvo, Ioannes Andreae videtur

---

[29] *Commentaria ad* III.viii.15 fol. 66ra, 'Item episcopus et capitulum conveniunt tanquam duo entia saltem respective, quia episcopus est caput et canonici membra. Unde, etiam si vox episcopi valeret tantum quantum omnes voces canonicorum simul, tunc vox aliquorum canonicorum nihil augeret vocem episcopi ex quo maior pars non consensit, nam tota potestas canonicalis est penes maiorem partem.'

stare primo quod standum sit papae. De hoc 4 *dist. in istis,* 15 *dist. sicut in fi.,* 9 q. 3 *nemo,* 24 q. 1 *quodcumque,* 19 *dist. pen.,* et ex notis in praemissis locis colligitur quod standum est Papae (nisi) in his quae concernunt fidem, in qua si erraret posset accusari, 40 *dist. si papa.* . . . Sed neque potest ea propter quae decoloratur status universalis ecclesiae, I q. 7 *et si illa,* 25 q. 1 *sunt quidam* . . . et haec littera debet intelligi cum hac limitatione, et dic ut dico infra eodem, *licet,* q. 44 et 45.[30]

Two of the passages from the *Glossa Ordinaria* to which he referred (*Dist.* 15 c. 2, *Dist.* 19 c. 9) clearly stated that in matters of faith a Council was superior to a Pope, but in both cases the original meaning seems only to have been that Pope and Council together, possessed greater authority than the Pope alone. The position of Joannes Teutonicus himself was ambiguous, but when he explicitly discussed the question of a dispute between the Pope and the rest of the Church (in the other three glosses cited by Zabarella in this series of references) he did not refer to these two chapters at all, apparently regarding them as irrelevant to the problem under consideration.[31] Zabarella, approaching the Decretist texts with a mind steeped in later corporation theories, took for granted a meaning that Joannes himself had probably never intended to convey.

He relied on the texts of the *Decretum* again in discussing the limitation of papal authority from yet another point of view. Not only was the Pope's power subject to limitation by a General Council in major matters affecting the faith and the state of the Church, but, according to Zabarella, it was also limited in its normal everyday exercise by the rights of other members of the ecclesiastical hierarchy. The argument brought forward was the familiar one that had come down from the controversies of a century earlier. Christ had not conferred power on Peter alone but on all the Apostles; hence all bishops exercised a divinely ordained authority which the Pope was bound to respect. Zabarella objected not only to specific abuses of papal power but to the whole Avignon tradition of ecclesiastical centralization. After referring to the usual Decretist texts he went on,

Quae iura sunt notanda, quia male considerata sunt per multos assentatores, qui voluerunt placere pontificibus per multa retro tempora, et usque ad hodierna suaserunt eis quod omnia possent. . . . Ex hoc enim infiniti sunt errores, quia papa occupavit omnia iura inferiorum eccle-

---

[30] *Commentaria ad* I.vi.4 fol. 104va. Joannes Andreae is a slip for Joannes Teutonicus, to whose glosses Zabarella was actually referring.

[31] The relevant glosses of Joannes Teutonicus are given in Appendix I.

siarum. Ita quod inferiores praelati sunt pro nihilo. Et nisi Deus succurrat statui ecclesiae universalis ecclesia periclitaretur. . . .[32]

This spirited defence of the rights of inferior prelates follows closely the views of the outspoken Bishop of Mende, but when he came to consider the status of the cardinals, who had been the target for some of Durantis's most biting invective, Zabarella found occasion to commend the very different opinions of Joannes Monachus. Indeed, he quoted at length the French cardinal's account of the consistory at which Pope Celestine's grants were revoked and, unlike some of his contemporaries, saw no reason to doubt its veracity nor to dispute its conclusion that the Pope was bound, legally as well as morally, to act in important affairs *de consilio fratrum*.[33] There was to be no identification between the personal powers of the Pope and the authority attributed to the *apostolica sedes* or *Romana ecclesia*, even when these latter terms were not used to designate the inherent powers of the whole *congregatio fidelium*:

> . . . intelligenda sedes Apostolica pro ecclesia Romana quae non censetur esse solus papa, sed ipse papa cum cardinalibus qui sunt partes corporis papae, sed ecclesia quae constituitur ex papa tanquam ex capite et ex cardinalibus tanquam membris.

This was almost a precise restatement of the doctrine put forward by Huguccio and others two centuries earlier, and Zabarella also recalled the view of the *Glossa Palatina* (which he knew through the *Rosarium* of Guido de Baysio) maintaining that the Pope could not promulgate a general law for the whole Church without the cooperation of the cardinals.[34] Even the emasculated *plenitudo potestatis* which he attributed to the Roman church (in its local sense) was not to be ascribed to the Pope alone:

> . . . licet dicatur papa habere plenitudinem potestatis, non debet tamen sic intelligi quod solus possit omnia. Sed intelligitur quod papa, i.e. Romana ecclesia quae repraesentatur in papa tanquam in capite et cardinalibus tanquam in membris.[35]

---

[32] *Commentaria*, fol. 109va (Schardius, pp. 703–4).

[33] *Commentaria*, fol. 109rb (Schardius, p. 701).

[34] *Ibid*. '. . . dicunt Laurentius et Archidiaconus, 25. q. 1 *sunt quidam*, Papa sine Cardinalibus non potest condere legem generalem de universali statu ecclesiae'. The Archdeacon always attributed quotations from the *Glossa Palatina* to Laurentius. Cf. *supra* p. 14 n. 34.

[35] *Ibid*.

The Pope could not act in important matters without consulting the cardinals, but the cardinals, if they saw fit, could withdraw allegiance from the Pope;[36] and during a vacancy or even a 'quasi-vacancy' they succeeded to the full powers of the Apostolic See, for Zabarella referred to them as 'iis qui succedunt loco papae, scilicet cardinalibus.'[37]

At this point his attempt to knit together the two opposing trends of fourteenth-century thought which can be described as the 'curialist' and 'conciliar' positions may seem to have produced only confusion, for at the beginning of his work Zabarella had stated quite explicitly that, during a vacancy, ecclesiastical power rested with the whole Church represented in a General Council. Yet the discrepancy was only a surface one and the underlying thought remained clear and consistent; Zabarella had indeed produced a synthesis and not a mere pastiche. He attributed to the cardinals all the powers in relation to the Pope that the extreme curialists had claimed for them, but he did not base his arguments on the assertion, often repeated since the days of the Colonna troubles, that the Sacred College was established by God himself *ab exordio nascentis ecclesiae*. He never departed from the principle that *plenitudo potestatis* rested unambiguously with the whole Church, *tanquam in fundamento*; but, just as the Pope represented the Church in the exercise of the powers that the Church had conferred on him, so too the cardinals who were 'parts of the Pope's body' exercised a derivative authority as representatives of the whole Church. 'Collegium cardinalium repraesentat universalem ecclesiam et eius vice funguntur.'[38] This view of the cardinals' status was common enough by the end of the fourteenth century, but Zabarella showed unusual interest in exploring its constitutional implications and incorporating them into his theory of Church government.

The cardinals succeeded immediately to the powers of a negligent Pope, but if the cardinals in their turn proved negligent then the inalienable *plenitudo potestatis* of the whole Church could come into play.[39] In the existing circumstances of the Schism he thought that it

---

[36] *Commentaria*, fols. 108vb–109ra (Schardius pp. 698–700).

[37] *Commentaria*, fol. 107vb (Schardius, p. 691).

[38] *Commentaria*, fol. 107va (Schardius, p. 690). The cardinals were referred to as representatives of the Church again at fol. 108vb (p. 698) and fol. 110vb (p. 711).

[39] The idea of a potential authority inherent in the cardinals or the Church as a whole had begun to penetrate into the works of even the more extreme papal publicists during the course of the fourteenth century. Augustinus Triumphus was at pains to define it with precision. During a papal vacancy the power of the Pope rested with the cardinals only *quantum ad radicem*. 'Comparatur enim Collegium ad Papam sicut radix ad arborem vel ad ramum . . . sicut potestas rami vel arboris, que floret et

was the duty of the cardinals to summon a General Council,[40] but that if they failed to do so and a Council could be brought together by any means whatsoever, then the assembled prelates could exercise the inherent authority of the whole Church. Again, he held that a withdrawal of allegiance from the two Popes should be initiated by the cardinals, but that if such a withdrawal was brought about in any other way the action should be regarded as a legitimate exercise of the authority of the *congregatio fidelium*.[41] Finally, he maintained that if any dispute arose between Pope and cardinals it should be referred to the General Council which most perfectly embodied that *plenitudo potestatis* of which Pope and cardinals alike enjoyed only a limited and conditional exercise:

> ... si inter papam et cardinales surgit discordia ... dic quod oportet congregare ecclesiam i.e. totam congregationem catholicorum et principales ministros fidei, scilicet prelatos, qui totam congregationem repraesentant.[42]

The old doctrine that the Roman church was 'head of all the churches' was now interpreted in the sense that Pope and cardinals together formed a corporate head of the Church; Zabarella was able to unite the discordant theories of the earlier canonists by applying the concepts

---

fructum producit remanet in radice ipso ramo vel ipsa arbore destructa, sic ... potestas Papalis remanet in Collegio vel in Ecclesia ipso Papa mortuo. In Collegio quidem tanquam in radice propinqua, et in Ecclesia prelatorum et aliorum fidelium tanquam in radice remote.' The jurisdiction of the Pope could be said to live on in Christ, but the actual exercise of that jurisdiction died with each Pope. 'Sed si nomine potestatis Papalis intelligimus actualem administrationem ... sic talis actualis administratio bene moritur, mortuo papa, quia nec remanet in Collegio ... nec remanet isto modo in Christo quia de commune lege Christus post resurrectionem non est executus talem potestatem nisi mediante Papa.' *Summa de Potestate Ecclesiastica* (Romae, 1584), Q. III, art. iii, p. 36. Augustinus Triumphus also held, however, that should the College of Cardinals become extinct, then, 'posset Concilium ordinare et terminare de omnibus que pertinent ad utilitatem Ecclesie', Q. III, art. ii, p. 29.

[40] *Commentaria*, fol. 110rb (Schardius, p. 708).

[41] *Commentaria*, fol. 109ra (Schardius, p. 700), 'Cum ergo maior et potior pars Catholicorum ab obedientia recesserit, sicut recessisse dicitur, tota ecclesia dicitur recessisse, quia quod maior pars universitatis facit tota universitas fecisse dicitur ... et in hoc non refert quomodo ventum sit ad hanc subtractionem. ...'

[42] *Commentaria*, fol. 109va (Schardius, p. 702). Zabarella, like John of Paris, put forward the argument, that, since the cardinals conferred authority on the Pope on behalf of the Church, they might also deprive him of authority. But whereas John of Paris, a philosopher anxious to carry his argument to its logical conclusion, accepted this doctrine, Zabarella, primarily a lawyer, admitted its logical force but rejected it as contrary to the actual provisions of canon law, '... si dicatur per hoc sequi quod cardinales possent papam deponere sine concilio ... respondeo quod standum esset arg. nisi aliter esset statutum' (fol. 110va, p. 708).

of corporation law not only to the relations between Pope and cardinals and between Pope and Council, but also to the status of the cardinals themselves in relation to the Universal Church.

His work gave a final formulation to the doctrine of the Church as at once a hierarchy and a corporation which had been implicit in the glosses of the Decretalists and especially in the work of Hostiensis. Just as each constituent corporation, each local church with its prelate, chapter, lesser clergy and people, could be regarded as a little hierarchy, so too the all-embracing hierarchy of the Universal Church could be treated as one great corporation.

Within that corporation ultimate authority rested with the *congregatio fidelium*, but the normal exercise of the power inhering in the Church was committed to the 'head of all the churches', i.e. the Roman church, itself a corporate body comprising Pope and cardinals. Within that corporate unity again the Pope was head and exercised the same type of *plena potestas* or *plenitudo potestatis* as the head of any other corporation. There was careful provision for the devolution of authority from head to members in all conceivable circumstances,[43] and a guarantee that the Church could never be finally brought to ruin by any failure of its leaders, since the authority which Christ had promised to his Church would always live on in the community of faithful Christians. Inspired by the urgent necessities of his own day, Zabarella had clothed the bare framework of Decretalist corporation theory with all the complex details of an integrated theory of Church government.

In the age of the Schism the whole theoretical edifice of papal pretensions seemed to be collapsing as though of its own weight, leaving the canonistic foundations exposed for new efforts at reconstruction. Zabarella's work was an attempt to devise a conciliar system of Church government that could rest without incongruity upon this basis of earlier canonistic doctrine. The degree of success that he could achieve in such a task may serve to remind us that the Conciliar Movement itself was no belated reaction against 'the Canonist theory of sovereignty', but a logical culmination of ideas that the canonists themselves had evolved in the greatest age of ecclesiastical law.

---

[43] He repeated the argument of Hostiensis that, should the College of Cardinals become extinct during a papal vacancy, it was for the Roman clergy to summon a General Council or themselves elect a new Pope 'tanquam gerens vices cleri totius orbis' (Gloss *ad* I.vi.6 fol. 105v*b*).

CONCLUSION

An adequate account of all the intricate schemes that were set on foot in the years of the Schism, the desperate expedients of exasperated churchmen, the evasions of the rival pontiffs, the manœuvrings of the Catholic princes, could be undertaken only in the context of a full-scale diplomatic and ecclesiastical history of Europe at the end of the fourteenth century. Yet a survey of the purely ideological concepts of the Conciliar Movement, and of the canonistic tradition upon which they were based, may shed some light on the pattern of events in those troubled years as well as on the broad movements of thought.

One paradox that has always interested students of the Conciliar Movement is the apparent incompatibility between the intentions of the cardinals who initiated the Schism and the actual influence of their revolt upon the constitutional structure of the Church in the following decades. The dissident cardinals sought to avenge the humiliations that Urban had inflicted on them, and perhaps to assert for themselves a dominant role in the government of the Church, but there was no hint that they favoured any doctrine of conciliar authority. To trace any affinity between the aims of the cardinals and the ideals of earlier Conciliarists on the grounds that both parties sought to 'broaden the basis' of Church government seems a mere evasion; it would be fantastic to attribute any 'democratic' tendencies to Robert of Geneva and his associates. The opposing point of view, which would insist on an inherent incompatibility between the 'oligarchic' ambitions of the Sacred College and the 'democratic' tendencies of the conciliarists seems more in keeping with the facts of the situation. Yet it fails to account for the actual course of events and still less for the developments in conciliar ideas in the later years of the Schism, for, eventually, it was the concerted action of the cardinals of both obediences that brought into existence the Council of Pisa, and the tenacity of the Sacred College that made possible the more constructive achievements of Constance. This change of front after thirty years of scandalous schism would raise no theoretical problem, if in turning to a conciliar solution of the Schism, the cardinals had abandoned the old curialist pretensions, but in fact one finds Zabarella and d'Ailly, the two most ardent conciliarists in the Sacred College, staunchly defending the traditional claims of the cardinals before the Council of Constance; and in Zabarella's treatise the conflict between curialist and conciliar principles did not end in a victory for one side or the other, nor even in a compromise, but in a genuine synthesis of the opposing traditions.

An investigation of the theoretical basis of both positions helps to explain this development, for it suggests that the earlier claims of both curialists and Conciliarists had been based on limited applications of the same canonistic theories to different problems of ecclesiastical authority. The immediate conflict of interests between the rival parties had concealed the underlying identity of their theoretical assumptions, but the views of Joannes Monachus and Guilielmus Durantis, which we have taken as typifying the opposing trends of thought, were at bottom complementary rather than contradictory. If the French cardinal's theory of the relations between Pope and cardinals had been extended to the corporate unity of the whole Church, it would have implied just such a relationship between the Roman church and the other churches as Guilielmus Durantis demanded. On the other hand, if Durantis had applied his theories as carefully to the structure of the Roman church as to that of the Universal Church, he would have been led to a thoroughgoing defence of the privileges and independent authority of the cardinals. Both theories were offshoots of the same canonistic tradition, and that is why, when the conflicting interests of all parties in the Church were submerged in a common desire for unity, they could be blended without incongruity into a coherent system of Church government.

The urgent, widespread desire for unity in the Church was the very life blood of the Conciliar Movement. On the need for unity all parties were agreed; but in the circumstances of the time it was perhaps inevitable that this universal aspiration should become associated with much more controversial ideas concerning the constitutional structure of the Church. The more radical conciliarists attacked the whole system of papal centralization because they believed that a survival of that system could no longer provide an effective guarantee of permanent unity. Meanwhile, as the evasive subtleties of the rival Popes rendered more and more unlikely any negotiated solution of the dispute, it became evident even to conservative churchmen that the Schism could be ended only by 'the royal way of the Council'. They were determined to unite the Church by giving it a single head, but precisely in order to bring about that result they had to assume that the Church could act as an effectively united organism even when it lacked such a head, to maintain, in effect, that the powers of the whole Church could be exercised by an authority other than the Pope. This was the central problem of conciliar thought. It seemed that Christendom could only be given a single Pope by a procedure which implicitly denied the unique competence of the Papacy; the steps necessary to end the Schism involved an attack on the very institution that had always been regarded as the indispensable key-stone of ecclesiastical unity.

The Conciliarists found an escape from this dilemma by emphasizing a hitherto somewhat neglected aspect of canonistic theory concerning the structure of the Church. Running through the glosses of the previous centuries were two separate doctrines on Church unity. The more conspicuous one, which has usually been regarded as the canonistic doctrine *par excellence* insisted that the unity of the whole Church could be secured only by a rigorous subordination of all the members to a single head, and to make that subordination effective, it developed the familiar theory of papal sovereignty. But side by side with this there existed another theory, applied at first to the single churches and then at the beginning of the fourteenth century, in a fragmentary fashion, to the Roman church and the Church as a whole, a theory which stressed the corporate association of the members of a Church as the true principle of ecclesiastical unity, and which envisaged an exercise of corporate authority by the members of a church even in the absence of an effective head.

It has often been pointed out in modern works that the medieval canonists played a significant part in the growth of the extreme theories of papal monarchy by crystallizing into a rigorous code of law the traditional doctrines on papal primacy which found their ultimate sanction in scriptural texts and patristic commentaries. It is also evident that the Conciliarists appealed to these same ancient sources in support of their very different views. Against the inevitable Matthew xvi of the papal publicists (*Tu es Petrus . . .*) they could cite Acts xv (the Council of Jerusalem), and in the *Decretum* of Gratian they found texts attributed to Cyprian, Augustine, Jerome and Gregory the Great which could be used to offset the papal examples, drawn from the same compilation, of Roman primacy in the early Church. So much is apparent from the most perfunctory reading of any conciliar treatise. But it has never been sufficiently emphasized that the traditional

doctrines employed by the Conciliarists had undergone the same process
of canonistic transmutation as those of their opponents, so that when
the rival publicists of the fourteenth century (Conciliarists and Papalists
alike) quoted the Scriptures and the Fathers, the connotations of the
terms they employed were determined less by their original contexts
than by the impress they had received from the thirteenth-century
canonists.

It seems possible now to trace the more important stages in this
canonistic adaptation of the concepts that were to be of fundamental
importance for the Conciliar Movement—above all the concept of
the Church itself. The ambivalence in canonistic doctrine to which
we have referred was already apparent in the works of the Decretists.
They were able to maintain a precarious harmony between the traditional doctrine of papal supremacy and the concept of the Church
as a *congregatio fidelium* possessing an inherent and indestructible authority of its own, only by taking advantage of the existing ambiguities in the use of the term *Romana ecclesia*. The phrase could be used
in some contexts to designate the Universal Church, the whole *universitas fidelium*, while in others it was taken to mean a local church
like the *ecclesia Anglicana* or *ecclesia Gallicana*, though indeed superior
to the others in dignity and power. This two-fold usage was again
only a reflexion of a more deep-rooted ambiguity in the meaning of
the word *ecclesia* itself, which sometimes designated the prelate who
stood at the head of an ecclesiastical corporation, sometimes all the
members of that corporation, and sometimes an intermediate group
of higher clergy.

The dominant movement of papal monarchy in the first half of
the thirteenth century produced a clarification of views concerning
the status of the Roman church, which now came to be defined as
a local church indeed, but one which had received from God the
exercise of all those powers and privileges which Christ had promised should dwell in his Church for ever. The other churches stood,
in relation to the Roman church, in a position of hierarchical subordination, dependent on it for all their authority, for their very life;
they were also united to it by the bonds of corporate unity, so that
the Roman church could be described as the 'head' to which all the
others were joined as 'members'.

While the canonists were shaping this comprehensive doctrine
concerning the structure of the Universal Church they were also called
upon to undertake the definition of the term *ecclesia* from a quite

different point of view, by a host of intricate problems relating to the internal structure of the local churches and of other ecclesiastical corporations. These problems they resolved in a spirit rather different from that of their large-scale synthesis. Yet in the growth of corporation theory itself one can trace the canonistic assimilation of ideas which, however one judges their conciliar applications, were certainly ancient and Catholic in their original form. Of the greatest importance in this connexion was the Scriptural insistence that all ecclesiastical authority was conferred for the good of the Church rather than for the personal glory of the prelates, that the clergy should be 'ministers' rather than masters. The task of the canonists was to ensure that this moral principle was observed in practice, and inevitably, in their juristic treatment of the problem, the moral obligation hardened into a legal obligation, with the necessary corollary of legal accountability for any breach of it; the final result was the canonistic doctrine of the prelate as proctor of his corporation. Thus, in the very years when the Decretalists were proclaiming most uncompromisingly that the Roman church as 'head' was 'mater et magistra' of all the churches, the Pope an absolute 'dominus mundi', they were also evolving a theory of corporation structure which had as its very corner-stone the principle, 'Praelati non sunt domini, sed procuratores'. Future critics would find in this principle, and in the whole complex of corporation ideas that surrounded it, an instrument peculiarly well adapted to sap the foundations of the doctrine of papal sovereignty that the canonists themselves had helped to build up.

It could be used, for instance, to protect the rights of diocesan bishops against the encroachments of papal centralization. The problems implicit in the relationship between Peter, the first Pope, and the other apostles, the first bishops, had already been apparent to the commentators on the *Decretum* who had avoided the implication that all the apostles received equal power with Peter by the suggestion that, although all were equal in orders, Peter was superior in jurisdiction. Innocent III carried the argument a step further, maintaining that the Pope was not only superior in jurisdiction, but actually the source of the jurisdiction of all lesser prelates in the Church; and this claim was developed by the papal publicists of the next two centuries and eventually stated in its most extreme form by Joannes de Torquemada. But meanwhile, in considering the internal structure of the local churches, the canonists had been analysing the different elements in a bishop's authority in a fashion that laid all the

emphasis on the act of election as the source of episcopal jurisdiction—an attitude closely connected with their definition of the prelate's
status as proctor of his church. This made it possible for defenders
of episcopal claims to follow up their assertion (usually based on texts
of the *Decretum*) that all the apostles received jurisdiction directly from
Christ with an explanation of how that jurisdiction had been transmitted to contemporary bishops. They did not need to admit that
episcopal authority was necessarily derived from the Pope's *plenitudo
potestatis* when, without departing from accepted canonistic principles,
they could maintain that all the powers of a bishop were obtained,
in the words of John of Paris, 'a Deo . . . immediate, et a populo
eligente vel consentiente'.

The same canonistic concepts produced even more striking results
when applied to the whole Church considered as a corporate entity
with the Pope as its head; then they made possible the development,
which was noticed in the work of Guilielmus Durantis, from mere
'episcopalism' to true conciliarism. The doctrine that all the members of a corporation should participate in decisions affecting the
well-being of the whole body could be developed into an argument
in favour of a representative General Council as a permanent element
in the government of the Church; the idea of a corporation as the
source of the authority of its head made possible a presentation of
the doctrine of papal *plenitudo potestatis* in a form consistent with the
most extreme conciliar ideas. A parallel process of argumentation
could be applied to the relations between Pope and cardinals. The
Sacred College too would claim to be a divinely ordained element in
the government of the Church; the cardinals, in their turn, would
assert a right to participate with the Pope in shaping the policies of
the Roman See, would even seek to present themselves as the source
of the Pope's authority.

During the fourteenth century the most respected canonists held
that in the corporate whole of the Universal Church all power was
concentrated in the head by a direct act of the divine will; but they
also held that, as a general principle of corporation structure, authority resided with all the members of a church, who conferred
upon the head only a limited and conditional right to act on their
behalf. This dichotomy in canonistic doctrine influenced profoundly
the growth of ecclesiological theories in the later Middle Ages and
made particularly difficult the formulation in juristic terms of a comprehensive and consistent theory of papal monarchy. The lack of

such a completely integrated theory might have had little practical significance in itself; it became a serious source of embarrassment to the Papacy in the fourteenth century because the policies of the contemporary Popes stirred into activity powerful enemies who were eager to seek out and to exploit to the full every weakness, theoretical or practical, in the Pope's claim to absolute authority over the Church. The disputes between Popes and secular rulers, the problems arising out of Pope Celestine's renunciation, and the conflicts within the curia itself, all stimulated a more critical analysis of the sources and limits of papal authority, and led to a renewed emphasis on the claims of other elements of Church government—bishops, cardinals and General Council—whose authority could be opposed to that of the Pope. Eventually the growing ambition of the cardinals precipitated the final crisis of the Schism, which in turn made Conciliarism, for a time, a practical programme rather than merely an academic theory.

The roots of the conciliar tradition lie deeper in the past than has usually been supposed. When the pressing demands of the Schism led the canonists to undertake a systematic investigation of the relations between Pope and Church it became apparent that, although their conception of the Church as a corporate entity was hardly compatible with the doctrine of absolute papal monarchy upheld in most of the glosses of the fourteenth century, it could lend itself quite readily to a restatement of certain early Decretist doctrines which had implied a very different conception of papal authority. The Decretist assertions that only the whole Church was unerring in faith, that a Pope could not act against the general well-being of the Church, that, in the last resort, he could be deposed by the Church provided essential ingredients in all the later theories of conciliar authority. The elaboration of conciliar systems of Church government in their more developed forms was made possible by the assimilation of these rather inchoate ideas of the Decretists into the framework of later corporation theory; the principal source of conciliar thought is to be found in the mingling of these two streams of canonistic ideas rather than in the *Streitschriften* of the imperial publicists or the constitutional examples of secular states. The law of the Church and the theories of the canonists, which had been moulded both by ancient doctrine and by the practical necessities of contemporary ecclesiastical life, formed an indispensable basis for any practicable system of Church government, not excluding a conciliar system. The Conciliar

✓ Theory, one might say, sprang from the impregnation of Decretist ecclesiology by Decretalist corporation concepts.

Accompanying all the other manifestations of this process was the gradual assimilation into canonistic theory of the ancient doctrine of the Church as the Mystical Body of Christ, with a consequent fusion between the theological concept of mystical unity in the Church and the juristic idea of legal incorporation. It was the blending of these ideas that gave both passion and precision to the work of the greatest Conciliarists. The idea of the Church as a corporation enabled them to give a more precise and concrete expression to the early idea of an ultimate authority inherent in the *universitas fidelium*; but the conviction that this corporate unity of the faithful was also an integral part of 'the whole Christ', that, in a sense, the body of Christ was lacerated by the continuing Schism in his Church, also inspired in the foremost Conciliarists that passionate will to unity which characterized all their works and without which the tortuous problems raised by the Schism could never have been resolved.

It is no part of our task to pass judgement on the theories whose development we have tried to explain. But it may not be superfluous to urge at least that the ideals and aspirations of the Conciliar Movement be judged in relation to the actual state of the Church at the end of the fourteenth century and in the light of the ardent sincerity that distinguished its first great leaders; for the Conciliarists have not altogether escaped the customary fate of those who leave no descendants to plead their cause before posterity. Neither Catholic nor Protestant can claim them as prophets, and so too often they have been dismissed as 'academes' or even decried as 'quislings'. In grappling with the grievous problems of their age they may have fallen into doctrinal errors, but they were not wilful partisans of heretical novelties. They thought that the doctrines they defended were ancient and orthodox; and there were substantial elements in the juristic tradition of the Church that could be adduced in support of their position. The dismal aftermath of Basle sheds a retrospective shadow over the early ideals of the Conciliarists, and makes it only tantalizing to speculate on the outcome of events if Zabarella had lived to become Pope, if Gerson and d'Ailly had found worthy successors in the next generation. It is probable that in any case the merely constitutional reforms emphasized in the conciliar programme could not have produced the much-needed regeneration in the whole life of the Church; it is certain that the collapse of all that the Conciliarists had stood for was followed within a century by the catastrophe that the Fathers of Constance had most feared, a new and more disastrous schism, cleaving irrevocably the fabric of ecclesiastical unity that they had laboured to restore.

APPENDICES

HUGUCCIO'S GLOSS ON THE WORDS
NISI DEPREHENDATUR A FIDE DEVIUS

Nisi deprehendatur a fide devius. Ecce de heresi papa potest condempnari a subditis, supra di. xxi *nunc autem* contra. Ibi dicitur quod Marcellinus heresim commisit, non tamen subditi eum condempnaverunt. Dicunt quidam quod noluerunt sed dico quod non potuerunt nec debuerunt eum condempnare inde quia sponte et humiliter est confessus errorem suum. Tunc enim demum potest papa condempnari de heresi cum contumaciter et pertinaciter resistit et errorem defendere et approbare conatur, ar. xxiii q. iii *dixit apostolus, qui in ecclesia.* Sed si admonitus vult resipiscere, a nullo potest inde accusari vel condempnari si non sit humilis (*a*) sive aliud crimen notorium.... Sed ex quo publice predicat talia admonitus non vult resipiscere conveniendus est et condempnandus et non ante.... Sed ecce, papa fingit novam heresim, aliquis vult probare illam esse heresim, papa dicit non esse heresim sed fidem catholicam, estne recipienda eius probatio? Credo quod non. Item sequitur heresim dampnatam latenter. Aliqui tamen hoc sciunt et volunt probare papam sequi talem heresim. Ille tamen negat. Debent audiri? Credo quod non. Tunc enim demum accusari potest de heresi cum constat quod illud factum sit heresim(!) et papa non negat se illud facere et admonitus non vult resipiscere sed errorem suum contumaciter defendit. Sed si non constat de facto quod sit heresis, vel si constat heresim esse sed papa infitiatur se illud facere, si constat heresim esse et quod papa illud facit et non infitiatur, vult tamen cessare et resipiscere nullus potest eum inde accusare vel condempnare. Vel nunquid de simonia vel alio crimine potest papa accusari? Dicunt quidam quod non sive sit notorium sive non, quia quod canon non excipit non debemus excipere, et isti assignant rationem diversitatis quare potius de heresi possit accusari quam de alio crimine, quia si papa esset hereticus non sibi soli noceret sed toti mundo, praesertim quia simplices et idiote facile sequerentur illam heresim cum credent non esse heresim. Sed si papa committit simoniam vel fornicationem vel furtum et huiusmodi sibi soli videtur nocere cum omnes sciant quod nulli licet fornicari vel furari vel simoniam committere et huiusmodi. Ego autem credo quod idem sit de quolibet crimine notorio quod papa possit accusari et condempnari si admonitus non vult cessare. Quid enim? Ecce, publice furatur, publice fornicatur, publice committit simoniam, publice habet concubinam, publice eam cognoscit in ecclesia iuxta vel super altare, admonitus non vult cessare, nunquid non accusabitur... nunquid non condempnabitur, nunquid sic scandalizare ecclesiam non est quasi heresim committere? Preterea contumacia est crimen ydolatrie et quasi heresis ut di. lxxxi *si quis presbyteri*, unde et contumax dicitur infidelis ut di. xxxviii *nullus*. Et sic idem est in alio crimine notorio quam in heresi. Quare ergo facit Bonifacius potius mentionem de heresi

quam de alio crimine notorio? Dico quod gratia exempli hoc posuit vel
forte in eo est differentia inter heresim et alia crimina notoria, scilicet quod
de crimine heresis potest papa accusari si heresim publice predicat et non
vult desistere quamvis tale crimen non sit notorium. Sed de alio crimine non
potest accusari nisi sit notorium. Ergo de occulto crimine non potest accusari. Sed ecce, duo vel iii vel quattuor sciunt crimen pape occultum, non possunt inde eum accusare? Possunt post amonitionem denuntiare illud crimen
iuxta regulam ecclesiasticam, *si peccaverit etc*? Nunquid illa regula evangelica
non habebit locum circa papam? Nonne nomine fratris intelligitur quilibet
fidelis et sic papa ut xi q. iii *ad mensam*? Respondeo, videtur quod illa regula
non habet locum circa papam propter defectum iudicis coram quo conveni-
retur, cum ipse sit superior iudex, aut cui ecclesie fieret denunciatio cum ipse
sit ecclesia? Item quero an papa possit istum casum excludere, scilicet ut nec
in heresi vel notorio crimine possit accusari. Respondeo, de facto sic, sed non
de iure, quia sic doceret heresim, preterea si papa esset hereticus publice et
inde non posset accusari tota periclitaretur ecclesia et confunderetur generalis
statutus ecclesie. Sed non credo eum posse constituere aliquid in preiudicium
generalis statutus ecclesie (*b*) ut di. xv *sicut.* . . . Item solent quidam querere
quare papa potuit suis successoribus hanc legem imponere ut possint accusari
de heresi. Sed dico nullam fuisse questionem. Non enim papa statuit quod
posset papa accusari de heresi sed constituit privilegium quod non posset accusari (de) crimine sed noluit illud privilegium extendere usque ad quodlibet
crimen, scilicet ut de nullo possit accusari. Generale enim et regulare erat quod
crimina punirentur in quolibet, ergo et in papa, sed illam generalitatem circa
papam restringit constituendo privilegium ut non posset accusari de quolibet
crimine sed propter periculum ecclesie vitandum et propter consuetudinem
generalis ecclesie est vitandam (*c*) noluit per illud privilegium removere heresim
vel notorium crimen. Sed nunquid papa potest isti privilegio renuntiare? Sic,
arg. ii q. v *mandastis, auditum* et q. vii *nos si.* Sed nullum ob hoc preiudicium
fieret successori quin possit idem statuere si vellet arg. ii q. v *mandastis, auditum.*

(*a*) Schulte, *sive sit haeresis.* (*b*) Schulte, *generalis status ecclesiae.* (*c*) Schulte,
propter confusionem generalem ecclesiae vitandam.

PASSAGES OF JOANNES TEUTONICUS ON THE AUTHORITY OF POPE, CHURCH AND COUNCIL[1]

Dist. 4 c. 3. *Iudicent.* Cum ergo papa vult condere canones episcopi possunt contradicere et dicere, canon iste non convenit consuetudini regionis nostrae ut supra c. *prox.* (c. 2). Sed nunquid potius stabitur sententiae Apostolicae vel omnium episcoporum? Videtur quod omnium episcoporum quia orbis maior est urbe, ut 93 *dist. legimus* (c. 24). Arg. quod sententia Papae praevalet, 35 q. 9 veniam (c. 5). Nam etiam error principis ius facit ... (Dicas quod sententiae Papae stabitur contra omnes, 9 q. 3 *nemo* (c. 13) et c. *cuncta* (c. 18) nisi contra fidem diceret, 25 q. 1 *sunt quidam* (c. 6).

Dist. 15 c. 2. *Praesumit.* Videtur ergo quod Papa non possit destruere statuta concilii, quia orbis maior est urbe, 93 *dist. legimus* (c. 24). Unde requirit Papa consensum concilii, 19 *dist. Anastasius.* Arg. contra, 17 *dist.* § *hinc etiam* (post c. 6) et *extra, de ele. significasti* (i.vi.4) ubi dicitur quod concilium non potest Papae legem imponere et 35 q. 9 *veniam* (c. 5). Sed intellige quod hic dicitur circa articulos fidei, 25 q. 1 *sunt quidam* (c. 6).

Dist. 17 ante c. 1. *Generalia.* In hac distinctione ostenditur qui possunt facere concilia. Sunt autem conciliorum quaedam universalia, quaedam particularia sive provincialia, quaedam episcopalia. Universale est quod a Papa vel eius legato cum omnibus episcopis statuitur, particulare sive provinciale est quod metropolitanus vel primas facit cum suffraganeis suis. . . . Sed universale non debet fieri sine auctoritate Papae ut hic. . . .

Dist. 17 c. 4 *Particularem.* . . . Videtur hic quod ad solum Papam spectat interpretari statuta universalis concilii, ut *extra, de conces. preb. dilectus* (iii.viii.12). Arg. contra quod ab omnibus episcopis, vel a saniori parte eorum qui inter-fuerunt, potest fieri interpretatio, quia ab eo iudice prodire debet interpretatio, qui ius statuit. *Extra. de senten. excom. inter* (v.xxxix.31). . . .

Dist. 17 c. 5. *Ad maiorem.* . . . Item hic appellatur a metropolitano ad concilium metropolitanum, infra 2 q. 6 *omnis* (c. 28) et sic concilium est maius ipso metropolitano et sic appellatur ab aliquo ad seipsum cum aliis. . . .

Dist. 17 *post* c. 6. *Iussione.* Habet ergo Romana ecclesia auctoritatem a conciliis sed imperator a populo ut 93 *dist. legimus* in fi. (c. 24). Contrarium huic signatur 21 *dist. quamvis* (c. 3) et 22 *dist. omnes* (c. 1) ubi dicitur quod Romana ecclesia habet primatum a Domino et non a conciliis. Sed dic principaliter habuit a Domino, secundario a conciliis.

Dist. 19 c. 7. *Nec portae.* Id est vitia vel etiam haereses, quia ecclesia non potest errare ut 24 q. 1 *a recta* (c. 9). Nec ecclesia potest esse nulla ut 24 q. 1 *pudenda* (c. 33) quia ipse Dominus rogavit pro ea ut non deficeret ut 21 *dist.* c. 1 in fine.

---

[1] Words in brackets at the end of a gloss are additions of Bartholomaeus Brixiensis.

Dist. 19 c. 9. *Concilio.* Videtur ergo quod Papa tenetur requirere concilium episcoporum, quod verum est ubi de fide agitur, et tunc synodus maior est Papa, 15 *dist. sicut* in fi. (c. 2). Arg. ad hoc 93 *dist. legimus* (c. 24).

Dist. 21 c. 7. *Marcellinus.* . . . Item quaeritur quare isti episcopi non deposuerunt Papam cum esset confessus de haeresi. Dicit Huguccio quia paratus erat corrigi. Licet enim Papa, vel alius sit haereticus, si tamen paratus est corrigi, non deponitur, ut 24 q. 3 *dixit Apostolus* (c. 29). Vel ideo non debebant ipsum deponere quia coactus fecit, 50 *dist. presbyteros* (c. 32).

Dist. 40 c. 6. *A fide devius.* Quod intelligit Huguccio cum Papa non vult corrigi. Si enim paratus esset corrigi non posset accusari, ut 24 q. 1 *aperte* (c. 36) et c. *ait* (c. 35) et c. *haec est fides* (c. 14) et 24 q. 3 *dixit Apostolus* (c. 29). Sed quare non potest accusari de alio crimine? Ponamus quod notorium sit crimen eius vel per confessionem, vel per facti evidentiam, quare non accusatur, vel de crimine simoniae, vel adulterii; etiam cum admonetur incorrigibilis est, et scandalizatur ecclesia per factum eius? Certe credo, quod si notorium est crimen eius, quandocunque, et inde scandalizatur ecclesia et incorrigibilis sit, quod inde possit accusari. Nam contumacia dicitur haeresis ut 81 *dist. si qui presbyteri* (c. 15) et contumax dicitur infidelis ut 38 *dist. nullus* (c. 16). Hic tamen specialiter fit mentio de haeresi, ideo quia et si occulta esset haeresis, de illa posset accusari, sed de alio occulto crimine non posset. Item nunquid potest denuntiari crimen Papae secundum regulam istam, *Si peccaverit in te frater tuus*; cum nomine fratris quilibet Christianus dicatur, ut 11 q. 3 *ad mensam* (c. 24)? Sed dico quod non potest denuntiari crimen de ipso, nisi inde posset accusari, nam inutilis esset denuntiatio. Item nunquid Papa posset statuere, quod non posset accusari de haeresi. Respondeo quod non; quia ex hoc periclitaretur tota ecclesia, quod non licet, infra 25 q. 1 *sunt quidam* (c. 6) quia hoc fit in eo casu quo desinit esse caput ecclesiae et ita non tenet constitutio.

Dist. 79 c. 8. *Contra fas.* . . . Sed quis erit iudex de hoc, an electio sit contra fas? Non ipsi Cardinales, quia si sic, essent iudices in proprio facto nam nullus superior potest inveniri ut *extra de elect. licet* in fi. (c. 6). Dic istud c. locum habere quando neuter est electus a duabus partibus. Vel dic, quod concilium convocabitur.

Dist. 79 c. 9. *Non apostolicus.* Videtur per principium istius cap. quod Papa de simonia possit accusari, quia non est apostolicus sed apostaticus, et quia simonia haeresis est, 1 q. 1 *eos qui* (c. 21) et cap. *fertur* (c. 28) et cap. *liqueat* (c. 13) et per primum cap. huius dist. Quod non credo. Et loquitur de eo qui per simoniam electus est ab illis qui non habebant potestatem eligendi, non a Cardinalibus. Simonia autem large dicitur haeresis, non secundum quod Papa, vel alius de haeresi potest accusari, cum scilicet errat aliquis in articulis fidei, sed antequam eligatur Papa, exceptione cuiuslibet criminis repelli poterit. Sed pone quod aliquis accusat Cardinales, quod simoniace elegerint Papam (hoc enim licite potest fieri ut infra cap. *proxi.*) numquid si probata fuerit simonia, Papa deponetur? Non, arg. 2. q. 5 *interrogatum* (c. 24). . . . Sed quid si dum uxor tua creditur mortua elegeris in Papam et consecraris et uxor tua te repetit, an ei reddendus es? Vel si tu neges eam tuam uxorem esse, apud quem cognoscetur, cum Papa iudicari non posset nisi de haeresi? Respondeo si revocetur in dubium, non est cogendus stare iudicio alicuius, immo excipere potest, Dominus est qui me iudicat, 9 q. 3

aliorum (c. 14). Si autem certum est, tenetur ei reddere debitum, nisi mulier induci possit ad continentiam observandam, vel abrenuntiabit papatui et satisfaciet uxori.

Dist. 93 c. 24. *Maior est.* Et ideo magis sequenda est consuetudo generalis ut supra *dist.* 12 *novit* (c. 10) et supra *dist.* 40 *nos qui* et c. *non loca* (cc. 3, 4). Et est hic argumentum quod statuta concilii praeiudicant statuto Papae si contradicant, ut dixi 9 q. 3 *nemo* (c. 14).

C. 2 q. 5 c. 10 *Potuissem.* Quia Papa a nullo potest iudicari ut 9 q. 3 *aliorum* (c. 14). Nec etiam ab universali concilio ut 17 *dist.* § *hinc etiam* (post c. 6) . . . (praeterquam in haeresi, 40 *dist. si papa* (c. 6)).

C. 2 q. 7 c. 41 *Aliena.* Hic Papa se subiicit aliorum iudicio, quod facere potest. . . . Non tamen eum possunt deponere, 9 q. 3 *nemo* (c. 13). Secundum Huguccionem possunt, quia et se ipsum potest deponere, ut 21 *dist. nunc autem* (c. 7).

C. 3 q. 6 c. 9 *Voluerunt.* Sic ergo concilia dederunt primatum Romanae ecclesiae, quod verum est secundario, sed ipse Christus principaliter, ut 21 *dist. quamvis* (c. 3), 17 *dist.* § *hinc etiam* (post c. 6) et 9 q. 3 *aliorum* (c. 14).

C. 7 q. 1 c. 7 *In ecclesia.* . . . Hic dicitur ecclesia episcopus; alibi est idem quod ecclesiastici viri ut 63 *dist.* c. 1; alibi ponitur pro maiori parte, ut supra 56 *dist. Apostolica* (c. 12); quandoque pro congregatione fidelium, infra *de cons. dist.* 1, *ecclesia* (c. 8). Et dic per exempla varias significationes. . . .

C. 9 q. 3 c. 13 *Nemo.* Nisi se alicuius iudicio submittat ut 2 q. 7 *nos si* (c. 41) et in causa haeresis, 40 *dist. si papa* (c. 6), et cum submittit se confessori suo, tenetur ei parere, et ligabit eum sententia illius. . . . Item cum Papa peccat potest eius peccatum etiam ecclesiae denuntiari secundum admonitionem Evangelii, ut supra 2 q. 1 *si peccaverit* (c. 19). Hoc determinavi, 40 *dist. si papa* (c. 6).

C. 9 q. 3 c. 13 *Neque ab omni clero.* Arg. quod concilium non potest Papam iudicare, ut *extra, de ele. significasti* (i.vi.4). Unde si totus mundus sententiaret in aliquo negotio contra Papam, videtur quod sententiae Papae standum esset, ut 24 q. 1 *haec est fides* (c. 14). Arg. contra quia orbis maior est urbe, 93 dist. *legimus* (c. 24).

C. 24 q. 1 c. 1 *In haeresim.* Hic est casus in quo Papa Papam potest ligare, in quo Papa in canonem latae sententiae incidit. Nec huic obviat regula illa, quia par parem solvere vel ligare non potest, *extra de elec. innotuit* (i.vi.20), quia si Papa haereticus est, in eo quod haereticus est minor quolibet catholico, 12 q. 1 *scimus* (c. 9), quia lex factum notat etiam sine sententia.

C. 24 q. 1 c. 6 *Reconciliat.* Arg. quod sententia totius ecclesiae praeferenda est Romanae si in aliquo sibi contradicat, arg. 93 *dist. legimus* (c. 24). Sed contrarium credo arg. infra, eadem. *haec est fides* (c. 14), nisi erraret Romana ecclesia quod non credo posse fieri, quia Deus non permitteret, arg. infra, eadem. c. *a recta* (c. 9) et c. *pudenda* (c. 33).

C. 24 q. 1 c. 9 *Novitatibus.* Quaero de qua ecclesia intelligas quod dicitur quod non possit errare? Si de ipso Papa qui ecclesia dicitur supra, eadem. *quodcumque* (c. 6), sed certum est quod Papa errare potest, 19 *dist. Anastasius* (c. 9), 40 *dist. si Papa* (c. 6). Respondeo, ipsa congregatio fidelium hic dicitur ecclesia ut *de consec. dist.* 1 *ecclesia* (c. 8), et talis ecclesia non potest non esse ut infra, eadem. *pudenda* (c. 33). Nam ipse Dominus rogavit pro ecclesia, 21 *dist.* 1 et voluntate labiorum suorum non fraudabitur.

C. 24 q. 1 c. 14 *Comprobatur*. Quia quod Papa approbat non licet aliis reprobare, arg. 50 *dist. si ille* (c. 58), 22 *dist. omnes*, 35 q. 9 *veniam* (c. 5), arg. 19 *dist. si Romanorum* (c. 1).

C. 25 q. 1 c. 3 *Nulla commutatione*. Ex hoc patet quod Papa non potest contra generale ecclesiae statutum dispensare, nec contra articulos fidei. Nam et si omnes assentiantur ei non valet statutum, sed omnes haeretici essent ut 15 dist. *sicut* (c. 2), et sic potest intelligi infra eadem. c. *sunt quidam* (c. 6) et c. *seq.* (c. 7). Sed contra statutum ecclesiae quod non est ita generale, sicut de continentia sacerdotum, bene potest dispensare.

C. 25 q. 2 c. 22 *Privilegia . . . nulla novitate mutari*. Quae sunt de generali ecclesiae statu, vel quae sunt de articulis fidei. Vel dic quod non possunt, id est non debent.

APPENDIX THREE

NOTES ON CANONISTS AND ANONYMOUS WORKS
MENTIONED IN THE TEXT

These notes are intended to provide a brief guide to the chronology, careers and literary activity of the various canonists mentioned in the text. For further details concerning the canonists and their works see Van Hove, *Prolegomena*, Kuttner, *Repertorium der Kanonistik* (1140–1234) and Schulte, *Quellen*. Kuttner's *Repertorium* is invaluable for the years it covers but the only detailed survey of the whole period is Schulte's old work. The best guide to the extensive modern literature concerning the various canonists is provided by the bibliographical notes in Van Hove's *Prolegomena*. Among the studies which have appeared since 1945, or which were not available to Van Hove at that time, the following seem of special interest.

On Gratian himself see Vol. xxi (1948) of the journal *Apollinaris*, a centenary celebration issue with articles by Kuttner, Le Bras, Stickler, Van Hove and Vetulani; the results of much current scholarship concerning the author of the *Decretum* are presented in the volumes of *Studia Gratiana*. Kuttner's 'Bernardus Compostellanus Antiquus', *Traditio*, i, 1943, pp. 277–340 contains much important information concerning the Bolognese canonists around the turn of the twelfth and thirteenth centuries. In this same field see also the same author's 'Johannes Teutonicus, das vierte Laterankonzil und die Compilatio Quarta', *Miscellenea Mercati* (Città del Vaticano, 1946) and 'Réflexions sur les Brocards des Glossateurs', *Mélanges Joseph de Ghellinck, S.J.* (Gembloux, 1951). The political views of Huguccio have been discussed by A. Stickler, 'Der Schwerterbegriff bei Huguccio', *Ephemerides Iuris Canonici*, iii, 1947, pp. 201–42, and a study of Huguccio's life and works by L. Scavo is promised in *Studia Gratiana*. S. Kuttner and E. Rathbone, 'Anglo-Norman canonists of the twelfth century', *Traditio*, vii, 1949–51, pp. 279–339 provides the first adequate introduction to the study of the Anglo-Norman canonists considered as a school in their own right—it includes a section on Caius MS. 676. An interesting contribution to the study of the French school in the twelfth century is T. P. McLaughlin's edition of the *Summa Parisiensis*, with a critical introduction (*The Summa Parisiensis on the Decretum Gratiani* (Toronto, 1952)). An edition of the *Summa Coloniensis* is being prepared by G. Fransen of Louvain. On the various recensions of the *Glossa Ordinaria* to the Decretals see S. Kuttner and B. Smalley, 'The *Glossa Ordinaria* to the Gregorian Decretals', *English Historical Review*, lx, 1945, pp. 97–105. N. Didier is producing a series of informative biographical articles on the career of Hostiensis ('Henri de Suse en Angleterre (1236?–1244)', *Studi Arangio-Ruiz* (Naples, 1952), 'Henri de Suse, prieur d'Antibes, prévôt de Grasse (1235?–1244)', *Studia Gratiana*, 'Henri de Suse, évêque de Sisteron (1244–1250)', *Nouvelle revue historique de droit français et étranger*, xxxi, 1953). Recent fascicles of the *Dictionnaire de droit canonique* have included articles on Berengarius Fredoli, Dominicus de Sancto Gemignano, Franciscus Zabarella, Gilbertus, Goffredus Tranensis, Gratian (see Corpus Juris Canonici, I. Le décret de Gratien), Guido de Baysio, Guilielmus Durantis (the Younger), Guilielmus Durantis (the Speculator), Guilielmus de Monte Lauduno, Guilielmus de Mandagato, Hostiensis and Huguccio. The treatment of the different canonists in these articles seems very uneven; the article on the Speculator, for instance, is a substantial treatise, that on Huguccio a trifling note of a dozen lines.

A number of recent works on the political theories of the canonists is considered in my article 'Some recent works on the political theories of the medieval canonists', *Traditio*, x, 1954.

ABBAS ANTIQUUS (Bernardus de Montemirato) (d. 1296). Studied at Bologna under Petrus de Sampsona (*c.* 1240) and, between 1259 and 1266 produced his *Lectura* on the Decretals. He also wrote commentaries on the *Novellae* of Innocent IV and *Distinctiones* on the Decretals. In 1266 he became Abbot of Montmajour and in 1286 he was appointed Bishop of Tripoli in Syria, but he never took possession of the see.

AEGIDIUS DE BELLAMERA (d. 1407). Collector of the decisions of the Roman Rota and author of *Consilia* and of Glosses on the *Decretum* and on the Decretals. He became Bishop of Lavaur in 1383, then of Le Puy (1390) and finally of Avignon (1393). He was present at the enthronement of Urban VI whose election he subsequently denounced; in 1398 he approved the policy of 'subtraction of obedience' from Benedict XIII.

ALANUS. An Englishman who lectured at Bologna in the early years of the thirteenth century. His principal works were a gloss on the *Compilatio Prima* (*c.* 1210) and his own collection of decretals, which formed an important source for the *Compilatio Secunda*. Most probably he was also the author of the apparatus *Ius Naturale* on the *Decretum*.

ALBERICUS DE ROSATE (d. 1354). Studied at Padua and subsequently lived at Bergamo and Rome. He wrote on both Roman law and canon law, his principal canonistic work being a commentary on the *Sext*.

ALBERTUS BENEVENTANUS (d. 1187). A distinguished glossator of the *Decretum*. He became cardinal (1155), Chancellor of the Roman church (1172) and finally was elected Pope in October 1187. He reigned for only a few weeks (as Gregory VIII) and died in December of the same year.

ALEXANDER III. See Rolandus Bandinelli.

ANDREAS DE BARBATIA (*c.* 1400–79). Lectured at Ferrara and then at Bologna. He acquired great fame as a consultant in legal cases and his works included a substantial collection of *Consilia*. He also wrote a commentary on the first three books of the Decretals, more detailed *Lecturae* on several titles of the Decretals, and treatises on selected topics of canon law.

ARCHDEACON. See Guido de Baysio.

BALDUS DE UBALDIS (*c.* 1319–1400). A most renowned jurist, equally famed as a civilian and a canonist. His principal canonistic work was a commentary on the first three books of the Decretals, but he also wrote notes on the *Commentaria* of Innocent IV and on the *Speculum* of Guilielmus Durantis. He left in addition many *Consilia*, including one on the legitimacy of the papal election of 1378.

BARTHOLOMAEUS BRIXIENSIS (d. 1258). A pupil of Tancred at Bologna. He produced original *Quaestiones*, but devoted himself mainly to re-editing stand-ard works of his immediate predecessors. He produced revised versions of Damasus's *Brocarda*, Tancred's *Ordo Iudiciarius* and Benencasa's *Casus Decretorum*. By far his most important work was a recension of Joannes Teutonicus's *Glossa Ordinaria* to the *Decretum* (*c.* 1245), which came to be accepted as the standard version of the *Glossa Ordinaria*.

BAZIANUS (d. 1197). A native of Bologna, he became a canon of the cathedral there, lectured on civil and canon law, and produced important glosses on the *Decretum*.

BERENGARIUS FREDOLI (d. 1323). A professor of Paris who became chaplain to the Pope, Bishop of Béziers and finally a cardinal. He is best known as one of the compilers of the *Liber Sextus*.

BERNARDUS COMPOSTELLANUS ANTIQUUS. Compiler of the *Compilatio Romana* (1208), a collection of decretals that was superseded by the official *Compilatio Tertia*; also the author of *Quaestiones* and glosses on the *Decretum* and on the *Compilatio Prima*.

BERNARDUS COMPOSTELLANUS JUNIOR (d. 1267). Chaplain to the Pope (*c.* 1261–67). Author of a commentary on the first book of the Decretals, an apparatus of glosses on the *Novellae* of Innocent IV, and notes on Innocent's *Commentaria*.

BERNARDUS PAPIENSIS (d. 1213). Compiler of the *Compilatio Prima* (1191), a work of the greatest importance since its division of the texts into five books according to subject matter was accepted in all the subsequent major col-lections. Bernardus also produced a *Summa* and glosses on his own compi-lation, glosses on the *Decretum, Argumenta* (or *Notabilia*), *Casus Decretalium* and finally a *Summa de Matrimonio* and a *Summa de Electione*. He became Bishop of Faenza in 1191 and subsequently Bishop of Pavia (1198).

BERNARDUS PARMENSIS (d. 1266). Author of the *Glossa Ordinaria* to the Decretals. He produced the first version of his gloss *c.* 1241, and continued to make revisions in it down to the time of his death. He also produced a *Summa* on the Decretals and wrote *Casus* on the *Novellae* of Innocent IV.

CAIUS MS. 676. A copy of the *Decretum* with an apparatus of glosses produced in England in the last years of the twelfth century.

DOMINICUS DE SANCTO GEMIGNANO (d. ante 1436). Professor at Bologna and subsequently auditor of the Apostolic Chamber. His most important work was his *Lectura* on the *Sext*. He also produced *Consilia* and wrote on the *Decretum* and Decretals.

FRANCISCUS ZABARELLA (*c.* 1335–1417). 'The foremost canonist of his day.' After studying at Bologna he lectured at Florence and then for many years at Pavia. He was the author of commentaries on the Decretals and Clemen-tines as well as of numerous *Consilia* and *Repetitiones*. Zabarella was created a cardinal in 1411 by Pope John XXIII, and attended the Council of Con-stance as Papal legate. He died during the sessions of the Council in 1417.

GILBERTUS. An Englishman who taught at Bologna and compiled a decretal collection (1202) which, with that of Alánus, formed the basis of the *Compilatio Secunda*. He wrote glosses on his own compilation.

GLOSSA PALATINA. An 'able and influential' compilation of glosses on the *Decretum*, produced at Bologna between 1210 and 1215 and containing many glosses of Laurentius Hispanus.

GLOSS ECCE VICIT LEO. An outstanding work of the French school. It is an apparatus of glosses on the *Decretum* produced between 1202 and 1210.

GOFFREDUS TRANENSIS (d. 1245). He taught civil law at Naples and canon law at Bologna, then entered the service of the Roman curia. Goffredus produced *Quaestiones* and glosses on the Decretals as well as his best known work, the *Summa in Titulos Decretalium*. He was created a cardinal in 1244.

GRATIANUS. 'The father of the science of canon law.' Very little is known of his life beyond that fact that he was a Camaldulensian monk who taught at Bologna. His immensely influential work appeared *c*. 1140.

GUIDO DE BAYSIO (d. 1313). Archdeacon of Bologna from 1296. His principal works were a gloss on the *Sext*. and the very influential *Rosarium*, an apparatus of glosses on the *Decretum*, 'in quo numero immenso glossas aliorum compilavit'.

GUILIELMUS DURANTIS (the Speculator) (1237–96). One of the most famous canonists of the late thirteenth century. He wrote a commentary on the *Novellae* of Gregory X, an important liturgical work, *Rationale Divinorum Officiorum* and, best known of all, the *Speculum Iudiciale*, produced *c*. 1272 with a later recension *c*. 1287. He became Bishop of Mende in 1286.

GUILIELMUS DURANTIS (the Younger) (d. 1328). Nephew of the Speculator whom he succeeded as Bishop of Mende in 1296. His *Tractatus de Modo Generalis Concilii Celebrandi* was written in response to a general request of Pope Clement V for suggestions concerning the reform of the Church to be undertaken in the approaching Council of Vienne. It was often attributed to Guilielmus's more famous uncle in the later Middle Ages.

GUILIELMUS DE MANDAGATO (d. 1321). One of the compilers of the *Liber Sextus* and author of a *Tractatus super Electione*. He became Archbishop of Embrun (1295) and was made a cardinal in 1312.

GUILIELMUS DE MONTE LAUDUNO (d. 1343). Professor at Toulouse and abbot of the Benedictine monastery there. He wrote glosses on the *Sext*., Clementines, and *Extravagantes Communes*.

HENRICUS DE BOHIC (d. *c*. 1350). A canonist of English descent who lectured at Paris. Author of an important volume of *Distinctiones* on the Decretals.

HENRICUS DE SEGUSIO. See Hostiensis.

HOSTIENSIS (d. 1271). A most distinguished and influential canonist. After studying at Bologna he lectured at Paris and then lived for some time in England in the service of Henry III. He became chaplain to Pope Innocent IV and then in turn Bishop of Sisteron (1244), Archbishop of Embrun (1250) and Cardinal-Bishop of Ostia (1262). He wrote on the *Novellae* of Innocent IV, but the works upon which his great fame chiefly rested were his *Summa* and *Lectura* on the Decretals, the first produced between 1250 and 1251, the latter completed only in the year of his death.

HUGUCCIO (d. 1210). Huguccio's *Summa* was the greatest achievement of twelfth-century Decretist scholarship. It was completed between 1188 and 1190. Huguccio was a native of Pisa who lectured at Bologna and became Bishop of Ferrara in 1190. He was the teacher of Innocent III but it has been suggested that his influence on his great pupil lay in providing the future Pope with 'juristic equipment' rather than in his 'actual political arguments'. Huguccio also had a considerable reputation as a grammarian and lexicographer.

INNOCENTIUS IV (d. 1254). According to Maitland, 'the greatest lawyer that ever sat upon the chair of St Peter'. After lecturing at Bologna he entered the service of the Roman curia and in 1227 was raised to the cardinalate. He became Bishop of Albenga in 1235 and was elected Pope in 1243. It was during his pontificate (c. 1251) that he produced his best-known work, the incisive *Commentaria* on the Decretals. He also promulgated as Pope three important collections of decretals.

JOANNES ANDREAE (c. 1270–1348). A prolific and very renowned canonist of the fourteenth century. He taught at Padua and Bologna and produced the *Glossa Ordinaria* on the *Sext.* and on the Clementines. Among his other writings were an important commentary on the Decretals (*Novella super Decretalibus*) and a second, shorter work on the *Sext.* (also called *Novella*).

JOANNES FAVENTINUS (d. c. 1220). Author of a *Summa* and glosses on the *Decretum*, composed between 1170 and 1180. He was a canon of the cathedral at Faenza.

JOANNES GALENSIS. Compiler of the *Compilatio Secunda* (after 1210) and author of glosses on this compilation and also on the *Compilatio Tertia* (before 1216). Joannes was a Welshman who lectured at Bologna.

JOANNES DE LIGNANO (d. 1383). Professor first of civil law then of canon law at Bologna and also a student of astronomy and natural philosophy. His canonistic works included commentaries on the Decretals and on the Clementines as well as a number of treatises on particular topics—among them 'the first systematic treatise on international law' (*Tractatus de Bello, de Repressaliis et Duello* (1365).

JOANNES MONACHUS (d. 1313). Studied at Paris and acquired a canonry there, becoming subsequently Bishop of Meaux and an adviser of Philip the Fair. (He was not a monk; the family name was Le Moyne.) In 1294 he was made a cardinal by Celestine V, and in 1302 was sent by Boniface VIII on an embassy to the French king. His principal canonistic work was a gloss on the *Sext.*; he also wrote on the *Extravagantes Communes*.

JOANNES TEUTONICUS (d. 1246). Author of the very influential *Glossa Ordinaria* on the *Decretum* which included materials from various earlier works, especially the *Summa* of Huguccio, the *Glossa Palatina* and the apparatus of Laurentius. The work was completed between 1215 and 1217. Joannes was also active as a Decretalist, producing glosses on the *Compilatio Tertia* and on the *Compilatio Quarta* of which he was himself the compiler. He also glossed the canons of the Fourth Lateran Council. He was a professor of Bologna and held the office of Provost of Halberstadt.

LABORANS (d. 1189). An able canonist of the late twelfth century who was raised to the cardinalate in 1173. His chief work was a re-arrangement of Gratian's *Decretum*, intended to present Gratian's texts (with some additional ones) in a more convenient form.

LAURENTIUS HISPANUS (d. 1248). Professor at Bologna in the early years of the thirteenth century. He was important not only for his own writings but also as the master of Tancred and Bartholomaeus Brixiensis. His works included a major apparatus on the *Decretum*, written between 1210 and 1215, and glosses on the *Compilationes* I, II, III, and V. In 1218 he became Bishop of Orense.

PANORMITANUS (Nicolaus de Tudeschis, also called Abbas Modernus, Abbas

Siculus) (1386–1453?). A Benedictine monk, he taught at Bologna, Parma and Siena, became Abbot of Maniaco (1425) and Archbishop of Palermo (1435). He produced many influential works including *Quaestiones, Repetitiones, Consilia* and glosses on the Decretals, *Sext.* and Clementines.

PAUCAPALEA. The first of the Decretists. He wrote glosses on the *Decretum* and also, between 1140 and 1148 a successful *Summa*. Furthermore he made a number of additions to the text of the *Decretum*, which, with other additions, were incorporated in later copies as *Paleae*.

PAULUS DE LIAZARIIS (d. 1356). Professor of Bologna. His works included glosses on the Clementines and *Quaestiones*.

PETRUS DE ANCHARANO (*c.* 1330–1416). Professor at Bologna and then at Siena. He wrote a vast commentary on the Decretals and also *Consilia, Repetitiones* and glosses on the *Sext.* and Clementines.

PETRUS BERTRANDI (1280–1349). Lectured at Avignon, Montpellier, Orléans and Paris. A brilliantly successful advocate, he came to play an important part in the ecclesiastical politics of France. He was made Bishop of Nevers (1320), Bishop of Autun (1320) and finally Archbishop of Béziers (1331) and a cardinal. His most important writings were glosses on the *Sext.* and Clementines.

PETRUS COLLIVACCINUS (or Beneventanus). Vice-Chancellor of Innocent III. At the Pope's command he undertook the compilation of the first official collection of decretals, the *Compilatio Tertia*, promulgated in 1209 or 1210.

RAYMUNDUS DE PENNAFORTE, S. (d. 1275). Compiler of the Gregorian decretals and also author of glosses on the *Decretum*, of a *Summa Iuris Canonici* and of a very influential *Summa de Poenitentia*. After lecturing at Bologna he entered the Dominican Order and subsequently became chaplain and penitentiary to Pope Gregory IX.

RICARDUS ANGLICUS (most probably Richard de Lacy). An Englishman who became a distinguished teacher at Bologna. His works included glosses and *Distinctiones* on the *Decretum*, an apparatus on the *Compilatio Prima, Casus Decretalium* and an *Ordo Iudiciarius*. These works were produced between 1190 and 1210.

RICARDUS PETRONIUS DE SENIS (d. 1348). A cardinal and Vice-Chancellor of the Roman church—one of the compilers of the *Liber Sextus*.

ROLANDUS BANDINELLI (d. 1181). A pupil of Gratian and one of the earliest Decretists. He produced both glosses and a *Summa*, or *Stroma*, on the *Decretum* (before 1148). He became a cardinal in 1150, and in 1159 was elected Pope. He ruled as Alexander III until 1181. Many of the decretals he issued as Pope were included in the early compilations, and subsequently in the *Gregoriana*.

RUFINUS. Author of a very influential *Summa* on the *Decretum* (1157–59). After lecturing at Bologna he became Bishop of Assisi and subsequently Archbishop of Sorrento (1180).

SICARDUS CREMONENSIS (d. 1215). Twelfth-century Decretist whose *Summa* on the *Decretum* was produced *c.* 1180. In 1185 he became Bishop of Cremona. The most recent study of his work suggests that it shows affiliations with the French school rather than the Bolognese.

SIMON DE BISIGNANO (d. 1215). A canonist of the Bolognese school who produced a Summa on the *Decretum c.* 1178.

SINIBALDUS FIESCUS. See Innocent IV.

STEPHANUS TORNACENSIS (1128–1203). Born in Orléans he studied theology at Paris and civil and canon law at Bologna. He was for many years Abbot of St Geneviève's in Paris, and his work provides an important link between the Bolognese school of canonists and the French school. His *Summa* on the *Decretum* appeared in the 1160s. In 1192 he became Bishop of Tournai.

SUMMA COLONIENSIS, SUMMA ET EST SCIENDUM, SUMMA PARISIENSIS, SUMMA PERMISSIO QUEDAM. These four anonymous *Summae* on the *Decretum* are all works of the French school composed in the second half of the twelfth century. The author of a recent edition of the *Summa Parisiensis* (T. P. McLaughlin) suggests that this work should be dated as early as *c.* 1160 and that it did not use material of Rufinus nor, probably, of Stephanus as had previously been supposed. The *Summa Coloniensis* was produced between 1169 and 1170 and it did make use of the works of both Rufinus and Stephanus. The *Summa Et Est Sciendum* is assigned to the pontificate of Lucius III (1181–5), and the *Summa Permissio Quedam* was written between 1179 and 1187. (The attribution of this last work to the French school is not certain.)

TANCREDUS (*c.* 1185–*c.* 1235). An influential canonist of the early thirteenth-century. He was a canon and subsequently archdeacon of Bologna. His works include the *Glossa Ordinaria* on the first three *Compilationes*, glosses on the *Compilatio Quinta*, an *Ordo Iudiciarius* and a *Summa de Matrimonio*.

VINCENTIUS HISPANUS (d. 1248). Author of glosses on the *Decretum*, on the *Compilatio Prima* and *Compilatio Tertia* and on the canons of the Fourth Lateran Council. He also produced two works on the *Gregoriana*, an apparatus and *Casus Decretalium*. He taught at Bologna and became Bishop of Idanha-Guarda in Portugal.

WOLFENBÜTTEL MS. HELMST. 33. This manuscript contains an apparatus of glosses on the *Decretum* composed towards the end of the twelfth century.

ZABARELLA. See Franciscus Zabarella.

ZENZELLINUS DE CASSANIS (d. 1334). A French canonist who wrote on the Clementines and composed the *Glossa Ordinaria* to the *Extravagantes Joannis XXII*. He was a professor at Montpellier, entered the service of the papal curia and died at Avignon.

LIST OF WORKS CITED

As a general rule works on canonistic sources listed in the bibliographies of Van Hove's *Prolegomena* have not been cited. There are a few exceptions, usually cases where direct quotations have been made from the work mentioned.

I. CANONISTIC SOURCES

(a) Manuscripts

Apparatus Glossarum ad Decretum:
  MS. 676 of Gonville and Caius College, Cambridge.
Glossa Palatina:
  MS. O.10.2 of Trinity College, Cambridge.
  MS. Pal.Lat.658 of the Biblioteca Vaticana.
Gloss Ecce Vicit Leo:
  MS. O.5.17 of Trinity College, Cambridge.
  MS. XI.605 of Sankt Florian, Stiftsbibliothek.
Huguccio, *Summa*:
  MS. 72 of Pembroke College, Cambridge.
  MS. 2 of Lincoln Cathedral Chapter Library.
Joannes Teutonicus, *Apparatus ad Compilationem Quartam*:
  MS. 17 of Gonville and Caius College, Cambridge.
Tancred, *Apparatus ad Compilationem Primam*:
  MS. 17 of Gonville and Caius College, Cambridge.
Tancred, *Apparatus ad Compilationem Tertiam*:
  MS. 17 of Gonville and Caius College, Cambridge.

(b) Printed editions

AEGIDIUS DE BELLAMERA. *Commentaria in Gratiani Decreta* (Lugduni, 1550).
ANDREAS DE BARBATIA. *De Prestantia Cardinalium, Tractatus Universi Iuris*, XIV (Lugduni, 1549).
BALDUS DE UBALDIS. *Baldus super Decretalibus* (Lugduni, 1547).
BERNARDUS PARMENSIS. *Glossa Ordinaria* to the Decretals in *Decretales Gregorii Papae IX . . . una cum glossis* (Parisiis, 1601).
DOMINICUS DE SANCTO GEMIGNANO. *Lectura super Sexto Libro Decretalium* (Tridini, 1522).
FRANCISCUS ZABARELLA. *Super Quinque Libris Decretalium Commentaria* (Venetiis, 1602).
  In Clementinarum Volumen Commentaria (Venetiis, 1602).
  Tractatus de Schismate in Schardius, *De Iurisdictione . . . Imperiali ac Potestate Ecclesiastica* (Basileae, 1566).
FRIEDBERG, A. *Corpus Iuris Canonici* (Lipsiae, 1879).
  Quinque Compilationes Antiquae (Lipsiae, 1882).
GOFFREDUS TRANENSIS. *Summa in Titulos Decretalium* (Venetiis, 1601).
GUIDO DE BAYSIO. *Rosarium seu in Decretorum Volumen Commentaria* (Venetiis, 1577).
  In Sextum Decretalium Commentaria (Venetiis, 1577).

GUILIELMUS DURANTIS. *Speculum Iudiciale* (Francofurti, 1592).
  Rationale Divinorum Officiorum (Venetiis, 1609).
GUILIELMUS DURANTIS (the younger). *Tractatus de Modo Generalis Concilii Celebrandi* (Parisiis, 1545).
HENRICUS DE BOHIC. *Distinctiones Libri Quinque ad Decretales Gregorianas* (Lugduni, 1557).
HOSTIENSIS. *Summa Aurea super Titulis Decretalium* (Coloniae, 1612).
  Lectura in Quinque Decretalium Gregorianarum Libros (Parisiis, 1512).
INNOCENTIUS IV. *Commentaria super Libros Quinque Decretalium* (Francofurti, 1570).
JOANNES ANDREAE. *Glossa Ordinaria* to *Liber Sextus* in *Liber Sextus Decretalium Bonifacii Papae VIII* (Parisiis, 1601).
  Glossa Ordinaria to *Clementinae* in *Clementis Papae Quinti Constitutiones* (Parisiis, 1601).
  Novella super Decretalibus (Venetiis, 1605).
  Novella in Sextum Decretalium (Lugduni, 1550).
JOANNES DE LIGNANO. *De Censura Ecclesiastica, Tractatus Universi Iuris*, XVI (Lugduni, 1549).
  Tractatus de Pluralitate Beneficiorum, Tractatus Universi Iuris, XV (Lugduni, 1549).
JOANNES MONACHUS. *Glossa Aurea super Sexto Decretalium Libro* (Parisiis, 1535).
JOANNES TEUTONICUS. *Glossa Ordinaria* to the *Decretum* in *Decretum Gratiani* . . . *una cum glossis* (Parisiis, 1601) (*Glossa Ordinaria* with additions of Bartholomaeus Brixiensis).
PAUCAPALEA. *Die Summa des Paucapalea*, ed. J. F. v. Schulte (Giessen, 1890).
Repetitionum in Universas fere Iuris Canonici Partes . . . *Volumina Sex* (Venetiis, 1587).
ROLANDUS BANDINELLI. *Die Summa Magistri Rolandi*, ed. F. Thaner (Innsbruck, 1874).
RUFINUS. *Die Summa Decretorum des Magister Rufinus*, ed. H. Singer (Paderborn, 1902).
STEPHANUS TORNACENSIS. *Die Summa des Stephanus Tornacensis*, ed. J. F. v. Schulte (Giessen, 1891).
SUMMA PARISIENSIS. *The Summa Parisiensis on the Decretum Gratiani*, ed. T. P. McLaughlin (Toronto, 1952).
ZENZELLINUS DE CASSANIS. *Glossa Ordinaria* to *Extravagantes* in *Constitutiones Ioannis Papae XXII* (Parisiis, 1601).

II. LITERARY SOURCES

ANDREAS RANDULF. *De Modis Uniendi* . . . *Ecclesiam in Concilio Universali* in Gerson, *Opera*, II.
AUGUSTINUS TRIUMPHUS. *Summa de Potestate Ecclesiastica* (Romae, 1584).
COLONNA, J. and P. *Die Denkschriften der Colonna gegen Bonifaz VIII*, ed. H. Denifle, *Archiv für Literatur- und Kirchengeschichte*, V (1889), pp. 493–525.
CONRAD OF GELNHAUSEN. *Epistola Concordiae* in Martène and Durand, *Thesaurus Novus Anecdotorum*, II (Paris, 1717).
D'AILLY, P. *De Ecclesiae et Cardinalium Auctoritate* in Gerson, *Opera*, II.
  De Jurisdictione Ecclesiastica in von der Hardt, *Concilium Constantiense*, VI (Francofurti, 1697–1700).
DIETRICH OF NIEM. *De Modis Uniendi et Reformandi Ecclesiam*, ed. H. Heimpel (Leipzig, 1933).
  De Schismate, ed. Erler (Leipzig, 1890).
FREDERICK II. Letters of Frederick II in *Monumenta Germaniae Historica, Constitutiones*, II, and in P. Huillard-Bréholles, *Historia Diplomatica Friderici II* (Paris, 1852–61).
GERSON, J. Sermons, treatises and letters in *Opera Omnia*, ed. Du Pin, II (Antwerpiae, 1706).
GILES OF ROME. *De Renuntiatione Papae* in Rocaberti, *Bibliotheca Maxima Pontificia*, II (Romae, 1698).
HENRY OF LANGENSTEIN. *Consilium Pacis* in Gerson, *Opera*, II.
JOHN OF PARIS. *De Potestate Regia et Papali*; ed. J. Leclercq (Paris, 1942).

MARSILIUS OF PADUA. *Defensor Pacis*, ed. C. W. Previté-Orton (Cambridge, 1928).
NICOLAUS CUSANUS, *De Concordantia Catholica*, in *Opera Omnia*, XVIII, (Basileae, 1566).
OLIVI, P. *De Renuntiatione Papae*, ed. P. L. Oliger, *Archivum Franciscanum Historicum*, XI (1918), pp. 340 ff.
RICHARD OF ST GERMANO. *Chronica Regni Siciliae*, ed. Gaudenzi in *Monumenta Storici della Società Napolitana di Storia Patria, Serie Prima* (Napoli, 1888).
WILLIAM OF OCKHAM. *Dialogus* in Goldast, *Monarchia Sancti Romani Imperii*, II (Francofordiae, 1614).
    Opus Nonaginta Dierum, ed. R. F. Bennett and J. G. Sikes in *Guillelmi De Ockham Opera Politica*, I (Mancunii, 1940).

III. SECONDARY WORKS

ANCIAUX, P. *La théologie du sacrement de pénitence au XIIe siècle* (Louvain-Gembloux, 1949).
ANDRIEU, M. L'origine du titre de cardinal dans l'église romaine.
    Miscellenea Giovanni Mercati, V (Città del Vaticano, 1946), pp. 113–44.
ARQUILLIÈRE, H.-X. L'origine des théories conciliaires. *Séances et Travaux de l'Académie des Sciences Morales et Politiques*, CLXXV (1911), pp. 573–86.
    L'appel au concile sous Philippe le Bel et la genèse des théories conciliaires. *Revue des questions historiques*, XLV (1911), pp. 23–55.
BARRACLOUGH, G. *Papal Provisions* (Oxford, 1935).
BLIEMETZRIEDER, F. *Das Generalkonzil im grossen abendländischen Schisma* (Paderborn, 1904).
BOASE, T. S. R. *Boniface VIII* (London, 1933).
BRADSHAW, H. and WORDSWORTH, C., eds. *Statutes of Lincoln Cathedral* (Cambridge, 1897).
BRESSLAU, H. *Handbuch der Urkundenlehre* (2nd ed., Leipzig-Berlin, 1912–31).
BROWN, F. BRENDAN. Canonical juristic personality. *The Jurist*, I (1941), pp. 66–73.
BRYS, J. *De Dispensatione in Iure Canonico* (Brugis, 1925).
CARLYLE, R. W. and A. J. *A History of Medieval Political Theory in the West*, V (London, 1928).
CASPAR, E. *Geschichte des Papsttums* (Tübingen, 1930).
CHROUST, A.-H. The corporate idea and the body politic in the Middle Ages. *Review of Politics*, IX (1947), pp. 423–52.
CONGAR, Y. M.-J. Incidence ecclésiologique d'un thème de dévotion mariale. *Mélanges de science religieuse*, VIII (1951), pp. 277–92.
COOPLAND, G. W. Un ouvrage inédit de Jean de Lignano. Le Somnium de 1372. *Actes du Congrès International d'Histoire des Religions*, II, pp. 344 ff.
DE LAGARDE, G. L'idée de représentation dans les œuvres de Guillaume d'Ockham. *Bulletin of the International Committee of Historical Sciences*, IX (1937), pp. 425–51.
    La naissance de l'esprit laïque au déclin du moyen âge (Paris, 1934–46).
DE LUBAC, H. *Catholicism*, transl. Sheppard (London, 1950).
DE WULF, M. L'individu et la groupe dans la scolastique du XIIIe siècle. *Revue néo-scolastique de philosophie*, XII (1920), pp. 341 ff.
    Dictionnaire de droit canonique (Paris, 1935–).
DIDIER, N. Henri de Suse en Angleterre (1236?–1244). *Studi Arangio-Ruiz* (Naples, 1952), II, pp. 333–51.
    Henri de Suse, prieur d'Antibes, prévôt de Grasse (1235?–1244). *Studia Gratiana*, II.
    Henri de Suse, évêque de Sisteron (1244–1250). *Nouvelle revue historique de droit français et étranger*, XXXI (1953), pp. 244–70, 409–29.
DIGARD, G. *Philippe le Bel et le Saint Siège, 1285–1304* (Paris, 1936).
DÖLLINGER, J. J. I. v. *Fables Respecting the Popes of the Middle Ages*, transl. A. Plummer (London, 1871).

DOUIE, D. *The Nature and Effect of the Heresy of the Fraticelli* (Manchester, 1932).

DUFF, P. *Personality in Roman Private Law* (Cambridge, 1938).

DUPUY, P. *Histoire du différend d'entre le Pape Boniface VIII et Philippe le Bel* (Paris, 1655).

EDWARDS, K. *The English Secular Cathedrals in the Middle Ages* (Manchester, 1949).

EICHMANN, E. *Die Weihe und Krönung des Papstes im Mittelalter*, ed. K. Mörsdorf in *Münchener Theologische Studien*, I (1951).

ERMINI, G. *I Trattati della Guerra e della Pace di Giovanni de Legnano* (*Studi e Memorie per la Storia dell'Università de Bologna*, I, 8) (Imola, 1923).

    Un ignoto trattato 'De principatu' de Giovanni de Legnano. *Studi di Storia e Diritto in Onore di Carlo Calisse* (Milan, 1940).

FEINE, H. E. *Kirchliche Rechtsgeschichte*, I, *Die Katholische Kirche* (Weimar, 1950).

FIGGIS, J. N. *Churches in the Modern State* (London, 1913).

    Studies of Political Thought from Gerson to Grotius (2nd ed. Cambridge, 1916).

FINKE, H. *Aus den Tagen Bonifaz VIII* (Münster, 1902).

GIERKE, O. v. *Das Deutsche Genossenschaftsrecht* (Berlin, 1868–1913).

GILLET, P. *La personnalité juridique en droit ecclésiastique* (Malines, 1927).

GILLMANN, F. Die simonistische Papstwahl nach Huguccio. *A.K.K.R.* LXXXIX (1909), pp. 606–11.

    Romanus Pontifex iura omnia in scrinio pectoris sui censetur habere. *A.K.K.R.* XCII (1912), pp. 3 ff.

    Zur scholastischen Auslegung von Mt 16, 18. *A.K.K.R.* CIV (1924), pp. 41–53.

    Die Dekretglossen des Cod. Stuttgart. hist. f. 419. *A.K.K.R.* CVII (1927), pp. 192–250.

GLANVELL, W. v. *Die Kanonessamlung des Kardinals Deusdedit* (Paderborn, 1905).

GLORIEUX, P. *La littérature quodlibétique de 1260 à 1320, Bibliothèque Thomiste*, V (Kain, 1925).

GRABMANN, M. *Studien zu Joannes Quidort von Paris O.P.* (Munich, 1922).

GRABOWSKI, H. St Augustine and the Primacy of the Church of Rome. *Traditio*, IV (1946), pp. 89–113.

HALLER, J. *Papsttum und Kirchenreform*, I (Berlin, 1903).

HARDT, H. v. d. *Magnum Oecumenicum Concilium Constantiense* (Frankfort, 1697–1700).

HAUCK, A. Die Rezeption und Umbildung der allgemeinen Synode im Mittelalter. *Historische Vierteljahrschrift*, X (1907), pp. 465–82.

HEILER, F. *Altkirchliche Autonomie und päpstlicher Zentralismus* (Munich, 1941).

HEIMPEL, H. *Dietrich von Niem* (Münster-in-Westfalen, 1932).

HINSCHIUS, P. *Das Kirchenrecht der Katholiken und Protestanten* (Berlin, 1869–97).

HIRSCH, K. *Die Ausbildung der Konziliaren Theorie* (Wien, 1903).

    Histoire littéraire de la France, XXVII, XXXIV (Paris, 1876, 1914).

HOFMANN, H. *Kardinalat und Kuriale Politik in der ersten Hälfte des 14 Jahrhunderts* (Leipzig, 1935).

HOLTZMANN, W. Die Register Alexanders III in den Händen der Kanonisten. *Quellen und Forschungen aus italienischen Archiven*, XXX (1940), pp. 13 ff.

    Über eine Ausgabe der päpstlichen Dekretalen des 12 Jahrhunderts. *Nachrichten der Akademie der Wissenschaften in Göttingen* (Phil.-Hist. Kl. 1945), pp. 15–36.

    Die Dekretalen Gregors VIII. *Festschrift für Leo Santifäller, Mitteilungen des österreichischen Instituts für Geschichtsforschung*, LVIII (1950), pp. 113–24.

HÜBLER, B. *Die Constanzer Reformation* (Leipzig, 1867).

HUILLARD-BRÉHOLLES, P. *Vie et correspondance de Pierre de la Vigne* (Paris, 1865).

JACOB, E. F. *Essays in the Conciliar Epoch* (2nd ed. Manchester, 1953).

JEDIN, H. *Geschichte des Konzils von Trient*, I (Freiburg, 1949).

JORDAN, K. Die Entstehung der römischen Kurie. *Z.S.S.R.* LIX (1939), pp. 97–152.

JUNCKER, J. Die Summa des Simon von Bisignano. *Z.S.S.R.* XLVI (1926), pp. 326–500.

KLEWITZ, H. W. Die Entstehung des Kardinalkollegiums. *Z.S.S.R.* LVI (1936), pp. 115–21.

KNEER, A. *Kardinal Zabarella: Ein Beitrag zur Geschichte des grossen abendländischen Schisma* (Münster, 1890).
Die Entstehung der konziliaren Theorie. *Römische Quartalschrift* (Erstes Supplementheft, 1893), pp. 48–60.

KOCH, J. Der Prozess gegen den Magister Johannes de Polliaco und seine Vorgeschichte. *Recherches de théologie ancienne et médiévale*, V (1933), pp. 391–422.

KÖSTLER, R. Zum Titel des Gratianischen Dekrets. *Z.S.S.R.* LII (1932), pp. 370–3.
Noch einmal zum Titel des Gratianischen Dekrets. *Z.S.S.R.* LIV (1934), pp. 378–80.

KUTTNER, S. *Repertorium der Kanonistik* (Città del Vaticano, 1937).
The father of the science of Canon Law. *The Jurist*, I (1941), pp. 2–19.
Bernardus Compostellanus Antiquus. *Traditio*, I (1943), pp. 277–340.
Cardinalis, the history of a canonical concept. *Traditio*, III (1945) pp. 129–214.
Johannes Teutonicus, das vierte Laterankonzil und die Compilatio Quarta. *Miscellenea Giovanni Mercati*, V (Città del Vaticano, 1946), pp. 608–34.
Quelques observations sur l'autorité des collections canoniques dans le droit classique de l'Église. *Actes du Congrès de Droit Canonique* (Paris, 1947), pp. 303–12.
Notes on a projected corpus of twelfth-century decretal letters. *Traditio*, VI (1948), pp. 345–51.
The scientific investigation of medieval canon law, the need and the opportunity. *Speculum*, XXIV (1949), pp. 493–501.
Réflexions sur les Brocards des glossateurs. *Mélanges Joseph de Ghellinck, S.J.* (Gembloux, 1951), pp. 767–92.

KUTTNER, S. and RATHBONE, E. Anglo-Norman canonists of the twelfth century. *Traditio*, VII (1949–51), pp. 279–339.

KUTTNER, S. and SMALLEY, B. The *Glossa Ordinaria* to the Gregorian Decretals. *English Historical Review*, LX (1945), pp. 97–105.

LE BRAS, G. Les écritures dans le Décret Gratien. *Z.S.S.R.* LVIII (1938), pp. 47–80.

LECLER, J. Les théories démocratiques au moyen âge. *Études*, CCXXV (1935), pp. 5–26, 168–89.

LECLERCQ, J. *Jean de Paris et l'ecclésiologie du XIIIe siècle* (Paris, 1942).
Simoniaca heresis. *Studi Gregoriani*, I (Rome, 1947), pp. 523–30.

LEWIS, E. Organic tendencies in medieval political thought. *American Political Science Review*, XXXII (1938), pp. 849–76.

LULVÈS, J. Päpstliche Wahlkapitulationen. *Quellen und Forschungen aus italianischen Archiven*, XII (1909), pp. 212–35.
Die Machtsbestrebungen des Kardinalcollegiums gegenüber dem Papsttum. *Mitteilungen des Instituts für österreichische Geschichtsforschung*, XXXV (1914), pp. 455–83.

MACCARRONE, M. Una questione inedita dell'Ollivi sull'infallibilità del Papa. *Rivista de Storia della Chiesa in Italia*, III (1949), pp. 309–24.

MAITLAND, F. W. Introduction to O. von Gierke, *Political Theories of the Middle Age*, transl. Maitland (Cambridge, 1938).
Selected Essays (Cambridge, 1936).

MANSI, J. D. *Sacrorum Conciliorum Nova et Amplissima Collectio* (Parisiis, 1901–27).

MARTIN, V. Comment s'est formée la doctrine de la supériorité du concile sur le pape. *Revue des sciences religieuses*, XVII (1937), pp. 212–43, 261–89, 404–27.
Origines du Gallicanisme (Paris, 1939).

MCILWAIN, C. H. *The Growth of Political Thought in the West* (New York, 1932).

MERSCH, E. *Le Corps Mystique du Christ* (Paris, 1936).

MERZBACHER, F. Wandlungen des Kirchenbegriffs im Spätmittelalter. *Z.S.S.R.* LXX (1953), pp. 274–361.

MICHEL, A. *Die Sentenzen des Kardinals Humbert* (Leipzig, 1943).
Die folgenschweren Ideen des Kardinals Humbert und ihr Einfluss auf Gregor VII. *Studi Gregoriani*, I (Rome, 1947), pp. 65–92.

MOHLER, L. *Die Kardinäle Jacob und Peter Colonna* (Paderborn, 1914).

MOLLAT, G. Contribution à l'histoire du Sacré Collège de Clément V à Eugène IV. *Revue d'histoire ecclésiastique*, XLVI (1951), pp. 22–112.

MÜLLER, E. *Daz Konzil von Vienne, 1311–1312* (Münster in Westfalen, 1934).

ONORY, S. MOCHI. *Fonti Canonistiche dell'Idea Moderna dello Stato* (Milan, 1951).

PANCIROLI, G. *De Claris Legum Interpretibus* (Lipsiae, 1721).

POSCH, A. Die Reformvorschläge des Wilhelm Durandus jun. auf den Konzil von Vienne. *Mitteilungen des österreichischen Instituts für Geschichtsforschung*, XI, *Ergänzungsband* (1929), pp. 288–303.

POST, GAINES. Parisian masters as a corporation. *Speculum*, IX (1934), pp. 421–5.

Plena potestas and consent in medieval assemblies. *Traditio*, I (1943), pp. 355–408.

Roman law and early representation in Spain and Italy. *Speculum*, XVIII (1943), pp. 211–32.

A Romano-canonical maxim 'quod omnes tangit' in Bracton. *Traditio*, IV (1946), pp. 197–251.

The theory of public law and the state in the thirteenth century. *Seminar*, VI (1948), pp. 42–59.

RAHNER, H. Navicula Petri. *Zeitschrift für katholische Theologie*, LXXIX (1947), pp. 5 ff.

RIVIÈRE, J. *Le problème de l'église et de l'état au temps de Philippe le Bel* (Louvain, 1926). In partem sollicitudinis ... évolution d'une formule pontificale. *Revue des sciences religieuses*, V (1925), pp. 210–31.

ROBERTI, M. Il corpus mysticum di S. Paolo nella storia della persona giuridica. *Studi in Onore di Enrico Besta*, IV, pp. 37–82 (Milan, 1939).

SÄGMÜLLER, J. B. *Die Thätigkeit und Stellung der Kardinäle bis Papst Bonifaz VIII* (Freiburg, 1896).

SARTI, M. *De Claris Archigymnasii Bononiensis Professoribus*, ed. M. Fattorini (Bononiae, 1888).

SCHOLZ, R. *Die Publizistik zur Zeit Philipps des Schönen* (Stuttgart, 1903).

SCHRAMM, P. *Kaiser, Rom und Renovatio* (Leipzig-Berlin, 1929).

SCHULTE, J. F. v. Zur Geschichte der Literatur über das Dekret Gratians, I. *Sitzungs-berichte der kaiserlichen Akademie der Wissenschaften in Wien* (Phil.-Hist. Kl.), LXIII (Wien, 1869); II, idem, LXIV (1870); III, idem, LXV (1870).

Die Stellung der Concilien, Päpste und Bischöfe (Prague, 1871).

Die Glosse zum Dekret Gratians von ihren Anfängen bis auf die jüngsten Ausgaben. *Denkschriften der kaiserlichen Akademie der Wissenschaften* (Phil.-Hist. Kl.), XXI (Wien, 1872).

Die Geschichte der Quellen und Literatur des canonischen Rechts von Gratian bis auf die Gegenwart (Stuttgart, 1875–80).

SIKES, J. G. John de Pouilli and Peter de la Palu. *English Historical Review*, XLIX (1934), pp. 219–81.

SINGER, H. Die Dekretalensammlung des Bernardus Compostellanus Antiquus. *Sitzungs-berichte der kaiserlichen Akademie der Wissenschaften in Wien* (Phil.-Hist. Kl.), CLXXI, ii (Wien, 1914).

SOUCHON, G. M. *Die Papstwahlen von Bonifaz VIII bis Urban VI und die Entstehung des Schismas 1378* (Braunschweig, 1888).

STICKLER, A. M. Der Schwerterbegriff bei Huguccio. *Ephemerides Iuris Canonici*, III (1947), pp. 201–42.

Sacerdotium et Regnum nei Decretisti e Primi Decretalisti. *Salesianum*, XV (1953), pp. 575–612.

SÜTTERLIN, B. *Die Politik Kaiser Friedrichs II und die Römischen Kardinäle* (Heidelberg, 1929).

TIERNEY, B. A conciliar theory of the thirteenth century. *Catholic Historical Review*, XXXVI (1951), pp. 415–40.

The canonists and the mediaeval state. *Review of Politics*, XV (1953), pp. 378–88.
Ockham, the Conciliar Theory, and the canonists. *Journal of the History of Ideas*, XV (1954), pp. 40–70.
TORQUEBIAU, P. Le Gallicanisme de Durand de Mende le Jeune. *Acta Congressus Iuridici Internationalis*, III (1936).
TRITZ, H. Die hagiographischen Quellen zur Geschichte Papst Leos IX. *Studi Gregoriani*, IV (Rome, 1952), pp. 191–364.
ULLMANN, W. *The Medieval Idea of Law* (London, 1946).
Origins of the Great Schism (London, 1948).
The delictal responsibility of medieval corporations. *Law Quarterly Review*, LXIV (1948), pp. 79–96.
Medieval Papalism (London, 1949).
Medieval views on papal abdication. *Irish Ecclesiastical Record*, LXXI (1949), pp. 125–33.
Cardinal Humbert and the Ecclesia Romana. *Studi Gregoriani*, IV (Rome, 1952), pp. 111–27.
VAN DE KERCKHOVE, M. *La notion de juridiction dans la doctrine des Décrétistes et des premiers Décrétalistes* (Assisi, 1937).
VAN HOVE, A. *Prolegomena* (*Commentarium Lovaniense in Codicem Iuris Canonici*, I, i) (Mechliniae-Romae, 1945).
VAN LEEUWEN, A. L'église, règle de foi chez Occam. *Ephemerides Theologiae Lovanienses*, XI (1934), pp. 249–88.
WASNER, F. De consecratione, inthronizatione, coronatione Summi Pontificis. *Apollinaris*, VIII (1935), pp. 86–125, 248–81, 428–39.
WENCK, K. Konrad von Gelnhausen und die Quellen der konziliaren Theorie. *Historiche Zeitschrift*, LXXVI (1896), 1–60.
WIERUSZOWSKI, H. *Vom Imperium zum Nationalen Königtum* (München-Berlin, 1933).
WILLIS, G. G. *St Augustine and the Donatist Heresy* (London, 1950).
ZEMA, D. B. The houses of Tuscany and Pierleone in the crisis of Rome. *Traditio*, II (1944), pp. 155–75.

INDEX OF NAMES AND PLACES

Aegidius de Bellamera, 192–194, 234
Alanus, xxiv, 14, 61 n. 47, 87, 116 n.
  61, 117, n. 66, 118, n. 70, 127, 193
  n. 38, 234, 235
Albericus de Rosate, 187 n. 19, 188,
  234
Albertus, *see* Gregory VIII
Alexander III, Pope, 13, 15, 22, 68, 88
  n. 27, 100, 101, 111, 112 n. 48,
  234, 238
Anacletus, Pope, 174
Anagni, 2
Anastasius, Cardinal, 86, 87
Anastasius II, Pope, 34, 35, 37–39, 45,
  64
Andreas de Barbatia, 187 n. 19, 188 n.
  26, 190 n. 32, 234
Andreas Randulf, 3, 4 n. 2
Aquinas, St Thomas, xvi, xviii, xix, 147
Aristotle, 10, 200 n. 3, 201
Augustine, St, xix, 27 n. 16, 28, 31, 33,
  123, 174, 217
Augustinus Triumphus, xix, 11, 166, n.
  13, 212 n. 39
Avignon, 2, 165, 175, 180, 181, 210,
  234, 238, 239

Baldus de Ubaldis, 188 n. 26, 195, n.
  48, 196 n. 52, 234
Baptista de S. Blasio, 60 n. 46
Bartholomaeus Brixiensis, 48, 234, 237
Bartholomew Prignani, *see* Urban VI
Bartolus, 94 n. 38
Bazianus, 65, 235
Benedict XI, Pope, 170, 188
Berengarius Fredoli, 16 n. 40, 234, 235
Bernardus Compostellanus Antiquus,
  46 n. 11, 235
Bernardus Compostellanus Junior, 14,
  129 n. 24, 193 n. 38, 235
Bernardus Papiensis, 14 n. 33, 235
Bernardus Parmensis, 15, 81, 147, 235;
  cardinals, 64 n. 10, 88; corpora-
  tions, 95, 96, 100–102, 104, 112,
  113, 118, 124–126, 183 n. 5, 202
  n. 10; Pope, and Council, 86; dis-
  pensing power, 83, n. 10; election,

  85 n. 16, 131 n. 26; supreme legislator, 82 n. 1, 86 n. 20; *status ecclesiae*, 46 n. 11
Bologna, 72, 98
Boniface VIII, Pope, 7, 118, 143–146,
  148, n. 13, 162–164, 166, 170, 171,
  173, 188, 189
Boniface, St, 52 n. 27

Caius MS. 676, 36 n. 41, 46 n. 11, 65,
  233, 235
Celestine V, Pope, 144, 145, 148 n.
  13, 164, 188 n. 22, 211, 221
Cicero, 128 n. 22
Clement V, Pope, 16 n. 41, 236
Clement VII, Pope, 2, 3
Colonna cardinals, 144, n. 3, 145, 155,
  157–158, 163, 166, 171, 189, 197,
  212
Conrad of Gelnhausen, 3, 4 n. 2, 5 n.
  5, 6, 43, 140, 185 n. 14
Conrad of Offida, 144 n. 2
Cyprian, St, 30, 31, n. 30, 115, 123,
  174, 217

D'Ailly, Pierre, xx, xxvi–xxvii, 3, 4 n.
  2, n. 3, 5 n. 4, 6 n. 6, 84, 165, 194
  n. 43, 216, 222
Damasus, Pope, 52 n. 26, 173
Damian, St Peter, 63, 166 n. 12
De Pouilli, Jean, 174, n. 34, 175 n. 35
Deusdedit, Cardinal, 63
Dietrich of Niem, xiv, 3, 4 n. 2, 5 n. 4
Dominicus de Sancto Gemignano, 188,
  234, 235

England, 10

Flandrin, Pierre, 179 n. 42
France, 7, 10, 180, 238
Franciscans, 2, 6, 7, 84, 144, n. 2
Franciscus Zabarella, xi, xxv, 3, 16, 62,
  68, 140, 222, 234, 235; cardinals,
  165, 166, 187 n. 19, 188 n. 26,
  211–214, 216; Church, as corporation, 184–185, 200–214 *passim*;
  superior to Pope, 4 n. 3, 204, 205;

corporation structure, 94 n. 39, 96, 97, 106, 115, 207, 208, 209; General Council, 5 n. 5, 201–203, 206–210, 213–214; Pope, and bishops, 210, 211; deposition, 4 n. 3, 205, 206; *plenitudo potestatis*, 131, 203, 204, 211–214

Frederick Barbarossa, Emperor, 51

Frederick II, Emperor, 1, 70–72, 132 n. 27, 166 n. 12

Gelasius I, Pope, 173

Geoffrey de Vinsauf, 181 n. 3

Gerson, Jean, xvi, xvii, xxii, xxvi–xxvii, 3, 5 n. 4, 11 n. 24, 76, 84, 135 n. 41, 201, 222

Gilbertus, 14, 234, 235

Giles of Rome, 11, 130, 146, 148 n. 14, 158, 162, 166, n. 13

Goffredus Tranensis, 15, 82 n. 3, 83 n. 8, 88, 109, 118 n. 68, 119 n. 72, 128, 129 n. 24, 147, 234, 236

Gratian, xix, xxii, 12–15, 22, 81, 125, 233, 234, 236; cardinals, 64, 65; General Council, 44, 45, 62, 217; Keys, power of, 28–32; Pope, and Roman church, 85; liable to judgement?, 7, n. 13, 51, 52, 57, 58; supreme judge, 26; supreme legislator, 26; teaching authority, 33–35

Gregory I, Pope, 34 n. 34, 44, 45 n. 8, 84, 123, 173, 217

Gregory IV, Pope, 133 n. 33

Gregory VIII, Pope, 13 n. 28, 234

Gregory IX, Pope, 15, 70, 71, 119 n. 72, 238

Gregory X, Pope, 15 n. 39, 165, 236

Guido de Baysio, xix, 16, 173, 180, 182, 234, 236; bishops and chapters, 116 n. 61, 118; cardinals, 160 n. 48, 116, n. 14, 168 n. 18, 187–193, 211; Church, as *collectio catholicorum*, 183; disobedience to, 26 n. 12; dominion of property, 109 n. 37, 129 n. 24; liable to judgement?, 192–194; Pope, abdication, 146 n. 6; source of authority, 51 n. 23

Guilielmus de Mandagato, 16 n. 40, 234, 236

Guilielmus de Monte Lauduno, 181 n. 3, 234, 236

Guilielmus Durantis, the Speculator, 123 n. 6, 163, 183, 234, 236

Guilielmus Durantis, the Younger, 123

n. 6, 163, 164, 172–178, 192 n. 35, 199, 211, 216, 220, 234, 236

Henricus de Bohic, 114 n. 56, 166 n. 14, 180, 183, 193, n. 38, 194, 195, 236

Henricus de Segusio, *see* Hostiensis

Henry IV, Emperor, 64 n. 8

Henry VI, Emperor, 51

Henry of Langenstein, 3, 4 n. 2, 6, n. 6, 196 n. 49

Honorius III, Pope, 14 n. 33

Hostiensis, xxv, 15, 147, 148, 199, 233, 236; cardinals, 136–139, 144, 166, 167, 171, 191, 192; Church, as corporation, 139, 140, 150, 208; *status ecclesiae*, 46 n. 12, 48 n. 18; corporation structure, 98–120 *passim*, 126–127, 155, 171–172, 207–209; General Council, convocation, 139, 196, 197, 203 n. 13, 214 n. 43; Pope, liable to judgement?, 193 n. 38

Hugh of St Victor, 123 n. 7

Huguccio, xxv, 13, 14, 147, 233, 234, 236; bishops and chapters, 110 n. 43, 116 n. 61, 119–120; cardinals, 38–39, 65, 66, 68, 69, n. 18, 72, 74, 75, 168 n. 18, 190, 193, 211; Church, as corporation, 124, 125; dominion of property, 109, 152; *status ecclesiae*, 48 n. 16; General Council, 44 n. 2, 45 n. 8, 50, 69, 70; Keys, power of, 29, n. 22; Pope, and Apostolic See, 71, 85; dispensing power, 83; liable to judgement?, 8, 53–61, 69 n. 18, 74, 75, 182, 193, 195, 227–228; *plenitudo potestatis*, 131 n. 26, 132 n. 28; supreme judge, 26, 33, 34, 35; teaching authority, 34 n. 34, 35 n. 39; *Tu es Petrus*, 24, 25, 26, 30, 32; *Romana ecclesia*, as local church, 36 n. 41; as unerring Universal Church 37–39; as Pope and cardinals, 38, 39, 211; source of authority, 50, 51

Humbert, Cardinal, 52 n. 27, 59 n. 44

Innocent III, Pope, 14, n. 33, 15, 17, 22, 41, 43, 81, 86–88, 111, 124, 133, 134, 166 n. 12, 182, 219, 236, 238

Innocent IV, Pope, 15, 88, 237, 239;

cardinals, 88, 160; Church, dominion of property, 130, 131, 152, 183; *status ecclesiae*, 47 n. 15, 48 n. 16, 82; corporation structure, 95–97, 98–118 *passim*, 126, 203 n. 13, 207, 208; Pope, liable to judgement?, 193 n. 38; *plenitudo potestatis*, 82, 132 n. 27, 135, 146; source of authority, 85, n. 16

Jacopone da Todi, 144
Jerome, St, xix, 28, 33, 36 n. 41, 37, 44 n. 2, 75, 217
Joannes Andreae, 16, 106, n. 30, 118, 119 n. 72, 125, 149 n. 16, 166, 168, 180, 181, 183, 187, 188 n. 22, 190–193, 195–197, 210 n. 30, 237
Joannes de Lignano, 16, 180, 184, 186, n. 17, 188, 191 n. 34, 195, 237
Joannes de Torquemada, 219
Joannes Faventius, 13, 24, 51 n. 23, 237
Joannes Galensis, 14 n. 33, 35 n. 39, 237
Joannes Monachus, 16, 118 n. 68, 119 n. 72, 163–173, 178, 180, 183, n. 6, 187–189, 199, 204, 211, 216, 237
Joannes Teutonicus, 14, 15, 81, 147, 199, 229–232, 233, 237; cardinals 64 n. 10, 67, 69, 70, 75 n. 41, 168 n. 18, 190; Church, principle of unity, 123; *status ecclesiae*, 47–48; unerring in faith, 40, 41; corporation structure, 38, 100, 103–104, 112,116 n.61,118 n.68, 119, n. 72, 120, 122 n. 4, 123, 183 n. 5, 208; General Council, 44 n. 2, 46, 47–49, 69, 70, 84, 85, 208, 209; Pope, dispensing power, 82 n. 1; liable to judgement?, 57, 58, 157, 182, 206 n. 23; supreme judge, 74; supreme legislator, 176; *Tu es Petrus*, 25
John XXII, Pope, ix, xxiii, 16 n. 41
John of Paris, xix, xxv, 4 n. 3, 5 n. 4, 53 n. 30, 130, 143–162, 167, 168, 173, 174, 176, 178, 197, 200, 204, 207, 213 n. 42, 220

Laborans, 13, 237
Laurentius, 14 n. 34, 51, 83, 111, 116 n. 61, 119 n. 72, 211 n. 34, 235, 237

Leo I, Pope, 133 n. 33
Leo IV, Pope, 52 n. 26, 173
Leo IX, Pope, 63, 64 n. 7, 86, 87
Lewis the Bavarian, 1, 72 n. 35
Lincoln Cathedral, 116, n. 63, 117
Lucius III, Pope, 117, 118, 239

Macchiavelli, 47
Marcellinus, Pope, 34, 52 n. 26
Marsiglio of Padua, xiii, xiv, xv, 6, 8, 9, 161, 163, 179, 202
Mary, guardian of faith, 40, 185 n. 14
Monteferrato, Count of, 87

Nicholas II, Pope, 63
Nicholas III, Pope, 15 n. 39
Nicolaus Cusanus, xiv, xx, 4 n. 3, 6 n. 6, 33, 49
Nogaret, 7, 143

Ockham, *see* William of Ockham
Olivi, Pietro, 8, 144 n. 2, 160 n. 50

Panormitanus, xx, xxv, 187 n. 19, 188 n. 26, 237
Paschal II, Pope, 85
Paucapalea, 13, 25 n. 9, 73, 238
Paul, St, 83, 121, 153, 174, 184
Peter, St, and the other Apostles, xvi, xix, 24, 25, 27, 30, 31, 83, 154, 159, 174, 210, 219; *Tu es Petrus*, 23–27, 32, 217; *see also* Pope *in Index of Subjects*
Petrus Bertrandi, 194, 238
Petrus Collivaccinus, 14 n. 33, 238
Petrus de Ancharano, 188 n. 26, 238
Petrus de Vinca, 70–73
Philip the Fair, 1, 72 n. 35, 143, 145, 162, 163 n. 1
Philip of Swabia, 132 n. 27
Photinus, 35

Raymundus de Pennaforte, St, 15 n. 36, 238
Ricardus Anglicus, 45 n. 5, 147, 238
Ricardus Petronius de Senis, 16 n. 40, 238
Richard of St Germano, 87
Robert of Geneva, *see* Clement VII
Rolandus Bandinelli, *see* Alexander III
Rufinus, 24 n. 3, 30 n. 26, 35 n. 31, 47, n. 14, 52, 73, 75 n. 41, 110 n. 43, 116 n. 61, 118, 206 n. 23, 238

Sicardus Cremonensis, 13, 75, 238
Simon de Bisignano, 24, 32 n. 31, 238
Sinibaldus Fieschus, *see* Innocent IV
Sixtus III, Pope, 52 n. 26
Spain, 10
Stephanus Tornacensis, 13, 23 n. 2, 24, n. 3, 30 n. 26, 53, 73, 74, 116 n. 61, 123, 127, 239
Symmachus, Pope, 52 n. 26

Tancred, 46 n. 12, 48 n. 18, 64 n. 10, 81, 82 n. 1, 83 n. 8, 84, n. 14, 85 n. 16, 87 n. 24, 100, n. 11, 134, 234, 237

Urban I, Pope, 173

Urban VI, Pope, 1, 2, 145 n. 4, 164, 215, 234

Vigilius, Pope, 133 n. 33
Vincentius Hispanus, 111, 119 n. 72, 193 n. 38, 239

William of Moerbeke, 202
William of Ockham, xiii, xiv, xv, xix, xx, 6, 8, 9, 40, 41, 59, 93, 163, 179
Wolfenbüttel MS. Helmst. 33, 32 n. 31, 38, 41 n. 57, 239

Zabarella, *see* Franciscus Zabarella
Zenzellinus de Casanis, 16, 166 n. 14, 180, 183, 185, 188, 191 n. 34, 239
Zosimus, Pope, 173

INDEX OF SUBJECTS

Archdeacon, *see* Guido de Baysio *in Index of Names and Places*

Bishops, and chapters, *see* Corporations; and Pope, 26, 30, 66, 130, 132–135, 154, 162, 172, 174–177, 210, 219, 220; successors of Apostles, 30, 31, 154, 174, 210, 220

Cardinals, and *plenitudo potestatis*, 88, 138, 171, 172, 188, 211–214; as corporation, 68, 73, 89, 108, 136–140, 167–169, 184–186, 190–192, 197, 213–214, 220; convoke General Council, 5, 66 n. 15, 69–72, 194, 203, 213; depose Pope, 75, 157 n. 38, 160, 193, 213 n. 42; during papal vacancy, 65–68, 88 n. 27, 137–139, 167, 172, 188–191, 196, 208, 212; electors of Pope, 1, 5, 55, 63, 66, 68, 160, 166, 178, 190, 196; limit authority of Pope?, 2, 4, 11, 64, 65, 70, 73, 84, 87, 88, 164, 168–172, 178, 186–188, 210, 211, 212; origins, 62–64, 166, 167, 212; represent Universal Church, 4, 76, 140, 160, 168, 195, 212–214; Senators of Church, 64, 160, 167, 187; subordinate to Pope, 86, 87, 162, 164, 186–189; superior to Pope, 1, 74, 75, 172, 189; *see also* Roman church

Centralization, ecclesiastical, 10, 63, 88, 90, 162, 165, 174, 177, 210, 216, 219

Church and State, 1, 10, 70–72, 82, 98, 128, 136, 153, 161; as *congregatio fidelium*, 3, 37, 39, 41, 49 n. 20, 62, 72, 109, 120–130, 140, 152, 168, 179, 183, 184, 201, 203, 206, 213, 214, 218; as corporation, 21, 42, 90, 92, 121–131, 135–136, 139, 150–152, 177, 184–187, 197, 201–214, 218, 220–222; as hierarchy, 10, 21, 125, 200, 214, 218; definitions of, 37, 115, 183, 184, 218; founded on Peter, 23–25, 32, 185 n. 16; indefectibility, 3, 7 n. 13, 21,

23, 32–42, 49 n. 20, 130, 195, 221; superior to Pope, 1, 3, 4, 32, 150–153, 159, 179, 197, 205, 206; well-being of (*status ecclesiae*), 2, 46, 47, 54, 70, 74, 75 n. 44, 82, 85, 130, 176, 209, 221; *see also* General Council, Pope

Churches, local churches and Rome, 26, 36, 37, 49, 50, 62, 172, 185, 186, 191, 217, 218

Compilatio Prima, 14 n. 33, 85, 87

Compilatio Quarta, 14 n. 33, 81

Compilatio Romana, 14

Compilatio Tertia, 14 n. 33, 88 n. 26

Conciliar Movement, and secular constitutionalism, 9, 130, 222; doctrines, 3, 6, 11, 41–43, 63, 68, 130, 146, 150, 215–217; origins, 8–12, 16, 17, 40, 41, 139, 146, 177, 179, 214, 218–223

Congregatio fidelium, *see* Church

Corporations, authority in head alone, 100, 105 n. 26, 114, 115, 125 n. 14, 129, 207, in all members, 89, 100, 108, 115, 137, 150, 155, 190, 207–209, 220; devolution of power from head to members, 97, 117–120, 126, 139, 140, 201, 202, 212–214, from members to head, 97, 106–108; election of head, 116, 117, 126, 131, 132, 150, 154; Gierke's theory of, 91–95, 124–127, 129, 167, 168; members limit authority of head, 97, 100–108, 113–115, 120, 155; particular rights within, 102–108; prelate as proctor, 108–117, 120, 132, 135, 150–152, 156, 171–172, 204, 219, 220; prelate *ut canonicus*, 103–108; vacant headship, 95, 99, 117–120, 190 n. 32, 191, 201, 217; *see also* Cardinals, Church

Corpus Iuris Canonici, 12, 16, 22

Counsel, and consent, 90, 100–103, 105–107, 112, 113, 116

Decretals, Gregorian, 10, 15, 16, 22, 86, 87, 99, 110, 148, 182

Decretum, xvi, xvii, xix, xx, xxi, xxiv, 10, 12, 14–16, 22, 23, 81, 122, 147, 177, 182, 217; bishops, and chapters, 100, 109, 110, 119, 125, and Pope, 153, 154, 174, 208–210; cardinals, 64, 69, 70, 75; General Council, 44, 45, 62, 153, 208–210; Peter, St, 23, 27, 30, 31, 154, 174, 219; Pope, and church, 31; election, 65, 69; heretical, 34, 52, 54; liable to judgement?, 52, 54, 55, 60, 157; *plenitudo potestatis*, 133; supreme judge, 26, 33, 34; supreme legislator, 26, 63 n. 4; teaching authority, 33, 153

Digest, 42, 68, 96, 111, 123, n. 6

Dominion of Church property, 109, 125, 128–130, 140, 150–153, 156, 183

Ecce Vicit Leo, 14 n. 34, 23 n. 2, 25, n. 9, 28 n. 21, 29 n. 23, 30 n. 26, 32 n. 31, 45 n. 8, 58, 67, 73, 109, 131 n. 26, 132 n. 28, 236

Emperor, 4 n. 3, 50, 51, 72, 85, 127, 133, 203, 205 n. 19

Extravagantes Communes, 16

Extravagantes Joannes XXII, 16, 185

Gallicanism, 7

General Council, and articles of faith, 45, 61, 153, 176, 194, 206, 208 –210; and *status ecclesiae*, 46–48, 175 n. 36, 176, 209; canons bind Pope?, 11, 44–48, 86, 87, 153, 165, 173, 176, 181, 197, 198, 208–210; composition, 43, 49, 50, 60, 201, 208–210; convocation, 2, 5, 69–72, 139, 194, 197, 203, 212, 214 n. 43; judge of Pope, 3, 6, 7, 22, 43, 52, 53, 59–61, 71, 72, 84, 143–145, 157, 177, 193–198, 206, 213; represents Universal Church, 3, 33 n. 32, 43–45, 48, 123, 139, 153, 157, 176–178, 201–202, 209, 212; role of Pope in Council, 49, 50, 61, 86, 87, 89, 208–210

General Councils, Basle, 222; Constance, 5, 201 n. 5, 216, 223; Third Lateran, 14; Fourth Lateran, 14 n. 33, 15 n. 35, 86, 87, 175 n. 36; First Lyons, 15; Second Lyons, 15, 165 n. 9; Pisa, 215; Vienne, 16 n. 41, 178

Glossa Ordinaria, Decretals, 15, 46 n. 12, 86, 87, 110, 147; *see also*

Bernardus Parmensis *in Index of Names and Places*

Glossa Ordinaria, Decretum, xxiii, 14, 23 n. 2, 25, n. 6, n. 9, 30 n. 26, 38, 40, 45, 51, 55 n. 32, 59, 60, 73, 81, 109, 145 n. 6, 147, 148, 157, 194, 206, 209, 210; *see also* Joannes Teutonicus *in Index of Names and Places*

Glossa Palatina, 14 n. 34, 235; cardinals, 69, n. 18, 70, 74–76, 84, 88, 108, 182, 187 n. 19, 211; Church, as corporation, 42, 123 n. 10; dominion of property, 109; liable to judgement?, 55 n. 32, 58, 59, 69 n. 18, 75, 76; *plena auctoritas*, 131 n. 26, 134; Pope, and Council, 45 n. 8, 46, 69–70; *Tu es Petrus*, 25, 26, 30 n. 26, 32 n. 31, 41; unerring in faith, 32 n. 31, 41, 42

Jurisdiction, and orders, 28–30, 116, 118, 129, 146, 150, 159, 160, 220

Keys, power of the, 23, 27–30, 32, 85, 174

Liber Sextus, 16, 118, 173, 180 n. 1, 190

Mystical Body, 120–124, 127–129, 184, 222

Natural law, 83

Ne Romani, 190–192

Plenitudo potestatis, 28 n. 21, 81, 82, n. 1, 88, 129–138, 146, 153, 162, 169–171, 175, 197, 198, 203, 204, 206, 211–214, 220

Pope, abdication, 143–146, 155, 196, 198, 220, 221; authority delegated by cardinals, 65, 66, 160, 171, 172, 190, 213 n. 42, 220, by Church, 4, 5, 50, 51, 134, 135, 156, 158–160, 195, 204, 205, 212; by God, 23–32, 81, 85, 123, 130, 135, 145, 151, 157, 158, 180, 189, 192; can err in faith, 3, 7 n. 13, 33–35, 37–41, 65, 205; defines articles of faith, 27, 33, 150; disobedience to, 26, 36 n. 41; dispensing power, 46–48, 83–85, 181 n. 3, 195; election, 2, 51, 55, 63, 66, 130, 132, 166, 200; head of Church, 11, 12, 21, 23, 25, 26, 30,

32, 35, 38, 124, 127–130, 144, 147, 150–152, 155, 217; heretic ceases to be Pope, 7, 8, 54–61, 194, 195; immune from judgement, 2, 4, 7, 26, 52, 55, 56, 82, 159; liable to judgement?, 2, 7 n. 13, 8, 51–61, 72, 75, 130, 144, 145, 155–159, 191–198, 205–208, 213, 221; person and office, 51, 71, 85, 146, 149 n. 16, 158, 159, 207; successor of Peter, 30, 36, 40, 66, 76, 82, 151, 154, 191, 219; supreme judge, 26, 28, 33, 45, 74, 133, 175, 180; supreme legislator, 26, 33, 82, 181, 188; symbolizes Church, 31–33, 37, 40, 44, 49, 85; *see also* Cardinals, Church, General Council

Quinque Compilationes Antiquae, 14
Quod Omnes Tangit, 44, 173, 176

Representation, 160, 167, 168; as delegation, 4, 32–33, 43, 44, 49, 115–117, 131, 212–214; as personification, 4, 31–33, 37, 41, 44, 49, 115–117
Roman church, distinguished from Universal Church, 3, 11, 35–40, 49, 62, 65, 128, 133, 185, 186, 191, 216–218; equivalent to Universal Church, 35–40, 128, 205, 216; equivalent to Pope and cardinals, 3, 6, 37–39, 62, 65, 73, 171, 172, 190, 213, 214; head of Church, 124, 127, 128, 138, 175, 198, 213, 214, 218, 219; unerring in faith, 34, 37–42, 49, 65, 205, 206

Sacrosancta, 5
Schism, equal to heresy, 8, 52, 206; Great, 2, n. 1, 3, 6, 9, 13, 16, 22, 70, 84, 143, 161, 165, 178–180, 190, 194, 195, 198, 200–203, 212, 214–217, 222
Simony, 55, 69
Status ecclesiae, see Church, General Council
Status regni, 46, 48 n. 16
Summa Coloniensis, 28 n. 21, 239
Summa Et Est Sciendum, 28 n. 21, 37, 38 n. 48, 46, 50 n. 21, 73 n. 36, 239
Summa Parisiensis, 24, 33 n. 33, 35 n. 39, 36 n. 40, n. 42, 44 n. 2, 45, 52, n. 29, 56 n. 34, 239
Summa Permissio Quedam, 46 n. 11, 239

Ubi Periculum, 165

Studies in the History of Christian Thought

EDITED BY HEIKO A. OBERMAN

1. McNEILL, J. J. *The Blondelian Synthesis.* 1966. Out of print
2. GOERTZ, H.-J. *Innere und äussere Ordnung in der Theologie Thomas Müntzers.* 1967
3. BAUMAN, Cl. *Gewaltlosigkeit im Täufertum.* 1968
4. ROLDANUS, J. *Le Christ et l'Homme dans la Théologie d'Athanase d'Alexandrie.* 2nd ed. 1977
5. MILNER, Jr., B. Ch. *Calvin's Doctrine of the Church.* 1970. Out of print
6. TIERNEY, B. *Origins of Papal Infallibility, 1150-1350.* 2nd ed. 1988
7. OLDFIELD, J. J. *Tolerance in the Writings of Félicité Lamennais 1809-1831.* 1973
8. OBERMAN, H. A. (ed.). *Luther and the Dawn of the Modern Era.* 1974. Out of print
9. HOLECZEK, H. *Humanistische Bibelphilologie bei Erasmus, Thomas More und William Tyndale.* 1975
10. FARR, W. *John Wyclif as Legal Reformer.* 1974
11. PURCELL, M. *Papal Crusading Policy 1244-1291.* 1975
12. BALL, B. W. *A Great Expectation.* Eschatological Thought in English Protestantism. 1975
13. STIEBER, J. W. *Pope Eugenius IV, the Council of Basel, and the Empire.* 1978. Out of print
14. PARTEE, Ch. *Calvin and Classical Philosophy.* 1977
15. MISNER, P. *Papacy and Development.* Newman and the Primacy of the Pope. 1976
16. TAVARD, G. H. *The Seventeenth-Century Tradition.* A Study in Recusant Thought. 1978
17. QUINN, A. *The Confidence of British Philosophers.* An Essay in Historical Narrative. 1977
18. BECK, J. *Le Concil de Basle (1434).* 1979
19. CHURCH, F. F. and GEORGE, T. (ed.). *Continuity and Discontinuity in Church History.* 1979
20. GRAY, P. T. R. *The Defense of Chalcedon in the East (451-553).* 1979
21. NIJENHUIS, W. *Adrianus Saravia (c. 1532-1613).* Dutch Calvinist. 1980
22. PARKER, T. H. L. (ed.). *Iohannis Calvini Commentarius in Epistolam Pauli ad Romanos.* 1981
23. ELLIS, I. *Seven Against Christ.* A Study of 'Essays and Reviews'. 1980
24. BRANN, N. L. *The Abbot Trithemius (1462-1516).* 1981
25. LOCHER, G. W. *Zwingli's Thought.* New Perspectives. 1981
26. GOGAN, B. *The Common Corps of Christendom.* Ecclesiological Themes in Thomas More. 1982
27. STOCK, U. *Die Bedeutung der Sakramente in Luthers Sermonen von 1519.* 1982
28. YARDENI, M. (ed.). *Modernité et nonconformisme en France à travers les âges.* 1983
29. PLATT, J. *Reformed Thought and Scholasticism.* 1982
30. WATTS, P. M. *Nicolaus Cusanus.* A Fifteenth-Century Vision of Man. 1982
31. SPRUNGER, K. L. *Dutch Puritanism.* 1982
32. MEIJERING, E. P. *Melanchthon and Patristic Thought.* 1983
33. STROUP, J. *The Struggle for Identity in the Clerical Estate.* 1984
34. 35. COLISH, M. L. *The Stoic Tradition from Antiquity to the Early Middle Ages.* 1.2. 2nd ed. 1990
36. GUY, B. *Domestic Correspondence of Dominique-Marie Varlet, Bishop of Babylon, 1678-1742.* 1986
37. 38. CLARK, F. *The Pseudo-Gregorian Dialogues.* I. II. 1987
39. PARENTE, Jr. J. A. *Religious Drama and the Humanist Tradition.* 1987
40. POSTHUMUS MEYJES, G. H. M. *Hugo Grotius, Meletius.* 1988
41. FELD, H. *Der Ikonoklasmus des Westens.* 1990
42. REEVE, A. and SCREECH, M. A. (eds.). *Erasmus' Annotations on the New Testament.* Acts —Romans — I and II Corinthians. 1990
43. KIRBY, W. J. T. *Richard Hooker's Doctrine of the Royal Supremacy.* 1990
44. GERSTNER, J. N. *The Thousand Generation Covenant.* Reformed Covenant Theology. 1990
45. CHRISTIANSON, G. and IZBICKI, T. M. (eds.). *Nicholas of Cusa.* 1991
46. GARSTEIN, O. *Rome and the Counter-Reformation in Scandinavia.* 1553-1622. 1992
47. GARSTEIN, O. *Rome and the Counter-Reformation in Scandinavia.* 1622-1656. 1992
48. PERRONE COMPAGNI, V. (ed.). *Cornelius Agrippa, De occulta philosophia Libri tres.* 1992
49. MARTIN, D. D. *Fifteenth-Century Carthusian Reform.* The World of Nicholas Kempf. 1992

50. HOENEN, M. J. F. M. *Marsilius of Inghen.* Divine Knowledge in Late Medieval Thought. 1993
51. O'MALLEY, J. W., IZBICKI, T. M. and CHRISTIANSON, G. (eds.). *Humanity and Divinity in Renaissance and Reformation.* Essays in Honor of Charles Trinkaus. 1993
52. REEVE, A. (ed.) and SCREECH, M. A. (introd.). *Erasmus' Annotations on the New Testament.* Galatians to the Apocalypse. 1993
53. STUMP, Ph. H. *The Reforms of the Council of Constance (1414-1418).* 1994
54. GIAKALIS, A. *Images of the Divine.* The Theology of Icons at the Seventh Ecumenical Council. With a Foreword by Henry Chadwick. 1994
55. NELLEN, H. J. M. and RABBIE, E. (eds.). *Hugo Grotius − Theologian.* Essays in Honour of G. H. M. Posthumus Meyjes. 1994
56. TRIGG, J. D. *Baptism in the Theology of Martin Luther.* 1994
57. JANSE, W. *Albert Hardenberg als Theologe.* Profil eines Bucer-Schülers. 1994
59. SCHOOR, R.J.M. VAN DE. *The Irenical Theology of Théophile Brachet de La Milletière (1588-1665).* 1995
60. STREHLE, S. *The Catholic Roots of the Protestant Gospel.* Encounter between the Middle Ages and the Reformation. 1995
61. BROWN, M.L. *Donne and the Politics of Conscience in Early Modern England.* 1995
62. SCREECH, M.A. (ed.). *Richard Mocket, Warden of All Souls College, Oxford, Doctrina et Politia Ecclesiae Anglicanae.* An Anglican Summa. Facsimile with Variants of the Text of 1617. Edited with an Introduction. 1995
63. SNOEK, G.J.C. *Medieval Piety from Relics to the Eucharist.* A Process of Mutual Interaction. 1995
64. PIXTON, P.B. *The German Episcopacy and the Implementation of the Decrees of the Fourth Lateran Council, 1216-1245.* Watchmen on the Tower. 1995
65. DOLNIKOWSKI, E.W. *Thomas Bradwardine: A View of Time and a Vision of Eternity in Fourteenth-Century Thought.* 1995
66. RABBIE, E. (ed.). *Hugo Grotius, Ordinum Hollandiae ac Westfrisiae Pietas (1613).* Critical Edition with Translation and Commentary. 1995
67. HIRSH, J.C. *The Boundaries of Faith.* The Development and Transmission of Medieval Spirituality. 1996
68. BURNETT, S.G. *From Christian Hebraism to Jewish Studies.* Johannes Buxtorf (1564-1629) and Hebrew Learning in the Seventeenth Century. 1996
69. BOLAND O.P., V. *Ideas in God according to Saint Thomas Aquinas.* Sources and Synthesis. 1996
70. LANGE, M.E. *Telling Tears in the English Renaissance.* 1996
71. CHRISTIANSON, G. and T.M. IZBICKI (eds.). *Nicholas of Cusa on Christ and the Church.* Essays in Memory of Chandler McCuskey Brooks for the American Cusanus Society. 1996
72. MALI, A. *Mystic in the New World.* Marie de l'Incarnation (1599-1672). 1996
73. VISSER, D. *Apocalypse as Utopian Expectation (800-1500).* The Apocalypse Commentary of Berengaudus of Ferrières and the Relationship between Exegesis, Liturgy and Iconography. 1996
74. O'ROURKE BOYLE, M. *Divine Domesticity.* Augustine of Thagaste to Teresa of Avila. 1997
75. PFIZENMAIER, T.C. *The Trinitarian Theology of Dr. Samuel Clarke (1675-1729).* Context, Sources, and Controversy. 1997
76. BERKVENS-STEVELINCK, C., J. ISRAEL and G.H.M. POSTHUMUS MEYJES (eds.). *The Emergence of Tolerance in the Dutch Republic.* 1997
77. HAYKIN, M.A.G. (ed.). *The Life and Thought of John Gill (1697-1771).* A Tercentennial Appreciation. 1997
78. KAISER, C.B. *Creational Theology and the History of Physical Science.* The Creationist Tradition from Basil to Bohr. 1997
79. LEES, J.T. *Anselm of Havelberg.* Deeds into Words in the Twelfth Century. 1997
80. WINTER, J.M. VAN. *Sources Concerning the Hospitallers of St John in the Netherlands, 14th-18th Centuries.* 2 vols. 1998
81. TIERNEY, B. *Foundations of the Conciliar Theory.* The Contribution of the Medieval Canonists from Gratian to the Great Schism. Enlarged New Edition. 1998
82. MIERNOWSKI, J. *Le Dieu Néant.* Théologies négatives à l'aube des temps modernes. 1998

Prospectus available on request

KONINKLIJKE BRILL — P.O.B. 9000 — 2300 PA LEIDEN — THE NETHERLANDS